BETWEEN
LABOR AND CAPITAL

BETWEEN
LABOR AND CAPITAL

Edited by
Pat Walker

SOUTH END PRESS   BOSTON

Dedication

Towards A Socialist United States

Preface

South End Press is a publishing collective committed to furthering the socialist movement in the United States. We are concerned with the totality of oppressions, especially those based on race, sex, and class; and we are striving for a world in which all people are directly and collectively in control of their lives.

Between Labor and Capital is the first volume in the **South End Press Political Controversies Series**. This series is designed as a forum for discussing contemporary political issues facing socially concerned people around the world. Beyond being a forum, it is our hope that the debate provoked by the series will lead to the forging of a theory and practice that can assist in the creation of genuinely democratic and liberating societies.

Each book in the series will consist of a lead article which develops a position on a particular political issue, various responses to the lead article, and a rejoinder by the author(s) of the lead article. Lead articles will be chosen on the basis of the strength of their arguments, and their ability to stir controversy and to raise strategical considerations. Responses will be both supportive and critical.

The Political Controversies Series stems from the belief that a powerful, democratic and united movement for socialism requires a process of vigorous discussion. There is not "one road to socialism." The way forward is often unclear. This series is intended to open debates, air positions, and pull together people's experiences and theories, eventually leading to programs for social change.

The first volume in the series focuses on the class position and consciousness of those people who work in jobs located between labor and capital, "the middle class." The responses develop several alternative positions in their critiques and extensions of the Ehrenreichs' thesis.

In our opinion, the contributions in this volume represent serious attempts to analyze the role of those between labor and capital in the social reproduction of capitalism, and their role in movements for social change.

While we feel that it is an important and valuable book, it does have certain drawbacks. It has not enabled us to reach substantially beyond a circle of previously published or well-known contributors. Correspondingly, in spite of our attempts to solicit responses which combine theory with experiential analysis, that balance is somewhat missing from this volume. We think this reflects, in part, a collective problem among leftists in the U.S. Many of us do not write; and those who do often produce work which tends to be accessible only to academics.

We would like the Political Controversies Series to be a means through which people who do theoretical work will feel compelled to root that work in experience, and to present it in understandable terms. At the same time we want this series to attract contributions from people who have not previously done theoretical work, but who have considerable organizing experience and skills. As these two kinds of contributions begin to merge, our controversy series will come closer to the ambitious goal of the development of an integrated theory and program relevant to social change.

The second and third volumes in the Political Controversies Series are, *Women And Revolution,* and *Ecology And Capitalism.* The lead article of *Women And Revolution* is "The Unhappy Marriage of Marxism and Feminism," by Heidi Hartman. This book focuses on the interaction of class and patriarchy in the shaping of our lives, the role of women in revolution, and the importance of sexism as a revolutionary issue.

Ecology And Capitalism discusses the issues of ecology and social change. Is ecological balance possible under capitalist or socialist societies as they exist today or are new economic arrangements called for? Can we continue to grow economically in coming decades or must there be "zero growth"? What are the revolutionary implications of ecological movements? Are they "merely" reformist or even reactionary? These issues and others are addressed by people of diverse political and ecological backgrounds.

Other proposed topics for the Political Controversies Series are: Race and Revolution, Socialism and Internationalism, Radical American History, Reform and Revolution, Unions and U.S. Socialism, Consciousness, Conformity and Revolution, Revolutionary Organization, High Culture and People's Culture, Gay Liberation and Socialism.

We encourage our readers to participate in this series. We welcome suggestions for other series books, and help in finding lead articles and contributions.

The South End Press Collective

Contents

III

Introduction

Revolution poses the question: what maintains society the way it is, and how can it be transformed?

Social reproduction refers to all the various social relations and institutions that serve to reproduce society without any fundamental change. In the past decade, marxists have become increasingly concerned with the forms of social reproduction in advanced capitalist countries. Attention has focused on the division of labor in the firm and in society at large, on the educational system and the state, and on the family and institutional racism. The left has sought to understand how these institutions and the social relations they embody influence people's consciousness so as to perpetuate race, sex, class and other forms of oppression. Where and how we work and learn, how we participate in the state, the family relationships we have grown up in, and the racial and ethnic oppressions which shape our life choices are all significant parts of the total process within which are expectations are formed.

But an analysis which explains why things remain the way they are, can also begin to make clear how they could be different. By revealing the manifold ways in which consciousness is influenced, an analysis of the relations of social reproduction opens the door for understanding how revolutionary class consciousness can be developed. By analyzing the specific positions and functions of people in these social relations, we can determine whose interests are in overthrowing the oppressive conditions of society. A dialectical understanding of social reproduction explains the forces which perpetuate these conditions and those which could serve to eliminate them.

The Marxist conception of class is integrally related to social reproduction. A thorough understanding of social reproduction reveals the determinants of class consciousness as well as the class position of those involved in the various forms of social reproduction.

Marx's concept of class provides a way of understanding capitalist society according to the place people occupy in the economy. Those who own and control the means by which society produces goods and services are the capitalists. Those who have been alienated from the means of production are the working class. The capitalist hires workers in order to make a profit. The workers, not having the means to provide for themselves, are forced to produce for the capitalist a greater value of goods and services than they receive as a wage. This surplus value becomes the capitalist's profit.

Capitalists and workers, according to Marx, are engaged in a continuous struggle: the capitalists to gain profits, the workers to regain control over their lives. This struggle is being continually waged, with varying degrees of class consciousness, in the factories, schools, families, and state institutions. Capitalist society is based on class struggle. Class then is a key concept for analyzing social forces in capitalist societies.

The concept of social reproduction broadens our understanding to encompass the total process of social development; class provides a specific criterion for analyzing this social totality. By analyzing those forces that maintain the status quo, social reproduction leads us into understanding the determinants of class consciousness. By revealing the specific arrangement of class forces and their class consciousness, class leads us into understanding the actuality of revolution—what can be done *now* to actualize the revolutionary *process*. By requiring us to thoroughly understand where we are (objectively and subjectively) and where we are to go, revolution leads us into understanding revolutionary philosophy and practice. Revolution is the art of the possible.

Social Reproduction. Class. Revolution. Key concepts for understanding society, our critical awareness of it, and our ability to transform ourselves in the process of eliminating the oppressive conditions we live under.

   These seem to me to be the main concepts around which to organize an introduction to the following debate. The debate centers on Barbara and John Ehrenreichs' position that there is a third class in advanced capitalist societies, called the Professional-Managerial Class (PMC). The PMC is defined by its role in the social reproduction of advanced capitalist countries. The proposition that there can be a third class, other than the capitalist and working classes, and that it can be defined by its role in social reproduction becomes a larger debate about the meaning and possible relevance of the traditional Marxist concepts of social reproduction, class and revolution.

   In the next part of this introduction, I sketch the breadth of the debate, and the practical implications of the various positions put forth. In so doing I also introduce some of the basic Marxist concepts involved. In the third part, I briefly discuss what I consider to be some of the main philosophical problems which underlie the debate. In the final section, I indicate some of areas which aren't covered in the debate.

II

SOCIAL REPRODUCTION

   In the essays that follow, five main aspects of social reproduction can be singled out: the technical division of labor in the firm, the social division of labor in society, the educational system, the state and the family. When an author is discussing social reproduction, it is important to clarify which of these apects is being referred to. The manner of reproduction and what specifically is being reproduced may vary significantly among the different authors. The developing of technologies which seek to assure worker passivity by the very design of the production process is a very different type of social reproduction from that which takes place in the family, where the satisfaction of sexual and nurturant needs takes place so as to produce passive workers and, perhaps more importantly, a class of exploited women.

   In regards to each aspect of social reproduction, I will follow the method outlined above. First I will discuss how each aspect influences people's consciousness, and then what the class position is of the people involved in these relations.

The Technical Division of Labor

   The technical division of labor refers to the manner in which work is organized in the capitalist firm. The capitalist seeks to organize the types of jobs and their relations to one another so as to assure the greatest profit possible. The Marxist way of explaining this is that the capitalist attempts to organize the labor process in order to extract the greatest amount of *labor* from the workers' *labor power*. Labor power is the capacity to work that the capitalist buys with the wage; labor is the actual work expended by the worker in the labor process. What appears to be an equal exchange in the labor market, the wage for the workers' labor power, becomes an unequal exchange in the factory where the capitalist tries to extract as much labor as possible from the worker.

Production for profit, however, is at the same time reproduction of productive workers. The workers must show up again tomorrow, and not with raised wrenches. One way certain technologies help the capitalist to keep the upper hand is by depriving workers of their understanding of the production process. By separating the conception of the work from its execution, the particular technology makes it seem natural that mental work is separated from and higher than manual work. Another way certain technologies can be used is to design production processes which physically separate workers or which make it seem that scientific requirements control the speed of work. Finally, technologies can be designed which fragment work tasks according to an arbitrary hierarchy of skill levels so as to increase both centralized control and competition among the workers to see who gets up the job ladder quickest.

The technical devision of labor is not "technical" in any "neutral" or "natural" way. Those technologies are implemented which fit the requirements of capitalist production—production for profit *and* social reproduction of alienated workers. In a society based on production for need *and* the social reproduction of self-managing workers, different technologies would be implemented.

Different theories of technology provide various explanations of the class positions of those in the technical division of labor. For example, an engineer in one instance is seen as a productive laborer (produces surplus value for the capitalist). In this case, the engineer is just like the rest of the workers, except that she or he has more skills. In another theory, an engineer's function *and* position in the firm are viewed as solely designed to control or manipulate labor. In this case, an engineer is not like the other workers, she or he does not contribute to production by her or his own labor, but rather is concerned with keeping the workers suppressed. According to yet another position, an engineer is both productive and reproductive, where the latter is separable from the former. This means that an engineer adds to the output and manipulates workers, but this manipulation function can be eliminated from the engineer's job, while the position of engineer is maintained as necessary to production. Or, finally, the two parts are seen as inseparable. The position of the engineer, because it embodies the separation of conception from execution in its very existence, must be reconceived according to a set of socialist work principles which establish the workers' needs to understand and control the production process as the basis for deciding upon how work will be organized.

Each one of these approaches would identify the engineer's class position differently. If an engineer is seen as a productive and exploited person, then differences between engineers and other workers will be minimized, both will be included in the same class, and unity against capital will be stressed. But if an engineer's function is seen as reproductive, then differences between engineers and workers will be stressed such that engineers might be put in another class, i.e., as part of the PMC, or at least issues concerning hierarchy will become primary organizing issues to be addressed in an organization which includes both workers and engineers (professionals and managers).

If engineers are seen as both productive and reproductive, then they may be considered to be a strata of the working class, or a strata of the petty bourgeoisie, or in a contradictory class location between classes. All of these positions make it possible for engineers to be in a working class organization. On the one hand they don't push engineers against the wall, afraid that their function will be eliminated (their productive function will remain). But on the other hand these positions are more likely to backslide on questions of elitism and technocratic tendencies (because the engineering position remains, the possibility of their controlling knowledge of the production process so as to perpetuate their position remains as well). If the final view above is taken, then the emphasis is on the formulation of a conception of work in a socialist society which can convince people of its viability within the context of present day work relations.

The Social Division of Labor

The social division of labor refers to the manner in which work is organized in society as a whole. When social reproduction functions within the firm become specialized to the extent that they form part of the broad social division of labor, e.g., when engineers start their own engineering firms, and when in addition there develop firms whose function is the management of mass consumption and culture, e.g., advertising agencies, how do these industries serve to reproduce capitalism, and what is the class position of those who work in these industries?

Social reproduction does not stop at the factory gate. For workers to keep working, all of society must work within the general contours of capitalism. Doctors, psychiatrists and lawyers; urban planners and architects; hollywood producers, advertising designers and T.V. announcers all help to shape a social reality whose values, culture and social institutions resonate with the racist, sexist and class based structures of power upon which our society is built. Whether it is the World Trade Center impressing you into the sidewalk, or Miller beer commercials triggering your psychic needs to seek ever greater false satisfaction, the whole ensemble of social architects tends to create passive, present-blinded individuals. Lacking self-confidence and critical awareness, people are geared to the consumption of goods and services whose very consumption tends to reproduce itself on an ever greater scale of future addiction.

It is important to distinguish between the technical and social division of labor, for in the former social reproduction is a part of production, whereas in the latter it has become a form of production itself. In the technical division, social reproduction is implicit in the structure of work. In the social division, it is more consciously evident in the content of what we physically and psychically consume.

Part of the debate on the class location of those who work in these industries hinges on the Marxist debate over *productive* and *unproductive* labor. Productive labor is labor which produces surplus value for capital; unproductive labor does not produce surplus value. Unproductive labor does not add value to the good or service being produced. It is an expense which does not produce a value greater than itself.

Some authors who argue against the PMC being a class argue that those whose function is social reproduction are unproductive. Because they do not produce surplus value, they are dispensable from the point of view of the capitalist, and from their own point of view they do not have the economic base upon which they could become an independent, third class. According to this position, the PMC can only be a derivative class. Moreoever, those who hold this point of view are bound to maintain that there can only be two main classes in capitalist society.

Some authors seem to use the term reproductive synonymously with unproductive. Though "the middle layers" may be both unproductive and reproductive, manipulation of the workers is clearly distinct from the production of surplus value. The strategical importance of this debate hinges on whether or not a group is expendable from the point of view of the capitalist. If the working class revolts there's no more capitalist. If the PMC revolts? The answer to this question depends not only on whether these people are unproductive, but also on how important their social function is for maintaining the status quo.

They may or may not produce a surplus, but will a surplus continue to be produced without them?

The Educational System

Perhaps in no other aspect of social reproduction have its structural and content dimensions been combined and refined as much as in the educational system. Both the process (as in the technical division of labor) and the content of learning (as in the social division of labor) have been organized to produce people who will fit into the social machinery. The educational system is structured like a factory: centralized, author-itarian control; impersonal, "natural" (IQ level) and social (bureaucratic rules) control systems; a hierarchy of tracks, grades and schools; and intense competition. And the educational system is designed to be consumed like a T.V. commercial: the student passively receives the "knowledge" necessary to consume and work under the prerogatives of profit. School is increasingly a principal mechanism by which the social fabric is held together.

Part of the debate over the class location of those in the educational system, as well as those in other social reproduction jobs, concerns the distinction between their *structural* place in the particular institution and the *function* they serve within that institution. Some authors argue that the class position of a person is determined solely by whether or not she or he has control over the institution, and has nothing to do with the person's particular function within the institution. In the case of the educational system, this debate is further influenced by the class structured nature of the educational system in this country, whether you're talking about Springfield Community College or Harvard. One's control over the teaching function diminishes the lower one is on the ladder. Teachers who have little if any control over what and how they teach would be included in the working class according to this position. Others would argue that all this may be true but the fact that a person is fulfilling the teaching function puts them in a relationship which perpetuates the elitism, the paternalism, the control of knowledge and the corresponding passivity and resentment which constitute significant class barriers between the two groups (e.g., between the PMC and the working class).

The State

Loss of control on the job is paralleled by the state's increasing control over our lives. Whether it is the violent subversion of progressive movements around the world, the intervention in labor/capital conflicts, the provision of all the various welfare services, the subsidization of private capital by its monetary and fiscal policies, or the acting as a planning board for international capital expansion, by its structure and by its specific actions, the state mediates intra- and inter-class struggles so as to keep the capitalist system intact. But perhaps even more important than all the coercive and remedial functions that the state serves is its role in trying to convince people that their democratic rights ensure that they can control their government. Voters must be convinced that they are deciding who the next president will be when in fact the range of their choice, and the basis upon which to choose, have all been decided behind their backs. Elections are an attempt to convince society that it has a choice when it doesn't.

The debate about the influence of the state on social reproduction and the class position of those who work for the state centers in part on the *autonomy* of the state. Autonomy here is a relative term which refers to the degree to which the state acts independently of the dynamics arising from the capitalist economy. Traditional Marxist theories of the state were based on the distinction between the economic *base* and the political and ideological *superstructure*. In the simplest of these models, the superstructure merely reflects changes in the base as determined by the forces of capital accumulation. In recent years, with the increasing intervention of the state into the economy, the base/superstructure formulation has been challenged by theories which give the state a much greater degree of autonomy.

In the previous section, we saw that some authors argue it is one's position in the structure of control that determines one's class position. But if the structures of control in the state are not determined in the same way as they are in the sphere of production, can class analysis be equally meaningful in both cases? To the extent that bureaucracies within the ideological and political institutions have a logic of their own determined by the political power groups and parties within them, there is no reason to think that people in a similar position in terms of control in the state and in the factory will necessarily have similar interests in either maintaining or overthrowing the system. A manual worker in a factory who is exploited by the capitalist will have much more interest in overthowing the system than a manual worker for the state whose job is due to the patronage of a reactionary party.

The degree of autonomy we see the state having thus affects not only the class location of individuals within the state apparatus, but also possibly the importance of class itself. To pose the question at its extremes: at one end, the state is the instrument of the ruling class, and/or the structure of the state is determined by the class struggle. The economy determines the state. At the other end, state intervention and the displacement of the class struggle to the political arena repoliticizes the economy to such an extent that the power groups and parties that determine state policies are the primary social movers. The state determines the economy.

Those who line up toward the former side will see the logic of capital dominating the state, and will correspondingly locate people and their revolutionary potential according to class analysis. Those who line up towards the latter side will use other types of institutional analysis for understanding revolutionary levers in society. An alternative theory posits an explanation in which neither the economy nor the state dominate. Both class analysis and other forms of political institutional analysis complement each other in their joint attempt to unravel how the state and the economy together shape social reality.

The Family

According to some authors, the family performs a dual role in social reproduction: in its production of domestic maintenance, procreation, nurturance and sexuality, the family reproduces the labor force, *and* it reproduces the sexist oppression of women. The authoritarian relationships between parents and children help contribute to the (present and future) worker's lack of self-confidence and acceptance of capitalist rule. At the same time this patriarchal domination systematically exploits women in their production of domestic goods and services. According to these authors, sexism cannot be explained by capitalism alone; rather it also has its own internal dynamics which are rooted in the family and which ramify throughout society.

The inclusion of the family brings up two related problems: what is the place of other *modes of production,* and of other forms of oppression in our conception of social reproduction? Within any society there may be many modes of production: family, slave, feudal or capitalist modes of production, for instance. Each has its own means of production and its own set of production relations which determine how goods and services will be produced and allocated. Each mode will have its own particular structure of classes or social groupings, which will further complicate the social forces at work in the whole society.

Racism and sexism may be considered as separate modes of production, perhaps slave and family modes, or as the vestiges of earlier modes of production. Alternatively, they may be seen as social forms of oppression which do not constitute a mode of production, and are not explainable by the dynamics of the capitalist mode of production alone. They have a life of their own.

The possibility of other modes of production, or of non-economically rooted forms of oppression, or the possible divergence of the internal dynamics of some of the institutions of social reproduction from the logic of capital all serve to question the general applicability of the Marxist concept of class.

CLASS

Our discussion of social reproduction has hopefully served the purpose of sketching parts of the totality that are being debated in the essays that follow. In this section we will focus on a concept we have been using rather loosely, class. The discussion is broken into three parts: the purposes that the authors see class analysis fulfilling, the criteria that constitute membership in a class, and the relationship between class and class consciousness. In the previous section the emphasis was on the social totality. In this section the emphasis will be on comparing how the various authors understand the development of class consciousness that is capable of transforming the oppressive conditions of this social totality.

Purposes of Class Analysis

Why study class? Towards what purposes do each of the following authors use their analyses? In order to meaningfully compare the following essays, and to self-consciously develop our own positions, it might be useful to clarify at the outset the various purposes that the authors see their class analysis as fulfilling.

One purpose of class analysis may be to systematically decode class locations in a capitalist society. Having *described* all possible class positions, one could use this framework to analyze specific historical processes and events. Similarly, a second purpose could be to use class analysis to understand the capital accumulation process. Class analysis would then be used to show how class structure and class struggle influence the nature and amount of surplus labor extracted from the exploited classes. On the one hand, if the working class is able to shorten the working day, or slow down the pace of work, or gain greater control over the production process, then less surplus will be available for capital accumulation. On the other hand, if society becomes increasingly stratified, the class struggle may subside, and the total surplus may increase, though more of it may go to the state and "the middle layers." From this perspective, the purpose of class analysis is often limited to explaining the dynamics of the economy, and would not be applicable to a general analysis of social forces.

A third purpose of class analysis is often to determine which is (are) the revolutionary class(es) in a society. With this intent, the process of analyzing the class structure of a society can reveal who is the most oppressed and exploited, or who is the most critical to the functioning of society, or who is most likely to develop revolutionary consciousness. This type of analysis would *prescribe,* at least potentially, who was to transform society. Following this line of reasoning, one would go on to determine the forms of revolutionary organization and the kinds of revolutionary issues most applicable, though of course other factors would affect this determination as well. The particular class structure would, however, at least influence whether one advocated mass working class parties, vanguard parties, autonomous parties and/or councils for different economic classes, as well as for different races and sexes. With this orientation, class analysis would further reveal the issues which divide the revolutionary class(es) and which unify them against capitalism (patriarchy, racism). In a highly stratified society, one may conclude that issues of status, cultural differences and educational background will determine that the various forms of elitism are the main issues to be struggled over amongst the people, while democracy and genuine, decentralized popular control of workplaces and communites are the issues which will unify the people.

Finally, a purpose of class analysis may also be to perceive the alternative aims of revolution. An analysis that shows the existence of many revolutionary classes or strata may indicate the potential for certain of these classes to usurp the general revolutionary interest in their attempts to preserve or extend their particular interests. The failure to acknowledge the existence of some class, say the Professional-Managerial Class, and thus the failure to develop the appropriate strategies to deal with these differences, may allow those in that class to gain excessive control in post-revolutionary political and economic institutions thereby creating a society which perpetuates the stratified character of the society supposedly being transformed.

In each essay that follows, one or more of these purposes will become apparent. Are these purposes mutually exclusive, or does the last logically follow from the first? Can class analysis both describe society and prescribe the manner of its transformation?

Class Criteria

These purposes influence the criteria chosen to define class. What one wants class analysis to do will influence what one defines as a class. This in not just a definitional debate—academic haggling. The criteria we use to define class deeply influence who one sees as the revolutionary class(es), what will be the forms of organization, the strategies, issues.

As mentioned above, the criterion most often used to define class is the ownership and control of the means of producing a society's goods and services. One class owns and controls; the other doesn't. The bourgeoisie, because of its ownership and control, is able to exploit the working class by forcing it to produce a value greater it receives for its own labor time. This surplus value becomes the capitalist's profit, the basis for further capital accumulation and luxury consumption.

Two related criteria are control over one's own labor, and control over others' labor. Though certain workers do not own the means of production, the fact that they exercize control either over their own or others' labor creates antagonistic relations between them and those who do not control their labor. For instance, antagonisms between middle level managers and workers on the line, between doctors and nurses are often over the issue of control.

Another economic criterion is social function. As in the case of teachers discussed above, certain occupations involve functions which separates some workers from others. For instance, the function of the engineer in conceiving how the work process will be organized separates him or her from the workers who perform the manual labor in the execution of the task.

Having a coherent social and cultural existence is also a criterion for class. To be a class a group must share a common social identity, have common forms of cultural expression, shared traditions, languages. In this view, a group to be a class would need to exhibit a certain degree of social cohesion arising from shared historical experiences, for instance the working class traditions of England and Western Europe. The issue that this criterion raises is the extent to which the economic sphere influences the non-economic dimensions? To what extent does geography, ethnic and linguistic backgrounds, pre-capitalist history, forms of community and family life, and various forms of cultural expression influence the development of a working class?

Similarly a political criterion may be specified. To be a class by this definition a group would have to develop past social and cultural forms of self-consciousness to the point where it can represent itself politically on a national basis. To be considered a class a group would have to defend and extend its interests in the political sphere.

A Class In-Itself and a Class For-Itself

The relations between the criteria outlined above can be illustrated in terms of the relation authors see between the in-itself and for-itself aspects of a class.

A class-in-itself usually refers to a class as being constituted of various socio-historic relations, as being formed by the system of which it is a part. A class-in-itself, for instance, shares the same ownership or control relations to the means of production, or the same place in the division of labor, or a common social and cultural background.

A class-for-itself refers to a class as being self-conscious of its socio-historic constitution, as being self-forming. Traditionally a class-for-itself forms a political party, develops a program and struggles for its implementation. A class-in-itself is made up of certain economic, and possibly non-economic relations; a class-for-itself makes itself.

Well enough, but what is the relation between the passive and the active, between being made and self-making, between systemic determination and self-formation? The authors differ in their opinions both as to what are the constitutive relations of a class-in-itself, and as to whether the criteria which represent a class being for-itself should be included in the determination of class.

On one side of the spectrum, is the position that the social relations of production are solely constitutive of class, that the logic of capital accumulation causes the working class to become self-conscious, and that the working class' vision of socialism is formed in the labor process. On the other side, is the position that a whole array of forms of institutional domination together constitute systemic determination, that there is no necessary relation between these institutions and revolutionary consciousness.

Between these poles, various authors focus on different social determinants that influence class consciousness in varying degrees. Some stress that in addition to occupying a common place in the social division of labor, a class must have a coherent social and cultural existence, and that these two factors together determine class consciousness (therefore not including a for-itself criterion in the definition of class). Others consider the economic, ideological and political structures to be co-constitutive of one's class location, and that life style, educational background, kinship networks, consumption patterns, and beliefs are dependent on class location (limiting the in-itself, and excluding the for-itself). Still another position maintains that economic and social determinants are pre-conditions, that one must be in the capital/labor conflict, but that there is no necessary relation between these pre-conditions and the sufficient condition of national political representation. If a class does not represent itself politically, it is not a class. Another position seeks to explain the full dimensions of class through a class' subjective experience of the totality of social relations which comprise itself.

These positions vary as to the degree of autonomy given to self-formation. Some authors see class consciousness arising inevitably out of the social relations of production, others see it as being given, dependent, or pre-conditioned, still others see the two as being discontinuous. The tension is either broken at the extremes or varies in degree and vagueness in between.

REVOLUTION

Who do the authors see as making the revolution, what will be the issues that unify them, and how will they be organized?

As might be expected, based upon the widely divergent purposes and criteria, the authors end up with quite different ideas as to who will likely become revolutionary. A number of authors conclude with a broad definition of the working class within which there may be different strata but whose primary identification is its opposition to capital. This position is based on the fact that this expanded working class does not own the means of production and is increasingly loosing control over their labor as proletarianization continues. Opposed to this position is the claim that there is a third class, i.e., the PMC, which has its own set of interests in opposition to both capitalist and workers.

In between, one author defines the working class narrowly, but doesn't posit a third class; rather maintains that there are contradictory class locations between the working class and the capitalists in which workers could be polarized in either direction depending upon a number of factors. Another author argues that there is a third class, the petty bourgeoisie, but that there are several strata within it, some of which are likely to align with the working class. Still another position holds to a narrowly defined working class and a narrowly defined "middle class" and maintains in addition that there are contradictory class locations between this third class and the working class.

Extending the concept of class, another author argues that women constitute a sex class who have the same revolutionary potential as the working class. Going beyond the concept of class, one theory holds that, in addition to class, certain races, sexes or levels in the hierarchy may become revolutionary agents alongside the working class but by different routes of development. Another position maintains that all those with radical needs constitute together the revolutionary basis upon which to transform society.

The more broadly one defines the working class, the clearer it becomes who is on which side and what the fight is over. But this clarity is gained at the sacrifice of being able to distinguish what the differences are between the revolutionary groupings, and what the multiple purposes of revolution might be.

External unity is the unity attained between groups as a result of their struggle against a common opposition; internal unity is the unity attained between groups as a result of their struggling over contradictions amongst themselves. Capitalism is the common enemy, the main basis of external unity, for most of the authors. Capitalism and patriarchy are the central issues for some. Capitalism, patriarchy, racism and authority are the central issues for others. All forms of institutional oppression are the central issues for yet others.

The more issues included, the more diffused become the focus, but the more total becomes the change. The inclusion of third classes, or different races, sexes or levels in the hierarchy suggest new factors which may be a basis of both internal and external unity—struggling against the reactionary forces which maintain these forms of oppression, and struggling over these contradictions as they arise amongst the revolutionary groupings.

The different organizational forms authors propose are based primarily on different analyses of particular historical traditions and conditions, who the revolutionary agents will be, how revolutionary consciousness is formed, and the type of socialist society envisioned. On the one side, a highly disciplined vanguard party is advocated; on the other, a loose alliance of autonomous councils. One side leans toward democratic centralism, the other towards participatory democracy. In between, some authors advocate mass working class parties, while others propose more binding alliances of revolutionary organizations. Some combine these organizational forms in different ways. The looser the organizational form, the more people can be directly involved, but also the more difficult it is to achieve the cohesion necessary to carry through the revolution.

III

In the previous part, I tried to introduce the main concepts and points of difference in the authors' treatment of social reproduction, class and revolution. Before concluding this introduction, I would like to offer a few observations on the problems raised in the previous part.

Beginning with social reproduction, I sketched out various parts of the social totality discussed in the following essays. But how do we understand this totality as a whole? Is it the sum of all the discreet parts, or are these parts particular expressions of an interrelated process? For the sake of simplicity, it might be useful to distinguish between the atomistic view of society and the relational view. The former sees social reality as a piece of glass broken into a zillion pieces, each of which can be understood by itself at a point in time. From the relational point of view, all aspects of social reality are like prisms through which you can see all the relations of that aspect extending throughout the present as well as backwards in time. The atomistic view is ahistorical and fragmented. The relational view sees all islands as peaks of an ever changing landscape.

As simple as the distinction may seem, it has profound implications once we begin to explore how it shapes our conception of human being. In the discussion of class, there is considerable debate over the purposes of class analysis, and the relation between "material conditions" and class consciousness. The debate over the purpose of class analysis concerns the relation between our study of society and society. How do we think? The atomistic view would lead us to hold that either we are blanks that passively reflect outside impressions, or that we are completely self-determining individuals, capable of apprehending the world according to our own set of concepts. Relationally, we are neither blanks nor completely autonomous.

According to the relational view, people are constituted of all the relations that have comprised their natural and social existence, and are thus determined by these relations—we are these relations. But right from conception we are in the process of self-formation. By acting upon our growing awareness of our interdetermination by the relations we grow up in, we are increasingly able to become *more* self-determining. According to this point of view, the process of thinking is seen as a process in which the knower (the individual) and the known (social reality) are both developing within a process of mutual interdetermination. Concepts themselves are seen as many sided tensions, specific to the socio-historic relations that they conceive and are conceived from, and at the same time they point beyond the specific moment (in the same way that the relations that they conceive of point beyond themselves in their prefiguration of what future outcomes are possible given the present configuration of relations).

Before, we asked if class analysis can both describe and prescribe. What I've tried to indicate above is that the debate becomes paralyzed unless we are explicit about the underlying theories of knowing and being behind our arguments. In this case, if we see ourselves as completely insular, there is just one or the other: description or prescription, the "scientist" or the priest. If we see the peaks as part of a larger landscape, the door is open for understanding the dynamics of historical development, and the possibilities for the future.

The second major debate is the relation between a class-in-itself and a class-for-itself—between "material conditions" and revolutionary consciousness. The problem of how material conditions influence the development of class consciousness is the flip side of the problem that we discussed above of how do we know of these conditions. How do we know of the social totality, and how does it develop?

All the rigorous critiques of capitalism will gain us nothing, if we do not have an even more thorough understanding of how revolutionary consciousness develops. Some readers may say that the way I've posed the question in terms of a class-in-itself and a class-for-itself bars the answer by assuming from the outset that the two are somehow qualitatively different. I do not think that the distinction needs to imply this, but the objection raises a fundamental assumption that needs to be aired.

Are material conditions and consciousness different in degree of extension in time and space, or are they two qualitatively different kinds of existence? Do material conditions necessarily have a greater influence on historical outcomes than, say, a theory about the overthrow of capitalism? The material conditions which influence consciousness to whatever degree are themselves the products, the embodiments, of human activity. To conceive of these conditions as completely separable things indicates the extent to which we have lost control of the world that we have created. If we understand human being as constituted of all the natural and social relations that comprise the world, then the products of human activity, society in all its aspects, are themselves seen as complex sets of relations created over time. The material world and the realms of consciousness are here understood as constituted of the same relations, as being co-extensive. One doesn't impact upon the other from the outside; they both change together in varying degrees dependent upon the importance of the particular relation to their constitutions.

Consciousness is always determined; revolutionary consciousness, based upon its putting into practice its understanding of the world that is, and the world it seeks to create, will be increasingly able to transform itself in its transformation of society.

The roots of individual self-determination are themselves grounded in the soil of revolutionary consciousness. The individual, by her or himself, can become more self-determing (but can only limitedly change the social relations in which she or he lives). Only a revolution which genuinely involves people in taking control of their lives will realize true liberation. A revolution which realizes the full implications of the relational view—that material conditions and consciousness both must change together—will develop the revolutionary compassion that follows upon the realization that the liberation of any one person, group or nation depends upon the full liberation of everyone.

What is the relation between class analysis and class consciousness? Our dialectical understanding of the world is integrally related to the dialectical development of the world. How we know, and how we become are the subjective and objective vistas onto one infinitely, interrelated process. If class analysis (or critical theoretical analysis in general) is made by those who have a clear philosophical framework, are involved in ongoing research, and are themselves personally engaged in day-to-day organizational work, then their analyses will heighten the revolutionary struggle. On the other hand, as the world capitalist crisis deepens, and as revolutionary movements around the world continue to expand, these struggles will deepen our analyses. Parts of the same process, our full understanding of society proceeds in hand with our greater ability to take control of it.

Are we islands, or are we peaks of expression, self-determined to realize ourselves as onekind?

Again, the reason for raising such questions in this introduction is twofold: first, the failure to be clear about the basic assumptions lying behind the various arguments severely limits the ability to compare them; secondly, in order to go beyond this debate, not only is more concrete research needed, but more careful elaboration of the philosophical premises that are to guide revolutionary practice.

IV

What isn't in this debate. Racism and the oppression of people of color. Only two articles discuss race at all, and only briefly at that. And much more: sexual oppression, especially that of lesbians and gays; religion and the control of the organized church; ageist oppression, the isolation of youths and the long living: and much more. Where do these other oppressions, realities which touch us all, fit into our understanding of class, social reproduction and socialist revolution?

Can the concepts put forth in the following essays comprehend these realities? Or should they? How broadly do we circumscribe our whole? How do we understand the tensions within it? Between it and people's consciousness? The inclusion of the people of the United States in the process of creating a socialist society critically depends upon how we understand and act upon these tensions. Theoretical struggle has deadly earnest results.

P. W.
Boston
12/11/78

BETWEEN
LABOR AND CAPITAL

I

The Professional-Managerial Class

Barbara & John Ehrenreich

To generations of radicals, the working class has been the bearer of socialism, the agent of both progressive social reform and revolution. But in the United States in the last two decades, the left has been concentrated most heavily among people who feel themselves to be "middle-class," while the working class has appeared relatively quiescent. This "middle-class" left, unlike its equivalent in early twentieth-century Europe or in the Third World today, is not a minority within a mass working class (or peasant) movement; it is, to a very large extent, the left itself. It has its own history of mass struggle, not as an ally or appendage of the industrial working class, but as a mass constituency in and of itself. At the same time, most of the U.S. left continues to believe (correctly, we think) that without a mass working class left, only the most marginal of social reforms is possible.

None of these historical anomalies about the U.S. left is explained by the theories to which most of the left now adheres. Orthodox Marxism describes capitalist society as being polarized between the bourgeoisie and the proletariat; it has nothing to say about a "middle class," or of course, about middle-class radicalism. Thus, the left today may sense the impasse created by the narrowness of its class composition, but it lacks even the terms with which to describe the situation, much less a strategy of overcoming it.

Theoretical confusion about class is endemic among all parts of the left. Some leftists (mainly associated with the "new communist movement") describe students, professionals, and other educated workers as "petty bourgeois" though more as a put-down than as a defensible analysis. Other contemporary leftists describe all salary and wage workers who do not own the means of production as "working class." The working class so conceived is a near universal class, embracing all but the actual capitalists and the classical petty bourgeoisie (i.e., small tradesmen, independent farmers, etc.). But this group, too, finds its definition practically untenable. In practice, and conversationally, these leftists use the terms "working class" and "middle class" with their colloquial connotations, knowing that the distinction is still somehow a useful one. Yet this distinction cannot be pursued in theory: the prevailing theoretical framework insists that all wage earners are working class and that the notion that some workers are "middle class" is a capitalist inspired delusion.

When analysis stops, the problem does not necessarily go away. Rather, it is at that point that the door opens to all kinds of irrational and subjectivist approaches. In the years since the New Left in the U.S. matured from a radical to a socialist outlook, the left has dashed itself repeatedly against the contradictions between its "middle class" origins and its working class allegiance. Some pursue the search for a "pure" proletarian line to an ever more rarefied sectarianism. Others seem to find comfort in the ambiguities of contemporary class analysis, fearing that any attempt to draw more careful distinctions will leave them in an undesirable category ("petty bourgeois," etc.). At this point the very emotion surrounding the subject of class provides a further impediment to analysis. Yet if the left is to grow, it must begin to come to an objective understanding of its own class origins and to comprehend objectively the barriers that have isolated it from the working class.

I. Classes In Monopoly Capitalist Society

The classical Marxian analysis of capitalist society centers on two classes and two alone—the bourgeoisie and the proletariat. The other numerically large class of mature capitalist society, the petty bourgeoisie, lies outside of this central polarity, and is in a loose sense anachronistic: a class left over from an earlier social order, which undergoes a continual process of "proletarianization" (i.e., its members are progressively forced down into the proletariat).[1] Meanwhile, the working class not only expands to embrace the vast majority of the working population, but also becomes more and more homogenous and unified.

As early as the turn of the century it was becoming evident that the class structures of the advanced capitalist countries were not evolving along quite so straight a path. The middle classes were simply not withering away; new, educated and salaried middle class strata had appeared and were growing rapidly. Most Marxists, however, either ignored the new strata or insisted that they, like the old middle class of independent artisans and entrepreneurs would become proletarianized. It was left to radical social theorists outside the Marxian mainstream (such as Emil Lederer and Jacob Marschak in Germany and C. Wright Mills in the United States) to analyze the "new middle classes." In these analyses, the salaried white-collar workers were not seen as a single class, but rather as a disparate group, ranging from clerical workers to engineers and college professors, connected to each other (and to the old middle classes) by little more than a common desire not to fall into the proletariat.

By early in the sixties, the explosive growth and continued social distinctiveness of the stratum of educated wage earners had become impossible for Marxists to ignore. But Marxian theorists were not yet ready to give up the attempt at forcing engineers, teachers, government workers and accountants into the proletarian mold. Pierre Belleville, Andre Gorz, and Serge Mallet were the first Marxists to chronicle and analyze the emergence of what they called, in opposition to Mills, et. al., the "new working class." The new working class, wrote Gorz in 1964, like the old working class, was defined by its antagonistic relation to capital.

> Technicians, engineers, students, researchers discover that they are wage earners like the others, paid for a piece of work which is 'good' only to the degree it is profitable in the short run. They discover that long-range research, creative work on original problems, and the love of workmanship are incompatible with the criteria of capitalist profitability....[2]

Despite their immediate consciousness as "middle class," the

1. "Our epoch, the epoch of the bourgeoisie, possesses...this distinctive feature: it has simplified the class antagonisms. Society as a whole is more and more splitting up into two great hostile camps, into two great classes directly facing each other—bourgeoisie and proletariat." Karl Marx and Friedrich Engels, *The Communist Manifesto.*

2. Andre Gorz, *Strategy For Labor* (Beacon Press, 1967), p.104.

growing body of educated workers are, according to this analysis, a stratum of the working class.[3]

A decade later, after the rise and decline of a New Left based heavily among students and educated workers, it had become apparent that the gulf between the "old" and "new" working classes was deeper than the earlier analyses had suggested. Nicos Poulantzas suggested making a distinction between labor necessary for production of commodities and labor necessary for the reproduction of capitalist social relationships. Thus, according to Poulantzas, workers in the state and other "ideological apparatuses"—schools, government agencies, welfare agencies, mass media, etc.—must be considered as being in a different class from production workers.[4]

In the early '70's Andre Gorz, too, broke with his own earlier analysis, arguing that it was not only workers in the ideological apparatuses who served reproductive roles, but also the engineers, scientists, managers, etc., in productive enterprises. The capitalist division of labor has been determined by the need to control the workers and the work process in the context of class antagonism, and *not* only by technological imperatives.[5] Thus, proposed Gorz, even at the point of production, a distinction must be made between productive and reproductive labor.

> We shall not succeed in locating technical and scientific labor within the class structure of advanced capitalist society unless we start by analyzing what functions technical and scientific labor perform in the process of capital accumulation and in the process of reproducing social relations. The question as to whether technicians, engineers, research workers and the like belong to the middle class or to the working class must be made to depend upon the following questions: 1) (a) Is their function required by the process of material production as such

3. For similar views see Pierre Belleville, *Une Nouvelle Classe Ouviere* (Juilliard, 1963); Serge Mallet, *Essays on the New Working Class* (Telos Press, 1975); Alain Touraine, *The May Movement* (Random House, 1971); Stanley Aronowitz, *False Promises* (McGraw-Hill, 1973); Francesca Freedman, "The Internal Structure of the American Proletariat: A Marxist Analysis," *Socialist Revolution*, #26 (Oct.-Dec. 1975), pp. 41-84.

4. Nicos Poulantzas, *Classes in Contemporary Capitalism* (Humanities Press, 1975), p.27.

5. Stephen Marglin, "What Do Bosses Do?", *Review of Radical Political Economics,* Vol. 6, #3 (Summer 1974); also see Katherine Stone, "The Origins of Job Structures in the Steel Industry," *Radical America*, Vol. 7, #6 (Nov.-Dec. 1973).

or (b) by capital's concern for ruling and controlling the productive process and the work process from above? 2) (a) Is their function required by concern for the greatest possible efficiency in production technology? or (b) does the concern for efficient production technology come second only to the concern for "social technology," i.e., for keeping the labor force disciplined, hierarchically regimented and divided? 3) (a) Is the present definition of technical skill and knowledge primarily required by the technical division of labor and thereby based upon scientific and ideologically neutral data? or (b) is the definition of technical skill and knowledge primarily social and ideological, as an outgrowth of the social division of labor?[6]

Both Gorz and Poulantzas conclude that there is an "unbridgeable objective class distinction," as Gorz puts it, between professional, technical and managerial workers and production workers. The problem, then, is where to place these mental workers in the class structure of capitalist society. But Gorz, so far as we know, has not extended his analysis of the class position of "technical workers" any further. Poulantzas refuses to break with Marx's two-class model, taking refuge in the dogmatic assertion that to "maintain that capitalism itself produces a new class in the course of its development" is *"unthinkable* for Marxist theory" (emphasis ours). He ends up by lumping the educated workers along with all other non-productive workers—wage earners (educated or not) in banks, commerce, service industries, government, etc.—in a stratum of the petty bourgeoisie which he calls the "new petty bourgeoisie."[7]

We will argue that the "middle class" category of workers which has concerned Marxist analysis for the last two decades—the technical workers, managerial workers, "culture" producers, etc.—must be understood as comprising a distinct class in monopoly capitalist society. The Professional-Managerial Class ("PMC"), as we will define it, cannot be considered a stratum of a broader "class" of "workers" because it exists in an objectively antagonistic relationship to another class of wage

6. Andre Gorz, "Technical Intelligence and the Capitalist Division of Labor," *Telos,* #12 (Summer 1972), pp. 27-28.

7. Nicos Poulantzas, "On Social Classes," *New Left Review,* #78 (March-April, 1973), p. 78.

earners (whom we shall simply call the "working class").[8] Nor can it be considered to be a "residual" class like the petty bourgeoisie; it is a formation specific to the monopoly stage of capitalism. It is only in the light of this analysis, we believe, that it is possible to understand the role of technical, professional and managerial workers in advanced capitalist society and in the radical movements.

Let us begin by clarifying what we mean by a "class." With E.P. Thompson, we see class as having meaning only as a relationship:

> ...The notion of class entails the notion of historical relationship. Like any other relationship, it is a fluency which evades analysis if we attempt to stop it dead at any given moment and anatomize its structure. The finest meshed sociological analysis cannot give us a pure specimen of class, any more than it can give us one of deference or of love. The relationship must always be embodied in real people and in a real context. Moreover, we cannot have two distinct classes, each with an independent being, and then bring them into relationships with each other. We cannot have love without lovers, not deference without squires and labourers.[9]

It follows that any class which is not residual—i.e., merely "leftover" from another era, like the European aristocracy in the 19th century—can be properly defined only in the context of 1) the totality of class relationships and 2) the historical development of these relationships. Thus, if we were going to fully and properly define a Professional-Managerial Class, we would not be able to restrict ourselves to a picture of this group as a sociological entity; we would have to deal, at all stages, with the complementary and mutually interacting developments in the bourgeoisie and the working class. The story of the rise and development of the PMC is simultaneously the story of the rise of the *modern* bourgeoisie and the *modern* proletariat as they have taken form in monopoly capitalist society. Here, of course, we can give only a fragment of this story. We will focus on the PMC itself, skimming lightly over the complementary developments in other classes.

8. "PMC" is, perhaps, an awkward term. But the more obvious "new middle class" has been used with a variety of definitions (e.g., by C. Wright Mills and Richard Hofstadter, who include sales and clerical workers in it), which could only lead to confusion. Moreover, "new middle class" obscures the fact that the class we are identifying is not part of some broader middle class, which includes both "old" and "new" strata, but rather is a distinct class, separate from the old middle class.

9. E.P. Thompson, *The Making of the English Working Class,*(Vintage, 1966), p. 9.

From our point of view, a class (as opposed to a stratum or other social grouping) is defined by two major characteristics:

1. At all times in its historical development, a class is characterized by a common relation to the economic foundations of society—the means of production and the socially organized patterns of distribution and consumption. By a common "relation" we do not mean a purely juridical relationship; e.g., legal ownership or non-ownership of the means of production.[10] Class is defined by actual relations between groups of people, not formal relations between people and objects. The former may or may not coincide, at any given moment in history, with the legal relationships evolved over previous years. The relations which define class arise from the place occupied by groups in the broad social division of labor, and from the basic patterns of control over access to the means of production and of appropriation of the social surplus.

2. However, the relation to the economic foundations of society is not sufficient to specify a class as a real social entity. At any moment in its historical development after its earliest, formative period, a class is characterized by a coherent social and cultural existence; members of a class share a common life style, educational background, kinship networks, consumption patterns, work habits, beliefs. These cultural and social patterns cannot be derived in any simple fashion from the concurrently existing relationship to the means of production of the members of the class. For one thing, culture has a memory: social patterns formed in earlier periods, when a different relation to the means of production (or even another mode of production) prevailed, may long survive their "owners" separation from the earlier relationships. (For example, the culture of an industrial working class newly recruited from a semi-feudal peasantry is quite different from that of habitually urbanized workers.) In addition, the social existence of a group of people is determined not only by its experience at the point of production, but by its experience in private life (mediated especially by kinship relations, production). The relationship between class as abstract economic relationship and class as real social existence has been all-but-unexplored; for our purposes we shall have to limit ourselves to insisting that a class has both characteristics.

Having stated these two general characteristics, we should strongly emphasize that class is an analytic abstraction, a way of putting some order into an otherwise bewildering array of individual and group

---

10. For more on the relationship between juridical ownership of the means of production and class see Ross Grundy, "More on the Nature of Soviet Society," *Monthly Review* (May 1976).

characteristics and interrelationships. It describes a phenomenon existing most clearly at the level of society as a whole. When, however, the notion of class is called on to explain or predict infallibly the actions, ideas and relationships of every individual, it ceases to be very useful.

Our description of the historical experience of the PMC will be abbreviated and episodic, leaving out many key developments in the history of the class (most importantly, any elaboration on the expansion of the state in the twentieth century) and restricting ourselves to the United States. We will begin with a schematic definition of the PMC, then describe the emergence of its distinctive class outlook and its consolidation as a class in the early part of the twentieth century, and finally return to the situation of the contemporary left.

II. A Definition

We define the Professional-Managerial Class as consisting of salaried mental workers who do not own the means of production and whose major function in the social division of labor may be described broadly as the reproduction of capitalist culture and capitalist class relations.[11]

Their role in the process of reproduction may be more or less explicit, as with workers who are directly concerned with social control or with the production and propagation of ideology (e.g., teachers, social workers, psychologists, entertainers, writers of advertising copy and TV scripts, etc.). Or it may be hidden within the process of production, as is the case with the middle-level administrators and managers, engineers, and other technical workers whose functions, as Gorz, Steve Marglin, Harry Braverman and others have argued, are essentially determined by the need to preserve capitalist relations of production. Thus we assert that these occupational groups—cultural workers, managers, engineers and scientists, etc.—share a common function in the broad social division of labor and a common relation to the economic foundations of society.[12]

11. We do not, of course, mean by "culture" merely "high" culture or the arts in general. By the culture of a social group we mean its total repertory of solutions and responses to everyday problems and situations. This is transmittable repertory, and the means of transmission may be anything from myths and songs to scientific formulae and machinery.

12. Throughout this essay, "manager," unless otherwise qualified, means lower- and middle-leveled managers. In advanced capitalism, the capitalists are the corporations, not the individual entrepreneurs of an earlier period. The people who as a group own a substantial portion of their stock, and as individuals have direct and dominant power over their functioning, can only be considered as part of the ruling class. The top officials of large non-corporate enterprises (i.e., government, large foundations, etc.) are also part of the ruling class.

The PMC, by our definition, includes people with a wide range of occupations, skills, income levels, power and prestige. The boundaries separating it from the ruling class above and the working class below are fuzzy. In describing the class standing of people near the divide separating the PMC from other classes (e.g., registered nurses, welfare case workers, engineers in routine production or inspection jobs at the lower end, middle levels of corporate and state bureaucratic managers at the upper end), we must emphasize two aspects of our definition of class: First (in Paul Sweezy's words), "It would be a mistake to think of a class as perfectly homogeneous internally and sharply marked off from other classes. Actually there is variety within the class; and one class sometimes shades off very gradually and almost imperceptibly into another."* Second, occupation is not the sole determinant of class (nor even the sole determinant of the relation to the means of production).

Consider the case of the registered nurse: she may have been recruited from a working class, PMC or petty-bourgeois family. Her education may be two years in a working-class community college or four years in a private, upper-middle-class college. On the job, she may be a worker, doing the most menial varieties of bedside nursing, supervising no one, using only a small fraction of the skills and knowledge she learned at school. Or she may be a part of management, supervising dozens, even hundreds of other RN's, practical nurses and nurses' aides. Moreover, over 98 per cent of RN's are women; their class standing is, in significant measure, linked to that of their husband. Some nurses do, in fact, marry doctors; far more marry lower-level professionals, while many others marry blue-collar and lower-level white-collar workers. So there is simply no way to classify registered nurses as a group. What seems to be a single occupational category is in fact socially and functionally heterogeneous.

Much the same kind of analysis could be made of most of the other groupings near the boundaries of the PMC. The situation of the groups near the PMC-working-class border, we should note, is especially likely to be ambiguous: it is here that the process of "de-skilling" —of rationalizing previously professional tasks into a number of completely routinized functions requiring little training—occurs. Moreover, a disproportionate number of people in these groups are women, for whom purely occupational criteria for class are especially inadequate.

Despite the lack of precise delineation of the boundaries of the PMC, by combining occupational data and statistics on property

* Paul Sweezy, *The Present As History* (Monthly Review Press, 1953), p. 124.

distribution we can make a very crude estimate of the class composition of U.S. society: by this estimate about 65 to 70 per cent of the U.S. population is working class. (We accept Braverman's conception of the working class: craftsmen, operatives, laborers, sales workers, clerical workers, service workers, non-college-educated technical workers.) Eight to ten per cent is in the "old middle class" (i.e., self-employed professionals, small tradespeople, independent farmers, etc.). Twenty to twenty-five per cent is PMC; and one to two per cent is ruling class. That is, the PMC includes something like fifty million people.

The very definition of the PMC—as a class concerned with the reproduction of capitalist culture and class relationships—precludes treating it as a separable sociological entity. It is in a sense a derivative class; its existence presupposes: 1) that the social surplus has developed to a point sufficient to sustain the PMC in addition to the bourgeoisie, for the PMC is essentially non-productive; and 2) that the relationship between the bourgeoisie and the proletariat has developed to the point that a class specializing in the reproduction of capitalist class relationships becomes a necessity to the capitalist class. That is, the maintenance of order can no longer be left to episodic police violence.

Historically, these conditions were met in the U.S by the early twentieth century. The last half of the nineteenth century saw: 1) the development of an enormous social surplus, concentrated in monopolistic corporations and individual capitalists; and 2) intermittent, violent warfare between the industrial working class and the capitalist class. The possibility of outright insurrection was taken very seriously by both bourgeois and radical observers. At the same time, however, the new concentration and centralization of capital opened up the possibilities of long-term planning, the refinement of "management" (essentially as a substitute for force), and the capitalist rationalization of both productive and consumptive processes. In the decades immediately following the turn of the century, these possibilities began to be realized:

1. At the point of production, the concentration of capital allowed for the wholesale purchase of science and its transformation into a direct instrument of capital. Science, and its practical offshoot engineering, were set to work producing not only "progress" in the form of new products, but new productive technologies which undercut the power of skilled labor. Labor was directly replaced by machines, or else it was "scientifically" managed in an effort to strip from the workers their knowledge and control of the productive process and reduce their labor, as much as possible, to mere motion.[13] As we have argued elsewhere,

13. Harry Braverman, *Labor and Monopoly Capital* (Monthly Review Press, 1975), pp. 85-123 and 155-168.

these developments drastically altered the terms and conditions of class struggle at the workplace: diminishing the workers' collective mastery cver the work process and undercutting the collective experience of socialized production.[14]

2. The huge social surplus, concentrated in private foundations and in the public sector, began to be a force for regulation and management of civil society. The Rockefeller and Carnegie foundations, each worth tens of millions of dollars, appeared on the scene in the first decade of the twentieth century; local governments increased their revenues and expenditures five-fold between 1902 and 1922.[15] Public education was vastly expanded; charity was institutionalized; public-health measures gained sponsorship and the authority of law, etc. These developments were of course progressive (in both the specific historical as well as the judgmental sense of the word). But they also represented a politically motivated penetration of working-class community life: Schools imparted industrial discipline and "American" values; charity agencies and domestic scientists imposed their ideas of "right living"; public-health officials literally policed immigrant ghettoes, etc.[16]

3. Beginning in the 1900's and increasing throughout the twentieth century, monopoly capitalism came to depend on the development of a national consumer-goods market. Items which had been made in the home or in the neighborhood were replaced by the uniform products of giant corporations. "Services" which had been an indigenous part of working-class culture were edged out by commodities conceived and designed outside of the class. For example, midwifery, which played an important role in the culture of European immigrant groups and rural (black and white) Americans, was outlawed and/or officially discredited in the early 1900's, to be replaced by professionally dominated care. [17] Traditional forms of recreation, from participant sports to social drinking, suffered a similar fate in the face of new commoditized (and privatized) forms of entertainment offered by the corporation (e.g., records, radio, spectator sports, movies, etc.). The penetration of

14. Barbara and John Ehrenreich, "Work and Consciousness," *Monthly Review* (July-August 1976).

15. U.S. Bureau of the Census, *Historical Statistics of the United States, Colonial Times to 1957* (U.S. Goverment Printing Office, 1960).

16. See Samuel Bowles and Herb Gintis, *Schooling In Capitalist America: Educational Reform and the Contradictions of Economic Life* (Basic Books, 1975); Barbara Ehrenreich and Deidre English, *Complaints and Disorders: The Sexual Politics of Sickness* (Feminist Press, 1973).

17. Barbara Ehrenreich and Deidre English, *Witches, Nurses and Midwives: A History of Women Healers* (Feminist Press, 1973).

working-class life by commodities required and continues to require a massive job of education—from schools, advertisers, social workers, domestic scientists, "experts" in child rearing, etc. As the dependence of American capital on the domestic consumer-goods market increased, the management of consumption came to be as important as the management of production.[18]

To summarize the effects of these developments on working-class life: The accumulation and concentration of capital which occurred in the last decades of the nineteenth century allowed for an extensive reorganization of working-class life—both in the community and in the workplace. This reorganization was aimed at both social control and the development of a mass consumer market. The net effect of this drive to reorganize and reshape working-class life was the social *atomization* of the working class: the fragmentation of work (and workers) in the productive process, a withdrawal of aspirations from the workplace into private goals, the disruption of indigenous networks of support and mutual aid, the destruction of autonomous working-class culture and its replacement by "mass culture" defined by the privatized consumption of commodities (health care, recreation, etc.).[19]

It is simultaneously with these developments in working-class life (more precisely, in the *relation* between the working class and the capitalist class) that the professional and managerial workers emerge as a new class in society. The three key developments listed above—the reorganization of the productive process, the emergence of mass institutions of social control, the commodity penetration of working-class life—do not simply "develop;" they require the effort of more or less conscious agents. The expropriation of productive skills requires the intervention of scientific management experts; there must be engineers to inherit the productive lore, managers to supervise the increasingly degraded work process, etc. Similarly, the destruction of autonomous working-class culture requires (and calls forth) the emergence of new culture-producers—from physicians to journalists, teachers, admen and so on. These new operatives, the vanguard of the emerging PMC, are not

18. Stuart Ewen, *Captains of Consciousness: Advertising and the Social Roots of the Consumer Culture* (McGraw-Hill, 1976); Paul Baran and Paul M. Sweezy, *Monopoly Capital* (Monthly Review Press, 1966), ch. 5.

19. For more thorough discussion of this phase in the history of the U.S. working class see Stanley Aronowitz, *False Promises* (McGraw-Hill, 1973); Stuart Ewen, *Captains of Consciousness* (McGraw-Hill, 1976); and Harry Braverman, *Labor and Monopoly Capital* (Monthly Review, 1975). The political implications of these phenomena for working class struggles are very great, though beyond the scope of this essay.

simply an old intellegentsia expanding to meet the needs of a "complex" society. Their emergence in force near the turn of the century is parallel and complementary to the transformation of the working class which marks the emergence of monopoly capital.

Thus the relationship between the PMC and the working class is objectively antagonistic. The functions and interests of the two classes are not merely different; they are mutually contradictory. True, both groups are forced to sell their labor power to the capitalist class; both are necessary to the productive process under capitalism; and they share an antagonistic relation to the capitalist class. (We will return to this point in more detail later.) But these commonalities should not distract us from the fact that the professional-managerial workers exist, as a mass grouping in monopoly capitalist society, only by virtue of the expropriation of the skills and culture once indigenous to the working class. Historically, the process of overt and sometimes violent expropriation was concentrated in the early twentieth century, with the forced Taylorization of major industries, the "Americanization" drive in working-class communities, etc. The fact that this process does not have to be repeated in every generation—any more than the capitalist class must continually re-enact the process of primitive accumulation—creates the impression that the PMC-working class relations represent a purely "natural" division of labor imposed by the social complexity and technological sophistication of modern society. But the objective antagonism persists and represents a contradiction which is continually nourished by the historical *alternative* of a society in which mental and manual work are re-united to create whole people. It is because of this objective antagonism that we are led to define the professional and managerial workers as a class distinct from the working class.

We should add, at this point, that the antagonism between the PMC and the working class does not exist only in the abstract realm of "objective" relations, of course. Real-life contacts between the two classes express directly, if sometimes benignly, the relation of control which is at the heart of the PMC-working class relation: teacher and student (or parent), manager and workers, social worker and client, etc. The subjective dimension of these contacts is a complex mixture of hostility and deference on the part of working-class people, contempt and paternalism on the part of the PMC.

The interdependent yet antagonistic relationship between the working class and the PMC also leads us to insist that the PMC is a class totally distinct from the petty-bourgeoisie (the "old middle class" of artisans, shopkeepers, self-employed professionals and independent farmers). The classical petty bourgeoisie lies outside the polarity of labor and capital. It is made up of people who are *neither* employed by capital *nor* themselves employers of labor to any significant extent. The PMC, by contrast, is employed by capital *and* it manages, controls, has authority over labor (though it does not directly employ it). The classical petty bourgeoisie is irrelevant to the process of capital accumulation and to the process of reproducing capitalist social relations. The PMC, by contrast, is essential to both.

3. The Rise of the PMC

In order to define more sharply the relation between the PMC and the other classes, we turn now to a closer examination of the initial emergence of the PMC, its ideology and its institutions. The PMC emerged with dramatic suddenness in the years between 1890 and 1920, a period roughly overlapping with that historians call the Progressive Era. (Table 1 summarizes the expansion of selected professional and managerial occupations at this time.)[20]

TABLE 1

(in thousands, except for total population in millions)

	1870	1880	1900	1910	1920	1930
Engineers	5.6	7	38	77	134	217
Managers* (manufacturing)	57	—	—	126	250	313
Social, recreation & religious workers (other than clergy)	—	—	—	19	46	71
College faculty	5.6	11.6	24	—	49	82
Accountants and auditors	—	—	23	39	118	192
Government officials, administrators, inspectors	—	—	58	72	100	124
Editors and reporters	—	—	32	—	41	61
Total population	39.9	50.3	76.1	92.4	106.5	123.1

*includes managers *and* manufacturers for 1870, managers only for all other years.
Sources: U.S. Bureau of Census, *Historical Statistics of the United States, Colonial Times to 1957;* U.S. Bureau of Census, *Statistical Abstract of the U.S., 1975;* H.D. Anderson and P.E. Davidson, Occupational Trends in the U.S., (Stanford, 1940).

20. Cf. Richard Hofstadter, *The Age of Reform* (Knopf, 1955), pp. 215-216: From 1870 to 1910, while the whole population of the United States increased two and one third times, the old middle class—business

We have already sketched the conditions which prepared the way for the expansion of these occupations: a growing and increasingly centralized social surplus, and intensified struggle between the bourgeoisie and the proletariat. But it would be wrong to think of the emerging PMC as being no more than passive recruits for the occupational roles required by monopoly capital. The people entering the class-in-formation were drawn from an older middle class. They were the sons and daughters of business men, independent professionals, prosperous farmers, etc.— groups which feared their own extinction in the titanic struggle between capital and labor. The generation entering managerial and professional roles between 1890 and 1920 consciously grasped the roles which they had to play. They understood that their own self-interest was bound up in reforming capitalism, and they articulated their understanding far more persistently and clearly than did the capitalist class itself. The role of the emerging PMC, as they saw it, was to *mediate* the basic class conflict of capitalist society and create a "rational," reproducible social order.[21] As Edward A Ross, a prominent professor and Progressive ideologue, wrote in 1907, after surveying the conflict and corruption of turn-of-the-century capitalism:

> Social defense is coming to be a matter for the expert. The rearing of dikes against faithlessness and fraud calls for intelligent social engineering. If in this strait the public does not speedily become far shrewder...there is nothing for it but to turn over the defense of society to professionals.[22]

Many people, of all classes, subscribed to parts of this outlook and stood to benefit one way or another from the Progressive reforms which were associated with it. For our purposes, the striking things about Progressive ideology and reforms are 1) their direct and material contribution to the creation and expansion of professional and managerial occupational slots; 2) their intimate relation to the emergence and

entrepreneurs and independent professional men—grew somewhat more than two times; the working class, including farm labor, grew a little more than three times; the number of farmers and farm tenants doubled. But the middle class (technicians, salaried professionals, clerical workers, salespeople, public-service workers) grew almost eight times, rising from 756,000 to 5,609,000 people....The new middle class had risen from 33% of the entire middle class in 1870 to 63% in 1910. Also cf. Robert H. Wiebe, *The Search For Order* (Hill and Wang, 1967), p. 111 fn.

21. Cf. Richard Hofstadter, *The Age of Reform* (Knopf, 1955), pp. 236-237; Christopher Lasch, *The New Radicalism in America (1889-1963)* (Knopf, 1965), pp. 147-149, 162, 168-177; Robert H. Wiebe, *The Search for Order, 1877-1920* (Hill and Wang, 1967), pp. 111-32, 145-55.

22. Edward A. Ross, *Sin and Society* (Houghton-Mifflin, 1907), excerpted in Otis L. Graham, Jr., *The Great Campaigns* (Prentice Hall, 1971), p. 237.

articulation of the PMC's characteristic ideologies; and 3) their association with the creation of characteristic PMC class institutions (such as professional organizations).

(1) **The Growth of the PMC**: Every effort to mediate class conflict and "rationalize" capitalism served to create new institutionalized roles for reformers—i.e., to expand the PMC. Settlement houses, domestic-science training courses, adult-education classes in literacy, English, patriotism, etc. provided jobs for social workers (who formed the National Conference of Social Workers in 1911) and home economists (who formed the American Home Economics Association in 1909), etc., Child-labor laws, compulsory-school-attendance laws, factory health and safety inspections, etc., created jobs for truant officers, teachers and inspectors of various kinds. Similarly, municipal reform meant the establishment of committees of city planners, architects, engineers, statisticians, sociologists, to plan and administer the health, recreation, welfare, housing and other functions of the metropolis. At the federal level, conservationist demands (pushed by the emerging engineering profession, among others) led to the creation of Federal agencies employing engineers to watch over and plan resource use. The Pure Food and Drug Act, the establishment of the Bureau of Labor Statistics, the Federal Trade Commission, etc., all, in addition to their direct impact in regulating business, gathering information, etc., offered thousands of jobs. Public policy in general became dependent on input from specialists, experts, professors. "It is a great thing," exulted political-economy professor Richard T. Ely, another major Progressive-era ideologue, on reading the report of the U.S. Industrial Commission established by Congress in 1898, "That there are in this country a body of economic experts, and that the state of public opinion is such so as to demand their employment."[23]

The rationalizing drive of the emerging PMC struck deep into the business enterprise itself. The early years of the century saw the transformation of the internal functioning of the corporation at the hands of a rapidly growing corps of managers—"scientific managers," lawyers, financial experts, engineers, personnel experts, etc. As early as 1886, Henry R. Townes had admonished the American Society of Mechanical Engineers (the source of much early management thought) that "The manner of shop management is of equal importance with that of engineering." By the early 1900's, Townes, Taylor, Gantt, the Gilbreths and other engineers were churning out papers on how to rationalize all aspects of the business enterprise. College-level schools and departments

23. Richard T. Ely, "A Government of Labor," in Robert La Follette, ed., *The Making of America*, Vol. III: *Labor* (Arno, 1969), p.26.

of business administration rapidly appeared to teach the new creed. (The American Association of Collegiate Schools of Business was founded in 1916.) The managers held conferences, formed associations (e.g., the Society to Promote the Science of Management in 1912, and the American Management Association, out of several already existing societies, in 1923), and published professional journals (e.g., *Engineering Magazine* in 1891, *Factory* in 1908, the *Bulletin of the Taylor Society* in 1916).

The introduction of modern methods of management was a reform which was understood by contemporary observers to be part of the overall Progressive cause. In fact, scientific management first became known to the public as a tool for the Progressive attack on corporate greed: In the "Eastern Rates" case of 1911, the Interstate Commerce Commission turned down an increase in railroad rates after scientific-management expert H. Emerson testified that proper management would cut a million dollars a day off the cost of rail shipments. Scientific management as taught in the new business schools, exulted reformer and writer Walter Lippmann, would produce a new professional breed of managers who would help lift American business out of the "cesspool of commercialism." To the managers themselves,

> ...scientific management became something of a "movement." In an age of growing achievement in the physical sciences, it offered the hope of resolving industrial problems also through the use of objective principles. For young and imaginative engineers it provided an *ethos* and a mission in life. The movement soon became replete with popularizers, traditionalists, and dissidents. After the initial periods of resistance, it conquered the citadels of old-fashioned industrial management in the United States, and had a tremendous effect on the practice. It had a major influence on the growing reform and economy movements in public administration.[24]

(2) **The Development of a Class Outlook**: From the beginning the nascent PMC possessed a class outlook which was distinct from, *and often antagonistic to*, that of the capitalist class. It is true that, with hindsight, one is struck by the ultimate concordance of interests between the two classes. Even at that time, *New Republic* editor Herbert Croley noted that Progressivism was "designed to serve as a counterpoise to the

24. Bertram Gross, *The Managing of Organizations* (London, 1964), Vol. 1, pp.127-128, cited in D. Gvishian, *Organization and Management* (Progess Publishers, 1972), p.184.

threat of working-class revolution."[25] And a wealthy philanthropist friend of Jane Adams noted appreciatively that Adams "was really an interpreter between working men and the people who lived in luxury on the other side of the city, and she also gave the people of her neighborhood quite a different idea about the men and women who were ordinarily called 'capitalists'."[26] "Class harmony" was the stated goal of many outstanding PMC spokespeople, and to many in the capitalist class as well, it was clear that "professionals" could be more effective in the long run than Pinkertons. But the PMC was not merely a class of lackeys: The capitalists fought vigorously to block or modify those PMC-supported reforms which they saw as threatening their interests. As for the PMC, the very ideals of "objectivity," "rationality," etc., which justified their role to the capitalists inevitably led them into *conflict* with the capitalists.

For one thing, the roles the PMC was entering and carving out for itself—as technical innovators, social mediators, culture producers, etc.—required a high degree of autonomy, if only for the sake of legitimization. Claims to "objectivity" cannot be made from an objective position of servility. The conflict over occupational autonomy was particularly visible in the universities. The enormous expansion of higher education in the latter part of the nineteenth century and the early part of the twentieth century had been underwritten by men like Johns Hopkins, Leland Stanford, and above all, John D. Rockefeller and Andrew Carnegie. Battles over academic freedom often brought faculty into direct confrontation with capitalist trustees, with the professors asserting their autonomy as "experts."

But the conflict between the PMC and the capitalist class went deeper than the issue of occupational autonomy. Early PMC leaders envisioned a technocratic transformation of society in which all aspects of life would be "rationalized" according to expert knowledge. For example, Frederick Winslow Taylor, the leader of the movement for scientific management, saw scientific management as much more than a set of techniques to streamline production:

> The same principles can be applied with equal force to all social activites: to the management of our tradesmen, large and small; of our churches, our philanthropic institutions, our universities, and our governmental departments...What other reforms

25. James Weinstein, *The Corporate Ideal in the Liberal State, 1900-1918* (Beacon Press, 1968), p.xi.

26. Anthony Platt, *The Childsavers* (U. of Chicago Press, 1969), pp. 87-88.

could do as much toward promoting prosperity, toward the diminution of poverty and the alleviation of suffering?[27]

Or, as E.D. Meier, the president of the American Society of Mining Engineers, put it in 1911, "The golden rule will be put into practice through the slide rule of the engineer."[28]

Of course, "efficiency," "order" and rationality are not in themselves capitalist goals. Even scientific management met with initial resistance from many in the business community, who saw it as a potential threat to their own autonomy from outside surveillance. (Scientific management, as already mentioned, was originally popularized as a tool for the public to use to judge the fairness of corporate prices.) Engineers, perhaps because of their workaday intimacy with capitalist concerns, often saw the recalcitrance of capital most clearly. To give a trivial, but telling, example: in 1902 and again in 1906, efforts of reform-minded engineers to get the American Society of Mechanical Engineers to support the campaign for conversion to the metric system were defeated by capitalist opposition. (Most capital equipment was already calibrated in English units.) "The businessman is the master, the engineer is his good slave," complained a writer in *Engineering News* in 1904.[29]

Out of these continual skirmishes—over academic freedom, Progressive reforms, consumer issues, etc.—many in the PMC were led to more systematic anti-capitalist outlooks. One widely publicized variety of PMC anti-capitalism was that represented by Thorstein Veblen's "technocratic" critique. Veblen portrayed the contemporary capitalists as a parasitical class no less decadent than the European aristocracy. The captains of industry, he argued,

> have always turned the technologists and their knowledge to account...only so far as would serve their own commercial profit, not to the extent of their ability; or to the limit set by the material cirumstances; or by the needs of the community...To do their work as it should be done these men of the industrial general staff i.e., engineers and managers must have a free hand,

27. *Frederic W. Taylor, Principles of Scientific Management,* cited in Edwin T. Layton, *The Revolt of the Engineers: Social Responsibility and the American Engineering Profession* (Press of Case Western Reserve University, 1971), p. 143.

28. Ibid., p. 67.

29. Ibid., pp. 110, 213: Raymond E.Callahan, *Education and the Cult of Efficiency* (U. of Chicago Press, 1962), pp. 19-22; Sammuel Haber, *Efficiency and Uplift (U. of Chicago Press, 1964).*

unhampered by commerical considerations and reservations....
It is an open secret that with a reasonably free hand the
production experts would today readily increase the ordinary
output of industry by several fold—variously estimated at some
300 per cent to 1200 per cent of the current output. And what
stands in the way of so increasing the ordinary output of goods
and service is business as usual.[30]

Progress demanded that the capitalists be swept away to make room—
not for the working class but for the rising class of experts. But Veblen's
vision of technocracy—a government by the experts—smacked too
overtly of PMC self-interest to gain a wide following, even within the
class. In fact Edward Ross, who in 1907 had himself called for extensive
"social engineering," was moved to write, somewhat defensively, in 1920:

> There is of course no such thing as 'government by experts.' The
> malicious phrase is but a sneer flung by the scheming self-
> seekers who find in the relentless veracity of modestly-paid
> trained investigators a barrier across their path.[31]

The strongest expression of PMC anti-capitalist ideology was to be
found in explicitly *socialist* politics—which in the early twentieth-century
United States meant the Socialist Party. "In the United States probably
more than anywhere else, socialism is recruiting heavily from the better
classes of society," boasted Party leader Morris Hillquit in 1907.
Although the party had a large working-class membership and people we
would identify as members of the PMC were clearly a minority in the
party as a whole, most of the top leadership and a vastly disproportionate part of the membership were engaged in PMC (and old middle
class) occupations (or had been so engaged before assuming full-time
party duties).[32]

30. Thorstein Veblen, *The Engineers and the Price System* (Viking, 1932),
pp. 61, 69-71.

31. Edward A. Ross, *The Social Trend* (The Century Co., 1922), p.171.

32. To give a few prominent examples, Victor Berger was a school teacher;
Morris Hilquit was a lawyer and journalist; Robert Hunter, A. M. Simons and
William Ghent were editors and journalists; and even Eugene Debs spent only
four years as a railroad worker, the rest of his pre-socialist life being spent as
billing clerk for the largest wholesale grocer in the Midwest, as elected town clerk
of Terre Haute, and as editor of a labor-union paper. Cf. Philip Foner, *History of
the Labor Movement in the United States,* Vol. 3 (International, 1964), p.391; Ira
Kipnis, *The American Socialist Movement, 1897-1912* (Monthly Review Press,
1972), pp. 173-177, 306-307, 312; David A. Shannon, *The Socialist Party of
America* (Quadrangle, 1967), pp. 53-54; James Weinstein, *The Decline of
Socialism in America* (Monthly Review Press, 1967), pp. 79-83.

In fact, socialism, as articulated by the pre-World War I Socialist Party, was frequently not far from the PMC's technocratic vision. Socialism meant government of the ownership of the means of production (which would still be administered by experts) and expansion of government social services (which would still be supplied by professionals—or "intellectual proletarians," as Hillquit called them).

Socialism in this version formed a continuum with non-socialist Progressivism. Party leader William Ghent even complained that Teddy Roosevelt's 1912 Progressive Party platform (a platform designed to attract the middle-class reform vote without fundamentally upsetting capitalist priorities) "begins its program with the brazen theft of half the working program of the Socialist Party." On the right wing of the Party, even such traditional socialist notions as class struggle were considered too radical and were replaced by Progressive ideals of class conciliation. Class hatred, wrote writer, social worker and Party National Executive member John Spargo, was a "monstrous thing...to be abhorred by all right-thinking men and women."[33]

3. The Consolidation of the Professional-Managerial Class: In the period up to mid-century, professional-managerial occupations expanded much more rapidly than the workforce as a whole.[34] The people filling these occupations (and their families) came more and more to constitute a socially coherent class. Collectively the PMC consolidated its cultural hegemony over the working class, as the army of counselors, psychologists, teachers, etc., swelled from the twenties on. But the early PMC's radical dream of a technocratic society was not, of course, to be realized. To the extent that the PMC established itself as a major class in twentieth century American society, it did so on terms set by the capitalist class.[35]

33. Kipnis, *American Socialist Movement*, pp. 216, 227-228.

34. A complete account of the development of the PMC would have to dwell on 1) the tremendous expansion of the state apparatus during World War II (and the accompanying triumph of what has been called—over simplistically, we think—corporate liberal ideology); 2) the expansion of the corporate bureaucratic apparatus and its extension from control of production to control of distribution and manipulation of demand; and 3) the post-WWII expansion of the universities and the mass media, etc.

35. It is necessary to emphasize this point. The PMC (or the managerial portion of it) has *not* become a new ruling class (as Berle and Means, Burnham, Galbraith and others have suggested). Top managers are part of the ruling class (see above, p. 13, footnote and Paul Sweezy, "The Illusion of the Managerial Revolution" in *The Present as History*, pp. 39-66; C. Wright Mills, *The Power Elite* (Oxford University Press, 1963), pp. 118-170, ch. 6 & 7. Most managers and administrators, along with all non-managerial salaried professionals, are part of the PMC, a subordinate and dependent class. This does not mean, however, that the PMC is *powerless* vis-a-vis the ruling class.

Individually, many PMC members scaled the highest pinnacles of power, either to bask there temporarily as constituents and advisors, or to remain as permanent members of the ruling class. Acceptance came gradually. Self-made capitalists like Andrew Carnegie initially had little use for "experts" and "college men" in their enterprises. But by the teens, "experts"—college professors, researchers, PMC civic reformers—had become indispensable and routine members of the boards of trustees of key capitalist-sponsored institutions (replacing the token clergyman of an earlier era). In 1918, when President Wilson went off to the Peace Conference in Paris, he publicly acknowledged the importance of the PMC by taking along with him a "grand conclave of expert advisors from several fields of knowledge which was known to contemporaries as The Inquiry."[36] Within industry, as the size and complexity of corporations increased, PMC occupations such as engineering, law and financial management became recruiting grounds for top management, i.e., into the ruling class itself.

For the great majority of the members of the PMC, however, the only guarantee of security—never mind autonomous power—lay in collective action. The characteristic form of self-organization of the PMC was the *profession*. The defining characteristics of professions should be seen as representing simultaneously both the aspirations of the PMC and the claims which are necessary to justify those aspirations to the other classes of society. These characteristics are, in brief: a) the existence of a specialized body of knowledge, accessible only by lengthy training; b) the existence of ethical standards which include a commitment to public service; and c) a measure of autonomy from outside interference in the practice of the profession (e.g., only members of the profession can judge the value of a fellow professional's work). The claims to specialized knowledge and ethical standards serve to justify the bid for autonomy, which is most commonly directed at the (capitalist) employing class. Furthermore, the possession (or claim to possession) of specialized knowledge ensures that the PMC can control its own reproduction as a class: "Lengthy training has barred working-class entrance to the professions and given a decided advantage to the children of the PMC itself. The claim to high ethical standards represents the PMC's persistent reassurance that its class interests are identical to the interests of society at large. Finally, all three characteristics of professions are aimed at ensuring that the relationship between the individual professional and his or her "client" (student, patient) is one of benign domination.

36. Joseph F. Wall, *Andrew Carnegie* (Oxford, 1970), pp. 834, 884; Hofstadter, *The Age of Reform*, p. 155.

Between the 1880's and 1920, medicine, law, social work, engineering and teaching emerged in their modern form, complete with professional organizations and journals and legally enforced criteria for admissions (i.e., accrediting of training institutions and/or licensing of individual practitioners). At the same time, the learned professions were sorting themselves out and taking organizational form: "natural philosophy" subdivided into the modern natural sciences; psychology detached itself from philosophy; sociology, history and political science began to go their separate ways, etc.

The device of professionalism was not universally or uniformly successful. Some occupations, like nursing, are "professions" more out of courtesy than social reality. Other, more clearly PMC occupations, such as engineering, can hardly claim to have a "professional" degree of autonomy. Between 1900 and 1920, many of the U.S. engineering societies were torn by struggle between "professional-minded" engineers, who saw themselves as professionals first and employees second, and business-oriented engineers, whose first loyalty was to their employing industry. The business-oriented faction triumphed, for the most part, even going so far as to permit untrained businessmen to join the engineers' "professional" societies.[37]

From the perspective of the entire class, professionalism had an inherent disadvantage as a strategy for class advancement. Specialization was the PMC member's chief selling point, the quality which justified his or her claim to a unique niche in society, but it acted as a centrifugal force on the class as a whole. Consider that in 1900 a scholar such as William James could flit from teaching physiology to psychology and finally to philosophy without unduly discomfiting the Harvard administration.

37. Layton, *Revolt of the Engineers*, pp. 79-83. The profession of medicine, at first thought, may seem to contradict our assertion that professionalism is the characteristic form of self-organization of the PMC, since most physicians, even today, are independent entrepeneurs (i.e., classical petty bourgeoisie). Professionalism does, of course, have pre-monopoly capitalist roots in the ancient "free professions"—medicine, law, theology. But in its modern form, medical professionalism in the U.S. was forged by a small handful of PMC doctors. The American Medical Association, in the crucial pre-World War I years when it gained hegemony over U.S. medicine, was dominated by academic physicians. And the public's belief in the expertise of doctors arose largely from the achievements and propaganda of (salaried) government public-health officials and medical school professors. Cf. Rosemary Stevens, *American Medicine and the Public Interest* (Yale Univeristy Press, 1971). Salaried physicians have made up an ever-growing and increasingly dominant fraction of the medical profession; and even the physicians still in private practice are, in real terms, completely dependent on and increasingly subject to the PMC-dominated hospitals, medical schools, and government health agencies. Cf. Health PAC, *The American Health Empire* (Random House, 1971).

And in 1919, Veblen (in *Engineers and the Price System*) could still lump together engineers and all sorts of managers and administrators under the common rubric "engineer." But by mid-century the class was so minutely splintered that even terms such as "scientist" or "engineer" no longer signified groups with common workplace concerns or even a common language.

The deepest rift, over-riding the petty occupational subspecializations, was the one which developed between the managers, administrators and engineers on the one hand, and those in the liberal arts and service professions on the other. The material difference between the two groups was that those in the first category are directly tied to business and industry; their jobs are, not infrequently, way stations on the road into the ruling class itself. Those in the second category are more likely to enjoy the relative shelter of the university or other sorts of non-profit agencies and to be firmly fixed within the PMC. Along with this difference in apparent sources of subsidy, went a difference in general political outlook: The managerial/technical community came to pride itself on its "hard-headedness" and even on its indifference to the social consequences of its labor (i.e., its helplessness). The second group, those in the more "liberal" pursuits, became the only repository of the traditional PMC antagonism to capital. Managers and engineers on the one side, liberal academics on the other, came to view each other across a gulf of distrust and contempt.

But we should not overestimate the significance of this division. The PMC at mid-century still constituted a single, coherent class. The actual employment experience and social attitudes of managers and engineers and those in the liberal professions are hardly more divergent than those of such working-class groups as, say, clerical workers and steel workers. The image of non-managerial professionals has little counterpart in reality. Seventy per cent of the country's scientists and engineers are employed in business and industry; half the rest are in government. (Even leaving out the engineers, only one-fifth of the physicists and two-fifths of the life scientists are employed by universities.) Well under half of the professional and scientific workers in all fields (including the social sciences) are employed by educational and other non-profit institutions. In the business and governmental organizations which employ most professionals, the professional typically is employed in a managerial or semi-managerial role. As for the minority of professionals who are in academic and similar institutions, they are hardly aloof from what C. Wright Mills called the "managerial demiurge." They greedily accept consulting positions with industry and government. And within their institutions, they take on a variety of managerial and administrative functions, administering grants, supervising research and teaching assistants, running departments and institutes.[38]

The image of the corporate middle manager as completely divorced from the academic world is equally overdrawn. Over eighty per cent of corporate managers (at all levels) in large corporations have college training (or graduate training)—about half in the liberal arts, the rest divided equally between engineering and business. "Professional" (graduate) training in law, engineering, or business schools—which, correctly, tell their students that they are being trained in "applied social science"—more and more becomes a prerequisite for advance on the management ladder.[39]

Moreover, the various groups within the PMC are socially coherent. Paul Sweezy has argued that the basic test of whether two families belong to the same class or not is the freedom with which they intermarry. The children of PMC members do overwhelmingly tend to marry within the class; marriage "down" to the working class or "up" to the ruling class is comparatively infrequent. In line with the frequency of intermarriage, the class exhibits a substantial degree of intergenerational stability: children of PMC families are more than twice as likely as children of working-class families to themselves enter PMC occupations.[40]

Moreover, the class is characterized by a common "culture" or lifestyle. The interior life of the class is shaped by the problem of class reproduction. Unlike ruling-class occupations, PMC occupations are never directly hereditary: The son of the Chairman of the Board may expect to become a successful businessman (or at least a wealthy one) more or less by growing up; the son of a research scientist knows he can only hope to achieve a similar position through continuous effort. Traditionally, much of this effort has come from the women of the class. Since, according to psychologists, a child's future achievement is determined by the nuances of its early upbringing, women of the class have been expected to stay at home and "specialize" in childraising. Both sexes, however, are expected to perform well in school and attend good colleges, for it is at college that young men acquire the credentials for full

38. U.S. Bureau of the Census, *Statistical Abstract of the United States, 1975* (U.S. Government Printing Office, 1975); National Industrial Conference Board, *Economic Almanac, 1967-68* (New York, 1967).

39. David Granick, *Managerial Comparisons of Four Developed Countries: France, Britain, United States, and Russia* (MIT Press, 1972), pp. 173, 207.

40. Paul M. Sweezy, *The Present as History*, p. 123; Otis Dudley Duncan, "The Trend of Occupational Mobility in the United Sates," *American Sociological Review*, Vol. 30, #4 (Aug. 1965), pp. 491-498; also cf. C. Wright Mills, "The Middle Classes in Middle-Sized Cities," *American Sociological Review*, Vol. 11, #5 (Oct. 1946).

class memberships and young women acquire, in addition to their own degrees, credentialed husbands.[41]

As a result of the anxiety about class reproduction, all of the ordinary experiences of life—growing up, giving birth, childraising—are freighted with an external significance unknown in other classes. Private life thus becomes too arduous to be lived in private; the inner life of the PMC must be continuously shaped, updated and revised by—of course—ever mounting numbers of experts: experts in childraising, family living, sexual fulfillment, self-realization, etc., etc. The very insecurity of the class, then, provides new ground for class expansion. By mid-century the PMC was successful enough to provide a new *mass market* for many of its own services—and unsuccessful enough to need them.[42]

The New Left and the PMC

We now use this analysis to understand some aspects of the development and current difficulties of the left in the U.S., starting with some observations on the New Left of the sixties. We will not try to give a complete and definitive account of the emergence of the New Left. Rather we will focus on the ways in which the PMC origins of the New Left shaped its growth and ideology, on how the originally PMC-based New Left ultimately began to transcend its own class, and on how it sought to deal with the resulting dilemmas.

The rebirth of PMC radicalism in the sixties came at a time when the material position of the class was advancing rapidly. Employment in PMC occupations soared, and salaries rose with them. The growth was so rapid that extensive recruitment from the working class became

41. Betty Friedan's book *The Feminine Mystique* (Norton, 1963) points out the inherent contradictions in this mode of class reproduction: Women of the class are educated along with men, then required to do the unpaid, menial labor of homemaking. Friedan herself feared that the degradation of PMC women was leading to the deterioration of the children and hence the entire class. Her book is a strongly class-conscious statement, concerned more with the future of her class than with the fate of women of all classes. Nevertheless she accurately pinpointed one major factor in the rise of the late-twentieth-century women's movement: the "over-education"—or under-employment—of PMC women.

42. Many of the characteristics of the PMC as a social class are shared, of course, by portions of the classical petty bourgeoisie, such as doctors in private practice. The PMC is integrated socially with these upper strata of the petty bourgeoisie (upper strata, we emphasize; *not* with the overwhelmingly larger lower strata of the petty bourgeoisie—the millions of proprietors of tiny shops, self-employed craftspeople, etc.). But, as we have argued earlier, this is not sufficient grounds for calling the PMC itself "petty bourgeoisie" [see above, pp. 19-20].

necessary to fill the job openings. (One early study indicated that no less than a quarter of the sons of skilled blue-collar workers and close to a fifth of the sons of semi-skilled workers were climbing into the PMC.)[43] It has become fashionable to argue that engineers, teachers, social workers and the like were becoming "proletarianized"—the fate Marx had predicted for the middle class.[44] But what was taken as a symptom of proletarianization, e.g., the expansion and bureaucratization of the university, was in many cases really a token of the rapid expansion of the class. The late fifties and early sixties were a golden age for the PMC, not a time of decreasing opportunities and compression into the proletarian mold.

With Sputnik in 1957 and Kennedy's election in 1960, the prestige and public visibility of the class reached new heights. Government and foundation funding for research, higher education and professional services began to skyrocket. Members of the class appeared in prominent public positions as presidential advisors, scientists, foreign-policy strategists, and social planners. New institutions—think tanks, consulting firms—engaged to meet the new demand for PMC skills.

The early student radicalism of the sixties had many sources—the civil-rights movement, the "Beatniks," the college experience itself, etc. For our present purposes, however, we only want to point out that this new radicalism also reflected the rising confidence of the Professional-Managerial Class. According to the sociologists' studies, the first wave of student activists typically came from secure backgrounds, and were, compared to other students, especially well-imbued with the traditional PMC values of intellectual autonomy and public service.[45] Their initial radicalism represented an attempt to reassert the autonomy which the PMC had long since ceded to the capitalist class. For example, SDS's seminal Port Huron Statement (1962) expresses both elements of traditional PMC class consciousness: scorn for the capitalist class and elitism toward the working class. Too many PMC elders, SDS argued, had capitulated to the demands of "the system."

43. Otis Dudley Duncan, "The Trend of Occupational Mobility in the United States," *American Sociological Review,* Vol. 30, #4 (Aug. 1965), pp. 491-95.

44. See, for instance, Stanley Aronowitz, "Does the United States Have a New Working Class?" *The Revivial Of American Socialism,* G. Fischer, ed. and *Ambiguous Legacy: The Left in American Politics* (Franklin Watts, 1975), pp. 125-128.

45. Richard Flacks, "Who Protests: the Social Bases of the Student Movement," in *Protest! Student Activism in America,* Julia Foster and Durward Long, eds. (William Morrow, 1970), pp. 134-157.

Many social and physical scientists, neglecting the liberating heritage of higher learning, develop "human relations" or "morale-producing" techniques for the corporate economy, while others exercise their intellectual skills to accelerate the arms race.[46]

But, the statement continued, the working class could not be relied on as the source of social renewal:

Any new left in America must be, in large measure, a left with real intellectual skills, committed to deliberativeness, honesty, reflection as working tools. The university permits the political life to be an adjunct to the academic one, and action to be informed by reason.[47]

The Berkeley Free Speech Movement in 1964 articulated the problem of the class forcefully: "History has not ended ... a better society is possible, and ... it is worth dying for" proclaimed Mario Savio, the voice of the Free Speech Movement. Yet the university had sold out; it was not training future members of the class for their historic and social and moral mission:

Many students here at the university ... are wandering aimlessly about. Strangers in their own lives, there is no place for them. They are people who have not learned to compromise, who for example, have come to the university to learn to question, to grow, to learn—all the standard things that sound like cliches because no one takes them seriously. And they find out at one point or another that for them to become part of society, to become lawyers, ministers, businessmen, people in government, that very often they must compromise those principles which were most dear to them .... The futures and careers for which American students now prepare are for the most part intellectual and moral wastelands.[48]

The Free Speech Movement made a direct appeal to the class consciousness of the faculty:

46. "The Port Huron Statement," in Paul Jacobs and Saul Landau, *The New Radicals: A Report With Documents* (Vintage, 1966), p. 159.

47. "The Port Huron Statement" cited in Kirkpatrick Sales, *SDS*, (Random House, 1973), p. 52.

48. Mario Savio, "An End to History", in Jacobs and Landau, *The New Radicals*, p. 230.

We challenge the faculty to be courageous. A university is a community of students and scholars: be equal to the position of dignity you should hold! How long will you submit to the doorkeepers who have usurped your power?[49]

PMC class consciousness, with its ambiguous mixture of elitism and anti-capitalist militance, continued to be a major theme of "the movement" thoughout the sixties. Expressions of it can be found in the "New Left," the anti-war movement, the ecology movement, the women's liberation movement—all of which defied "the system," but often with moralistic contempt for the working class.[50] Ultimately, however, a significant part of the New Left decisively broke with this tradition and sought to transcend the imperatives of its own class base. It is to this evolution that we now turn.

As late as 1966, many New Left leaders held to Veblenesque theories of the unique importance of PMC-type occupations or of the students themselves. Carl Davidson (then SDS Vice-President), for example, argued in a highly influential article that a student movement to control the university could be the base for the transformation of all of society.[51] But then—somewhere around 1967 or 1968—there was a decisive break which made the sixties totally unlike the earlier (Progressive Era) period of PMC radicalism: Large numbers of young people pushed PMC radicalism to its limits and found themselves, ultimately, at odds with their own class.

There are reasons why this development should have occurred in the sixties rather than in earlier periods of PMC radicalism. One has to do with the evolving role of the university. The university is the historical reproductive apparatus of the PMC and a historic center for the production of new knowledge, disciplines, techniques, heresies, etc.: both

49. Quoted in *The Berkeley Student Revolt: Facts and Interpretations*, Seymour Martin Lipset and Sheldon S. Wolin eds.

50. By the "New Left" we mean the consciously anti-racist and anti-imperialist (and later, anti-capitalist) white movement, centered initially in the universities but ultimately extending well beyond them (e.g., it came to include underground newspapers; organizations of teachers, social workers, and medical workers; theater groups; community-organizing groups; etc.). Students for a Democratic Society (SDS) was its most important organizational expression from 1964 to 1969. The New Left interacted with or was part of most of the other movements of the sixties, but it was not identical to them. To take two examples, the anti-war movement was far broader than the New Left; and the women's liberation movement emerged in part in opposition to the practices of the New Left.

51. Sales, *SDS*, pp. 289-292.

functions which have acquired a semblance of autonomy from capital. In the fifties and sixties, however, the university was being called on to play a much more direct role in the functioning of the capitalist state as well as private enterprise. It had become, as University of California President Clark Kerr described it, "a prime instrument of national purpose." As in the Progressive Era (and the New Deal), public-policy makers turned to the university for expert consultation in designing anti-poverty programs, health-care programs, etc., but on a vastly expanded scale. Beyond that, in the mid-sixties, the state also increasingly relied on the university for military assistance, not only from engineers and natural scientists, but from anthropologists, sociologists, etc.

The university's involvement with business or even with the defense establishment was one thing; its complicity in the war in Vietnam was quite another. In the bleak Eisenhower years and in the brief glow of Kennedy's New Frontier, the university, despite its compromises, had seemed to many to be the repository of all that was good in the PMC-liberal tradition. For a while, it had been possible to ignore the conflict between the university's actual functions and its liberal ideology. But the liberal facade could not be maintained in the face of genocide. In the blinding light of the bombs raining on Vietnam, the brutality of American foreign policy was starkly revealed—as was the university's role in maintaining it. As far as the students were concerned, the self-righteous cold-war liberalism of the previous generation simply and abruptly collapsed. The moral legitimacy of the university, the older generation of the PMC, and the entire American system were thrown into question.

Student fury against the war in Vietnam inevitably turned against the government's accomplice, the university itself, and hence against one of the central institutions of the PMC. In response to the student attack on the university, liberal and even some Marxist faculty members began to dissociate themselves from the New Left. The older generation had a stake in the university: their grants, their careers, their image of themselves as being morally "above" the business world were tied to the university.

Furthermore, the older generation were more cautious—they had matured in the Depression and the cringing forties and fifties; the New Left was filled with the ebullience of the New Frontier. The gap in generational experience was just too great to be bridged by abstract class interests.

At the same time that many students of PMC origin and destiny were becoming disenchanted with their own class and its institutions, they began to find themselves challenged by the previously alien working class. For one thing, as the university struggled to keep pace with the booming growth in PMC jobs, the characteristics of students were changing. Unable to meet the demand for engineers, teachers, social workers, etc. with sons and daughters of the existing PMC alone, the colleges were increasingly filled with sons and daughters of the working class. As the student rebellion spread from elite PMC training grounds such as Berkeley, Columbia, and Harvard to the much less elite Kent State, Penn State, and San Francisco State, the class background of the activists shifted as well. Instead of student activists "well imbued with the traditional PMC values," there were student activists who had always viewed the PMC—their teachers, social workers and the like—at the very least with some unease and hostility.

But the wedge that finally separated a chunk of the New Left from its own class was the Black liberation movement. White student involvement in the Southern civil-rights struggle had often been tinged with paternalism: something like that settlement-house experience for so many middle-class young people in the early twentieth century. The Northern Black movement was more challenging. Ghetto uprisings— especially the massive 1967 upheavals in Detroit and Newark—seemed to raise the possibility of an armed revolution, led by working class Blacks, in which students would have to take sides. Black students, admitted to even the elite white colleges in response to the civil-rights movement, brought the Black rebellion to the campuses. Black students demanded that the white left support Black working class demands (e.g., the demands for open admissions and for stopping university expansion into Black neighborhoods).

Contacts between the white student left and Black non-student groups (most notably the Black Panther Party) were characterized by arrogance on the latter side, near servility on the former. White PMC youths began to feel that their own radicalism, even their entire life experience, was a pale abstraction compared to this militance which came from "the streets." There was an acute consciousness of "privilege"—a static and fragmentary prelude to the notion of class.

Even more important to the student radicals' break with the PMC was the content of urban Black militancy. Consider the relationship which had developed between the PMC and the Black community: lower-stratum occupations, teaching and social work, had been in a close service/social-control relation to the Black community since north-ward migration of the fifties. In the sixties, the official concern about poverty, much heightened by the Watts rebellion of 1965, led to a massive federally-sponsored PMC penetration of the ghetto. Job opportunities multiplied for (largely white) planners, community organizers, psychologists, anthropologists, trainers, etc. The Black community came to play the same role with respect to the PMC of the sixties as the white immigrant community had played in the 1900s: It was a nourishing medium for expansion, a bottomless mine of "social pathology." But it was far from a passive medium. By late 1966, Black militants and Black community groups were raising the demand for "community control" of the very agencies and institutions which were providing opportunities for the white PMC.

This demand did not fit into the traditional categories of the Old Left. (In the case of the New York City school struggle, the Progressive Labor Party decided that the community-control demand was a ruling-class plot against the only "workers" in sight—the teachers!) But it was a clear declaration of class warfare: the Black community (largely working class) against the invading PMC. In many instances, it was Black members of the PMC who won out under the banner of community control; but the radical, class conscious thrust of the demand was "power to the people"—replace the professional and administrative elite with ordinary citizens.

Most white student radicals identified themselves with the community-control struggle without question. For one thing, it was the direct descendant of the civil-rights struggle which had, in part, given birth to the New Left. It also seemed to be a living link between foreign Third World struggles for self-determination (e.g., Vietnam) and the struggle to change U.S. society. In identifying with the community-control movement, the young PMC radicals were taking a position which ran counter to their own objective class interests. "Let the people decide," said the front page slogan in SDS's newspaper, *New Left Notes*, even if they decided they didn't want you.[52]

By 1967 or 1968, the New Left was approaching a crisis: It had been born when the war in Vietnam forced thousands of PMC youths to confront the conflict between their class' supposed values and American social reality. It had been bred in the institution where these contradictions appeared most sharply—in the elite universities which

52. The conflict between ideals and self-interest felt by some in the PMC is illuminated by the 1969 community and worker takeover of the Lincoln Hospital Mental Health Sevices in New York City. Only a few days before the administrators were locked out of their offices by 150 demonstrators, led by Black and Puerto Rican non-professional community mental-health workers. Dr. Harris Peck, the designer and director of the center, had written in *Reader's Digest* : "When there's a foot planted in the seat of my trousers to kick me out of here, I'll know we've succeeded. It will mean that the people want to take over the running of their own community. And that's the way it should be." But after the takeover, Peck commented that, while he still favored the principle of community control, "It's a long-term goal. We don't think it is possible to implement it at this time." [Health-PAC, *The American Health Empire* (Random House, 1971), pp. 253-254]

both taught the old PMC values and abjectly served capitalist interests. But the student rebellion had spread to universities whose students often came from working class families. Originally committed to the university, the New Left was now locked in battle with the university. And it was increasingly committed to supporting Black working class-based movements which, for their part, rejected the traditional PMC attitudes toward the working class. The New Left was forced to examine its own class composition and class attitudes. Could it survive as a primarily PMC-based movement? How could such a movement change society? What relationship would it (or could it) develop with the traditional agent of social change, the working class (and especially with the militant Black movement)?

The problem of the New Left's relation to the PMC as a whole was partially solved by the reaction of the older generation of the PMC. Many of the latter responded to the growing militance of the students with all the venom at their command. Psychiatrists theorized publicly that America's youth was searching for a father figure (and had found one in Mao, according to Bruno Bettelheim); educators blamed the rise in "anarchy" on Dr. Spock's permissiveness, and seconded Spiro Agnew's call for a collective spanking. College administrators and sometimes faculty cooperated with the police and the FBI during the violent repression which began in 1968. On their part, student radicals often turned on the University, not in order to "free" it from complicity with imperialism, but to destroy it. In the fall of 1967, University of Wisconsin demonstrators handed out a leaflet announcing: "We pick this week to demonstrate against DOW (Chemical Corporation), against the university as a corporation and against the war because they are all one."

Criticism of the university, by a twisted kind of logic, soon led to criticism of students themselves. Carl Davidson, who only a year before had seen students as the mass base for social change, wrote:

> What can students do? Organizing struggles over dormitory rules seem frivolous when compared to the ghetto rebellions... We organize students against the draft when the Army is made up of young men who are poor, black, Spanish-American, hillbillies or working-class. Everyone except students... Students are oppressed. Bullshit. We are being trained to be the oppressors and the underlings of oppressors.[53]

By the end of the sixties, SDS was so repulsed by its own class that it would have nothing to do with the emerging ecology movement and held

53. Sales, *op. cit.,* pp. 382, 390.

back from mass anti-war activities such as the nationwide student "moratorium" and the massive student strike of May 1970. Mark Rudd went so far as to reject SDS itself (of which he was then the National Secretary) as a "weird pile of liberal shit."

It was a serious impasse: Where does a movement go when it comes to feel that the concerns which motivated it were trivial, if not illegitimate? Or that the people in it are irrelevant, if not objectively enemies? The "Weatherman" tendency in SDS took self-loathing to its logical extreme, resolving, in 1969, that white babies are "pigs" and pledging themselves to a suicidal strategy of direct confrontation with the police. For many women, the emerging feminist movement became the last legitimate refuge from the guilt which was engulfing the New Left at this time. The newly articulated understanding that women were oppressed as a sex allowed many white PMC women to continue to assert the demands for meaningful work, self-fulfillment, etc., at a time when these demands had lost all moral legitimacy to most male leftists.

By 1969, two overall approaches to handling the class problem were emerging for the New Left: one which we will call the "radicals in the professions" strategy; the other the strategy represented by what came to be called the "new communist movement." The "radicals in the professions" approach developed quite naturally out of the student life cycle; the undergraduates of 1963 were, by 1969, teachers, social workers, journalists, lawyers, or students in graduate or professional schools. Stated very simply, the idea was to use these positions, or at least whatever skills went with them, to advance the radical cause—which was now generally understood to be the cause of poor and working class people, oppressed minority groups, etc., and only indirectly of the professionals themselves. For example, the Student Health Organization (medical and nursing students) worked on setting up preventive health-care programs in Black ghettos; the New University Conference (college and junior-college teachers and graduate students) worked for open admissions to the colleges; the Social Welfare Workers Movement attached itself to the cause of the National Welfare Rights Organization; and so on. Other "radical professionals" set up alternative law firms, health centers, etc., or dedicated themselves to providing technical resources and support for Black and Puerto Rican community organizations.

Certain streams of the radical professionals' movement could be interpreted as being little more than attempts to salvage PMC interests in the face of the Black working class challenge. There was a search for more acceptable professional roles, such as "advocacy planning," and even some hopes that community control would bring an expansion of PMC opportunities:

Struggle by communities for control of their own development and services prepares the basis for a decentralized and democratized civil society. It is obvious that all such developments have profound need for the services of professional, intellectual, cultural, and scientific workers.[54]

But on the whole, the radicals-in-the-professions took a dramatic step beyond traditional PMC class interests. The great importance of this direction, or strategy, of New Left activism is that it embodied a critical self-consciousness of the PMC itself—a kind of negative class consciousness. The radicals-in-the-professions challenged the PMC not for its lack of autonomy (as the student movement had in the early sixties), but for its very claims to autonomy—objectivity, commitment to public service, and expertise itself. "Demystification" was the catchword. Radical doctors wanted not only to free their profession from the grip of the "medical industrial complex," but to demystify medicine. Radical lawyers would open up the law books and make elementary legal skills available to the people. Radical psychiatrists would lead the assault on psychiatric mythology and show that any sensitive community person could easily replace them. Radical teachers would expose the capitalist functions of education. And so on. Credentialing barriers would tumble. The rule of the experts would be abolished—by the young experts.[55]

It was, at best, a difficult approach to sustain. Clients, patients, students, etc., often turned out to resent their radical professionals' very lack of professionalism. Black aspirants to the PMC (briefly in demand in the late sixties and early seventies) had little interest in "demystifying" the positions they were for the first time attaining. Furthermore, conditions made it less and less possible to give the radicals-in-the-professions approach a fair test. Repression destroyed the radical elements of the Black movement which had held the radical professionals in some sense accountable. Government grants and money for community programs began to dry up. Finally, the economic downturn of

54. Richard Flacks, cited in *The New Professionals*, Ronald Gross and Paul Osterman, eds. (Simon and Schuster, 1972), p. 26.

55. It would be hard to overemphasize how sharp a break this was with the dominant traditions of the Second and Third Internationals. The latter, for instance, following the model of the USSR, believed that technology was neutral: In capitalist societies it served the interests of the capitalists; in socialist societies it would be directed toward popular ends. The New Left, influenced by the Cultural Revolution in China, came to believe that the technology itself embodied bourgeois social relations. The contrast between Old and New Left attitudes toward professionalism and the privileges accompanying it are equally sharp. The New Left position, of course, was in no small measure the descendent of the militantly egalitarian SDS and SNCC tradition of "participatory democracy."

the seventies placed stiff penalties on radical activty among professionals or anyone else: Teachers who defied the administration by giving out all A's, social workers who attempted to organize their clients against the welfare department, etc., found themselves in case after case out of a job. The Student Health Organization, Social Welfare Workers Movement, New University Conference, Medical Committee for Human Rights, all collapsed in the early seventies, and radical caucuses in professional associations became at best centers of radical scholarship, at worst, little more than job-placement networks for the hordes of ex-student radical professionals.

The "New Communist Movement" arose out of the shambles of SDS in 1969 and picked up recruits with the collapse of the radicals-in-the-professions approach in the early seventies.[56] The New Communists explicitly dissociated themselves from the New Left and adopted a political outlook which was superficially not very different from that of the earlier generation of PMC radicals who had been Communists in the 1930s. They advocated the primacy of the working class in revolutionary struggle and the need to build a vanguard party to lead that struggle. But exactly who constituted that working class was not entirely clear. Sometimes (e.g., in describing teachers' strikes and the spread of union-like attitudes in professional organizations of engineers and nurses) the New Communists adhered to the orthodox Marxian two-class model and included all wage earners within the "working class." But most of the time, by "working class" they meant the traditional blue-collar (and in some cases, lower-level white-collar) working class.[57] Students and young professionals joining New Communist organizations were urged to 'proletarianize" themselves in outlook, life style, and even occupation. Factories replaced universities as the key setting for political activity. Issues which had preoccupied the New Left—personal fulfillment, community, participatory democracy, etc.—were dismissed as "petty

56. By the "New Communist Movement" we mean those "Marxist-Leninist" organizations which grew out of the New Left, rather than out of prior left organizations such as the Socialist Workers Party and the Communist Party, plus individuals and study groups which identify with these organizations or their ideologies. National "new communist" organizations at this time include the October League, the Revolutionary Communist Party, and the Communist Labor Party. Although not affiliated with any of these groups, the weekly *Guardian* is the most widely read advocate of New Communist ideas.

57. In common New Communist Movement parlance, most of the PMC is lumped together with self-employed professionals, shopkeepers, small business men, etc., as the "petty bourgeoisie"—a distinctly pejorative description. As we have argued in the first part of this paper this is a grossly incorrect class analysis.

bourgeois" or even "decadent."

On the face of it, it was the New Communists, out of all the tendencies arising from the New Left, who seemed to come closest to transcending their own (PMC) class interests and to achieving an unambiguously revolutionary outlook. But in many ways, they had taken a step backwards: In discarding all traces of their "petty bourgeois" origins, they had thrown out the most radical insights of the New Left— *including the incipient New Left critique of the PMC itself.* Where the radicals-in-the-professions had agonized over the issues which haunt the PMC/working class interface—those which have to do with authority, knowledge, skill—the New Communists by and large simply abandoned the problem. Insisting that the working class is concerned only with issues of economic self-interest, the New Communists have tended to define all other issues as "cultural" or "superstructural" and consequently of secondary importance. Thus the very issues on which the historical antagonism between the PMC and the working class rests—those related to the division of labor, the ideological content of science and technology, etc.—are (conveniently?) shelved.

The real problem is, that having abandoned consciousness of the PMC/working class relationship, the way is open to replicating that relationship within the left. The vanguard/mass relationship comes to duplicate the PMC/working class division of labor within capitalism, with the vanguard providing the expertise and managerial skills. Educational requirements (the study of Marx, Lenin, Mao, etc.) and the mysteries of meeting decorum tend to bar actual working class people from the vanguard itself. Leadership becomes restricted to "professional revolutionaries, who like professionals generally, are drawn from the PMC. In this kind of situation, conventional PMC prejudices towards the working class—that the latter are anti-intellectual, authoritarian, "square," interested only in their material comfort, etc.—go unchallenged, and these prejudices feed directly into a narrowly economic approach to program. It is no doubt in part due to their inability to analyze and confront PMC/working class tensions that the various New Communist groups have remained small and unable to gain significant working class support.

V. Conclusion

Traditional Marxist analyses of capitalist society centered on the polarization between two classes and two alone—the capitalist class and the proletariat. We have presented a very different model, one which is meant to describe the class dynamics specific to monopoly capitalist society. In this model there is a *three-way* polarization, between the capitalist class, the working class and a third class which emerges in force only with the transition to modern monopoly capitalism—the Professional-Managerial Class.

In positing the existence of a Professional-Managerial Class, we do not mean to suggest that society has entered some new, "post capitalist" phase of development. The central dynamic in our society still lies in the contradiction between the socialized nature of the production process and the private appropriation of the fruits of production. The interests of the capitalist class remain fundamentally antagonistic to the interests of wage earners of all kinds, including those we have defined as members of the PMC. In fact, as we have argued, within the U.S., this antagonism has turned the PMC into an enduring reservoir of radicalism (from Progressivism and the Socialist Party to the New Left).

But as we have said, not only is there an objective antagonism between the working class and the PMC on the one hand and the capitalist class on the other; there is, in addition, an objective antagonism between the working class and the PMC. This latter antagonism has severely undercut the revolutionary chances of the working class (or of a combination of elements of both the PMC and the working class).

In the first place, as we have seen, PMC radicalism emerges out of PMC class interests, which include the PMC's interest in extending its cultural and technological hegemony over the working class. Thus the possibility exists in the PMC for the emergence of what may at first sight seem to be a contradiction in terms: anti-working class radicalism. This possibility finds its fullest expression in the PMC radicals' recurring vision of a technocratic socialism, a society in which the bourgeoisie has been replaced by bureaucrats, planners, and experts of various sorts. Nor is this vision restricted to the right-wing socialists and social democrats who come forth from the PMC; it has been advanced with great militancy by many who style their views as the "proletarian line." In fact, with any left ideology which fails to comprehend the PMC and its class interests, there is always a good possibility that the "dictatorship of the proletariat" will turn out to be the dictatorship of the PMC.[58]

Turning now to the effects of the PMC/working class polarization on working class consciousness, we should recall first the very existence

58. At the risk of considerable over-simplification, we would suggest that this is in a sense just what happened in the USSR: a "new class" of technocrats—government and party bureaucrats, industrial managers, professional ideologues, etc.—has come to preside over a society in which more or less capitalist relations of production persist, despite the absence of a capitalist class. In this context, Lenin's well-known interest in adopting the methods of Taylorism [see Harry Braverman, *Labor and Monopoly Capital* (Monthly Review Press, 1975), p. 12] and conversely, the Chinese concern with restricting the privileges of managers

of the PMC is predicated on the atomization of working class life and culture and the appropriation of skills once vested in the working class.[59] The activities which the PMC performs within the capitalist division of labor in themselves serve to undermine positive class consciousness among the working class. The kind of consciousness which remains, the commonly held attitudes of the working class, are as likely to be anti-PMC as they are to be anti-capitalist—if only because people are more likely, in a day-to-day sense, to experience humiliation, harassment, frustration, etc., at the hands of the PMC than from members of the actual capitalist class.

Now, add to the fact of working class hostility to the PMC two observations we have made already: 1) the historic association in the U.S. of socialist radicalism with the PMC; and 2) the PMC's proclivity for a technocratic vision of socialism in which the PMC would be the dominant class. The result is that there emerges in the working class another seemingly contradictory ideology, which we might call class conscious anti-communism. This working class anti-communism receives continual encouragement from right-wing demagogues who emphasize exactly these points: the role of PMC members ("pinko intellectuals," "effete snobs," etc.) in radical movements and social-control activities, and the supposedly totalitarian nature of socialism. But working class anti-communism is not created by right-wing demagoguery (or bad leadership, or ignorance, though all these help); it grows out of the objective antagonism between the working class and the PMC. Often enough it comes mixed with a wholesale rejection of any thing or thought associated with the PMC—liberalism, intellectualism, etc.

We hardly need to emphasize the dangerous, potentially tragic, nature of this situation. It is reflected with painful clarity in the condition of the U.S. left today: isolated and fragmented, still based largely in the PMC, more a subculture than a "movement."

and reducing the gap between mental and manual workers in order to avoid the Soviet mistakes [see John Ehrenreich, "The Dictatorship of the Proletariat in China," *Monthly Review* (October 1975)] are worth recalling. Similarly, "Arab socialism," "African socialism," and "military socialism" (e.g., pre-1975 Peru) can also best be understood not as "petty bourgeois socialism" but as "PMC socialism," based on the rising of civilian and military government mental workers.

59. We do not mean to suggest, of course, that the PMC alone holds the working class in check, or that restraining the development of working-class consciousness is always, or even usually, a conscious goal of the PMC. On the former point, other sources of control over the working class certainly include the direct use or threat of state and private employer power: pre-capitalist authoritarian mechanisms of control such as the Catholic Church; and the many forces leading to the segmentation of the labor market along lines of race, ethnicity, sex, and to the physical dispersion of the working class.

Is there a way out? Is there anything in the experience of either PMC or working class which could lead them to transcend their antagonism, to join together in some sort of mass radical alliance for social change. If so, how can such an alliance be built?

To answer these questions it seems to us we have to draw on the experience of the New Left. In a sense, the New Left represents a historic breakthrough: a first conscious effort to recognize and confront the conflict between the PMC and the working class. Learning in part from the Cultural Revolution in China, with its emphasis on the gap between mental and manual labor and its populist approach to technology, and in part from their uneasy alliance with (mainly Third World) working class community movements, the radicals of the sixties began to develop a critique of their own class. The feminist movement extended that critique, exposing the ideological content of even the most apparently "neutral" science and the ideological functions of even the most superfically "rational" experts.

But the New Left was not able to complete its incipient critique of the PMC and its role. With the collapse of the New Left as a mass movement in the seventies, the very effort ceased: Guilt replaced self-confidence, sterile efforts at remolding the consciousness of individual members of the PMC along "proletarian" lines replaced the more fruitful search for ways in which the PMC-based left could help stimulate and unite with a working class movement.

But the possibility of developing the emergent insights of the sixties and applying them to the development of a truly broad-based anti-capitalist movement is perhaps more alive now than ever. Unlike the early sixties, there are thousands of PMC leftists who remain aware, in however unsystematic a way, of the tensions at the PMC/working class interface. And, also unlike the early sixties, there is a growing number of young radical working class intellectuals—people who were given a brief exposure to higher education (and to the New Left) in the period of university expansion in the sixties, and were then thrown back into working class occupations by the economic crisis of the seventies. Thus, if only in terms of personnel, the opportunity exists for developing a politics which can address and overcome the class stalemate of the contemporary left.

What directions might such a politics go? We can only suggest a few beginning directions:

(a) The way out does not lie in falling back on romantic visions of the historical mission of the working class, manifested in efforts to expunge "petty bourgeois"—i.e., PMC—ideology from the left so as to uncover the "pure proletarian line." The relationship between the PMC and the working class is complementary; neither class has a "pure" ideology, uninfluenced by the other, or by the capitalist class. It is in the nature of this relationship that "culture" (in the loose sense of knowledge, ideas, history), including the systematic critique of capitalism itself, is dominated by the PMC. In a sense, Lenin's perception in *What Is To Be Done* remains true: the possibility of building a mass movement which seeks to alter society in its totality depends on the coming together of working class insight and militancy with the tradition of socialist thinking kept alive by "middle class" intellectuals.

(b) The antagonism between the PMC and the working class cannot be wished away in the name of anti-capitalist unity—any more, for example, than the antagonism between men and women, or between Black and white can be. The left, which is now predominately drawn from the PMC, must address itself to the subjective and cultural aspects of class oppression as well as to material inequalities; it must commit itself to uprooting its own ingrained and often subtle attitudes of condescension and elitism. The tensions between PMC leftists and the working class can only be dealt with by starting with a clear analytical perception of their origins and nature. Guilty self-effacement on the part of PMC radicals and/or simplistic glorification of the working class simply perpetuate the class roles forged in capitalist society.

(c) Moreover, in order to forge an alliance between elements of the PMC and the working class, the left must address itself not only to "bread and butter" issues but to all the issues it has too readily shelved as "cultural": the division of labor, the nature (and ideological content) of science and technology, art, psychology, sexuality, education, etc. For it is on these issues that the historic antagonism between the PMC and the working class rests. Both classes confront the capitalist class over the issue of ownership and control of the means of production. They confront each other over the issues of knowledge, skills, culture.

II

1.

A Critique and Extension of The Professional-Managerial Class

Al Szymanski

The Ehrenreich's must be congratulated for their analysis of the professional and managerial strata. In my opinion it ranks heads and shoulders above most of the class analysis produced within the American left in recent years. Its strongest points are their sharp refutation of the "new working class" theory and their, by and large, solid analysis of the class interests and social function of these strata. As they point out, major political mistakes follow from the "new working class" theory. A theory which they have rightly rejected in favor of a far more sophisticated analysis.

Other major contributions of the article include its insightful analyses of the development of professionalism (seen as a bid for autonomy of the professional stratum), and of the rise of the new left of the 1960's (seen as a reflection of the interests of the professional stratum). I would like, however, to take exception to two important points in their argument: 1) Their treatment of the "professional-managerial class" as a class distinct from the old petty bourgeoisie, together with their definition of class on which this claim is based; and 2) the political conclusion of the article which rejects Leninism. After redefining the class of which the professional and managerial strata are a part, I will attempt to extend the argument that this sector of the population can play an important progressive, while at the same time not a leading, role in the revolutionary process.

They define the "professional-managerial class" as "consisting of salaried mental workers who do not own the means of production and whose major function in the social division of labor may be broadly described as the reproduction of capitalist culture and capitalist class relations." This definition encompasses two parts: 1) relations of production, and 2) the social function of this group. The validity of definitions of class, must of course, be judged by their analytical power as tested by both their empirical correlates and the success of political practice based on the competing definitions. Nevertheless, it should be noted that the Ehrenreich's definition differs from the classical unidimensional Marxist one, which defines class solely in terms of relations of production.[2] Traditionally Marxists have defined proletarians as those that are able to, and must in order to live, sell their labor power; capitalists, as those that own or control the means of production, and hire the labor power of those that are free to sell it; and the (traditional) petty bourgeoisie as those who both own or control their means of production, and primarily work them themselves, rather than hiring the labor power of others.[3] Social function never enters in. Therefore, both capitalists who produced productive goods (such as food, houses, etc.) *and* unproductive goods and services (such as weapons, insurance, etc.) are equally and fully part of the capitalist class, just as workers, whether they produce food, weapons, houses, or work in sales, insurance or banking, are equally part of the working class. By bringing in the component of social function as part of their definition the Ehrenreichs seem to be accepting a Poulantzian type categorization that adds criteria beyond relations of production to class.[4] If it is valid to define a class in terms of whether or

2. See, for example, Karl Marx, *Capital*, 3 Vols. (Moscow: Foreign Languages Publishing House, 1962 [1894]), Vol. 3, Ch. 52 (On Classes).

3. See, for example, Judah Hill, "Class Analysis: the United States in the 1970s, " Pamphlet, Class Analysis, P.O.Box 84944, Emeryville, California, 1975; Charles Loren, *Classes in the United States* (Davis, California: Cardinal Publishers, 1977).

4. See Nicos Poulantzas, *Classes in Contemporary Capitalism* (London: New Left Books, 1975).

not their function is to reproduce class relations, then it is but a minor step to define bank or insurance workers out of the working class because their labor is unproductive, or workers in munitions industries out of this class, because their labor allows the capitalists to maintain a world empire, i.e., because their *economic* function is to *reproduce capitalist class relations,* just as surely as is that of the professionals who propagate ideology. Why is it that the Ehrenreichs' put professional ideologists in a separate class, but apparently would keep munitions workers in the working class? This is indeed an inconsistency.

Another inadequacy in their mode of conceptualization is that they are forced to define self-employed professionals as in a different class from employed professionals who do essentially the same job, and have the other characteristics of social class which the Ehrenreich's use, i.e., intermarriage, common culture and lifestyle, and anxiety about ordinary life experiences. Thus, according to the Ehrenreich's, a doctor who goes to work for Kaiser hospitals or a lawyer who leaves General Motors to set up his own practice, changes classes. By the Ehrenreich's own criteria this does not seem to be reasonable.

Still another problem with defining the professional and managerial groups as a class, in terms of both their distinctive relations of production and their social role, is that it excludes a lot of professionals who do not in fact function primarily to reproduce capitalist class relations (or who do so less than proletarians in banking, sales, offices or munitions). For example, employed doctors must reasonably be considered to be performing a socially useful function, most engineeers to be performing a useful productive function (to the extent they increase the efficiency of the productive process, rather than just saleability), most physical and biological scientists (unlike social "scientists") to be advancing, however selectively, knowledge (both theoretical and practical), most corporation employed lawyers to be lubricating the relations *among* capitalists (rather than those between workers and capitalists); and many teachers, to be teaching, either practical skills, such as shop, mechanical drawing, typing or scientific knowledge (who must then be treated either as adding to the productivity of students or to their scientific understanding). Indeed, a head count of the various professions would seem to show that *most* professionals probably can not be considered to be primarily engaged in the reproduction of capitalist culture and capitalist class relations.

While it certainly is true that there has been a rapid expansion of those whose primary function is the reproduction of capitalist culture (namely sociologists, economists, social studies and often literature teachers, literary apologists, etc.), and of capitalist class relations (social workers, lower level managers, time and motion analysts, etc.), it is not the case that this social function can be usefully considered a defining characteristic of a class. To do so would artifically divide people with identical relations of production, common culture and lifestyles, and overlapping marriage patterns, falsely placing them in different classes; namely, a Class I, composed of all lower level managers and the minority of the professionals whose primary function is to reproduce capitalist culture or class relations, and a Class II, composed of the majority of professionals whose primary social function is to add to productivity, develop or teach knowledge, lubricate relations among capitalists, health care, etc.

Further, a consistent application of the Ehrenreich's definition to other groups would produce a proliferation of (rather artifical) classes. Not only would the working class have to be divided into productive and unproductive sectors, but so would the capitalist class and the independent petty bourgeoisie. The independent petty bourgeoisie too, (as is the capitalist class itself), is divided into those whose primary function is to reproduce capitalist culture (independent authors and artists—most prominent artistic apologists for capitalism are *not* employed by the state or corporations), *or* to reproduce capitalist relations (e.g., sales, advertising or managerial consultants). Thus, if the Ehrenreich's carry through with their dual definition of class in terms of both relations of production and social function they are forced to conclude that contemporary capitalist society has not four major classes, but at least eight. If they reject this conclusion, they are forced to reject the class criteria on which it is based.

In any event, the question of the class nature of managers and professionals must finally be resolved in terms of the ability of competing definitions to give us an understanding of how classes behave. Are there in fact *two* socially distinct groups, an old petty bourgeoisie and a new professional-managerial class, i.e., do they tend not to intermarry, do they have distinctive cultures and lifestyles, does one, but not the other, have an inordinate amount of anxiety, etc.? Which definition is the most useful in explaining and changing the world? The question of whether the professional and managerial strata are part of the petty bourgeoisie (which includes the old independent middle class), or a separate class must be resolved on an empirical and practical basis.

While it is easy to see that the proletariat and the capitalist class are clearly socially distinct and usefully defined as separate classes, and that intermediate groupings exist between them, it can not, in fact, be demonstrated that *two* socially distinct groups exist between the proletariat and the capitalist class. In fact the intermediate group is more or less socially homogeneous, as well as having essentially similar relations of production. Thus, we must speak of a single petty bourgeoisie, which for many purposes must be considered to have an "old" and "new" component. While there are differences between these sectors of a single petty bourgeoisie in terms of how exactly they relate to capital and the capital accumulation process, as well as in their social function, these differences are secondary compared to their essential identity.

When the Ehrenreichs argue that the "hardheaded" managerial sector, and the "liberal" professionals are both part of a "professional-managerial class" they argue that: 1) there is little difference in their material conditions; 2) the two groups are socially coherent, i.e., they intermarry; 3) they share a common culture and lifestyle; 4) they share a common anxiety about ordinary life experiences, such as birth, education, marriage, etc.; and 5) they are not really all that different in terms of either education or managerial functions. In all but the last of these arguments they can mobilize significant evidence in favor of their case, and indeed because of this, present a convincing argument that these two groups can be usefully defined as part of a single class. However, precisely the same arguments can be successfully raised that both the professional and managerial strata are part of a broader petty bourgeois class which also includes the old independent middle class. The empirical evidence does not support the claim that two socially distinct intermediate strata exist.

Both the independent *and* the professional and managerial strata have similar relations of production. Both are intermediate between capital and labor. And as a result, they tend to be socially coherent, share a common culture and lifestyle, and a common anxiety about ordinary life experiences. Both the independent and the employed groups typically have a high degree of autonomy over their own labor (compared with proletarians), while being essentially dominated by capital, as well as a degree of authority over others (but mostly without essential control of other's labor power.)

It is not true, as the Ehrenreichs suggest, that the classical petty bourgeoisie is "irrelevant to the capital accumulation process." They have been just as important to it as the professional and mangerial strata. And because they have been as integral to it as this latter group they have been and are very much a part of the network of capitalist social relations. Small farmers traditionally produced the food that monopoly capitalists transported, processed and sold. Small businessmen traditionally sold the products produced by monopoly capitalist corporations. In no way can small farmers and small businessmen then be considered irrelevant to capitalist accumulation, for without their role in production and sales capitalism would not have functioned. What *is* happening is an increasing socialization of the central role of the independent petty bourgeoisie in the accumulation process. More and more agricultural production is being appropriated by corporate farms, while sales is being taken over by giant chains. The same functions continue to be performed, but now more and more by the managerial stratum, and less and less by the old independent petty bourgeoisie. Because of their role in the capital accumulation process as producers and sellers the old petty bourgeoisie was very much dominated by capital in the form of banks (which hold their mortgages), railroads, grain elevator companies, and slaughter houses (which took a considerable share of the income of small farmers), as well as food processing, distribution and wholesale companies and supermarkets. Thus while the old petty bourgeoisie had significant autonomy in their labor, they were essentially controlled (and indirectly exploited) by the logic of capital and thus subordinate to the capitalists. While the forms of control (indirect versus direct) differ, the amount of control by capital of the old petty bourgeoisie, and of the professional and managerial strata, is essentially the *same.*

Likewise, the amount of control over the labor power of others is *essentially* similar in the two groups. While the managerial stratum has *direct,* although delimited power, over the labor power of workers, the professional stratum does not. Professionals benefit from the services of secretaries, research assistants, and janitors, and have authority over students and clients (an authority while somewhat analogous to control of their labor, does not involve essential control). Professionals are not typically in a position to hire, fire, promote or otherwise exercise control over the labor power of those who serve them. The managers and administrators where the professionals work have this power. The traditional petty bourgeois farmer, shopkeeper or independent professional typically has power over the labor of others (a few employees, workers during the harvest, school kids on weekends, a bookkeeper or receptionist, his own family members, etc.), although the allocation (and hence, essential control) of their labor is in good part dictated by the constraints and compulsions put on small business by capital. It is not reasonable to define the (rather large) difference between the managerial and professional stratum in control over the labor of others as being less than the difference between either of the two and the small business sector. In fact all three groups are generally intermediate in this dimension. And thus all must be treated as members of a single class—the petty bourgeoisie.

A Class Analysis of the Petty Bourgeois

We can perhaps usefully sub-categorize the petty bourgeoisie by two dimensions: 1) *their social function*: whether their role is to, a) reproduce capitalist culture and indirectly capitalist class relations (e.g., social "scientists," literary apologists, social studies teachers, social welfare workers, etc.), b) directly administer and reproduce capitalist class relations through supervising and directing labor power (i.e., managers, managerial consultants), c) produce goods or add to productivity e.g., small farmers, artisans, engineers, d) sell goods or provide non-professional services (e.g., high level salesmen, small retail businessmen), or e) provide professional services (e.g., doctors and lawyers); *and* 2) *their employment status;* whether they are, a) self-employed, b) employed by private corporations, or c) employed by the state. Each of the possibilities on these two dimensions (five on the first, three on the second) has different consequences in terms of the life experiences, and hence, politics, of the various sectors of the single petty bourgeoisie.

Independent professionals (along with corporate managers) are traditionally the most conservative section of the petty bourgeoisie, while professionals employed by the state are usually the most progressive, with corporate employed professionals intermediate.[5] The life experience of independent professionals leads them to fear the expansion of the public sector as a threat to their autonomy and privilege, while state sector professionals generally welcome the expansion of the public sector as an opportunity to expand their authority. Within the business sectors of the petty bourgeoisie, small farmers and artisans are traditionally the most progressive, while the private managerial stratum is the most conservative, with shopkeepers intermediate. This is because the small producers are indirectly exploited by the banks and corporations who deprive them of the value they produce with their own hands, while the corporate managerial stratum materially benefits from increasing the direct exploitation of proletarians, or the indirect exploitation of the independent petty bourgeoisie. Thus, being part of the old or independent sector of the petty bourgeoisie would seem to have the *opposite* political effect on professionals than on business people, suggesting that a class division in terms of independent or employed status (as the Ehrenreichs do) has problems in terms of its political usefulness.

Although the managerial stratum should be included in the petty bourgeoisie its interests could well be considered essentially anti-working class. For managers, especially those in the corporate sector, to support full socialism, i.e., workers' control of industry, they would necessarily abolish themselves as a class along with their privileges. Such is not the case with any other sector of the petty bourgeoisie. A socialist regime need not negatively affect the independent businessmen, nor need it undermine the role of scientists, teachers, engineers, doctors, etc. (although a socialist regime would re-orient their energies). Thus if any

5. See Albert Syzmanski, *The Capitalist State and the Politics of Class* (Boston: Winthrop Publishing Co., 1978), Ch. 4.

single sector should be defined out of the petty bourgeoisie and into a separate class (as characterized in terms of the political usefulness of a definition) it has to be the managerial stratum, a stratum whose very existence is, unlike the rest of the petty bourgeoisie, tied up with the preservation of capitalist-worker relationships.

However, it must be said, that even the lower level managers would not suffer greatly in the short run in a socialist society. Workers will only gradually take direct charge of day-to-day administrative and co-ordinating tasks. Socialism in the short run, as the experience of all socialist revolutions of the twentieth century have shown, will essentially mean worker's power over basic decision making and general policies, i.e., the directive power over lower managers will change from the corporate capitalists to the workers, thus not requiring a total loss of position of the lower managers.

We should expect a significant difference between managers employed by private industry and those employed by the state ("administrators" and "officials") in these regards. While the former group should be expected to be fearful of socialization of industry, the latter group, who in the short run may well experience an expansion of authority and job opportunities with socialization, should be expected to be less resistant and sometimes even supportive.

In spite of the qualifications expressed above, the petty bourgeoisie's most fundamental division, as the Ehrenreichs suggest (although they do not conceptualize it this way) *is* between its "old" and "new" sectors, i.e., the self-employed independent small businessmen, professionals, and small farmers on the one side, and the employed professionals, intellectuals, scientists, and lower level management personnel on the other. (Although for some purposes the corporate managerial sector could best be grouped with small retail businessmen and independent professionals as the more conservative strata.)

Traditionally the old petty bourgeoisie was so large compared to employed professionals and lower management that it was identified as *the* petty bourgeoisie. The rapid growth of corporations both in the cities and on the land over the last 100 years has, however, driven almost all of the old independent small businessmen and farmers bankrupt, forcing them to sell out to the corporations which now produce, and sell, most everything made and sold in the advanced capitalist countries. The growth and consolidation of monopoly capitalism, on the other hand, has produced the rapid expansion of a new petty bourgeoisie of scientists, university teachers, professional state workers (e.g., social workers), architects, accountants, writers, lower level managers who do not have fundamental control of corporate policies, etc. In many ways the class interests of these two basic segments of the petty bourgeoisie are identical, but in some important ways they diverge.

Both segments of the petty bourgeoisie have the same dual antagonism to the corporate capitalist class on the one side and to the revolutionary working class on the other. While the petty bourgeoisie's antagonism to monopoly capitalism was based on the economic competition between them, which was being won by the more efficient monopoly capitalists who were driving them into the proletariat, the petty bourgeoisie's antagonism (especially its professional sector's) is based on its lack of fundamental control over the conditions of its labor and the uses of its "product" (or "service"). Scientists are not really able to determine what kind of research they will do or how their work will be used because of corporate funding and direction of their work; university teachers are under great pressure to mass produce students without raising fundamental criticisms of the way things are; social workers are forced to act like policemen; architects are made to design monstrosities, rather than socially useful buildings; engineers are required to design cars which fall apart and factories that pollute, etc. Although faulty as general analysis, it is useful to examine Serge Mallet's, *Essays on the New Working Class,* Andre Gorz', *Strategy for Labor* and Thorstein Veblen's, *Engineers and the Price System,* in this context.

There is continuing pressure to "proletarianize" the new petty bourgeoisie (in a fashion analogous to the pressure on the old petty bourgeoisie). The teaching load of college professors and class sizes go up, architects and engineers are subjected to increasing productivity demands, social workers must take on higher case loads, etc. It should be noted that the material privileges of much of the new petty bourgeoisie have been exaggerated, the average income of employed professionals in recent years has averaged only about 30% more than that of skilled workers (comparing males only to eliminate the effect of sexism). It is also true, especially since the occurrence of a surplus of college graduates which developed in the early 1970s, that there has been considerable downward pressure on the salaries of the new petty bourgeoisie.

While the new petty bourgeoisie has fundamental antagonisms with the capitalist class that controls and pressures them, it is *not* initially in as desperate a situation vis-a-vis this class as is the independent petty bourgeoisie who are about to go bankrupt (except, of course, for those engineers and teachers, etc., who are being laid off or can't find work). This sector of the petty bourgeoisie continues to grow (although not as rapidly as before) while the old petty bourgeoisie continues to shrink. On the other hand the potential antagonism of much of the old petty bourgeoisie (namely those that employ a few workers) to the working class is more intense than is that of the new petty bourgeoisie (except perhaps its corporate managerial stratum). As the violently anti-union efforts of small growers in California and small farmers in Northern Italy after World War I, as well as the strongly anti-union efforts of small employers almost everywhere, show, this class is very badly hurt by unionization of its work force, which results in wage increases which this sector can only meet at the cost of profits (it can not, like monopoly businesses, pass on wage increases to consumers by increasing prices). This class periodically becomes violently hostile to the Communists and Socialists it sees as trying to take away the little property they have. The fact that the new petty bourgeoisie has already been "socialized," i.e., has no private property and does not directly depend on profits to survive makes a fundamental difference in their attitude about both unions and the socialization of private business (although not, of course, about the preservation of their own relative privileges vis-a-vis the working class). Unionization and the improvement in the conditions of workers do not adversely affect the new petty bourgeoisie (so long as they can maintain their pay differentials, which, by the way, are often geared to the increases in union settlements). Proposals for the nationalization of enterprises and the expanison of social services, and the public sector in general, not only do not hurt the petty bourgeoisie, but positively help it by increasing its job opportunites in working for the state, raising its prestige and status by elevating the importance of the socialized sector and expanding funds available for scientific research, medicine, etc., from which it benefits. (Joseph Schumpeter in his *Capitalism, Socialism, and Democracy* has an interesting discussion of these points). These differences between the old and new petty bourgeoisies have major implications for how these groups respond to appeals from the revolutionary left and the monopoly capitalists in a crisis situation where they are forced to side with one side or the other.

To an extent, the new petty bourgeoisie still maintains the ideal of a "third path" between monopoly capitalism and proletarian socialism as manifested in such phenomena as the "small is beautiful" trend, fighting for secure tenure for teachers and other professions and generally trying to increase job autonomy, minimize interference from administrators and owners etc., on the one hand, while preserving privileges vis-a-vis workers on the other. The general strike of professional workers in Sweden a few years ago, whose goal was to restore the traditional pay differential with manual workers, is an important example of this latter point, as have been the various doctors' strikes around the world. But the ideals of the new petty bourgeoisie are in the last analysis as much a fraud as the old Jeffersonian ideal of the old petty bourgeoisie because of the insatiable drive for greater and greater productivity and control demanded by capital. The new petty bourgeoisie, like the old, is faced in the final analysis with having to side with either the monopoly capitalists or the revolutionary proletariat. Because of the significant difference in the conditions of work of the new petty bourgeoisie, which considerably weakens this class's traditional hostility to the proletariat in crisis situations, we can expect it to have a considerably greater likelihood of siding with the working class, a class which need offer much less of a threat to its immediate interests than the monopoly capitalists.

It is of course true that the goal of a socialist revolution is to begin the transformation to a communist society in which the division of labor between mental and manual work will be abolished, and thus that in the long run there can be no preservation of the privileges of the new petty bourgeoisie. But this is the long term goal of socialist revolution, not the immediate prospect. Just as the Cuban, Russian, Chinese, Vietnamese, etc., revolutions held out the promise of full and socially useful employment in fulfilling a great historical task, and only a gradual withering away of their material privileges, to their intellectuals and professionals, there is no reason that revolutions in the West will not do the same. Such an alternative may well prove to be more attractive than the "proletarianization" offered them by the monopoly capitalists in a *crisis* situation. (It is unlikely, of course, that this class will move as a class in anything but a vacillating way until a revolutionary crisis forces it to choose between the two viable options.)

While the traditional opposition of the old petty bourgeoisie, because of its nature as property owners, has always been exerted against the socialization of property by a socialist revolution which would expropriate its property (e.g., the opposition of the Kulaks to collectivization in the Soviet Union), the professional sector of the petty bourgeoisie has no interest in opposing full socialization by a fully socialist revolution, since it owns no productive property and in fact in the short run, stands to gain by the increasing opportunities socialization provides, e.g., more scientific research, creative architecture and construction, efficient cars, more money for medicine, etc. The various segments of this class can thus be expected to diverge politically at the stage of the revolutionary transformation which moves from anti-big and middle capitalism, which socialized only medium and large businesses (which is in the interest of the independent and employed petty bourgeoisie, excepting perhaps its private managerial stratum), to full socialization (which is only in the interest of the employed professionals and intellectuals, and perhaps state managers). It is not until the third phase of a revolutionary transformation, the transition to full communism, which implies the abolition of all privilege and division between mental and manual labor, that the employed professional's, intellectual's and state manager's interests diverge from those of the proletariat. This is the current stage of development in both the Soviet Union and China. The struggle between the new petty bourgeoisie and the proletariat and peasantry has been manifested in both the Chinese Cultural Revolution and in the trend towards "revisionism" (or as the Chinese say, the movement towards the "restoration of capitalism") in the Soviet Union. The bureaucrats in the party, industries and state want to maintain and secure their privileges vis-a-vis the working masses and thus they resist the movement from socialism to communism, while the working masses demand progress which entails the elimination of all privileges inherent in a socialist (as opposed to communist) form of social organization. Thus what was a contradiction among the people at both the stage of the original revolution against the bourgeoisie and imperialism, as well as at the stage of full socialization, has recently, in both China and the Soviet Union, become the primary contradiction within the society.

Petty Bourgeois Movements

Twentieth century advanced capitalist society has seen the three major classes play central roles in the historical process. Although these three classes have engaged in an on-going struggle with one another, with the petty bourgeoisie often seeking its own "third path," modern conditions present only two real historical options for the middle run: socialism (a society organized under the leadership of the working class) and monopoly capitalism (organized under the leadership of the corporate capitalist class). The various movements of the petty bourgeoisie, e.g., American Populism and progressivism, radical farmers' movements of the 1930s, French Poujadism, the German Nazi party before 1934, Italian fascism before 1923, and most out of power fascist and proto-fascist movements, as well as most populist type movements the world around, demonstrate consistently the non-viability of any "third path." The ideal of the "little man," of hostility to both "big labor and big business," of a return to the idyllic state of Jeffersonian Democracy with every person a king or queen on his or her own small farm, running his or her own small business or being a successful doctor, lawyer or professor, proves itself to be an unrealizable romantic chimera. Independent movements of the petty bourgeoisie, because of the absolute impossibility of reversing the course of historical development, which would be necessary in order to realize their goals, are necessarily merged into movements led by either the bourgeoisie or the working class. Because neither monopoly capitalism nor socialism adequately reflects their interests, this class, by its very nature, vacillates between the two historically viable movements of the twentieth century. In a time of decisive battle between the two greatest modern classes, the petty bourgeoisie, being forced to take sides, can go *either* way. Which way it goes is in good part determined by the effectiveness with which one or the other viable class reaches out to it and mobilizes it, and further, in good part determines the outcome of the test of strength between the two viable classes.

In the period between the two world wars fascism became the leading expression of the petty bourgeois (both its "old" and " new" sectors) interest in finding a "third path" that was both opposed to monopoly capitalism and proletarian socialism. The fascists (out of power) never tired of directing their venom against both communists, socialism, unions and workers' co-operatives, which were squeezing the petty bourgeoisie from the left, *and* the big banks, department stores, and corporations that were squeezing them from the right. Fascist programs throughout the world promise both the destruction of independent trade unions and working class parties *and* the breaking up of the big corporations, banks and landed estates and their redistribution to the petty bourgeoisie. The story of what happened to the fascists once they came into power is familiar to all. Being brought into power by the corporate capitalists who established a firm alliance with Hitler and Mussolini they fulfilled the anti-working class half of their program admirably, but forgot the anti-monopoly half. In Germany the Storm Troopers, who actively pressed for the *full* realization of the Nazi program, i.e., the breaking up of big business, were violently purged and disbanded. In spite of the great hopes raised in the petty bourgeoisie, at least its independent sector faired poorly during the period of Nazis and fascist rule. Monopoly profits went up, the rate of monopolization increased; big business never had it so good. But for the independent petty bourgeoisie, there was nothing but more bankruptcy and an acceleration of their descent into the proletariat. The new petty bourgeoisie, especially its managerial section, on the other hand fared relatively better, with the expansion of administrative functions in both the public and private sectors.[6]

Although the petty bourgeoisie gives birth to fascist movements all around the world, movements which are inevitably captured by the bourgeoisie whenever they achieve a massive following, the petty bourgeoisie also gives birth to progressive movements which focus their struggle against big business, and thus are open to following the leadership of the working class, once the bankruptcy of their independent pursuit becomes clear. Such have been the paths of the left wing of the

6. Some of the best sources on the nature of fascism include Lewis Corey, *The Crisis of the Middle Classes*; Daniel Guerin, *Fascism and Big Business*; Arthur Schwatzer, *Big Business and the Third Reich*; Angelo Tasca, *The Rise of Italian Fascism*; and E. Palme Dutt, *Fascism and Social Revolution*.

Populist movement in the U.S., which after their right and center were captured by the big business-planter controlled Democratic party in 1896 merged into the Socialist Party, and the progressive movements of peasants and urban petty bourgeoisie which came to accept the leadership of Marxist parties in China, Vietnam, Chile and throughout the Third World, as well as in Italy, France, Spain, and other European countries.

The international Communist movement once made the nearly fatal mistake of not understanding the dual (vacillating) nature of the petty bourgeoisie. Directing its appeal almost exclusively to the working class and in practice rejecting outreach to these groups, the "Third Period" of the Comintern (1928-1935) facilitated the growth of fascist movements throughout the advanced capitalist countries by isolating itself in a sectarian fashion from those it should have been reaching out to and mobilizing behind working class leadership. The 7th Comintern Congress held in 1935 analyzed these serious ultra-left mistakes and developed a corrective policy encapsulated in the Congress report of Georgi Dmitrioff:

> In its agitation fascism, desirous of winning these masses to its own side, tries to set the mass of working people in town and countryside against the revolutionary proletariat, frightening the petty bourgeoisie with the bogey of the "Red peril." We must turn this weapon against those who wield it and show the working peasants, artisans and intellectuals whence the real danger threatens. We must show concretely who it is that piles the burden of taxes and imports onto the peasant and squeezes usurious interest out of him; who it is that, while owning the best land and every form of wealth, drives the peasant and his family from their plot of land and dooms them to unemployment and poverty. We must explain concretely, patiently and persistently who it is that ruins the artisans and handicraftsmen with taxes, imposts, high rents, and competition impossible for them to withstand: who it is that throws into the street and deprives of employment the wide masses of the working intelligentsia.[7]

The international Marxist-Leninist movement thus set itself the task, to which *both* the Chinese and Soviet leaning Communist parties

7. Georgi Dimitrioff, "The United Front Against War and Fascism," Report to the Seventh World Congress of the Communist International, 1935 (New York: Gamma Publishing Co., 1972).

have adhered, of attempting to win the petty bougeoisie to working class leadership against their greater enemy—the monopoly corporations. The program outlined by 7th Comintern Congress was designed as more than a temporary expedient to stop the growth of fascism in Europe in 1930s. It was the outline of a general strategy meant to have validity until the total collapse of capitalism. Fascism was seen as a necessary outgrowth of decaying capitalism which would always tend to come to power in crisis situations unless its popular base, the petty bourgeoisie, could be won by the proletariat. Dimitrov goes on to argue that American Marxist-Leninists should organize a Farmer-Workers' Party which would direct itself against the "banks, trusts, and monopolies, against the principle enemies of the people" which must defend "the interests of members of the liberal professions, small businessmen and artisans."[8] The 7th Comintern Congress did not confuse the Popular Front, which included petty bourgeois organizations, with the united front of working class organizations which was designed to provide the leadership to the Popular Front. The point is that the interests of the proletariat required it to mobilize the petty bourgeoisie behind an anti-monopoly popular front as a necessary condition for making a socialist revolution.

Conclusion

By far the weakest part of the Ehrenreichs' article is their conclusion. The contrast between the insightful class analysis of the body of their paper and the confusion and contradictions of the end is astounding.

The clear thrust of their whole class analysis is the decisive rejection of new working class theory, while at the same time, the recognition of the progressive potential of the petty bourgeoisie. The Ehrenreichs argue that the only consistently revolutionary class is the working class. Yet neverthless, they draw back from the logical step that the working class is the leading (or vanguard) class in the revolutionary process, using such "new left" or "new working class" phrases as "The way out does not lie in falling back on romantic visions of the historical mission of the working class...," or the apparent rejection of the very concept of a working class analysis and politics as expressed in the placing of "proletarian line" in quotation marks whenever it is used. These conclusions are in absolute contradiction to the Ehrenreichs' own brilliant analysis. If the professional and managerial strata are not clearly revolutionary then only the working class is. If only the working class is, then the analysis and politics indigenous to this class is the guide to the revolutionary process, i.e., the historical mission of the working class is human liberation.

Another clear aspect of the Ehrenreichs' analysis is that a socialist

8. Idem.

revolution can only be won through an alliance of the working class and the professional and mangerial strata (under the leadership of the working class). Yet in their conclusion they stress the importance of emphasizing the issues which *divide* these two groups, rather than those that unite them. At this point in the revolutionary process, a point where it is necesssary to stress the unity of the working class and the petty bourgeoisie, it is not wise to emphasize the elimination of the need for professionals or small businessmen. To do so is both foolish and unscientific. To stress such questions is to drive the petty bourgeoisie to fascism, and thus prevent socialist revolution. To seriously believe that professionals will be abolished in the first generation after a revolution is romantic anarchism unsubstantiated by any real revolutionary process in the twentieth century. However (and this is a contradiction within a contradiction), when they actually talk about what issues they would stress, most of them; e.g., the ideological content of science and art, education, sex, cultural issues, etc., seem not to be issues that divide these classes but rather issues which stress how capitalism oppresses *both* the petty bourgeoisie and the working class.

Perhaps the most blatant contradiction of all in the Ehrenreichs' conclusion is the virtually back-to-back statements that "The possibility of building a mass movement which seeks to alter society in its totality depends on the coming together of working class insight and militancy with the tradition of socialist thinking kept alive by "middle class intellectuals" and "The vanguard/mass relationship comes to duplicate the PMC/working class division of labor within capitalism, with the vanguard providing the expertise and managerial skills."[pp. 45, 41] On the one hand the Ehrenreichs understand that because of the pervasive cultural and educational subordination of the working class and the special training and freedoms of the socialist intelligentsia, that the latter (and the organizations they can form), have a special responsibility to play in initiating the development of revolutionary consciousness (as they in fact have in all twentieth century revolutionary movements), while on the other, in an anarchist fashion, they seem to suggest that expertise and vanguard organizations are inherently petty bourgeois and obstacles to the development of revolutionary consciousness. Again their own analysis leads them to the brink of admitting that the socialist segment of the petty bourgeoisie and a disciplined party (which, although it might have been started mainly by such people, soon has a predominantly working class membership) must play the catalytic role in the development of the revolutionary process. But rather than following the logic of their own careful analysis of the cultural oppression of workers, and the special skills of professionals, they instead slip back into a muddle.

The Ehrenreichs have made an important contribution to the class analysis of contemporary capitalism and to our understanding of the new left of the 1960s. However, their major failing is in not drawing out the logical conclusions of their analysis. While, in their class analysis, they radically remove themselves from the popular new left ideas of the 1960s, yet they continue to give credence to many of the political notions of this movement. In spite of the clear implications of their arguments, they still reject the leading political role of the working class, the necessity of a vanguard organization which is able to successfully combat the ideological hegemony of the bourgeosie, and organize the petty bourgeoisie and the proletariat around issues which unite rather than divide them.[9] In short, the Ehrenreichs' analysis brings them to the brink of Leninism. But shying away from this logical conclusion they end with confusion and muddle which does nothing to advance our practice organizationally or strategically. Appreciating the power of their analysis, we must take the step from which the Ehrenreichs themselves draw back.

9. For a summary discussion of the necessity of a disciplined "vanguard" party to successfully combat the ideological hegemony of the bourgeoisie over the proletariat see Albert Syzmanski, "Leninism and the Culture of Resistance," *Socialist Revolution, #20 (October 1974).*

2.

Why Class?

Jean Cohen & Dick Howard*

On first reading, the Ehrenreichs' account of the New Left in terms of the class constellation of monopoly capitalism seems to unite the best of Marxism with the innovations of the sixties' radicalism. They try to clarify the new phenomena out of which the New Left emerged, and to situate this novelty historically within the pattern of capitalist development and class struggle. Only when one comes to their political conclusions and, disappointed by their meagerness and by their hidden orthodoxy, returns for a second reading, do the analytic weaknesses and unchallenged assumptions become apparent. The Ehrenreichs' Marxism seeks to present itself as open-ended, flexible, and oriented toward the new. Yet, the essay begins with the assumption of a mass working class as the revolutionary subject, and despite statistical and historical evidence claiming the emergence of a new "PMC," concludes with Lenin's relegation of the radical members of the 'middle classes' to keepers of the tradition. A comparison with the new working class theories which they quickly reject shows the superficiality of their transcendence of Marxist dogmatism. But the problem of class is more complex, even in Marx's own theory. Therefore, when applied indiscriminantly to account for new social strata, its own ambiguities both distort and oversimplify. Hence, the political analysis that emerges will also have to be called into question.

I

The Ehrenreichs try to apply the spirit of Marx's method to the problems and institutions which the New Left confronted. Marx's claim was that his theory was the conceptual expression or structural analysis of the actual, ongoing struggle of the proletariat. It was to be a theory *of* praxis, whose own praxical, political relevance was guaranteed by its roots in the dynamics of struggle. The Ehrenreichs attempt to thematize the practice of the New Left in the same manner. They pose the question: what kind of social and economic structures could have called forth and developed a movement of this peculiar type? They don't want to give up the uniqueness of the New Left in favor of the schemata of orthodoxy. They want to remain true to their origins; and be Marxists. They are asking: if this movement and its phases were socio-economically rooted, how can we understand these roots; and, in terms of that understanding, how can we see where we went wrong, where we misunderstood ourselves and our potential, where elan took the place of reflection and the movement became either an end in itself or simply a means or tool toward an end that was wholly foreign to it?

True to its Marxist background, this proposed class analysis will have to be both structural and dynamic. The Ehrenreichs present first a structural analysis of the transformation of capitalist forces and relations of production in their "monopoly" phase. Scientized production and the commodification of essential human services are shown to be inherent in the intensive capitalist growth which emerges once the extensive implantation of colonialism is checked. Then, following Thompson's injunction that classes are not simply objective economic categories but rather forms of self-organization in struggle, the Ehrenreichs interpret these structural changes dynamically in terms of class conflict. But their analysis runs into difficulty when they have to further define the notion of class. "Class" is given a double definition: a dose of historical materialism

*Discussed and agreed upon by both, Parts II, III, and IV were written by Jean Cohen and parts I and V were written by Dick Howard.

and a dash of academic sociology. From the former:

> A class is characterized by common relations to the economic foundations of society—the means of production and the socially organized patterns of distribution and consumption... Class is defined by actual relations between groups of people, not formal relations between people and objects. [p. 9]

But insofar as the formative nature of the labor process on the forms of consciousness and interaction is not sufficiently stressed in this definition, academic sociology paradoxically comes to the rescue:

> However, the relation to the economic foundations of society is not sufficient to specify a class as a real social entity... a class is characterized by a coherent social and cultural existence; members of a class share a common life style, educational background, kinship networks, consumption patterns, work habits, beliefs. [p. 9]

To this is added a double caveat: a class cannot be analyzed in isolation from its relation to other classes; and the relation between class as an abstract economic concept and class as a "real social existence" is all but unexplored. But, instead of exploring this vital issue, the Ehrenreichs simply assure us that "class" has the two above characteristics, and proceed to define the new middle strata, from intellectuals to technicians to bureaucrats, as members of the "PMC." The historical illustrations they bring only cover up the conceptual ambiguity.

The meagerness of their political conclusions is certainly due to this conceptual problem. There are suggestions that we must understand structurally both "anti-working class radicalism" and "class conscious anti-communism." On the other hand, the (uncritical) praise of the Chinese Cultural Revolution and the women's movement implies a more open-ended dynamic approach which stresses self-organization. Structure returns when we are warned to avoid romantic visions which could prevent us from seeing the PMC for what it is; and to beware of the lure of a (false) anti-capitalist unity which denies the "objective" antagonism of the PMC and the working class. Then, the other side returns, and we are admonished to take seriously cultural issues, while being told that Lenin was right after all about the relations between intellectuals and the working class. Finally, the conclusion denies the originality of the three-class model after all, because "the central dynamic in our society still lies in the contradiction between the socialized nature of the production process and the private appropriation of the fruits of production." [p. 42]

Playing on the ambiguity of a structural, then a dynamic analysis, the Ehrenreichs' three-class model ultimately reverts to the standard two-class variety in its political implications. However independent its structure, the PMC is dynamically caught between the polar structure of the capitalists and the proletarians. The radicals of the PMC must attach themselves to one or the other. The Ehrenreichs would argue that unless one considers the structural position of the PMC, struggles by its leftist members in the name of the working class would become a disguise for a technocratic socialism draped in the robes of the dictatorship of the proletariat. Yet, while welcoming an analysis which resists both the betrayal of the leaders/bourgeoisification thesis, as well as the Trotskyist nonsense of a degenerate, but still workers' state, and agreeing that technocratic ideology is a danger for our own movement, we wonder whether the addition of a new class without any change in the "basic contradiction" implies that the new class is at best epiphenomenal. If so, the Ehrenreichs' political account remains economistic, and the structure triumphs over the dynamics of political struggle.[1]

The apparent strength of the analysis was its unification of the dynamics of the class struggle and capitalist accumulation with an account of the birth of a new class whose position could be structurally specified and to whose "objective possibilities" the analysis could point. This was to give a stance from which to grasp the class position and problems of the New Left, and to understand the political choices it made. It was hoped that this would permit us to see what the radical members of the PMC must do in order to loosen themselves from their own class background and partial ties to the capitalists. Above all, the objective obstacles lying in the way of an alliance with the working class and the necessary strategy to catalyze their dormant energies would become apparent. *But this transforms the original goal of the analysis.* Instead of seeking a theory *of* ongoing praxis of the New Left, one now aims at a technical, ultimately manipulative theory *for* realizing a pre-given end (defined by the "central dynamic" of socialized labor with private appropriation). The reader becomes leader, i.e., is supposed to grasp a new set of objective conditions and adjust his or her—and his or her followers'—actions to the new necessities. This is a return to the Second International (of which Leninism is but a variant); it is based on a metaphysical notion of the working class; and it distorts social and political reality.

In the last resort, the dogmatic and unargued assertion of the working class' priority as revolutionary subject negates the advances the

---

1. The Ehrenreichs admit that one must analyze the changed role of the state in monopoly capitalism, and explain that they were forced to omit this reconsideration in their essay. But given the thrust of their analysis, as we shall show, the kind of arguments they might have offered would have been but another instance of judging categories within a fixed framework.

Ehrenreichs might have made. The apparent openness of the essay lies in its insistence on the *self-formation* of classes in struggles around *new* conditions of production. It would seem therefore that just as capitalist development generates new social strata, so too the working class itself changes. The old, pure revolutionary subject of history surely could not be unaffected by the process in which it is an actor. Granted, the Ehrenreichs speak of the PMC's stealing from the proletariat its own skills, ability to manage its own affairs and form a self-subsistent community. On the basis of the structural changes in capitalism, and the changed nature of work itself, they might have been led to reconsider the primacy of this class, and to ask whether its goals and "objective possibilities" remain the same. But they don't. They see the PMC's "anti-working class radicalism" as something structured into modern capitalist relations, to be overcome if the famous melting of mental and manual labor occurs. And their discussion of the "negative class consciousness" supposedly achieved by the radicals in the professions—if not pure metaphysical gibberish—is once again based on that model of proletarian consciousness which they periodically warn us not to romanticize, but never themselves put into question. The referent of all radical activity remains the proletariat, which permanently carries the revolutionary project despite all structural and historical changes.

The metaphysics of the working class rests on an implicit category of work or labor based on the model of a subject transforming an external object. Workers are potentially revolutionary *as producers*. Revolution is declared necessary because of the constraints that class domination places on a rational organization of work, hence distribution and hence of society. Since the workers are the subject from the start, there is no real process of interaction, no debate concerning ends, no learning—none of that self-formation that the Ehrenreichs wanted to stress. Instead, the means to revolution are calculable in terms of "objective" structural contexts of precisely the type that they set out to clarify. Politics is reduced to goal-oriented economic choice. In short, the revolutionary and the capitalist entrepreneur operate according to the same logic, that of a theory *for* practice, a technique.

To avoid this kind of position, the Ehrenreichs draw on another facet of the metaphysics. When they discuss the antagonism that "objectively" exists between the PMC and the working class, they point to the process of deskilling which weakens the workers' leverage, reducing them to interchangeable cogs in an automated production process directed by science and technology. Aside from the fact that this process is coincident with the birth of capitalism as described by Marx or Thompson, and is thus nothing new, it implicitly glorifies the skilled worker who, if only left alone, if only given control of production, would automatically produce the good society. This implies an *instinctive* lucidity on the part of the working class. If carried to the extreme, it becomes an aggressively anti-Leninist syndicalism of the kind to which the New Working Class theories also lead. On the other hand, this assumption is rooted paradoxically in bourgeois attitudes: the glorification of work is specific to capitalist society. That this glorification reappears in so-called socialist societies in the course of "modernization" ought to make us wonder about their revolutionary claims. Why should revolutionaries think of work and workers as the salt of the earth, the unconscious bearers of a new social form, just because they are "productive?"

Why are the Ehrenreichs pushed to conclusions which, in this form, they surely would not accept? The clue can be found first in their discussion of the New Working Class theory. The context in which this falls is revealing—a discussion of structural economic analyses of modern society. Running through the French positions, they conclude with the pseudo-structural empiricism of Poulantzas, whom they easily reject for his orthodox two-classism (with its dogmatic assertion that any other position is "unthinkable" for a Marxist). But with this economistic framing of the question, the political context in which the New Working Class theory was formulated is lost. While Poulantzas' work represents the worst of ahistorical structuralist category-juggling, Belleville, Mallet and Gorz formulated their conceptions as part of, and a reflection on, actual political struggles.[2] From the new forms of political struggle they saw emerging, they were driven to rethink the economic analysis hitherto accepted. As opposed to this, the Ehrenreichs start from an economic analysis from which, then, they want to draw political conclusions.

The weakness of the Ehrenreichs' positions from a Marxian point of view can be brought out by a comparison with the analysis of Serge Mallet, who first coined the term "new working class." The Ehrenreichs

2. Gorz's work emerged through an analysis of the innovative trade union strategies developed by the CGIL in Italy; and influenced the student union, the UNEF in the early 60's and found supporters among trade unionists in the CFDT. Mallet's theory emerged from his experience as a party organizer. After he left the party and reformulated his theory, it was a major force in the independent development of the CFDT, and in the PSU, who were able to see and act on the self-management implications of May '68. One might mention that Mallet's next work, *The Peasants Against the Past*, applied a similar analytic strategy and political intervention to a very different domain, again however, in a political context.

3. C.f., the essays collected in Serge Mallet, *Essays on the New Working Class,* eds. Dick Howard and Dean Savage (St. Louis: Telos Press, 1975). On the New Working Class, besides the citations by the Ehrenreichs, see the Preface to that

look at society in order to find there a play of force-vectors which delineate a set of "objective possibilities" within which a strategy towards a fixed, pre-given goal can be elaborated. Mallet had a similar theoretical orientation when he worked as a PCF union organizer. However, he soon found it impossible to fit the new forms of struggle and organization that he confronted in his travels into a pre-given categorical framework. Unlike the Ehrenreichs, he did not reduce the forms of struggle and their legitimation to economic categories. Rather, he tried to rethink the Marxian insight that the forms of consciousness and struggle are developed in the social relations of the work process. If the nature of the work process changes, so too will the forms of struggle and the goals chosen (although the correlation is not that of cause to effect). The structural and the dynamic are interwoven here, as Marx himself already noted in *Capital* when he observed that a history of technology could be written as a history of class struggle, since the capitalists introduce new technology only when forced to do so in order to maintain their domination.[4] From this point of view, the "new" working class is neither an appendage of the old, nor its aristocracy, nor a hindrance to its struggles. Rather, insists Mallet, the "new" working class is defined *politically* as the most advanced sector of the working class which puts forth demands and invents forms of struggle that incarnate future possibilities for the class as a whole. The stress here, unlike the Ehrenreichs' constant concern with "objective possibilities" built into an economic structure (a point of view which leads one to misunderstand new possibilities, or reduce them to variants of the old), is on forms of struggle, on the development of new needs and new capacities which imply a radical challenge which capitalism cannot integrate. These new forms of struggle bear a new principle of socialization, a new form of society, a new thrust of politics. To give but one indication, the kind of skills and the form of work relations of those in the "newer" sectors means that the kinds of strike movements, slow downs and work demands they can and will make are different from those of workers on the classical production line. Mallet stresses the flexibility of their strike

volume, and "New Situation, New Strategy," in *The Unknown Dimension: European Marxism since Lenin*, eds. Dick Howard and Karl E. Klare (New York: Basic Books, 1972); and on Mallet's life, see Howard, "In Memory of Serge Mallet," *Telos* #20, (Fall, 1974).

4. The problem is tricky, and peripheral to our argument. If one sees capital as introducing new technology simply because competition forces the increase of relative surplus-value rates, then one remains at the level of an economic analysis and ignores the class struggle. If on the other hand one opts, as we suggest here, for the assertion that technology is a form of social control, then one is doing a *political* economic analysis of capitalism as a system.

tactics, and the manner in which they are led to demand control over a work process which they understand and in which they are not just cogs. In this way, the dynamic, changing and historical nature of the socialist goal is preserved.

Mallet's case studies, and the generalizations he drew from them, have been criticized by sociologists; moreover Mallet (like the Ehrenreichs) privileges the sphere of production. But it is the political thrust of his work that is vital. Mallet was concerned with the forms of *working class self-organization,* i.e., with the manner in which the struggle at the point of production is translated into the political sphere in a way which cannot be co-opted or fitted into the standard party functioning. Thus, when challenged to define the "New Working Class," Mallet always refused to apply structural parameters, insisting that it is the forms of struggle that count. Indeed, in the early 1970's, he even asserted that, because of the new forms of struggle that they were developing, it was the foreign manual workers in France (the "O.S.") who were the "new" working class. One must be aware, of course, of the dangers of *ouvrierisme,* i.e., the glorification of the worker *qua* worker. One way around this dilemma (which we have labelled the polarity of structure and dynamics) is seen in Andre Gorz's development, which has apparently led him beyond his earlier "New Working Class" position to a critique of the division of labor and the role of science and technology as forms of domination. What Gorz recognized is that a structural account can demonstrate what kind of demands and activities are immanent to, present no threat for, the capitalist form of domination. Gorz's analyses of new forms of struggle against the repressive implications of the forms of the division of labor, his critique of science and technology as artificially preserving unnecessary hierarchy, are attempts to combine the structural with the dynamic in the framework of a political analysis. Gorz's purpose is to analyze and further new forms of needs, new kinds of struggle with new goals. As opposed to this, when the Ehrenreichs do talk about the political potential of the PMC, because they reduce its nature to the economic structures in which it is embedded, they are forced to see its needs as elitist, and to recognize as legitimate only those aspects of the PMC which work in consort with the working class.[5] Indeed, this

5. As to their discussion of the working class itself, it simply stands there, unmoving and self-identical. There is no discussion, for example, of the forms of action which it, with or against the PMC, has developed over the years. When they talk about how working class students, and then the "content" of black militancy affected SDS, these are presented as if the middle class PMC students of SDS finally discovered the truth of an age-old process of working class militancy—which, in a sense, is true as a description of SDS's reaction, but wrong in that it doesn't point out that the newness could/should have been seized upon.

objectivist economism regarding work relations is directly linked to their Leninist solution.

To be sure, the working class struggle is first of all a defensive reaction to the pressures of capitalism; and here it is waged on the soil of capitalism and on its terms. It becomes a political struggle when it puts into question the captialist forms of social relations (and not simply the form of capitalist work relations). The "New Working Class" theory and strategy tries to show how this political translation in fact takes place in contemporary conditions. Hence it stresses the repoliticization from below of the sphere of production due to the emergence of new needs and new forms of working class organizations (councils, new forms of strike, slow downs, self-management demands). Marx's point, after all, was not that the goal of working class revolution is simply to free production from irrational or outdated social constraints.[6] The working class was revolutionary for Marx precisely because it was the "nothing" that could become "all"—its goal is the elimination of class society altogether which means the elimination of the working class as well. Economic and social struggles must be seen from this political optic. The working class does not fight to be simply a better paid working class, nor to preserve a form of culture which too many middle class radicals of the 60's suddenly discovered and romanticized. Its struggle is against the life and work conditions of capitalism. When the Ehrenreichs descry the "moralistic contempt for the working class" which they see in the early SDS, the rhetorical form distorts the issue. Workers don't want to be defined by their work; and the pitfalls of crude communism were long ago attacked by Marx. Perhaps the New Left was right; perhaps it represented a *political* vision, in modern capitalist conditions, of the goals of a contemporary revolution which points beyond the class relations of modern society.

The logical schema of Marxian revolution has always postulated that capitalism would create its own gravediggers. Marxists have always looked for them in the sphere of production. Accordingly, both the "New Working Class" theorists and the Ehrenreichs look to the Marxian notion of class as the key to understanding the new strata that have emerged. They differ only in that the Ehrenreichs have a static account whereas the "New Working Class" theorists look to the changing structure of work relations as providing the dynamics of new political struggles around new needs. *But*, can one analyze the new phenomena

---

6. Marx does sometimes talk in this manner, transposing the model of the bourgeois transformation of feudalism onto the socialist transformation of capitalism. We shall show, however, that such a conception remains within the confines of the capitalist forms of logic and domination.

with categories derived from, and applicable to, the old capitalist form? Might it not be that the PMC represents not a new economic class, but rather the elimination of economics as the dominant framework of social life and the birth of a new set of problems and questions that demand *political* resolution? This new political sphere could not be dealt with on the model of goal-oriented strategic action; and not in terms of class either. In a marvellous passage, the Ehrenreichs cite the President of the American Society of Mining Engineers: "The golden rule will be put into practice by the slide rule of the engineer." The golden rule, a moral or political imperative concerning forms of societal interaction, is here translated into a merely technical imperative. Politics is reduced to economics (itself reduced to the rationality of technology).The questions that the "old" New Left raised, and which the Ehrenreichs tend to dismiss as moralistic and ideological maskings of "objective" conditions, were political questions.[7] To see how the political dimension is lost, we need to return to the notion of class itself.

II

The difficulties inherent in the attempts to provide a class analysis of late capitalism do not derive solely from the complexity of the phenomenon; they are rooted in the problematic premises of Marxism itself. The Ehrenreichs begin by rejecting more orthodox Marxian attempts to maintain the two-class model either by relegating the middle to the anachronistic or peripheral category of the petty bourgeoisie, or by extending the categories of proletariat and capitalist so that they encompass respectively all lower level salaried workers and upper echelon managers. They argue for the specificity of the new, educated, salaried middle strata, insisting on their historical situation and particularity. But for the truly open-minded Marxist, it would seem obvious that the appearance of new social strata, unforeseen and indeed impossible for classical Marxism, would call for a self-critique of Marxian class theory. However, instead of interrogating the Marxism which they only apparently transcend, the Ehrenreichs, like "New Working Class" theorists, presuppose all the fundamentals of Marxian class analysis in their otherwise inexplicable attempt to force the new middle strata into the

---

7. It is worth mentioning here that the New Working Class approach, though closer to seeing this political dimension, was also unable to conceptualize the political dimension in its own terms. The syndicalist or *ouvrierist* orientation seemed to block its development. But it is worth mentioning that just before his tragic death, Mallet had planned to return to his native Bordeaux away from the centralized Parisian scene, to take part in the Free Occitania movement. When asked about this his justification was framed in *political* terms.

straight jacket of class. The class theory is not reexamined but directly imposed onto the new social groups.

One wonders why it is so terribly important to understand the new middle strata in terms of "class?" What explanatory value does this category offer as opposed, for example, to Mills' approach which analytically relates the new strata to the changed structure not only of labor, but of political, military and educational institutions as well? Mills' refusal to squeeze the disparate strata into a single class with a single general interest stems not from an ill-tempered anti-Marxism, but from the insights of a sociological analysis of the different institutional bases of the new professionals which cannot be collapsed into one logic through the levelling force of the concept of class. Indeed, in a sense Mills is truer to the spirit of the Ehrenreichs' model, E. P. Thompson, insofar as he takes seriously the idea that "class is not a thing" which can be defined with mathematical exactness by virtue of relations to the means of production exclusive of the awareness of individuals that they have something in common. While one can of course identify social classes objectively, according to their mode of labor, relation to the means of production and to other strata, one cannot impute a uniform, action-orienting class interest to the variety of new strata: technicians, intellectuals, professionals, bureaucrats, managers, etc., merely because they compose a middle stratum between capital and labor. In the context of contemporary U.S. society the strata grouped under the class rubric of the PMC in fact seem to dissolve into conflicting interest groups rather than coalesce into a coherent class. At issue, then, is not the presence and importance of the new social strata "between capital and labor," but the effort to conjure away ambiguity and indeterminacy through the dogmatic use of the Marxian notion of class.

The Ehrenreichs' introductory comments make clear the difficulties confronting the Marxian analysis of class in late capitalism. Their intent in looking at the new middle strata as a class stems from the Marxist idea that class is a critical category—if employed vis-a-vis the New Left, it could both delegitimize contemporary capitalist relations and reveal to the left the contradictions that its class status imposed on its radicalism. We have pointed to some of the unintended implications that marr their analysis. If we can show that these problems are rooted in the analyses of Marx himself, we will have cleared the way for a rethinking of modern capitalist social relations. Above all we want to argue that the critical function of Marxian class theory is itself defused by its overextension within Marx's own analysis of modern society resulting in an antinomic class concept which Marx never was able to rectify.

For Marx, the category of class serves first of all to designate the historically specific form of stratification of capitalist society. Marx distinguishes between pre-modern (estate, caste, and slave systems) and modern (class) forms of stratification. Modern classes are socio-economic forms found in a society where a formerly democratic state exists separately from an independent civil society. Thus, arguing against Hegel's attempt to reintroduce the medieval estates into his analysis of civil society, Marx insists that class relations are unique precisely because of the absence of politically and legally established corporate groupings. Expressing the uniquely modern separation of the political state from a depoliticized civil society, the category of class serves as a critique of both the attempt to mediate between the two through a politicization from above (Hegel's estates, fascism's corporations), and the opposite proposal (of the natural law theory and political economy) that freedom and equality are established once the state abolishes such corporate entities and limits its own intervention to that of night watchman.

Initially, the concept of class is used by Marx to demystify the formal democratic state's claim to legitimacy through the fact that it recognizes only independent legal persons and accords no privileges to particular groups. The concept of "class" plays the critical role of demonstrating that the explicit political articulation of modern society conceals its internal relations of domination and stratification. By articulating socio-economic distinctions within civil society, the concept of class reveals that the emancipation of the state from the particularistic limitations of estate representation (absolutism) does not in fact free individuals from these restrictions but only relegates them to the depoliticized sphere of civil society where the differentiations of status, wealth and religion properly retain their powers. This is the message of "On the Jewish Question:" political emancipation is not the same as human emancipation. Political emancipation *is,* however, the precondition for the formation of the social identity of economic, as opposed to political, classes.

But Marx moves beyond the sociology of inequality (and analysis of political alienation), to the use of the category of class to express the fundamental relations of domination and crisis in modern society. He turns from the state to an analysis of the capitalist economy, reformulating the notion of class as a correlate of production relations. Socio-economic strata are linked to categories of production within a systematic analysis of capitalist accumulation, with the result that the category of class must now express:

1) internal mechanisms of social stratification (i.e., relations to the means of production);
2) relations of domination of modern capitalism (i.e., the wage

labor/capital relation);
3) dynamics of capitalist accumulation and reproduction (i.e., the class struggle);
4) internal contradictions of capitalist social relations (i.e., socialized production along with private accumulation);
5) the dynamics of revolutionary overthrow of capitalist social relations.

But, this is not all! The (questionable) assumption that *relations of domination* in modern society can be reduced to *social relations of production* and thus comprehended as *class relations* is deprived of its historical specificity to capitalist society when, with Engels' help, Marx comes up with the theory of historical materialism. The theory which proclaims all history to be the history of class struggle projects the category of class together with the forces/relations model of production backwards as the motor of all history and the key to understanding relations of domination and struggles for emancipation in all dynamic societies. Not only does this destroy Marx's own insight into the historical specificity of class as opposed to estate, caste, or slave stratification; it also precludes any investigation of the state as an independent institution. Historical materialism sees the state according to the parameters of the class theory as merely a parasitic body of officials under the control of that thoroughly ambiguous entity, the ruling class. Perhaps the meagerness of Marxist (including the Ehrenreichs') analysis of the political state can be attributed to this overextension of class theory. For example, the awareness that bureaucracy is inherent in (Hegel) and contradictory to (Marx) the democratic principles of the modern state never leads to an adequate theory of political institutions because the class theory reduces the state first to a superstructure and second to an instrument of socio-economic class domination. Yet, as Mills points out, the term "ruling class" is a loaded phrase insofar as it implies that a socio-economic class rules politically, thus denying any autonomy to the political order and its agents.[8] Granted, Marx points to situations in which the capitalist class does not rule even though capitalist relations predominate (Bonapartism). However, these situations are seen as extraordinary and appear as an historical deviation from the general paradigm of class rule.

One might argue that Marx's overextension of the notion of class implies only a criticism of his theory of historical materialism while his specific class analysis of capitalism remains valid. Lukacs was the first

8. C.W. Mills, *The Power Elite* (New York: Oxford University Press, 1956), p. 277.

Marxist to restrict the primacy of economic relations to the logic of capitalist development alone, arguing that the ideological moment of historical materialism manifests itself precisely when applied to pre- or post-capitalist social formations.[9] But the logical next step (which Lukacs never took) of limiting the adequacy of the concept of class to the critique of capitalism is also problematic.[10] The sociological analysis of the principle of stratification unique to capitalist society as entailing the formation of socio-economic classes is valid and retains its critical force. Further, the critical analysis of the capitalist logic of accumulation and social reproduction correctly uncovers the structural relations of domination of capital over wage labor. *The difficulty arises in relating these two analyses.* Marx derives a two-class model from the structural analysis of capitalism; and then imputes objective class interests to the classes on the basis of the logic of the accumulation process which entails the centralisation of capital in ever fewer hands and the corresponding proletarianization of ever greater sectors of the population. But this deduction rests on a *methodological confusion* similar to that pervading the theory of historical materialism: there is a *collapse of logic and history.* It is legitimate to consider, as Marx does in *Capital*, the capitalist mode of production in its purity, abstracting from historical influences, the role of the state, etc. But to move from here to sociological predictions regarding class formation is a category mistake. What Marx wanted is clear: a concept of class that is both an objective structure rooted in production relations *and* a dynamic result of the self-organization of groups coalescing around common needs and interests in a struggle for emancipation. But if the imputation of interests to the sociologically real actors is made on the basis of an abstract logic of contradiction of wage labor/capital, then a panlogism determinism triumphs over historical contingency.[11]

The result of the collapse of logic and history is the overburdening of the concept of class, even when it is limited to the critique of capitalism.

9. Georg Lukacs, *History and Class Consciousness* (London: Merlin Press, 1968), pp. 223-256.

10. Lukacs was probably inhibited from this step due to his belief in the Marxian dogma that the end of class struggle must mean the end of domination. If class is limited to capitalism, however, this would mean that there are significant forms of domination which are not class relations and that therefore the abolition of classes does not necessarily equal the abolition of domination. Only the non-Marxist, Max Weber recognized the implications of this problem.

11. Jean Cohen, "False Premises" *Telos* #24 (1975), pp. 135-158. With panlogical assumptions, it becomes possible to juggle the facts in order to fit them into the pre-existing schema, which in itself is argued for not on the level of history but as a kind of meta-theory unrefutable by historical development.

The logic of capital is presumed to delimit the actual forms of domination in civil society—as class domination. But simply because capitalism rests on the domination of the working class (among others) it does not follow that domination must exist exclusively as the power of one socio-economic class over another; nor does it follow that the road to emancipation of workers and other oppressed strata must be that of class formation and class struggle around class interests. The bias resulting from this panlogism is twofold: the logic of the economy is mistaken for the logic of society as a whole, and forms of domination are restricted to class relations with the result that both political structures and struggles appear as epiphenomena of socio-economic relations.

Significantly, Marx himself points to the limits of what can be derived from the logic of the wage labor/capital relation. From the opposition of *interest* inherent in this relation one can only derive "class in itself"—that is, classes formed through the reproductive logic of capitalists competing and struggling with each other for the satisfaction of interests which are part and parcel of the dynamic of capitalist development, *not of its overthrow!* The revolutionary project of a class cannot be deduced from this logic whose result is what Lenin called "trade unionism." Struggles around interests do not challenge the logic of a society whose nature it is to impose a competitive interest structure on individual actors. After all, Marx believed that the proletariat is a revolutionary class not because of the interests imputable to it, but because it develops radical needs which challenge the logic of capitalist reproduction.[12] The proletariat does not become a "class for itself," a revolutionary subject, because it presses for satisfaction of particular interests within the framework of capitalist relations, nor because its class interest is really universal. It is revolutionary because it struggles around *radical needs* that point beyond the competitive egoistic and economistic structure of interest and production specific to capitalist society. The opposing class interests rooted in the objective structure of capitalist relations express the competitive, goal-oriented logic of the economy. Since the goal is to abolish both capitalism and socio-economic classes, only a struggle around needs that subvert this objective logic could be radical. However, the inconsistencies first in associating needs with a collective class subject and second in limiting the emergence of radical needs to classes alone (the proletariat in particular), are glaring.[13]

The tension in Marx's work between an open-ended philosophy of

12. Agnes Heller, *The Theory of Need in Marx* (London: Allison & Busby, 1976).

13. Jean Cohen, "Agnes Heller: The Theory of Need in Marx" *Telos* #33 (1977), pp. 170-184.

history with practical intent which speaks to radical needs articulated by individuals in their collective struggles against domination, and the scientific analysis of the objective logic of modes of production, is reproduced as an antinomy internal to the concept of class itself. Necessity/freedom, universality/particularity, as well as the classical antinomies of bourgeois philosophy (as presented by Lukacs) return in the concept of class as the conflict between need and interest. Insofar as radical needs can be defined as those needs of individuals that challenge the structure of domination, they can appear in any and all aspects of social-political life—there is no reason to limit the notion of need to the category of class. Only the speculative Hegelian concept of the negation of the negation, formulated in terms of a metaphysics of labor (i.e., alienated labor magically represents species activity in a negative form awaiting its return through the negating action of revolution) enabled Marx to associate radical needs and the proletariat as an indissoluble pair. But if the correlate of the wage labor/capital relation, i.e., of production relations, is class interest and not radical needs, then there is no basis for assuming that an analysis of the relations of production, or a class analysis of these relations, will lead to the discovery of radical needs pointing to struggles for emancipation. If, on the other hand, one seeks the objective possibility of emancipation in the logical contradictions of capitalism, in conflicts over interest, one necessarily reduces the political dimension of class formation and struggle to the objectivistic contradiction of forces and relations of production.

This political dimension, however, is precisely what the Ehrenreichs miss. Since unlike a host of theorists from Castoriadis to Gorz to Mallet, they do not analyze new needs, new forms of organization, as well as the new structure of labor, they are forced to resort to objectivism to ground the radical potential of the working class and the absence or presence of such potential in the PMC. Their essay is shot through with terms like "objective class interest," "objective situation," objective this, objective that. One encounters countless "reflections" of structures, "representations" which, ideologically distorted, seem to emerge naturally from the "objective situation." This all terminates of course in "objective contradictions" which, if critically analyzed can then be resolved strategically. The Ehrenreichs thus lost a major merit of "New Working Class" theory—the focus on new needs and new forms of struggle at the point of production which uncovers radical potential of individuals struggling against their class position albeit not as an exclusive or uniform revolutionary class subject.[14] Having drawn from only one side of Marx's

14. If, in other words, one procedes in the manner of Gorz and Mallet to analyze changes in the structure of labor and new forms of struggle around new needs, without however totalizing the groups in motion into a single class with a

extremely complicated concept of class, the Ehrenreichs reduce classes to the sociological expression of production categories despite their protestations to the contrary. Having banished the political dimension from the objective and subjective constitution of classes they, once again, are led to the Leninism they seemed to reject.

III

Marx never resolved the tensions between the various levels of his class theory. Even in *Capital* he never overcame the dogmatic presupposition of the *Communist Manifesto*: that the process of capitalist reproduction both simplifies class antagonisms and creates its own gravedigger—the proletariat as revolutionary subject. The collapse of logic with present and future history led to the double error of presuming the oppressed class (wage laborers) to be the emancipators of society, and identifying the dynamic of institutions in capitalist society with that of production relations. The move from the sociology of class structure to the theory of class domination proved to be overambitious and abortive.

But the Ehrenreichs should have the advantage of hindsight. Instead they employ the same overburdened concept of class to explain the emergence of a new class, its interests, its relation of domination over the proletariat and subordination to capital, and the potentialities for and against its radicalization. *For us, however, it is thoroughly untenable to refer to the groups in question as a class at all!* To lump together technical workers in corporations, college professors, state bureaucrats, managers with technical knowledge or those who are but corporate bureaucrats, professionals, *et tutti quanti*, as a coherent class of "salaried mental workers who do not own the means of production," whose function in the division of labor is "the reproduction of capitalist culture," is absurd. Only by collapsing the "objective analysis" of the structure of labor attributed to "monopoly capitalism" with the various social strata that make their appearance in this phase of capitalist development could the Ehrenreichs maintain such a position. Just as they fail to account for the

uniform interest, without presuming that a radical revolution can only be a revolution of the (new and/or old) working class, and finally, without reducing the structure and dynamic of non-economic institutions to that of production, one can indeed identify one among many locii of potential radical struggles. The "New Working Class" theorists insist on a working class subject, albeit one which forms itself and leads itself. To avoid the Leninist position, they return to a somewhat mythical syndicalism. But Leninism turns out to be the truth of class politics because *the myth of a single revolutionary class subject always requires an agency of totalization and unification other than itself*. To dispel this myth is not, however, to deny the really radical needs and movements emergent at the point of production—it is only to make the groups which constitute themselves there one among many potential revolutionary actors.

transformation, stratification and fragmentation of the working classes when their direct manual labor becomes mediated by machines, so too they fail to make distinctions internal to the catchall rubric of "mental labor." But if, as they have to concede, it is illegitimate to define the proletariat as a class in terms of the category of wage labor, then surely it is unacceptable to define the new middle strata as the PMC and to impute common interests, cultural coherence, and the like simply from the concept of mental labor![15]

The failure to distinguish between technicians, managers, bureaucrats, professors, and state employees of all sorts can be traced to the concept of "monopoly capitalism." It leads to the erroneous conclusion that all these groups share a class interest because they exercise control over the working class. Yet civil servants do not regulate the labor of others as do managers and technicians in the corporate sector; their power is a form of domination and manipulation of the *consumers* of state services. Furthermore, whereas the technicians employed by corporations sell their labor power and technical knowledge as a commodity to capital, state bureaucrats are salaried civil servants whose labor power is not exchanged through the market. As Claus Offe points out, the labor of civil servants is "decommodified:" "...an 'equilibrium' price between partners in an exchange transaction is not arrived at; the state does not 'buy' the work performed by its civil servants and salaried employees, just as it does not 'sell' the results of this work."[16] Accordingly, the political relation between civil servants and the state takes precedence over the fact that, like managers and corporate technicians, these "mental workers" receive a salary. Moreover, they have a different relation to the employer institution and a different type of qualification of their labor (since the bureaucrat is not a technical expert, but only has the ideology of technical expertise at his disposal), hence within capitalism they have different interests. Their relation to the "economic foundations of society" is different, as are their skills.

The Ehrenreichs' interesting analysis of the ideology of the Progressive Movement which expresses the consciousness of technocratic class interest is needlessly weakened by a faulty sociology which seeks to include all "intellectuals" from bureaucratic managers in corporations and in the state to teachers in high school in the same class. The interest in occupational autonomy and rationalization of social activities according

15. The Ehrenreichs blindly accept Braverman's concept of the proletariat which is an arbitrary grouping of craftsmen, operatives, laborers, sales workers, clerical workers, service workers and non-college educated technical workers.

16. Claus Offe, "Crisis of Crisis Management" *International Journal of Politics*, (Fall 1976), p. 42.

to expert knowledge can be imputed to the increasingly important technocratic stratum; but it cannot be imputed to the non-expert bureaucratic managers in either sphere, for their position rests on the irrationalities of capitalism and uncoordinated state regulation within a capitalist system. As Claude Lefort has shown, the relative autonomy of the technician and engineer by virtue of their professional knowledge and the importance of the work performed over the office held, distinguishes these groups from the bureaucrat who, lacking real expert knowledge, is wholly dependent on the institutional role from which he or she derive his or her power and privilege.[17] Far from developing an interest in overthrowing capitalist irrationalities in the name of expertise and rational economic planning, the bureaucrat's interest is above all in the proliferation of bureaucratic offices *within* the existing institutions of the corporation and the state. Given the uncoordinated framework of bureaucracies within capitalist societies, the bureaucrat's interest is not the concentration and consolidation of bureaucracies into one centralized apparatus, for this would imply the elimination of posts. The resistance encountered by Carter to streamlining the state bureaucracy can only be explained if one recognizes the conflicting particular interests of different bureaucratic offices which fight to preserve their institution even after its original purpose is fulfilled or obsolete. The same, of course, holds true for bureaucrats in the corporation.

A similar difficulty arises concerning the unity of function and interest attributed to professionals in institutions outside the sphere of production (hospitals, schools, etc.) with the technocrats, administrators, or bureaucrats in those institutions.[18] How else is one to understand the incessant struggles between professor and administration, doctor, and hospital, etc., over issues of autonomy, ethics, service, money, and the like? "Class," as the relation to the means of production, to the economic foundation of society, or to other social classes simply cannot account for the formation, power, interests or real potential of these groups. One might add here that while it is indeed the function of some intellectuals and professionals to reproduce capitalist or mass culture—and we might note that this "culture" remains to be defined by the Ehrenreichs—certainly the ideology of the technocrat and the culture of professionalism also run counter to the interests of capitalism. The rationalized planned social system implied by technocratic ideology is predicated upon the abolition of market irrationalities, and the private decisionmaking of capitalists. Indeed, the crucial function of intellectuals vis-a-

17. Claude Lefort, "What is Bureaucracy?" *Telos* #22, (1974-5).

18. Of course the distinction between bureaucracy and technically necessary functions remains an empirical question.

vis the social formation in which they exist is a varied and ambiguous one, hardly touched upon by the Ehrenreichs. But the bad sociology inherent in the concept of the PMC is predicated upon an even worse structural analysis of late capitalism that precludes investigation of its varied institutional organization, to which we now turn.

IV

We have already indicated that the Ehrenreichs ignore the role of the state in contemporary capitalist society. Because they operate on the narrow basis of the productivist structural model of *Capital*, they perforce are blind to the institutional transformations of many aspects of everyday life from production to education to culture, resulting from the changed role of the state, as well as its implications for class analysis. This is not the place to discuss in detail the theories of state intervention recently developed by such different thinkers as Bell, Touraine, Offe, Habermas, O'Connor, etc. But what is significant is that all of their analyses lead to the following consequence; the partial repoliticization from above (through state intervention) of both economic and socio-cultural life alters the fundamental presupposition on which Marx based his class theory: the separation of the state and civil society.[19] Habermas and Offe in particular have stressed the implications of this repoliticization for class analysis. State intervention entails a partial repoliticization of the wage structure (in the monopoly and state sectors) such that the framework in which socio-economic classes develop their social identity is radically altered.[20] If the economic system is no longer independent of state intervention, if the exchange of commodities and the setting of prices (including that of labor power) is at least partially politically determined, it becomes meaningless to define power struggles and the formation of interest groups strictly in terms of socio-economic classes and economic interests.[21] Whereas in liberal capitalism, the depoliticization of civil society allowed for the institutionalization of the class relationship through the labor market and through class conflicts in production, in late capitalism, "...the political anonymity of class

19. Politicization from below would mean instead the resignification of socio-economic issues and questions into questions of power, autogestion, self management and the like from the part of the individuals involved in the sphere in question.

20. Claus Offe, "Political Authority and Class Structures—an Analysis of Late Capitalist Societies" *International Journal of Sociology*, (Spring 1972), pp. 73-108. See also Jurgen Habermas, *Legitimation Crisis* (Boston: Beacon Press, 1973), pp. 37-39.

21. Offe, "Political Authority," pp.80-81.

domination is superseded by social anonymity."[22] In other words, in liberal capitalism, given the separation of the political and economic spheres, individuals in the same relation to the means of production were able to organize as classes around common interests and to identify and struggle against their oppressors as another socio-economic class—the capitalist owners of the means of production. For both groups, the very absence of an explicit political structuration of society into estates or orders, the absence of a political identity, allowed for the emergence of the socio-economic identity of classes. But the situation in late capitalism has fundamentally altered.

If the production and appropriation of surplus value and the determination of wages are increasingly dependent on relations of political power rather than the market mechanism, then the forms of domination and the formation of interest groups will increasingly transcend the realm of production and develop in terms of the state itself. When the economy was sheltered from state intervention, classes could form and confront one another directly over issues of economic power. Today, as Offe maintains, the question of power must be reformulated: "What mechanisms ensure the dominant influence of social interests on the functioning of the political system even though these interests *are no longer able to assert their former independence of the system within a free sphere beyond state power?*"[23] Since need articulation is no longer dependent primarily on private economic power, it is necessary to investigate those institutions which prestructure the field and delimit access to the media of public expression and satisfaction of needs: political parties, unions, and parliaments among others. Because these political and quasi-political institutions create new forms of social inequality and domination which cannot be economically defined, their internal logic must be examined, their systematic imperatives analyzed, and their internal contradictions clarified. In short, the crises of late capitalism, the impetus to struggle, the target of critique, and the types of potential radical groups can neither be deduced from an analysis of economic contradictions nor analyzed in terms of class struggle.

The Ehrenreichs also talk about the "social atomization" of the working class in advanced capitalism. But rather than examine this phenomenon in terms of the changed relation of the state to economic life, they focus on the realm of production, talking about the fragmentation of work and workers in the production process resulting from the concentration and accumulation of capital. Clearly the similarity of terminology is misleading. What the Ehrenreichs are referring to is not new in capitalist history—Marx described it long ago. But whereas Marx

---

22. Habermas, *Legitimation Crisis*, p. 37.
23. Our emphasis. Offe, "Political Authority," p. 103.

could legitimately expect that workers could overcome their mutual competition to organize themselves as classes struggling around common interests (unionization, wages, hours, conditions of work, etc.) against capital, the Ehrenreichs' claim, under modern conditions, of inside knowledge into the real coherence of the working class becomes pure metaphysics. If, as they maintain, the culture of the proletariat has been stolen by the PMC, and if, as Habermas and Offe argue, the repoliticization of the economy prevents the emergence of clear-cut class interests, then only faith serves as the basis for the belief in the persistence of the old class struggle.[24]

The increasing political intervention into the economy should dispel the expectation of a traditional class confrontation. What is more likely is the emergence of various groups struggling for the power to express their *needs* both within and outside of the institutions which provide for public articulation of *interests*. The eclipsing of traditional relationships of class inequality by a politically determined disparity between various social needs—transportation, health, unemployment, etc.—implies a relation of confrontation between the affected groups and the state itself. Once the state engages in active crisis management, its own rationality and legitimacy can be called into question by those who remain systematically underprivileged and powerless. But, and this is the main point here, "Because the lines of conflict are no longer drawn between classes, but between vital areas affecting the same individuals, disjunctions in living standards are no longer a fit basis for the organization of conflicts of broad social relevance."[25] In other words, neither crises nor political struggles can be assumed in advance to take on a purely economic and class character. The chances for groups to effectively challenge the structures and institutions that oppress them can no longer be evaluated on the basis of an expanded critique of political economy—only a multi-leveled systemic analysis of the institutional structure of late capitalism could help in this regard.

The nature of the political sphere can be further specified by contrasting our approach to the Ehrenreichs' anachronistic Marxist presuppositions. Their dogmatic use of the Marxian category of class blinds them not only to the complex institutional structure and

24. The idea, especially as far as the United States is concerned, that there ever was a coherent working class culture has been disproved by S. Aronowitz in *False Promises*. The corollary notion, that the PMC has consciously been the agent of the de-skilling and fragmentation of the proletariat, rests on the untenable inference that the beneficiary of a process must also have been its initiator. The constant shifts in qualification and dequalification of labor are a complex process which cannot be understood voluntaristically.

25. Offe, "Political Authority," p. 103.

stratification of western society; it also prevents them from understanding the nature of domination in what they so aptly term "anti-
working class" socialist societies. Because they believe that the PMC is a
coherent class in the West, they readily adopt Djilas' new class thesis
regarding the Soviet Union, thereby saving themselves the effort of
interrogating the specificities of that new social formation. The inherent
defect of all forms of modern Marxism, the inability to analyze forms of
domination in the Soviet Union from any standpoint other than that of
the categories of *Capital* (exploitation, class inequalities, etc.), is not
overcome by the Ehrenreichs. Indeed, the mechanisms through which
technocrats, managers, bureaucrats, etc., coalesce into a dominant and
ruling stratum must remain concealed as long as they insist that in
capitalist society these groups already compose a class whose inherent
goal is to replace capitalist domination with their own. In actual
historical fact, the welding together of the disparate groups of bureaucrats, technocrats and managers into a coherent ruling stratum required
the mediation of the Leninist party which, integrated with the state
apparatus, in turn invaded all aspects of social life.[26] If one focuses only
on relations of exploitation in production, and the economic privileges of
those in control, then one would locate privileged strata, but one would
not understand the nature of the *political strata* whose power stems
neither from this technical skill, nor this expert knowledge, nor their
private wealth, but from the *positions* they occupy within the party and
the state. These groups do not have coherent and convergent class
interests before the appropriation of power. A constant process of
unification is necessary, which is impossible without the integrative
structures of the party and the state. This is why Lefort insists that the
result of this political process is the emergence of a new social formation
with a new structure of domination, not to be confused either with the
features of late capitalist states nor with inherent tendencies of non-
capitalist and non-proletarian strata within these societies. The implication here is that it is misleading to see the PMC as a class within
bourgeois society, for there is no mechanism through which their
particular and conflicting interests are smoothed into a unity. Therefore,
Lefort observes:

> ...bureaucracies exist full-fledged within mass institutions: in
> parties, unions, in various branches of production, and various
> cultural sectors. In each of these contexts, they attempt to grow
> and monopolize an increasing part of social capital in order to

26. Lefort, "What is Bureaucracy."

expand in as broad a field as possible. There is no pre-established harmony within the bureaucracy, and the unity of the class does not 'naturally' prevail: it involves a constant activity of unification. The rivalry of bureaucratic apparatuses reinforced by the struggles of inter-bureaucratic cliques is only managed by the intervention of a political principle at all levels of social life. But the party which applies this principle is itself the broadest and most complete bureaucracy. If class unity is inconceivable without it, since its mediation 'politicizes' all of society so that the state tends to merge with civil society, its presence and its natural tendency to control and subordinate everything to its own power generates the sharpest tension within the ruling class. Thus, the bureaucratic system is unceasingly torn by internal conflicts.[27]

While this analysis focuses on political domination in the Soviet Union, it contains an important caveat for the analysis of capitalism: "The bureaucracy is not a class so long as it is not a ruling class, and when it becomes so, it remains essentially dependent on a political activity of unification."[28]

The implications of this analysis for both bureaucratic collectivist and capitalist societies are significant. In the Soviet Union there has been a change in the function of the political, and with it the forms of stratification dependent on the bureaucratic political institutions are transformed. Once the party has intertwined with the state apparatus and begun to structure all areas of "civil society," from production through education; once it has succeeded in destroying all independent sources of power (i.e., socio-economic classes such as the bourgeoisie, peasantry, and the independent working class organizations such as unions)—the question of class takes on an entirely different meaning. While one might posit there the existence of a new *political* class consisting of bureaucrats, technocrats and professionals, it must be admitted that the power of these groups exists only in and through the bureaucratic institutions of party and state. The interpenetration of these strata within the apparatus, the tensions and internal contradictions generated by this *new* structuration of society, and the potential struggles generated by this new mode of domination remain to be seriously analyzed. What is certain at this point, is that they cannot be reduced to the logic of a different social formation—capitalism.

This is not to suggest that since economic rationalization and bureaucratization are associated in capitalist societies they follow the

27. Ibid., p. 51.
28. Idem.

same internal logic, nor that each is carried forth in the interests of a particular class. Although the Ehrenreichs comment perceptively on the quasi-progressive reformist and potentially anti-capitalist logic of technocracy in capitalism, they ignore the basically conservative thrust of bureaucracies in corporate and state institutions. As noted earlier, one must decide empirically in a given social-historical context which functions are technically necessary, and which are bureaucratic functions of domination. Although bureaucracy indeed responds to technical needs and legitimates itself through the same technocratic ideology as the technicians, although it too poses itself as an end, in the absence of a unifying framework giving it direction, it appears conservative. The Russian example indicates that a fusion can occur in the context of a political party advocating rational administration of social and economic life, unifying these strata around a common goal of state power. Such a unification, however, is not deducible from the actual existence of these strata in capitalist society; and above all, it can not be imputed to them as a class interest from an analysis of their relation to the means of production. In other words, professionals, managers, technicians, intellectuals, may act in a unified manner—or may not. If they do the reason for their unification will not be common "objective" economic interests and possibilities, but a *political process.*

V.

There is an uncanny Hegelian echo in the reconstruction of the odyssey of the New Left consciousness presented to us by the Ehrenreichs. The New Left begins in the immediacy of its "PMC" origins, which it has to struggle to transcend. Fortunate coincidences (of course dictated by the logic of "objective possibility"—in this case, the shift from elite to mass universities) permit it to encounter its negation or Other, the working class. Pathologically at first it takes itself as its own Other, errs about in black, then white and yellow robes, until it gradually learns the secrets of self-limitation in the professions or as the adjunct to a pure class movement. Finally, with the Ehrenreichs' help, it will find itself once it comes to be self-conscious about its own origins and situates itself within the grand objective whole. What renders this drama Hegelian is not only the structure of negation and negation of negation; the structure itself is made possible by the doubly loaded dice of the authors: as with Hegel, the subject has its end or *telos* already inscribed in its starting point (the class analysis of the "PMC" and its relation to the proletariat-as-revolutionary-class); and the authors know in advance where the path must lead, a cue that permits them to integrate the unexpected as a merely structural permutation.

The Ehrenreichs' attempt to understand and to revive the New Left succeeds only in explaining *away* its newness. We agree with the need to pose many of the questions they open up concerning the changed function and status of students and intellectuals today; but we cannot accept the idea that class origins and class situation explain both its growth and its ideology. While seeming to give an objective class basis to the New Left, in fact the Ehrenreichs deny it and its particular needs any real legitimacy by reducing its political role to that of "organic intellectual" of the working class. The "class" straightjacket into which they fit phenomena so opposed as demands for self-determination and participatory democracy on the one hand, and the technocratic claims of Veblenesque engineers, optimistic liberals like Lippman and prophylactic sociologists like Ross on the other, is useless in constraining the patient. When Mario Savio is quoted, only to be placed in the sack of anti-working class elitism, one wonders what kind of paranoid friend/ enemy world even an open Marxism creates. Only a dogmatic and reductionist class analysis would refuse legitimacy to the needs articulated by the New Left because they appear to run counter to, or do not come from, the working class itself. Now and again the Ehrenreichs slip out of the absurdities to which they are led by their model, asserting for example that—

> The newly articulated understanding that women were oppressed as a sex allowed many white PMC women to continue to assert the demands for meaningful work, self-fulfillment, etc., at a time when those demands had lost all moral legitimacy to most white male leftists. [p. 38]

What would "oppressed as a sex" mean in the context of their class analysis? Probably it could mean no more than their assertion that the Free Speech Movement made "a direct appeal to the class consciousness of the faculty." The seeming historical concreteness of their analysis only masks its dogmatic abstraction.

A friend who had read the Ehrenreichs' essay, and the first parts of our own, accused us first of theoretical overkill (which makes for a bad rhetorical strategy), and second of wasting our time. One might legitimately wonder why we choose to make so much of the Ehrenreichs' inadequate analysis of the Russian situation; and then go on to accuse us too of living out the legacy of old Marxian quarrels, pursuing our scholastic exposition of the "five senses of class", of "theories of" and "theories for" etc., etc. But the problem is not too much Marx, rather too little and undigested. Marxism does not remain a reference point for all of us who want to achieve a political understanding of our present and the meaning of our actions because it offers a fixed, closed set of categories into which—with a little or much juggling—we can fit a set of "objective possibilities" or some apparently novel facts. A self-understanding of the New Left requires a self-critique of Marxism, preserving its project but dispensing with its dogmas. The "theoretical overkill" was necessary to reproblematize Marx. Beyond the Ehrenreichs, our target was a kind of theorizing towards which too many are tempted when a movement slows down, when the horizon is clouded with doubts and self-doubt, and when the need for objective certainty becomes an almost neurotic necessity.

This theoretical concern is also political. Marxist revolution is supposed to occur when an objective crisis of the system's foundations coincides with the emergence of a collective will ready actively to transform the old order. If the working class' immediate interests are caught up within the logic of capitalist reproduction, then the only hope for transforming these interests into a political will comes from an intervention from outside, from the Party. We reject the *premises* of this analysis just as much as we reject its (Leninist) *conclusions*. Too many today accept the premises, after which, twist or turn as they may, they can come only to either a spontaneism or a version of the Party theory. No economic situation—unemployment, falling rate of profit, degree of exploitation, or whatever—can *of itself* bring about a class-based socialist revolution.[29] Without a political will to seize the occasion, economic crisis would lead only to the barbarism about which Rosa Luxemburg warned. This puts the stress on the "subjective" factor. The panlogism of class analysis and its imputation of interests on the basis of objective conditions unsuccessfully attempted to solve this problem. But if not to Leninism, or to syndicalism, anarchism, spontaneism or some other variant, to what are we to turn?

It is significant that the Ehrenreichs' discussion of the New Left remains at a level of vague generality as far as the actual everyday activities of the Movement are concerned. All of those activities revolved around a practical critique of the *legitimation* which the present so-ciety offers; they were a refusal to accept its motivating principles and they were a defetishization if its ideology. Recall the strategy of the local organizing projects (ERAP), the tactics of the civil rights and anti-war movements, or the struggles at the University. The manner in which all of these were undertaken—the *participatory democracy* which was both means and end—cannot be ignored in favor of structural analysis or cost-accounting our victories and defeats. When we look back at this phase, we may tend to think of it as naive, innocent, and somehow the wild oats of privileged youth. But we do so only if we measure our actions

---

29. It is only the dogmatic translation of the truism that radical needs can emerge at the point of production into a class subject that leads to the logical basis of Leninism.

against presupposed standards of Marxist revolution, only when we are haunted by, and try to recreate, the revolutions of the past. Ironically, when we do this we sometimes sound like our old bourgeois (and old left) critics: they too accused us of idealism, of ignoring what is "objectively possible."

The "old" New Left used to worry about being co-opted by the establishment. The Ehrenreichs, on the other hand, imply that co-optation is in a sense inscribed in the class situation from which the New Left emerges. But this concern with co-optation is itself a false problem: the former position implies an original purity which is somehow subjectively betrayed, while the later makes it impossible for the movement to achieve any independent status. But the subjectivism and voluntarism which appear to characterize the New Left cannot be countered by the objectivist and economistic approach of the Ehrenreichs. Rather what is needed is an analysis that looks at the changed nature and function of the university in the context of a new capitalism integrated increasingly by state intervention, without dissolving the response of students to these changes (the bulk of the New Left) in a dogmatic stratification theory. On the one hand, as the Ehrenreichs insightfully argue, the tendency towards professionalization of the university, the new availability of lucrative posts both in business and the state for aspiring young managers, bureaucrats, professionals, etc., created in part through the scientization of the labor process (and we would add, state interventionism) lends credence to the suspicion that student movements, whatever their claims, represent power aspirations of future technocrats against the irrationalities of capitalism. But it is not so clear that the same trends were also directed against truly emancipatory struggles. And, on the other hand, one must also argue for an opposite interpretation of this transformation: i.e., that the vocationalization, democratization (which opens the door to broader and more varied publics), but also the bureaucratization of the university, created a tendency towards the "proletarianization" of students which set off a genuinely anti-authoritarian, anti-bureaucratic revolt. This revolt both challenged the very legitimacy of the university, and with it that of capitalism and the bureaucratic state of which it was increasingly the microcosm. The contradictory demands of the New Left itself, for example the demand for "relevance" which affirmed professionalization and vocationalization, as opposed to the demand that the university remain a space freed from the corrupting influences of the economy and the state and be transformed into a genuine public (free university, critical university, new university), suggests that both of these analyses have their grain of truth. If a (however renewed) class analysis is incapable of grasping the novelty of the 60's revolt, that does not mean that the revolt itself is inexplicable nor that the conditions which engendered it have disappeared. A class analysis can ground the student movement only in interests imputed to heterogeneous strata and groups. It must necessarily disregard both new needs and projects expressed and formulated on the most heterogeneous levels from individual psychology to experimental politics.

The alternative to objective necessity is not the option for an existential moralism or a strategy of praxis-first. Theoretical and empirical research and strategic innovation are called for. The strategic innovation must be guided by the imperatives of critical publicity, counter-institutions, political experiment, in a word, participatory democracy. Cultural, empirical and theoretical research must come to grips with the nature and impact of the political aspects of late capitalist society. One must be able to determine the historical plausibility of New Left type politics in the structural development of late capitalism. Our critique of the Ehrenreichs has made use of insights gleaned from Habermas and Offe on the one hand, and Lefort and Castoriadis on the other. Our goal was not to present the (quite different) positive analysis to which they come; we wanted, rather, to reemphasize the *New* Left which the Ehrenreichs distort, and to unfasten the dogmatic blinkers to which a Marxism disguised as objective science must lead. The New Left was not the "finally discovered form of the revolution," as Marx said of the Commune. But the New Left was new, its interest in emancipation was genuine, and even this much can never again be said of a theory that is dogmatically based on class analysis and a practice relying on the myth of the revolutionary proletariat.

3.

Class Conflict:
The Human Dimension

Sandy Carter

John Murphy is a thirty-five year old construction worker, married
and father of two children. Reflecting on his life, he comments:

> I don't know, I guess I've done alright with my life, but I'd like
> my kids to have it a little better, have a little more respect. Be
> somebody people look up to you know, like some professional
> person. It's not that I've done so bad, but I want to see them (the
> children) develop more as people.[1]

1. The interviews and comments quoted in this article, when not otherwise
noted, are drawn from conversations and formal interviews occurring over the
last two years in the Boston area. Many of the interviews were conducted while I
was working as a therapist in the psychiatric unit of a small hospital in Somerville,
Massachusetts. Other comments are taken from conversations with friends,
neighbors and fellow workers with whom I've worked at various factory and
warehouse jobs during the past year.

Later he adds:

> It's not that they're (professional people) any better than me. I
> mean some people get more breaks than others. It's not right,
> but that's the way it is. Some guy has to bust ass all day, while
> another guy gets paid to sit around and think. You call that fair?

Mary, a twenty-five year old printer, recalls her experience in a
"socialist group" in the early '70s

> I was terrified at those meetings. Every time I opened my mouth
> I was afraid I was going to say something dumb. Everyone else
> could talk so well and seemed to know so much. It reminded me
> of how I used to feel in school—only this time I was in a whole
> roomful of teachers. Jesus was I out of place. I felt kinda like
> some creature from another planet.

For too long now the feelings expressed by John Murphy and Mary
Gregor have been either avoided or misread by the U.S. left. This
combination of feelings of awe, resentment, self-blame and hostility that
working class people often express toward 'pie-in-the-sky' intellectuals,
'bureaucrats,' 'college radicals' and 'bleeding heart liberals' has too often
been characterized as a simple lack of class consciousness, anti-
intellectualism and/or anti-communism. At best, the left has seen these
feelings as arising from lifestyle differences, differences between educated
and non-educated workers, or perhaps divisions emanating from within a
highly stratified working class. The peculiar hostility between the
working class and the left, between manual and intellectual labor, has
remained largely unexplained by marxist thinkers.[2] No doubt this
problem is linked to the confusion and complexity surrounding the
subject of class analysis.

In the seventies there has been a rebirth of 'working class politics' in
the U.S. left. This awakening has demanded a more serious look at the
class structure of modern capitalist society. Undoubtedly the major
complicating factor in this renewed effort at class analysis is the existence
of a very large group of 'middle class' professional and managerial
workers (engineers, technicians, scientists, social workers, etc.). The
significance of this phenomenon has been difficult to comprehend not
only because it is 'new,' but also because marxists have remained

---

2. This is not to deny the important effects of imperialism, repression, the
Cold War, racism, immigration, etc. on the outlook of the working class.
However, these historical forces do not, in themselves, fully explain the difficult
relationship between "middle class radicalism" and the working class.

shackled to antiquated theory.

This is perhaps most clearly exemplified by 'the new communist movement' as they dissolve professionals and managers, and other mental labor into that ill-fated and dying class—the petty bourgeois.[3] On the other hand, other leftists recognize that vast technological and scientific developments have greatly transformed the class structure to the point where nearly everyone is working class. This view, characteristic of the early New American Movement,[4] relies on the orthodox notion that all those who do not own the means of production and who must therefore sell their labor power for a wage in order to survive constitute the working class.[5] From this point of view society is composed only or primarily of an immense working class and a small ruling class. This analysis takes partial account of a 'proletarianization' of various professional and technical occupations, yet this 'expanded working class theory' blurs class distinctions so thoroughly that the concept of class becomes virtually meaningless.

To these unsatisfactory formulations must be added a third view, which refuses to shove the 'professional and managerial worker' into the petty bourgeoisie or the working class. In this analysis the new scientific and technical labor of advanced capitalism cannot be clearly situated in class terms. To Harry Braverman, these new workers are 'middle layers,' and to Erik Olin Wright they stand in 'contradictory class locations.'[5] According to this perspective, a new middle strata, not a class, is between and pulled back and forth by the ruling class and the working class. This middle strata feels some unity and contradiction with the two major classes, but is compelled by no objective historical forces to develop its own autonomous class outlook. To Wright and Braverman, the middle strata is too heterogeneous, too contradictory, and too free from the forces of history to become an important historical agent. Braverman

3. The 'New Communist Movement' refers to Marxist Leninist organizations deriving from the New Left. The two largest and most well known new communist organizations are the Communist Party (M.L.), formerly October League, and the Revolutionary Communist Party, formerly the Revolutionary Union. The newsweekly, "The Guardian," also shares the new communist view that the "middle strata" is petty bourgeois.

4. The New American Movement defines itself as a revolutionary socialist organization committed to democratic socialism. This national organization with origins in the New Left is a multi-tendency socialist organization.

5. Harry Braverman, *Labor and Monopoly Capital,* (New York: Monthly Review, 1974), pp. 403-410; and Erik Olin Wright, *Class Crisis and the State* (London: NLB, 1978).

and Wright define the distinctiveness of professional and managerial labor more precisely than the 'new communist' and 'expanded class theorists,' yet in the end all join hands in agreement that this 'category' of labor plays a limited role in class struggle. As in classical marxist theory, the focus remains on a two class model of conflict.

In sharp contrast to these views Barbara and John Ehrenreich argue that the explosion of technical, managerial and professional workers in advanced capitalist society has created a new class—the professional-managerial class (PMC), a class in contradiction with both the ruling class and the working class.[6] The PMC is defined by the Ehrenreichs as

> ...consisting of salaried mental workers who do not own the means of production, and whose major function in the social division of labor may be described broadly as the reproduction of capitalist culture and capitalist class relations. The PMC thus includes such groups as scientists, engineers, teachers, social workers, writers, accountants, lower and middle-level managers and administrators, etc.—in all some twenty to twenty-five per cent of the U.S. population. [pp. 12-14]

The Ehrenreichs hold that the consciousness of the PMC is shaped by its *objectively contradictory* position and function within modern capitalism's social division of labor. The PMC manifests this contradiction by sharing some of the class characteristics of the ruling class and some of the working class. Like the working class, the PMC is forced to sell its labor to capital. But like the capitalist, the PMC engages in planning, managing and rationalizing capitalist institutions and ideology. The PMC as it plans and rationalizes often comes in conflict with the capitalist drive for profit. However the PMC is also in an objectively antagonistic relation to the working class since its function is to manage, maintain and service the working class. The Ehrenreichs argue further that the PMC/working class antagonism has deepened as the skills, culture and knowledge of the working class have been taken away by the PMC. They add:

> Thus the PMC's objective class interests lie in the overthrow of the capitalist class, but not in the triumph of the working class; and their actual atittudes often mix with hostility toward the capitalist class with elitism toward the working class.[7]

6. Ehrenreichs, "The Professional-Managerial Class," pp. 9-10.

7. Ehrenreichs, "The Professional-Managerial Class," *Radical America,* Vol. 11, #3 (May-June 1977), p. 8. This quote does not appear in the article in this book because it was taken from the introduction written especially for the *Radical America* publication.

Buried beneath this seemingly heterogenous and contradictory surface the Ehrenreichs claim to have uncovered a 'commonality of function' defining a class interest independent of the working class or the bourgeoisie.[8] While one might quibble over the exact class boundaries separating the PMC from the working class, and while one might wish its function to be defined a bit more precisely, the PMC theory does bring an immediate spark of recognition.[9] It begins to clarify the origins and specificity of a social group that has remained hazy in the eyes of both left and bourgeois thinkers. It helps us understand the power of the colloquial phrase, "middle class." Most importantly, here is a theoretical framework that speaks to the experience of John Murphy and Mary

8. The Ehrenreichs emphasize, however, that a "commonality of function" or a common relation to the mode of production is insufficient for determining class as a real phenomenon. While their article does not develop the notion, they contend that a class must be characterized by a "coherent social and cultural existence; members of a class share a common life style, educational background, kinship networks, consumption patterns, work habits, beliefs."

9. The boundary that the Ehrenreichs establish between the PMC and the working class, as they admit, is fuzzy. This problem bears most heavily on the lower sections of the PMC. Here we find many low-level engineers, technicians, computer programmers, welfare workers, etc., whose social role and culture seems divergent from the higher and more pure PMC positions. To briefly mention these differences, many workers at the lower end of the PMC: 1) have very little autonomy in their labor; 2) exercise no supervisory role; 3) add value to the production of goods and services; 4) come from traditional working class backgrounds; 5) receive an income and maintain a lifestyle comparable to that of the working class; and 6) while their labor may contribute to the subordination of the working class to the PMC and the ruling class, they play only a minimal role in elaborating the technology and ideology of social control. Nevertheless, whether these groups are PMC or not, at present, they seem socially and politically distinct from the working class. They do embody many of the characteristics and contradictions discussed by the Ehrenreichs. A more detailed discussion of the diversity and unity within the PMC is beyond the scope of this article.

My primary purpose here is to confront the realities that differentiate the PMC from the working class. This is the starting point for a more full discussion of the nature of the PMC and its effect upon class struggle. With this in mind, "PMC" will be used to designate what others may refer to as the "middle strata." When referring to the working class I am using Harry Braverman's conception of the traditional working class. The working class by this definition is estimated to be about 65% of the workforce. It includes production workers, as well as low level service and office workers.

Class analysis cannot account for everyone. The full complexity of social life eludes our most careful abstractions, particularly when class is understood as a human "class." With the rich intermingling of subjective and objective aspects, it often moves above analytic maps.

Gregor. And this should be our starting point.[10]

No matter how internally consistent, a theory must at some time be tested against the raw experience of everyday life. The contradictions of society are nurtured in the blood, flesh and nerves of human beings. The debate over the "middle strata" can only persist for so long until someone must ask—does this phenomenon really exist? Does the working class really experience the PMC as a separate and distinct social group? Do working people really feel "hostility and deference" toward the PMC? Does the PMC feel contempt and paternalism toward the working class? So to begin to answer some of these questions, let us re-approach the subject of class relations by examining the working class experience of itself and of the PMC.[11]

***

In recent years the U.S. left has not been alone in waking up to the realities of working class life. Social scientists who a decade before had proclaimed the insignificance of class distinctions in U.S. society suddenly discovered a voice of pain and anger. The illusion that upward mobility was widespread, that the embourgeoisment of the working class was near complete and that the class as a whole was fat, affluent and content has gradually lost credence. Sociological portraits revealing a working class full of rage and frustration have become more and more common.[12] More recently this discontent has been reflected in popular films, rock music and nightly television.[13] If anything becomes clear from

10. In reality the issues and problems surrounding the subject of class are intimately linked to questions of kinship and race. Male supremacy and racism have greatly determined, both objectively and subjectively, the formation of the American working class. Thus the abstraction of class from the social totality of which it is a part does injustice to the present discussion. However, a more full treatment of the interpenetration of these relations is beyond the bounds of this article.

11. By basing an argument on a small, random set of interviews and conversations I am well aware that I am open to criticism. This "non-scientific" approach makes my generalizations suspect. My only response is that I have tried to select comments and data that reflect and elucidate the basic conflicts of the PMC/working class relation. If I have in fact touched upon this reality, much of the presentation should ring true in the experience of the reader.

12. See Andrew Levison, *The Working Class Majority* (New York: Penguin Books, 1975); Lillian Rubin, *Worlds of Pain* (New York: Basic Books, 1976); Richard Sennet and Jonathon Cobb, *Hidden Injuries of Class* (New York: Vintage, 1972); and Studs Terkel, *Working* (New York: Pantheon, 1974).

13. *Saturday Night Fever, Blue Collar,* and *Rocky* are among the recent group of films whose subjects are working class characters. These films speak only partially and indirectly to the lives of working class women; they

these characterizations of working class life it is a distinct line, objectively and subjectively, separating the working class from the PMC. While it is true that terms like "blue collar," "white collar," "manual" and "non-manual" labor hold less and less water, the difference in lifestyle, work, self-conception, culture, etc. distinguishing the "professional middle class" from the working class have come more sharply into focus.[14]

In the sixties it was often assumed that the U.S. working class was financially secure and living a life of middle class affluence. References to the wages of a few plumbers, electricians, steel and auto workers were used to depict the typical worker with two cars in the garage, a color T.V., and other creature comforts. In actuality this affluent worker made up, at best, 12% to 15% of the working class. The Bureau of Labor Statistics showed in 1970 that the average working family earned $9,500.[15] For this same year the B.L.S. calculated an "intermediate budget" for a family of four at $10,700.[16] The same survey revealed that thirty per cent of the employed work force made less than $7,000. At this income level the life style associated with the American Dream is simply beyond the reach of most workers. A more realistic picture of the average working family would show us a home with furnishings from Sears, clothing from J.C. Penny, two used cars traded in every five to ten years, and a small savings.[17] A middle aged meat cutter describes his economic situation:

> I take it day by day and try not to worry too much what's down
> the road. We always make it somehow. But I do wonder

nonetheless reveal many of the contemporary conflicts in working class life. In rock music, the songs of Elvis Costello, Patti Smith, Bruce Springsteen and The Clash explode with bitterness, despair and rebellion common to working class youth. And though short lived and often farcical, the *Mary Hartman* television series exposed a wide variety of blue collar discontents.

14. Levison's *Working Class Majority,* Rubin's *Worlds of Pain,* and Sennet and Cobb's *Hidden Injuries of Class* are all strongly argued cases detailing the social and economic differences between the working class and the middle class.

15. "Guide to Living Costs, 1970," Special Publication B.L.S., U.S. Dept. of Labor. This income figure includes the earnings of all members of the family. It should be added that the income of white working families would only increase marginally (roughly 2.5%) if black workers were excluded from the calculations.

16. B.L.S. budgets are laid out for rather frugal families. For instance, the budget allows a husband and wife a visit to the movies every three months; it permits the husband to purchase a suit every four years; a refrigerator and range are expected to last for 17 years, and so on. For a more thorough breakdown of B.L.S. budgets see Levison, op.cit. p. 32-33.

17. Levison calculates that three out of every four working class families earning an average income of $9,500 are in debt. One out of every three of these families owes more than $1,000. See Levison, op. cit. p. 105.

sometimes where the next dollar is gonna come from. And I get
tired of feeling guilty every time I stop for a beer.

One major illness, a period of unemployment, an unexpected
pregnancy and the affluent worker faces economic disaster. A working
mother and wife of a bricklayer says:

We make ends meet, not much more. And pray to God that
nobody gets sick or needs the dentist.

Turning to a comparison of PMC workers versus the working class,
we immediately confront the truisms regarding similar lifestyles and
income. Here we discover the PMC earns an average income of $14,500, a
difference in income of $5,000 between the PMC and the working class.[18]
The income distance between the PMC and the working class is, in fact,
as great as the income gap between the black and white labor force.[19] If
through the 50's and 60's bourgeois and left intellectuals discussed the
disappearence of class or the proletarianization of everyone, workers
nonetheless could not close their eyes to the inequality that confronted
them. Time and again this inequality is measured against the middle
strata. A thirty year old carpenter put it this way:

Shit these professors really got the life. Teaches a few hours
each day, writes some useless article every now and then, gets
three month vacations, makes three or four thousand dollars
more than me and never breaks a sweat.

Speaking of this inequality as perceived by the average worker
Andrew Levison writes:

The auto assembly line worker who owns a five year old Chevy
he bought second hand, spends eight or nine or even ten hours a
day building Cadillacs or Torinos he will never buy, and he
knows that it is the middle class that is buying them. As middle
class people go flying to Acapulco or San Juan for Christmas,
they leave under the watchful eyes of mechanics, maintenance
men and cab drivers, who get two weeks vacation a year and

18. These figures are taken from the 1970 B.L.S., *The Handbook of Labor
Statistics.* The comparison I make is between professional and technical,
managerial and proprietor occupations and those of the working class. The
income figure that I give for the PMC is not exact, but it is I feel a reasonable
approximation.
19. The income gap between black and white workers stands at about
$4,000. Black income remains at about 60% of white income.

usually spend it at home, or perhaps take a drive with the family to Disney World or a national park for a few days. Social inequality is not abstract for these people. It is a visible daily reality.[20]

Yet the visibility of PMC economic privilege is hardly the most significant class difference recognized by the working class. More basic is the feeling that human potential has been blunted and stifled. These feelings are no more evident than when people speak of their work— labor that is often physically hard and dangerous, most always routine, boring and permitting of little individual expression.[21] Here again we hear the working class person compare his or her labor to that of the professional. Though these feelings have been extensively documented, we should recall some of the more typical expressions of discontent.

Guys in the plants nowadays, their incentive is not to work harder. It's to stop the job to the point where they can have lax time. Maybe to think. We got guys now that open a paper, maybe read a paragraph, do his job, come back, and do something else. Keeping himself occupied other than being just that robot that they've scheduled him to be.[22]

—a thirty year old auto worker

A lot of time I hate to go down there. I'm cooped up and hemmed in. I feel like I'm enclosed in a building forty hours a week, sometimes more. It seems like all there is to life is to go down there and work, collect your paycheck, pay your bills, and get further in debt. It doesn't seem like the circle ever ends. Everyday it's the same thing; every week it's the same thing; every month it's the same thing.[23]

—a twenty-nine year old warehouseman

For women wage labor is yet another burden on top of housework and the rearing of children. However on the positive side it gives an escape from the isolation and boredom of household chores and it grants some independence. But still labor in the factory, the office or the department store brings many of the same gripes.

20. Levison, op. cit. p. 39.
21. For comprehensive treatment of this subject see *Work in America: Report of the Special Task Force to the Secretary of Health, Education and Welfare* (Cambridge: M.I.T. Press, 1973).
22. Quoted in Terkel, *Working,* p. 190.
23. Quoted in Rubin, *Worlds of Pain,* p. 158.

I enjoy the work, I guess. I mean it gets me out of the house. That's good. But it is kind of a dumb job. Anybody could do it. In fact, I could do it in my sleep and sometimes I do.
> —a thirty-five year old mother of four working
> in an electronics factory

These comments, of course, should not be taken to mean that there are no workers with fulfilling and meaningful occupations. The statements represent some of the primary complaints of the U.S. working class regarding their labor. But for our purposes these remarks also reflect the extraordinary differences in the nature of the work of the working class and the PMC. In fact, a systematic comparison of PMC labor to that of the working class reveals striking differences in control of labor, health and safety, job security, compulsory overtime, graveyard shifts, vacation and sick leave. One can only be shocked that these two types of work are equated.[24]

This alienation of labor cannot be disconnected from everyday life. The anger and despair generated at work freely spill over into community and family life.[25] In some cases this frustration is translated into physical violence against self, family, friends or strangers. In other cases, the pain of alienated labor is expressed more subtly through psychological withdrawal or a numbing fatigue that leaves one too drained to do anything but "die before the television." Studs Terkel's interview with a steelworker portrays both forms of violence.

24. These differences are nowhere more evident than in the area of occupational health and safety. In 1970, 14,200 workers died from accidents on the job. Another ten to twenty million were injured, and at a minimum another 100,000 died from occupationally related diseases. Needless to say, very few of these "accidents" and job related deaths occurred in PMC occupations. For futher treatment of health and safety issues see Ralph Nader, "The Violence of Omission," *The Nation,* Feb. 10, 1969; and Brendan and Patricia Sexton, *Blue Collars and Hard Hats,* (New York: Random House, 1971), p. 103. See Levison, op. cit. p. 53-97 for a complete comparison of working class labor to that of the "middle strata."

25. Marx's concept of alienation does not allow for a rigid separation between the sphere of production and the social relations of everyday life. The separation from the ownership and control of one's product and producing activity violates the social and creative nature of human beings. Thus for Marx, alienated labor transforms not only material objects; it also produces changes in consciousness, human nature and the social relations of society in general. The experience of alienation is therefore pervasive in a society based on alienated labor. It cannot be forgotten as one passes beyond the factory gates or office doors. It lives on in all psychological and social life.

Yeah. When I was single I used to go into hillbilly bars, get in a lot of brawls...
Why did you get in those brawls?
Just to explode. I just wanted to explode.
You play with the kids...?
When I come home, know what I do for the first twenty minutes? Fake it. I put on a smile. I don't feel like it. I got a kid three-and-a-half years old. Sometimes she says, Daddy where you been? And I say, work. I coulda told her I'd been in Disneyland. What's work to a three year old kid? I feel bad, I can't take it out on the kid. Kids are born innocent of everything but birth. You don't take it out on the wife either. This is why you go to the tavern. You want to release it there rather than do it at home. What does an actor do when he's got a bad movie? I got a bad movie every day.[26]

The bad movie running eight hours a day at U.S. workplaces has its sequel at home. The drudgery and authoritarianism of the factory, the warehouse and the office merges with familylife to produce a distinctive set of experiences. Sexual relations, parental discipline, the quality and quantity of leisure, consumption patterns all bear a particular cultural stamp.[27] Here one offers only a taste of that reality.

On leisure and consumption:

After the kids go to bed and things settle down, we're just here. I guess we watch TV or something (angrily). What am I saying? It's not 'or something;' that's what it is. It's the same every night; we're just here.[28]

Oh, after supper I sometimes work on the house, fix things, or tinker with the car or bike a little bit. I can relax a little bit that

---

26. Quoted in *Working in America,* op. cit., p. 29-30.

27. When speaking of culture I am referring to the ideas, values and general patterns of living common to particular groups of people. In capitalist society, the ruling class naturally exercises cultural dominance—the ruling ideas are those of the ruling class. These ideas furnish a certain homogeneity in values and behavior that cuts across various regional, ethnic, class and racial differences. Still, within the context and limits of the larger social whole, subordinate classes and social groups live and create their peculiar realities expressing the distinct conditions of their existence. These particular cultures and subcultures are constantly being born, absorbed, eliminated and remolded within the parameters established by "ruling ideas" and institutions.

28. Quoted in Rubin, *Worlds of Pain,* op. cit. p. 185.

way. And sometimes I take the bike out for a long ride in the country on the week-end.

—a thirty-three year old mechanic

We go to a movie sometimes, not often. And I go bowling with a girlfriend every now and then. But mostly he falls asleep watching TV, and me, after doing some chores, maybe washing dishes, ironing, I might sew or work a crossword puzzle. After that it's time for bed.

—a forty-three year old mother and beautician

I'd like to read more. I like to stay informed, but when I get home from work I'm just too tired to read much. I try to get through the newspaper a little bit, but even that's hard, except for the sports page.

—a forty-eight year old butcher

On sex and family life:

Basically the kids know the rules around here and who makes them. I try to be fair, but when I say something I don't want a lot of questions and static. When they get out on their own that's when they can start saying what goes.[29]

—a thirty year old trucker

I think my husband drinks a little too much. He tries to forget about all the things that have happened during the day and have a good time. But when he has too much, he gets angry about most anything and we end up at each other's throats. It can be kinda scary and crazy sometimes.

—a twenty-six year old woman married
to a construction worker

Our sex life is alright. I would like to do it more often and more different ways. But she seems to think it's wrong and feels guilty. I don't understand her maybe like I should. And in some

---

29. The relation between child rearing practices and social class has long been a favorite topic of social scientists. Numerous studies have shown that middle class parents, as compared to working class parents, use less physical punishment and more verbal control in the education of their children. In line with the role they are later to play in the production process, middle class children are expected to be more questioning and self-directing. By contrast, working class children are expected to be more conforming and unquestioning of social rules and authority. For a more broad treatment see Melvin Konn, *Class and Conformity: A Study in Values* (Homewood, Illinois: Dorsey Press, 1969).

ways she don't understand me.

Well I guess I give him what he wants. Even when I don't feel
like it, I do it. But there's more to love than just sex and I wish
he'd understand that.

> —a young couple in their mid-twenties

The picture that emerges from these interviews and surveys portrays
vividly the particular socio-economic situation of the working class in
relation to that of the PMC. Around income, jobs, community, family
and sexual relations, working class life is so enormously different from
that of the "middle strata" that to disregard the difference can only smack
of blindness, condescension and arrogance.

If the U.S. left has been relatively oblivious to these glaring
differences, that has certainly not been the case with the working class'
perception of the PMC. One of the nuances of class is that it manifests
itself, at the experiential level, by "instinctively" and spontaneously
making a person aware of being in or outside one's own "crowd." While
this is most often not viewed in any definite class terms, fundamental
differences are nonetheless felt and observed. In the case of the working
class / PMC distinction, working people are acutely aware of this
distinction and articulate it through a mixture of entangled feelings. At
times there is guilt and profound feelings of inferiority as workers justify
the "superiority" of the PMC. At other points there is deep resentment as
someone describes the social injustice in this relation—a relation that
judges and measures the life of the working class individual against that
of a person from the PMC. Sennet and Cobb comment on this perception
and relation in *Hidden Injuries of Class:*

> ...people felt that an educated, upper middle class person was in
> a position to judge them, and that the judgement rendered
> would be that working class people could not be respected as
> equals; to this people responded in one of two ways—either by
> trying to show that the position they held in society was not
> personally their fault, or that it was wrong in general for people
> to make judgements on other people based on social standing.[30]

Noting the basic obstacle to their study, they add:

> ...trust was finally established when people felt they could
> express anger to us about the barriers they felt between people
> in our class and theirs. 'You mean Dick,' a plumber said to

---

30. Sennett and Cobb, *Hidden Injuries,* p. 38.

Richard Sennet, 'You mean you make a good living just by sitting around and thinking? By what right? Now don't take that personally—I mean I'm sure you're a smart fellow and all that—but that's really the life, not having to break your balls for someone else.[31]

Here the plumber is not merely recognizing economic privilege; he is also keenly aware that the "upper middle class" person has more freedom to develop human potentials. This freedom permits more control over one's existence, and, in the eyes of society, it allows more dignity. The realization of this disparity in social roles and status cannot be escaped. The pipefitter who makes twice as much salary as the schoolteacher, still calls the schoolteacher "Mister" and in return is called by his first name.[32] The role models for social respectability that appear on nightly television are not "people like us."[33] The buzzer at work that signals the beginning and end of the workday, lunch and breaks emits a calming bell-like tone for the office and management "employees" and an irritating, growling blast for those on the shop floor. And at school when the teacher asks each student to stand up and announce to the class the occupation of his or her father, one young boy grows quickly uncomfortable for he is ashamed that his father is a mechanic. These are only a few of the infinite ceremonies of social distinction surrounding everyday life. Needless to say, these insults and rewards are not easily forgotten.

I don't know, I guess I always feel funny around people like that (the PMC). I feel like I'm not quite as good or at least they feel I'm not as good as them. That may not be right. Maybe they don't feel like that. But that sure is the feeling I get when I'm around them—that they think they're better.

I think everyone should be treated decent. The doctor, scientist, professor, should get no more respect than the bricklayer, the housewife, the steelworker or the janitor. That's not the way it is of course, but that is the way it should be.

We do hope one of our children can get a college education and

31. Ibid.
32. Ibid. p. 35.
33. See *Work in America,* p.35, where it is argued that:
Today there is virtually no accurate representation...of men and women in working class occupations...Research shows that less than one character in ten is a blue collar worker, and these few are portrayed as crude people with undesireable social traits.

get a job like that (a professional position). It's a better life.
People treat you better and you can see more and do more. You
kinda grow as a person, you can really make something of
yourself. My husband and I never had the chance to do
anything like that but we hope our children can.

For the working class these feelings represent years of accumulated
and unexpressed anger and self-blame. However this experience is
composed of more than recognition and resentment of a higher social
status. The working class perception of the PMC also contains the
awareness that members of the PMC perform a very different social role.
"They get paid to think." "They dream up ways to control my life." "I feel
judged by them,"—these fragments taken as a whole make up an
awareness that the PMC maintains a special relation to knowledge,
science, culture, and morality. The particular ways that members of the
PMC dress, speak, write and live—all the habits of everyday life contain
within them the rituals of power and judgement.

These habits obviously did not drop from the sky. The patterns of
living that separate the working class from the PMC are tied to definite
social divisions of labor and the roles necessary to uphold these. The
differences in income, status, self-concept, control of labor, family, etc.
are the products of and help reinforce a set of class relations that allow
some the power to manage, teach, and plan while others remain the
object of this activity. In the end, as the Ehrenreichs argue, these
differences amount to a confrontation "over the issues of knowledge, skill
and culture." This confrontation does not go unnoticed by members of
the working class.

***

A thirty-seven year old housewife speaks of her suspicions of child
care workers:

I think little kids belong at home with their mothers not in some
nursery school that's run by a bunch of people who think they're
experts and know all about kids and how they're supposed to
act. I saw some of these kids in a nursery school once. They act
like a bunch of wild Indians, and they're dressed terrible, and
they're filthy all the time.[34]

A forty-one year old garment worker talking of his feelings toward
technical and management workers:

---

34. Rubin, *Worlds of Pain,* op. cit. p. 87.

> I know they do work, but they don't do work like I do. They keep their eye on us; they make sure that everything runs smooth. But we're the ones who do the production. They're just here to make sure we do it like they want.

A forty-six year old mother of three children, diagnosed as suffering a "character disorder" says of her social worker:

> God I hate that woman. She makes me feel so stupid. Seems like everything that I do is wrong—the way I am with my kids, with my husband, even my sex life. She knows it all. Personally, I think her ideas are a little screwed up, but I can't tell her that.

And finally the bitterness of a young steelworker:

> As far as I'm concerned I got no use for the intellectual—the so-called expert, who sits around all day dreaming up new ways to control my life.

***

This brings us to the relationship between the U.S. left and the working class. Today, with the exception of the Communist Party USA, the left is largely derived from the PMC—either in origin or current class position. A left without roots in the working class is the result of the peculiar historical conditions that have shaped U.S. political life. While this history may explain the lack of class consciousness among U.S. workers, it does not absolve the left of a responsibility to address the very real differences in culture, power and knowledge that distinguish it from the class it hopes to reach. To pretend that a vast cultural, psychological and economic chasm does not stand between the working class and the left is simply to deny a profound reality of modern class society. Calling attention to this reality should not be looked upon as divisive, but rather as an initial first step toward overcoming a division that already exists. This in no way demands a guilt-ridden turn toward "proletarianization," employment in industrial jobs, short hair-cuts, the artificial assimilation of working class slang and lifestyle, etc. More realistically, the recognition of this class antagonism means that the left must become more self-conscious of its origins and the intrinsically oppressive assumptions attached to that history.

PMC attitudes of elitism toward the working class must be challenged. In place of the deeply engrained "need" to instruct, lead and control must be substituted an understanding that knowledge and skill must be dispersed, shared, and mutually developed. And most important, the PMC must come to realize that it has much to learn. The working class need not be glorified and the PMC need not take on any false humility. What is required is a willingness to recognize and struggle with the differences that left unchallenged will continue to replicate the relations of capitalist society.

But today there can be no doubt that this struggle is just beginning. "Middle class radicalism" does not yet see itself historically. It remains only vaguely aware of its roots, its interests, its relation to other classes. And it retains only the dimmest awareness of how it is perceived by those outside its insular sub-culture. As a result working class persons who have been attracted to the left have often had only a very brief and unpleasant encounter with socialist politics. One young woman in her twenties relates her experience:

> My first real experience with the left was when I joined a study group that was going to study Marx and Lenin and Mao. Everyone in the group, except me and this working class man, had college degrees. Naturally I was terrified to speak. It seemed like they had all the knowledge and I felt judged by it. The other working class person and I didn't ever say much. When we would talk, we'd always feel stupid. But finally I began to raise some questions about class—the class composition of the group, the feelings and lives of real people and I began to question the relevance of some of the things we were reading. For that I was called "workerist." Later I realized that it wouldn't work. The same people dominated meetings—all white, male and middle class, and nobody wanted to own up to the class problems. It was almost like you had to drop a bomb on people to wake them up! It was like they wanted to fit you to their view of what working class people are. If it didn't fit, they didn't want to hear it. About the same time, this working class guy and I dropped out.

Recalling a similar experience is a thirty-two year old man now "pretty turned off by the left":

> In the group I was in, I always felt very crude and vulgar. I didn't express myself the way they did and I felt bad about it. Back then I didn't really see this in any class way. I just saw them as intellectuals, with knowledge that I could never have. It made

me feel like I'd always felt—"I can't measure up, I'm not smart." They were all confidence and control. They were winners and me the loser. It brought back all the feelings of failure that I'd picked up in school and the family.

I remember once they were having this discussion on feudalism. Of course, three-fourths of the discussion I didn't understand. So finally, I asked a question. One of the women in the group told me my question was 'too simple'—that the issue was 'actually much more complicated' than that. After that I felt like shit, really stupid. But it was more than that. There were two worlds meeting there and they couldn't be reconciled. I couldn't imagine those people doing the same work as we did or relating like we did. I'd go to work the next day after one of those meetings and it was a totally different reality.

The experiences of these two workers are not atypical. They capture some of the basic conflicts felt by working class people entering the present day left. It is a conflict that reflects the relations of domination and subordination of society as a whole. Attitudes of elitism, mysterious differences in language and lifestyle, are not merely the characteristics of a few insensitive leftist intellectuals. The discomfort that the PMC and the working class feel around each other is the natural outgrowth of living two disparate social realities.

I remember how shocked one of these people was when they heard me griping about all the shitty jobs I'd had. One of them asked me 'haven't you ever had a job you felt good about?' I said, 'No.' It was beyond him, outside his reality. Factory workers are exotic creatures to these people.

...whenever I'm with educated people, you know, or people who aren't my own kind...um...I feel like I'm making a fool of myself if I just act natural, you know? See it's not so much how people treat you, it's feeling like you don't know what to do.[35]

Their advantages, you know, wealth, education, the suburbs, all that, make them think they can be more moral. They can understand you, with all their fancy words, but you can't understand them cause you're just part of the scenery. Well, actually, nobody can understand them, they think, you know,

---

35. Sennett and Cobb, *Hidden Injuries,* p. 115.

because they each got their individual problems, their shrinks, they're always special.[36]

***

As we reflect further on these two widely divergent but interpenetrating realities, it is helpful to reconsider the concept of class. E.P. Thompson writes that class is "an historical phenomenon, unifying a number of disparate and seemingly unconnected events, both in the raw material of experience and in consciousness." He adds that class happens when humans:

> ...as a result of common experiences (inherited or shared) feel and articulate the identity of their interests as between themselves, and as against others whose interests are different from (and usually opposed to) theirs.[37]

Thompson's notion of class is not a "thing," a "category," or "structure." Class is a lived human experience founded in actual life situations and owing "as much to agency as conditioning." This experience is based largely on one's relationship to the productive processes in a particular society—in this sense class is an objective relationship. Nevertheless, and what classical Marxism easily forgets, class always remains *more than an objective relation.* Marx makes this clear when he writes that the mode of production "must not be considered simply as being the reproduction of the physical existence of individuals. Rather it is a definite form of expressing their life, a definite mode of life on their part."[38]

Class then is not merely an objective or economic relationship; it is also the reproduction of class in all aspects of life. Class is a political, economic and ideological set of relations encompassing a complex mix of objective and subjective factors. Class is a human relationship lived not only in production, but also in families and sex relations, through religion and morality. It touches and shapes the personality giving a picture of self, of needs, and of power.

At all points class relations are power relations. Every class has its common life, its particular interests. These interests, in turn, are satisfied

36. Ibid. p. 147.

37. E.P. Thompson, *The Making of the English Working Class* (New York: Random House, 1966) p. 9.

38. Karl Marx, *The German Ideology,* edited and translated by Lloyd D. Easton and Kurt H. Guddat in *Writings of the Young Marx on Philosophy and Society* (Garden City, N.Y.: Doubleday, 1967) p. 409.

in opposition to the interests of other classes. Class struggle, understood in this more total sense, can be seen in relations of domination and subordination at all levels of human existence—political, ideological, economic, social and psychological. In essence, *class is defined by human beings as they live and create their history.*

Unfortunately, the understanding of class as a human experience has often been opposed in theory and practice by a stubborn tendency in the Marxist tradition to define class as an abstraction, an object, or in Thompson's words, an "it." When this occurs the object tends to assume human qualities and a real existence. The working class becomes a mythical entity with definite objectives, interests and consciousness. Often "it" is defined with "scientific accuracy" as so many things standing in a certain relation to the mode of production and thereby determined to perform a fixed historical task. On the other hand, the working class is sometimes deemed absent from history unless it can define a coherent and self-conscious "class consciousness." Approached in this manner, there is no need to examine a real class situation or listen to the experience of a real working class person.

These lifeless conceptions of class remain implanted in the U.S. left. In this tradition, class analysis continues to be a fairly simple undertaking demanding a primary and often singular focus on the working class and the bourgeoisie. In Marx's day the two class model was more justified since the small and politically insignificant intermediate classes played a limited historical role. However as this analysis ossified into religion it failed to account for the expanding middle class in Western Europe and it denied the revolutionary potential of the peasantry in underdeveloped capitalist countries.

In regard to contemporary capitalist society and the sweeping changes in class structure occurring during the last half-century, Marxist theoreticians have gradually come to see the problems of the two class model while nonetheless being bound to it.[39] It is agreed that a broad middle strata has come into existence, yet this development is not held to alter, in any fundamental way, the nature of the class struggle. A new category has been added to the old game plan. Or to put it another way, a new "it" has been attached to the old "structure." The human conflict has not yet been discovered.

Historically this reified approach to class and class analysis has been most dominant during periods of relative calm in the class struggle. During such periods the gaps between theory and practice, intellectuals

---

39. Various radical thinkers since Marx's day have examined the "intermediate strata." Yet these investigations have in the main been schematic and have not challenged the theoretical dominance of the two-class model.

and masses, loom large. One of the many conditions promoting this fragmentation is the fact that the experts on revolution and the working class have not themselves been of working class origins. To classical Leninists who "declass" themselves and come to identify "the laws of history" that carry the "objective interests" of the working class, this contradiction poses no great problem. But for those concerned with who defines the objectives and process of socialist revolution, it is a major contradiction—a contradiction reflecting and perpetuating the relations of class society. Today this question is perhaps more important than it has ever been.

Inadequate theory and "objective conditions" cannot alone explain the confusion surrounding the issue of the "middle strata." In this time of relative calm in the class struggle, a left with origins in the middle strata has been allowed to define itself "outside" the class struggle. "Middle class radicalism" has defined itself in relation to *how it sees itself*—this includes a vision of how the middle strata sees the working class and how the middle strata thinks the working class sees the middle strata. In these circumstances the words that the working class speaks between themselves have remained part of an internal dialogue.

> They seem very confused about their backgrounds and that was something we could never really talk about. Just to bring up the issue was a 'guilt trip.'

> Whenever they talked about the Working Class, the emphasis was always on what they had to teach. They acted like missionaries going out to educate the savages.

> I don't think they really like working class people. They think we are childish and irrational.

> I'm glad the sixties are over. Maybe they'll be more humble now that they know they can't build the whole world over in their image.

***

Can these be the words of people addressing a contradiction *within* the working class? Does this resentment, expressed so strongly and consistently, stem from simple differences in income and status? Do we not see here a barrier between the common life of two distinct social groups? Is this not a very real clash of political interests?

At the level of lived reality a social relation is definitely being called into question. Over and over we hear workers using the phrases "our kind," "we," and "us" against "them" and "people like that." The social division is being described imprecisely. Sometimes the terms of description are contradictory. Often enough the relation is even justified by those oppressed by it. Still these broken words eventually find coherence. The working class cannot forget the inequalities in work, income, lifestyle and social function that it absorbs daily. In relation to the PMC, workers not only recognize the social and economic advantages of this "more valued social group," they see members of the PMC, justly and unjustly, as authorities who unravel how and why things happen. They know that the PMC gives and withholds knowledge that effects and restricts their lives—at school, work, over TV, in the welfare office or at the family counseling center. In these arenas and so many others, members of the PMC personify the control that society holds over their lives. However wrong it may be, when workers rail against "the system" their words often lash out as much at the PMC as at the capitalist.

> This distrust is compounded by the fact that most left-wingers have been to college. In the experience of most people in the plants college trains people (e.g., teachers, social workers, engineers) to do one thing: to keep the workers in line.[40]

But the antagonism between the working class and the PMC is not unbridgeable, nor is it desireable. A complementary role in the revolutionary process has historically existed between the working class, radical intellectuals, and elements of intermediate classes. Radical intellectuals have an important role to play in aiding the working class in its struggle to take hold of its science, culture and history. Socialist thinkers can help make the spontaneous and unsystematic working class critique of capitalist society more cohesive. This coming together however is complicated by the PMC.

The PMC holds a one-up position over the working class. As the Ehrenreichs and others have argued, it possesses the knowledge and power that helps keep the working class in check and we would be naive to expect that that power will be willingly relinquished. The PMC's objectively contradictory position in the social division of labor makes it a dubious and wavering ally in the course of class conflict. It cannot be expected to be a primary base of social discontent. Working class victories mean losses not only for the capitalist class, but at least partially for the PMC as well. This is not to argue that an alliance between the PMC and the working class is impossible. On the contrary, the PMC's contradictory nature means that a substantial section of the PMC—most

40. John Lippert, "Fleetwood Wildcat Anatomy of a Wildcat Strike," *Radical America* (Sept.-Oct., 1977), p. 18.

likely at the lower end of the class—will politically align with the working class. This alliance should be encouraged, but not at the expense of the working class and other subordinate groups. We can not afford to forget that a socialist movement and its political organizations are challenging the power relations in its own ranks as well as society as a whole. The totality of the struggle, in theory and practice, depends on the coming together of left intellectuals, the working class, elements of the PMC, women, minorities, and other oppressed groups in a common fight to eradicate, not replicate the relations of exploitation and oppression common to advanced capitalism. This unity, however, cannot come about without struggle and a critical assessment of differences.

4.

The PMC: A Critique

David Noble

The Ehrenreichs have formulated the notion of the Professional-Managerial Class (PMC) for a purpose, but their notion defeats their purpose. Recognizing that the "middle class left" to which they belong suffers from a subjective confusion, an ambiguous self-identity, that it has "dashed itself repeatedly against the contradictions between its middle-class origins and its working class allegiance," and that it has thus developed a proclivity for self-effacement, proletarian piety and indulgent subjectivism, the Ehrenreichs have tried to "objectively comprehend" their dilemma, who they are, where they came from, what they should do. They are seeking something solid, something firm, some thing to lean on, to refer to, to struggle against—something above all unambiguous, a touchstone with which to demystify reality. However well intentioned, it is this very quest for a hard and fast, unproblematical, unambiguous reality that leads them into trouble. Emphasizing the contradictions in thought, they minimize the contradictions that obtain in reality and seem not fully to realize that objective comprehension entails more often a confrontation with ambiguity than a reprieve from it. True to their purpose, the Ehrenreichs identify a "single coherent class," fixed in time and space, defined in terms of its structure and function. But it points nowhere; it is objective but lifeless. For all their rhetoric of fluency, process, subtlety and contradiction, for all their genuine political concern and commitment, the Ehrenreichs offer us a glimpse of what is essentially a cardboard reality.

The Ehrenreichs are correct in pointing out that the swelling of the ranks of professionals, managers, and administrators—paralleling and, in part, reflecting the growth of the state apparatus, of the service sector and of private firms themselves—raises important questions for radical critics of capitalism. But in this regard the Ehrenreichs are following in what is now a rather mature, if not altogether insightful, tradition of inquiry (some would say, dating back to Marx himself). There are certainly real challenges here. Where the Ehrenreichs go wrong is in their reliance upon seriously degraded Marxian concepts, concepts which neither retain the potency of the originals nor point us beyond them. Of course, the Ehrenreichs are not to be blamed for the degradation of these concepts; rather, their work merely reflects an unfortunate tendency on the left to appropriate the one-dimensional approaches of mainstream social science, approaches marked by dualistic, either-or type thinking (reality is either this or that, never both; things are good or bad, never both good and bad), a relatively static, short time-frame view of history, and a decided emphasis upon descriptive rather than normative analysis. In short, conceptually the Ehrenreichs approach, like the genre it reflects, constitutes a regression not an advance on classical Marxism, however up-to-date their language and familiar their references.

This critique, then, is directed less against the Ehrenreichs than against a general tendency in radical thought, which is itself a product, like the Ehrenreichs work here, of a too hurried quest for certainty. Using the PMC as a springboard I will examine two concepts which are critical to the Ehrenreich analysis but are also significant in themselves for any radical social criticism of modern capitalism: "class" and "reproduction." (The PMC is a "class" and it has a special function, "reproduction.") Again, my aim here is not to argue dogmatically for the integrity and inviolability of the original Marxist concepts nor to criticize them (an ambitious undertaking which demands rigorous historical analysis and defies facile theorizing). My purpose is a much more modest one, to try to distinguish the Marxist conceptions of class and reproduction from what the Ehrenreichs offer in their name, and to suggest that something has been lost, not gained, in the newer version.

Class

The Ehrenreichs recount and dismiss some previous attempts which have been made to situate the professionals and managers within the framework of a consistent and coherent theory of modern society (Mills, Gorz, Mallet, Poulantzas, Galbraith, Burnham) and come up with their own version of an "objective"middle class: the PMC. The PMC, they argue, "must be understood as comprising a distinct class in monopoly capitalism;" composed of salaried managers and professionals of many varieties. The PMC is defined in terms of its relationships to the ruling and working classes, and by its relation to, its part in, the process of social production. Its rise in the twentieth century reflects, and in itself embodies, the evolution of capitalist class/ working class relations in monopoly capitalist society. Nevertheless, the PMC is a distinct, coherent class in, of, and for itself, defined not only by these relations to the other major classes but by the position it occupies in the "broad social division of labor," its access to and control over the means of production, and its own unique culture (a shared "life-style," educational career patterns, kinship networks, consumption and work-habits, ideology, etc.). The PMC then, according to the Ehrenreichs, is not a broader class of workers, not simply a new, vaguely defined, disparate middle class resisting proletarianization at all costs. Nor is it a vestige of an older day, a petty-bourgeois strata of self-employed professional peddlers, or an emergent class, heirs of the managerial revolution whose destiny it is to eclipse capitalism and the class struggle once and for all. The PMC is thus specific to (and limited to) monopoly capitalism, a class without much of a past and without promise of a future beyond this particular historical epoch.

Fixed in time and place by its relations to the two "dominant" classes in monopoly capitalist society, the PMC is neither an anachronism nor a vanguard; caught up in the struggle between capitalist and worker, it owes its mixed fortunes to the fate of each. The PMC is composed of salaried, educated mental workers, wage earners who do not own the means of production and yet are not members of the working class (the Ehrenreichs use Braverman's category: craftsmen, operatives, laborers, sales workers, clerical workers, service workers and non-college educated technical workers). The PMC's major function in monopoly capitalism is described broadly as "the reproduction of capitalist culture and capitalist class relations." "Specializing in the reproduction of capitalist class relationships," this new class is divided roughly into those who carry out their function explicitly (teachers, advertising copy writers, social workers, psychologists, propagandists, entertainers, etc.) and those who do so implicitly, through the performance of those technical roles in the production process which exist as a reflection of, and the means of furthering, this reproduction function (engineers, college-educated technical workers, managers and administrators).

The PMC constitutes nearly one-quarter of the U.S. population (almost 50 million people); members share a coherent, common culture and marry overwhelmingly within their class. Having no legal means of transmitting or inheriting class status over generations, the PMC reproduces itself primarily through a certification process based upon formal higher education (to which members enjoy ready access). Despite rifts between the various sub-classes within it—such as that between conservative engineers and more progressive liberal arts intellectuals—the PMC constitutes a "single, coherent class" no less than the variegated working class, which is itself composed of people as diverse as secretaries and steel workers. Although objectively in the service of capital against the working class, the PMC identifies its interest with that of society as a whole (and progress), an ideology grounded in notions of professional autonomy, scientific rationality, and the disinterested political objectivity of expertise.

The PMC was forged as a class in the heat of the class struggle between capital and labor. The time of its formation was set by an historical condition and marked by an historical need: the existence of sufficient social surplus to support a new 'nonproductive' class of functionaries and the demand of the bourgeoisie to find ways of ameliorating the intensifying class struggle and to secure capitalist control over the actual process of production (to regulate output in the face of intensifying competition). The PMC emerged then, not "naturally" or automatically as a product of increasing scale of complexity or technological sophistication or any other such disembodied demiurge but as part and parcel of the transformation in the relations between capital and labor: the creation of mass institutions of social control that went beyond sporadic police actions, the reorganization of production to place even the minor prerogatives of production in the hands of management, and the creation of a consumer culture to absorb the fruits of mass production (and turn more potent labor power into surplus value). Representing the agency whereby capital took for itself the resources of the working class and turned them to profitable advantage, the PMC existed "only by virtue of the expropriation of the skills and culture once indigenous to the working class." Thus, the PMC led a shadow life between the classes, living off borrowed power from the one, borrowed talents from the other.

The ideology of the PMC, however, did not reflect such a lack of substance. Viewing itself as a mediator between warring classes, cautious expert in the service of Science and Reason, the PMC believed itself to be speaking for civilization, not capital, furthering scientific progress, not robbing the artisans of their art. However much this self-serving ideology might have deluded the PMC, tempting them into hubris and bad faith, it nevertheless neatly complemented and camouflaged the aims of capital. At the same time, though, it fueled the zeal for "progressive reform," reform which was at once a means of extending and reinforcing capitalist hegemony and, potentially, in the eyes of many a threat to that hegemony. Thus, although they stood in an "objectively antagonistic" relationship to the working class—in their capacity as capitalist functionaries—members of the PMC who pushed forward the ideological principles of autonomy, reason, and efficiency often found themselves in conflict with capitalists as well. The Socialist Party, the technocratic and liberal progressives, the radicalism and communism from the Thirties through the Sixties, all could be understood, in part, as instances of "PMC radicalism"—what happens when the PMC mistakes its ideology for reality.

The New Left of the Sixties, moreover, pushed the ideology of the PMC to its limits, further than ever before, beyond mere criticism of capital for thwarting the realization of the PMC vision or of the PMC itself for failing to live up to its own ideology, for failing to strive toward realization of its vision. The New Left adopted the perspective of the working class, the objective antagonists of the PMC, to launch a critique of the PMC ideology itself as elitist and exploitative in its own right as well as a mystification, a camouflage for capitalist domination; the cult of professionalism, expertise, objectivity all came in for attack. As a result, the New Left radicals, children of the PMC, found themselves estranged from their own homes, their parents, and that bastion of the PMC— repository of both radicalism and reaction—the university. The working class, however, and minority movements, with their long-standing and deep-seated distrust of and hostility toward the PMC, rejected the New Left's claims of identification with them. Thus, ultimately, the PMC were set adrift, without moorings, without a direction. Having rejected capitalism and the PMC itself, and charged them with elitism, condescension, and (worse) liberal guilt, the New Left floundered in its own isolation, confused, dejected, and politically superfluous. Enter the Ehrenreichs.

In their search for solid ground, the Ehrenreichs have done their best to describe an "objective" class, in terms of ideology, sociology (position in the social structure and membership), relationship with other classes, historical development, culture and function. In essence their notion of class boils down to a functionalist one as we will see; much of the rest is rhetoric, a gloss of sophistication and subtlety that doesn't penetrate very deeply into the analysis itself.

When the Ehrenreichs write about PMC ideology—of progress, Science, Reason, elitist technocratic notions of destiny, the managerial revolution, expertise, objectivity, the eclipse of the class struggle—they do so only in the sense of "mere ideology," a straw man to be knocked down under the glare of "objective comprehension" of reality. Thus in their analysis they never really try to come to grips with the connection between ideology and reality, to attempt to understand why such notions were (and are) so compelling to so many. What aspects of reality are reflected in, and reinforce, the ideology? Since the Ehrenreichs raise the matter of the PMC ideology simply in order to dismiss it as a mystification of reality, (and to dismiss those who are imbued with it as deluded or guilty of bad faith) they never seriously confront the fact that capitalism underwent a profound and dramatic transformation in the twentieth century and that the ideology of the PMC is rooted in reality, however much it might exaggerate certain aspects of that reality and deny others. For present purposes, it is enough to point out that the Ehrenreichs' cursory examination of PMC ideology serves more to direct our attention to "objective reality"—that is, away from ideology—than to define the PMC in terms of its ideology.

If the Ehrenreichs never take the PMC ideology seriously in their analysis, they take the PMC culture even less seriously. They talk about it because social historians talk about it; if you have a class, it's got to have a culture. So the Ehrenreichs make mention of life-styles, family life, marriage patterns, education, and the anxieties of living in a world where credentials precede existence, but their discussion remains superficial and impressionistic, carelessly lumping together the culture of industrial engineers with that of art dealers, dental technicians, and professors of neurophysiology. If the culture has a single defining characteristic, it is probably that it is eminently purchaseable. But again, the Ehrenreichs talk about culture because they think they must; it is certainly not central to their notion of the PMC. Indeed, they have not undertaken any of the empirical labors that would be required in any serious discussion of culture. The reason for this failure of effort is plain enough: culture is a minor matter here.

Unlike Marx himself, who took great pains to ground his discussion of classes in France upon empirical detail, the Ehrenreichs shy away from the drudgery positivist social science normally requires of its adherents (such work is, of course, the great strength—if, albeit, also the great weakness when left at that—of positivist social science). Thus, it is more sleight of hand than careful social analysis that magically lumps together advertising executives, practical nurses, and design engineers in a single class. But before we begin to quibble over who is a member and who isn't (reminiscent of the sterile debates over who is productive and who isn't) we should recognize that the question is of little consequence for the Ehrenreichs; their notion of PMC is immune to such nit-picking, as they themselves acknowledge: "the very definition of the PMC—as a class concerned with the reproduction of capitalist culture and class relationships—precludes treating it as a separable sociological entity."

If ideology, culture, and sociological categories are not central to the definition of the PMC, its relationship to other classes, and its historical development appear to be. The Ehrenreichs are emphatic in their insistence upon the fluid, subtle character of class; class is not a thing, it is a process, an historical relation. But here too sophisticated rhetoric substitutes for sophisticated analysis. The Ehrenreichs use a quote from E.P. Thompson's famous "Preface" to the *Making of the English Working Class* to make their point about class being an historical relationship and then go on to describe the nature of the various relationships the PMC has with the other classes. In the process, however, it becomes apparent that they have missed a crucial aspect of Thompson's description of class (an aspect that Thompson learned from Marx) that class is not simply a relation, it is a particular bipolar relation, namely, the dialectical relation of opposites: masters and slaves, squires and laborers, lovers. As Thompson suggests in the same passage from which the Ehrenreichs have quoted: "we cannot have two distinct classes each with an independent being, and then bring them into relationship with each other. We cannot have love without lovers, nor deference without squires and laborers. And class happens when some men...feel and articulate the identity of their interests as between themselves, and *as against* other men whose interests are different from (and usually *opposed to*) theirs (emphasis added)." [p. 10] The point to be made here is that class for Thompson, as for Marx, is an historical relation which means it, first, is not simply a place in society but also a time in history and, second, that it is not merely a thing but a relation; and in particular, the relation of opposites. Moreover, it is precisely the fact that class is the relation between dialectical opposites that gives it its tension, and it is this tension that makes history move. Thus, neither class (nor history) can be comprehended by looking only at a single class; any class is defined, and defines itself, in terms of the "other" class.

Marx, of course, derived his dynamic conception of class from Hegel. Class was a way of grounding Hegel's Spirit in history, in "sensual" reality, while retaining a sense of motion, a way of locating the Historical subject in time and place. History, for Marx—as for Hegel— was the medium of human self-development; for Hegel this self-development entailed successive modes of consciousness, each being eclipsed in its comprehension of the "whole" by the next. For Marx, this development entailed successive modes of production (interaction with

Nature) and corresponding forms of social life, each eclipsed in making possible the fullest realization of human potential by the next. Class society for Marx was "false" society, society in which the struggle between modes of existence was still going on, society in which mankind was not fully free to enjoy its birthright as a species. Marx begins his analysis of society with this assumption of human potential and it is against this benchmark that he measures historical development, evaluates reality.

Marx first uses the term "proletariat" in his philosophical critique of Hegel's *Philosophy of Right* to describe not the class that produces surplus value but the locus of the Historical Subject, the embodiment of the further potential of human self-development. History has seen many a class claim to represent the complete and final realization of human potential in its rise to power only to succumb to a new class whose claims superceded its own. Thus the bourgeoisie announced its efforts to overcome feudal domination by declaring the rights, not of the bourgeoisie, but of Man. Marx's criticism of bourgeois hegemony was not only that the bourgeois rights themselves had not been granted to everyone but that they did not speak to economic realities, to the rights of all people to exercise control over and reap the fruits of their own productive labor. The proletariat, alienated from its own labor, its own humanity, owners of no property in a society based upon the ownership of property, thus stood in opposition to the bourgeoisie as its living negation, its dialectical opposite. The two classes were inherently antagonistic, mutually exclusive manifestations of humanity, and the struggle between them, the motor of history, was a fight for survival for both. The proletariat ascendance was identical to the bourgeois descent; and it signalled a step forward for the Historical Subject, mankind.

There are three important things to be said about Marx's concept of class. First, it entails the relation between opposites. Second, it tells us something about the movement of history. And third, it is itself a political construct, not merely a device for describing things as they are but also a means of making things move in the right direction; that is, it is at once a descriptive and a normative heuristic. The Ehrenreichs, in their use of class, have drained it of such meanings. The PMC has relations with other classes but these merely produce ambiguity about what the PMC is, not real tension between it and something else, a tension which implies movement. The relations between the PMC and the two other classes seem to dissolve the PMC rather than clarify what it is. On the one hand, it exists "only by virtue of the expropriation of the skills and culture once indigenous to the working class," that is, its existence vis a vis the working class is "derivative." The PMC has no real substance of its own. On the other hand, the PMC has established itself as a "major class" but has done so only "in terms set by the capitalist class." Here too, it has no "terms" of its own, no claims to separate identity, other than a fanciful, wrongheaded ideology of expertise. The PMC, in short, as the Ehrenreichs have described it, is a phantom class; it has members perhaps (whoever they are) but no substance independent of the other classes. "The story of the rise and development of the PMC is simultaneously the story of the rise of the modern bourgeoisie and the modern proletariat as they have taken form in monopoly capitalist society." Doesn't the PMC have a story of its own?

This brings us to the second point. Because the PMC has no dialectical relationship with another class—because the PMC has no identity of its own to distinguish it from its opposite—it tells us very little about the movement of history. The PMC has something to do with the emergence of scientific industry and rational, bureaucratic enterprise as well as with the evolution of capital-labor relations, but the role of the PMC itself *in history*, that is, in terms of the development of the species, of freedom, of human fulfillment, is never made clear. If it is merely an extension of capitalist authority, as the Ehrenreichs often imply, why call it another class? However they might be used (wittingly or unwittingly) in an apology for capitalism (and a critique of Marxism), the notions of the "managerial revolution" and of the technocratic "overturn," at least suggest movement beyond capitalism, an eclipse of the class struggle, a step toward human fulfillment. They tell us something (true or not) about the course of human events. The notion of the PMC tells us nothing of the sort. Why ought we to pay so much attention to it?

Finally, and perhaps most important, the PMC remains merely a descriptive concept, describing things as they are, whereas Marx's concept was both a guide for action and a front line of action. For Marx, to define society as a class society was already to render a judgment, give direction to history, and begin to move in that direction. Class analysis was never merely anatomy, it was revolution. Class itself was never just a locus; it was a lever. "We should strongly emphasize," the Ehrenreichs warn their readers, "that class is an analytic abstraction, a way of putting some order into an otherwise bewildering array of individual and group characteristics and interrelationships. It describes a phenomenon exist-ing most clearly at the level of society as a whole...and ceases to be useful...when it is called on to explain infallibly the actions, ideas, and relationships of every individual."[p. 11] With this caveat, the Ehrenreichs free themselves of worry about the details; their notion can't be tested empirically. More important, they fail to realize that class, however vague, is not simply a way of putting *some* order into social complexity but a particular type of order; it is a way of distinguishing between exploiter and exploited, classes with opposing interests, freedom and unfreedom, the present and the future. The concept of class offered by the Ehrenreichs tells us nothing about these things, and worse. As a formless "abstract analytical concept" carelessly draped over the class struggle, it offers little guide for action, little glimpse of "what might happen if" (the most any Marxian analysis has to offer). And as a one-dimensional, static, description of class, defined in terms of its place in the social structure and, most of all, by its function, the concept reifies reality, freezes an indeterminate situation, stills history in the here and now. Thus, the very "objectivity" of the concept denies the possibilities and, with them, the Ehrenreichs' original purpose as well.

Reproduction

If the Ehrenreichs' concept of class tells us little about where we are going or how we might get there, what does it tell us about what is? How valuable is the notion of the Professional-Managerial Class as a merely descriptive device? As we have seen, in the last analysis the Ehrenreichs define the PMC primarily in terms of position in the social structure and function in the social division of labor (despite discussion of relations, ideology, culture). Thus, their first definitional sentence reads: "we define the PMC as consisting of salaried mental workers who do not own the means of production and whose major function in the social division of labor may be described broadly as the reproduction of capitalist culture and capitalist class relations." [p. 12] These characteristics then, are the adhesive that binds together an admittedly heterogeneous class. But, here again, the Ehrenreichs are less than firm. The details of social position—in terms of occupations, skills, income levels, power and prestige—defy such facile inclusiveness, which, on the one hand, links a minor administrative assistant with a corporation vice-president and, on the other, excludes non-college trained technical workers while including their college-trained brethren who do the same work, occupy the same positions, etc. The Ehrenreichs acknowledge these difficulties only to sweep them under the theoretical rug, all the while emphasizing the centrality of the functional definition: "the *very definition* of the PMC—as a class *concerned with the reproduction of capitalist culture and class relationships*—precludes treating it as a separable sociological entity (emphasis added)." [p. 14] The PMC, in short, are "reproduction" specialists. Here is the hard ground of the analysis; all else is epiphenomenon or mystification. We will now examine that ground. What is reproduction? Is it something people can specialize in?

As with their (mis)use of the Marxian concept of class, the Ehrenreichs have here too substituted a static, one dimensional notion for a dynamic, contradictory one, with similar consequences. Again, they have lost a sense of potential, motion, history; their concept kills. When they use the term "reproduction," they mean only reinforcement; to reproduce capitalist social relations is to strengthen, repair, revitalize, renew, sustain those relations and nothing more. Reproduction stops history, for the Ehrenreichs. Marx had other ideas. As the Ehrenreichs use the term, reproduction represents only one side of a process, the positive side (in the Hegelian sense). In Marx's use of the term, it had another side too, a negative (revolutionary) side. The Ehrenreichs have lost sight of this other side because they have divorced the process of reproduction from the process of production itself, setting it aside as something apart, something people can specialize in. This is a mistake no Marxist can afford to make; the reproduction of capitalism is, after all, the reproduction of a mode of production. Production and reproduction are not so easily disentangled. In the Marxian scheme, reproduction and production are but two aspects of the same, single process of social production. In overlooking this, the Ehrenreichs miss two central Marxian insights: First, the process of production itself, the production of commodities, is the primary means of reproducing capitalist social relations (a one sentence summary of *Capital*). Production and reproduction are not separate tasks to be assigned to different specialists; they are one and the same task, assigned to all. This is not to say that there are no reproduction activities external to the workplace—family, state, media, etc.—but just that production itself is a medium of reproduction. To produce is to reproduce. Second, the dialectic of social production, the historical relation between "forces of production" and "relations of production," has a *double* significance: it both reinforces (reproduces) capitalist relations and undermines them, laying the material foundations for socialism. Reproduction thus has a twin identity: it is at once the strengthening of capitalist relations and movement beyond them.

These two insights are valuable for social analysis. The first enables us to place the particular activities of people in the context of society as a whole; the second enables us to comprehend the significance of those activities in terms of the larger movement of history. In this section of the critique, we will begin with a brief discussion of the Marxian notion of social production and then examine the social and historical significance of the activities of a particular subset of the PMC, engineers. Engineers are employed in what the Ehrenreichs call one of the "more clearly PMC occupations" and constitute the largest single profession outside of teaching in the U.S.; they are also very heavily represented at all levels of management, a reflection of the fact that the typical career pattern of an engineer is ten years (or less) of technical work followed by entry into middle management (and promotion to top management in many cases during the next two decades). The engineers, in short, are central to the notion of a professional-managerial class. Without their inclusion, the PMC would consist merely of state functionaries, ideologues, propagandists, perhaps teachers—that is, the professional-managerial class would leave out a large proportion of professionals and managers as well as the people who play perhaps the central role in capitalist production. This would be a different kettle of fish from the one the Ehrenreichs are trying to cook up. It is in the work of engineers that the unity of production and reproduction is most clearly seen, and with it, the folly of defining a class which includes engineers merely in terms of a function called "reproduction."

Marx derived his dialectical notion of social production from Hegel's conception of the dynamic, self-creating process of human labor. The individual, according to Hegel, defines his/her relationship to Nature, and to other human beings, in the activity of labor. At the same time, as he/she refashions the world in his/her own image, the individual remakes him/herself, developing new powers, new perceptions, a new identity. Marx's concept of social production is, in essence, Hegel's concept of individual labor raised to the level of society as a whole; both concepts describe a process of becoming, of change which preserves the past as it moves beyond it.

Social production both provides the material means of social survival (vis a vis Nature) and establishes the basic patterns of social life and the relations between people. Thus, production and reproduction are two different aspects of the same process; society, that is, the complex of social relationships corresponding to a particular mode of production, is reproduced "automatically" in the very process of production itself. Under capitalism, for example, production is not simply the creation of commodities but also the routine re-creation of the commodity production system (and thus of the alienation of labor, the routine exploitation of workers through the surplus value-generating wage labor system, the relations of domination, etc.). Production is the medium of capitalist social relations, the means whereby labor is extracted from labor power, embodied in commodities, and transformed into exchange value which in turn is the basis of capitalist power and the wherewithal to sustain control over the means of production and thus of society itself.

This loop of domination, however, is not eternal. It is true, of course, that modes of production are passed from one generation to another. Indeed, it was precisely because of this that, according to Marx, "a coherence arises in human history."[1] But, and this is the crucial matter,

1. Karl Marx, *Poverty of Philosophy* (New York: International Publishers, 1963), p. 181.

the forces of production are themselves undergoing change, change which is (potentially) mirrored in the structure of social life. Thus, social production is dynamic, a means of social self-development through history, the analog of labor activity in the self-development of the individual; and history therefore is more than a simple repetition of patterns set once and for all.

Because the forms of social production undergo change, as society discovers new ways of doing its work, the continued hegemony of those whose power rests upon an historically particular mode of production is contingent upon their being able to keep abreast of, and on top of, change. This is especially the case in a dynamic social system like capitalism where the spur of competition drives producers continually to find better ways of doing things. Those in power, in short, must strive to ensure that changes in the mode of production will take only those forms which will tend to sustain and perhaps reinforce their domination rather than pose a threat to it. Thus, while the forces of production condition the patterns of social relationships from generation to generation, and foster changes in those patterns as they undergo change themselves, so social relations of domination in turn condition the development of the forces of production, guiding it down certain paths and not others. But, whatever the outcome at a given time and place, the net result is a continual tension between forces of production and social relations, a tension, like that of class struggles that makes history move.

The key factor in Marx's theory of social production is the twofold significance of the independent development of the forces of production; although the forces of production are the product of previous generations and the reflection of the present one, insofar as they undergo their own internal evolution they also point beyond the present. Thus the development of the forces of production both serves to reinforce and (potentially) to eclipse the society in which it is embedded. Social relations and forces of production are at once in correspondence and contradiction. The production done under capitalism, for example, daily reproduces capitalist social relations. At the same time, however, the same development of productive power holds out the promise of a new social order. Industrial capitalism, in Marx's analysis, was based upon the private appropriation of the social surplus, dehumanizing labor and the routine exploitation of the many by the few. But it also gave rise to potent new modes of production—science-based, labor-saving, socially integrated—that hold out possibilities of cooperative enterprise, rational allocation of resources, and the fuller development of the human individual, possibilities through which to critically examine the present social system.

Given the requisite consciousness on the part of the exploited class (who catch a glimpse of their own latent potential in the actual process of socialized, scientific production)—itself a recognition of the disparity between the actuality and potentials of social production (the existent and possible social relations)—the contradiction erupts into revolution. In Marx's own words,"On the present false basis, every fresh development of the productive powers of labor must tend to deepen social contrasts and point out social antagonisms." Thus, although "forces of production and social relations...appear to capital as mere means, and are merely means for it to produce on its limited foundations...in fact, they are the material conditions to blow this foundation sky-high."[2]

Where do the PMC—in particular, the engineers—fit into this process of social production, a process, as we have now seen, that, on the one hand, reflects and reinforces (reproduces) capitalist social relations and, on the other, points beyond them, laying the foundation for a new social order? How meaningful is it to characterize engineers merely as "reproduction specialists?" Our discussion will be divided into two sections. First, we will critically assess the notion that engineers are "essentially non-productive" specialists in reproduction by attempting to clarify the nature of capitalist production and the nature of the transformation of capitalist production reflected in the emergence of the engineers in the first place. Are engineers involved in production? Do they make a contribution beyond simply doing what workers used to do without them? Second, we will examine the contradictory meaning of this transformation in the nature of production from the perspective of the larger sweep of human history. What is the relationship between "reproduction of capitalist social relations" and the creation of the material foundation of socialism?

To argue that the PMC is "essentially non-productive" is a curious assertion, especially with reference to that "more clearly PMC occupation," engineering. Engineers, the master-builders who brought science into the workshop, the hard-working no-nonsense heroes of boyhood pulp novels, the quintessential utilitarians whose motto was and is "production, production, and more production" are "essentially non-productive?" How have the Ehrenreichs come to such a strange conclusion? One possibility is that, after having recognized the ways in which various non-work-related activities of the family and the health-care system serve to reproduce capitalist social relations, the Ehrenreichs have pushed their insight back into the workplace. Another, not unrelated, explanation is that the Ehrenreichs are forced into such a seeming paradox by their mechanical separation of reproduction from production, and their implicit understanding that production is some-

---

2. Karl Marx cited in Shlomo Avineri, *Social and Political Thought of Karl Marx* (Cambridge: Cambridge University Press). p. 173, and *Grundrisse* (New York: Vintage, 1978), p. 706, Nicolaus translation.

thing good and reproduction is something bad. Since the good guys in the the story are the workers, and they are the producers, the bad guys— the bosses, the engineer managers—must be non-productive reproducers. To concede that engineers are productive too would muddle the analysis.

Engineers, of course, are productive *within the capitalist mode of production*. To argue otherwise would be to deny that capitalism is productive altogether. The Ehrenreichs themselves acknowledge this in another essay, "it is the host of managers, engineers, supervisory personnel, planners, etc.—not the average workers—who now *appear* necessary and essential to the production process and, of course, *are* necessary given the basic class antagonism inherent in capitalist production."[3] Engineers, then, *are* necessary in maintaining and promoting the capitalist mode of production, which is a mode of *production*. Hence, they are themselves productive in the capitalist sense of the term; they are involved in the production of commodities and thus in the reproduction of the commodity production system.

"Reproduction" is often distinguished from "production" in an effort to distinguish the specific relations of capitalism from the general capacities of human labor at a given time in history, or, more specifically, to distinguish "control over the workforce" from the production of goods. Here reproduction is bound up with the notion of "control" where control can mean, alternatively, preservation of capitalist class hegemony; the establishment, preservation, and extension of managerial prerogatives to determine the social organization and material means of production; the detailed managerial supervision of the actual production process, the ability to get the work out. Rarely are these several levels of control distinguished. Thus, prevention of mass strikes; the maintenance of managerial authority within a plant; the fragmenting and deskilling of workforce by means of minute division of labor, design of equipment, incentive pay schemes, job ladders, etc.; and the maintenance of shop discipline are all lumped together under "control of the workforce" (or "reproduction"). But, all of these forms of control over the workforce can be understood as means of capitalist production, which is, in part, *defined* as capitalist control over the workforce. It is precisely this fact, of course, that makes it so easy for people like engineers and other middle management to do their job. They are not exploiting people, or "controlling the workforce." They are just trying to get production through the plant as "efficiently" as possible. And they are. The only problem is that their sanitized, seemingly eternal and incorruptible language, like the work it describes, is already loaded with capitalist imperatives (centralization of control, lower labor cost, rational elimina-

2. John and Barbara Ehrenreich, "Work and Consciousness," *Monthly Review* (July 1976), p. 12.

tion of uncertainty—"human error," etc.). Efficiency means capitalist efficiency, the efficiency of men as machines. Production means reproduction.

The engineers are productive, then, in the sense that they render capitalist production more potent and profitable. In essence, this means that they intensify capitalist/managerial control over the process of production in order more effectively to extract labor from the workforce (or magnify that labor) and turn it into surplus value in the marketplace. And this generates profits which reinforce capitalist prerogatives and power to exercise command over production. Thus, production begets reproduction, which in turn begets production, etc. In this way, the particular productive activities of engineers, which reinforce the social relations of the workplace, are linked as well to the social relations of society as a whole.

If engineers are indeed productive within the capitalist mode of production, as supervisors of labor and creators of ever more potent (and profitable) means of production, what is the historical significance of their efforts? We have already seen that, to some extent, they function as agents of social reproduction, reinforcing capitalist relations of domination, but given the fact that the forces of production under their command change over time, as a consequence of their technical work, what are the implications of these new forms of productive activity in terms of the continued survival of capitalism as a social system? As we discussed above, in the Marxian scheme there is a fundamental tension between the evolving forces of production and the social relations of capitalism. The Ehrenreichs admit of such a tension when they intimate that "of course, efficiency, order and rationality are not in themselves capitalist goals," that such impulses, however much informed by capitalist imperatives are not wholly reducible to them. Something remains after the capitalist purposes are removed, a drive embedded within capitalism that points beyond it, and this creates a tension in the edifice, a tension embodied by the engineers themselves.

By emphasizing only the reproduction side of the engineers' function in society, and neglecting their productive role, the Ehrenreichs miss the contradictory significance of that productive role for capitalism, that it is at once a constructive and a potentially subversive agency. This contradictory nature of the engineers' social activity was seen most clearly by observers at the dawn of the twentieth century, many engineers being among them. Having given issue to what was perhaps the most dramatic transformation in the productive powers of the human species, the engineers found themselves caught up in a struggle between capitalists, on the one hand, and socialists, technocrats and other radicals , on the other, over what society would become as a consequence.

The central contradiction of capitalist society, the Ehrenreichs note, is that between "the socialized nature of the production process" (a good) and the "private appropriation of the fruits of production" (a bad). But how, one wonders, did the production process get "socialized" to begin with? What, and who, brought that about? The answer is capitalism and that means capitalists, managers, scientists and engineers (with substantial help from bankers, lawyers, judges, politicians and generals). The Ehrenreichs describe the PMC as having emerged solely to specialize in reproduction—to reinforce capitalist class relations that were, by the turn of the nineteenth century, strained to the breaking point. This interpretation provides a valuable corrective to liberal conventional accounts which characteristically leave out the class dimension, but the liberal blindspot here becomes the exclusive focus. They minimize the significance of the revolutionary transformation of production that was taking place and thus the role of the engineers in that transformation. They barely acknowledge the scope of the change: the concentration of control over manufacturing, the wedding of science to the useful arts (in the electrical and chemical industries but also in extractive, rubber, automobile, petroleum etc.), the enlargement of plants, the extension and interpenetration of industrial and consumer markets, the standardization of processes, the development of scientific disciplines, the growth of government regulation and planning functions. There were a number of different things going on here at once. Capitalists were indeed working to secure their control over production but, in addition, the material nature of that production itself was undergoing a dramatic transformation and capitalists were struggling to stay on top of it. The engineers embodied both of these developments. Thus it is absurd to argue as the Ehrenreichs do (twice!) that they (the PMC) "exist as a mass grouping *only* by virtue of the expropriation of skills and culture once indigenous to the working class." Such an argument accounts perhaps for the managerial expropriation of the craft skills of machinists (Taylorism), with the resulting creation of "process engineers," "method planners" and the like, but it hardly suffices to explain the emergence of electrical engineers or organic chemists, or statisticians. However much some new social types may have emerged solely in order to exercise managerial control functions, that is not to say that their skills (or culture) are merely derivative. That would suggest that their functions were formerly performed by workers, which they were not. The Ehrenreichs have identified a distinct new class, with its own function and culture, only to deny it its own function and culture because they fail to appreciate the major social changes which the emergence of this amorphous class reflected, changes which went beyond the mere appropriation of working class skills and culture by the capitalist class.

With their exclusive, reductionist emphasis upon the reproduction aspect of the engineers' work—their role in the expropriation of working class knowledge and the reinforcement of capitalist hegemony—the Ehrenreichs overlook the production aspect, with its double meaning. It was this second aspect, of course, that was emphasized by liberal technocratic radicals and socialists during the Progressive period of American history. These were people who were witnessing a major transformation of social production, one unprecedented in recorded history. The former were thus led to believe that capitalism had overcome its own evils; the latter were convinced that socialism was just around the corner.

Many liberals who were genuinely concerned about the horrors of capitalism developed a faith in the self-correcting capacities of the system early in the century. The Ehrenreichs themselves provide evidence for the plausability of the liberal interpretation, despite contrary intentions, in their example of the metric conversion debate. The Ehrenreichs portray the struggle as one between reform-minded engineers and conservative businessmen, between rationality and greed. In fact, it was a struggle between the newer science-based industries (allied with the "school culture" engineers and scientists in the professional associations) against the "shop culture" engineering profession which dominated the American Society of Mechanical Engineers and the machine metal-working industries. The latter stood to lose both status and power within the engineering profession—based upon their craft-type knowledge of the English system—as well as their investment in English standard capital equipment. Thus, to argue that the metric reform effort was "defeated by capitalist opposition" is to misrepresent what was happening. It fosters an image of a conflict between science and capitalism, between reason and greed, which could not possibly account for the fact that, in 1896 for example, *supporters* of metric conversion included Andrew Carnegie, Thomas Edison, George Westinghouse, Alexander Graham Bell and Henry Ford. Something "progressive" *was* happening to capitalism; this fact converted many radicals to liberalism and facilitated (while it reflected) the entry of many scientists and engineers (and social scientists) into the shiny new world of corporate capitalism.

If liberals viewed the transformation of social production as a new lease on life for capitalism, as the realization of an enlightened, scientific, humane social order, the socialists viewed the same process as a *prelude* to freedom and social regeneration. Thus Charles Steinmetz, like many social democrats of his day, identified the large, science-based, seemingly rational corporations, like his own General Electric, as agencies of the socialization of production and thus, willy nilly, as harbingers of socialism. Veblen similarly identified the scientific, no-nonsense engineers as the new revolutionaries, champions of reason and industry against the greed and wastefulness of commerce, the irrationality and anarchy of the market, the human suffering and degradation of capitalism. The engineers, Veblen believed, were the new vanguard who would lead the "social overturn" and usher in a new day of human freedom and freedom from want.

What then was the significance of this transformation, this change in capitalism that the "PMC" embody and reflect? Was it simply the reinforcement and elaboration of capitalist control over social production, as the Ehrenreichs suggest, and nothing *more*? Was it instead the emergence of a new, progressive, enlightened and rational capitalism, as the liberals maintained (and still maintain)? Or was it a signal that capitalism was on the way out, creating on its own "limited foundation" the material means for its (self) destruction, as the socialists believed? Ample evidence could be marshalled in support of each interpretation. Capitalism *was* strengthening its hold on social life, both within and without the workshop, as management became a "science" and markets were created to absorb the output of larger, more mechanized, better coordinated and more efficient manufacturing operations. Capitalism *was* changing for the better in the United States; grounded upon an expanding imperialism and a new scientific base, it was slowly moving from the sordid "paleotechnic" era into a cleaner "neotechnic era" (as Lewis Mumford viewed it), of electricity and government welfare programs and higher incomes.[4] And, finally, capitalism *was* at the same time, for purposes of economy, power, control, and stability bringing about more scientific, socially integrated production—the much heralded precondition for socialism. What then was the meaning of it all in terms of the larger movement of history?

Drawing upon recent critical historical scholarship, the Ehrenreichs emphasize that this transformation reflected changing relations between capital and labor, that it reinforced the position of the former vis a vis the latter, and that it was the work of a new breed of "reproduction specialists" (the PMC) rather than the logical outcome of some automatic, natural process of "increasing complexity" and "technological sophistication." In short, the Ehrenreichs have strived to reintroduce the role of purposive human action and the central significance of the class struggle into the discussion of recent American history, two very worthwhile goals. But their functionalist conception of the PMC is a distortion; the harsh glare of their spotlight blinds us to everything else, exaggerating and reifying just one side of a subtle and contradictory reality. Thus, they emphasize the "reproductive" aspect of the work of the engineers—exemplary members of the PMC—and ignore its reverse,

4. Lewis Mumford, *Technics and Civilization* (New York: Harcourt Brace)

productive, side within a more scientific, extended, and complex capitalism. And in doing this, they lose sight also of its double significance, especially its significance as productive activity that transscends capitalism. To be sure, the Ehrenreichs are right as far as they go. The vast majority of engineers diligently dedicated themselves to enhancing the profitability and stability (in securing greater managerial control over) capitalist social production. In so doing, they materially contributed, daily and devotedly, to the reproduction of capitalist social relations. That was their social purpose and more often than not they understood their role in the class struggle, however much it was obscured in the abstract, technical, depoliticized jargon of their trade: output, rationality, efficiency, productivity. But the Ehrenreichs end their discussion where they should, in reality, begin it. They neglect to look "behind the backs" of their protagonists, to try to comprehend the Cunning of Reason, the historical meaning of the engineers' work of which the engineers themselves have been perhaps unaware. Thus, they reject the liberal notion of an eternal, self-adjusting capitalism only to end up seconding such a notion themselves with their one-dimensional "objective comprehension" of social production, their cardboard PMC: it gets us nowhere. Are we to suppose that the "reproduction of capitalist social relations" has put an end to history, that capitalist forces of production are not at the same time socialist forces of production in embryo, that Science and Reason have abandoned the revolution for a split-level and a pension? The functionalist notion of the PMC, of specialists in reproduction, begs all these important questions; at the same time, it defies the original purpose with which the Ehrenreichs undertook their analysis in the first place, to find direction.

Conclusion

These final questions are not meant to be merely rhetorical; they demand answers. Marxists must begin to entertain the possibility that since the forces of production are designed and deployed not merely to maximize production but to maximize *capitalist* production, (that is, to reproduce capitalist social relations of production as well as "increase output") they might somehow bear the "imprint" of capitalism, of exploitative relations, of alienated labor, of domination. And if this is, in fact, the case, these forces of production might not suffice as the material basis for socialism. Moreover, in immediate terms, they might not appear on the surface to contradict capitalist social relations but to reaffirm them, to reinforce the notion that this is the only way of doing things. In short, Marxists must begin to critically reassess their simple and naive faith that every step toward greater efficiency and productivity is willy nilly a step toward socialism and they must cease to rely upon the internal contradictions of industrial capitalism—between scientific socialized forces of production and anachronistic capitalist social relations—to do their revolutionary work for them. They must confront these questions undogmatically and undertake to answer them historically, theoretically, empirically. Is there an historical discontinuity, a fatal disjuncture, between "capitalist forces of production" and "socialist forces of production?" In what ways have science and technology become merely—and finally, in their present form—the handmaidens to capitalist domination? (Do engineers design and deploy the forces of production in order to soften the contradictions of capitalism and stay the revolution?) Have the capitalist forces of production lost their second identity as the material basis for socialism? Recent critical scholarship has barely begun to raise such questions, much less answer them. Essentially, there are three, interrelated questions: 1) how does "capitalist production" differ from "socialist production?" 2) in what ways is capitalist production specific to and limited to capitalism? 3) what contradictions remain between capitalist forces of production and capitalist social relations?

As we struggle to answer these critical questions, we must keep in mind that Marxism is not the simple telling (or foretelling) of an automatic history. The contradiction between the two poles of social production—forces of production and social relations—is less apparent now than in Marx's time, or at the turn of the century, owing largely to the fact that science and engineering have themselves have become permeated with capitalist imperatives; thus, or so it seems, scientific production has merely strengthened capitalist production rather than eclipsing it altogether. But such appearances are not the end of the matter, they are the beginning. Appearances do not exist, they are perceived. The contradiction between forces of production and social relations has not disappeared: our perception of it has faded.

Marxists have during the twentieth century adopted hook, line, and sinker dominant liberal conceptions of production; in so doing, they have tacitly accepted the premise that capitalist forms of production are natural and immutable, the best—indeed the only—way of going about things. This means, of course, that radicals have incorporated notions of productivity most suitable for enhancing a mode of production grounded upon exploitation within their own analysis. At the same time, and most important, they have lost the capacity to identify capitalist production as such, owing to a restricted vision of the possible. In short, we tend to hold onto the only form of production we know and thus end up casting our stones at "reproduction." The only way we are ever going to get beyond this mimicry of capitalism is to begin to conceive of alternatives to capitalist production, alternatives which must arise, conceptually, from the juxtaposition of basic assumptions about the potentials of human beings—gleaned from the historical record of human accomplishment—with a rigorous identification of the possibilities latent in capitalist social production. That is, we must again take up the task Marx began and not be satisfied with superficial explanations. We must again become visionaries, as Marx was a visionary, with our feet on the ground. Only then will we be able to perceive the contradictions and make history move. For history does not move "by itself" any more than it can be stopped by the efforts of "reproduction specialists."

And this, finally, brings us to politics. The notion of the PMC is a feeble guide for those who would like to change things. The concept hypostatizes what is in actuality a rather contradictory, fluid, essentially indeterminate situation; it reduces people to a function, a social position, a particular place and time and, in so doing, denies the possibilities. Thus, it ought not be surprising that the Ehrenreichs should end their journey where they began it. Starting off their analysis with a criticism of the middle-class propensity toward subjectivism, they end with a call for more self-awareness, self-scrutiny, self-effacement, not less. Having failed to discover any promising paths along which to move, they urge their fellows to turn inward, to try to overcome the handicaps of their PMC heritage, their elitism and condescension toward the working class. The big hurdle is getting your head straight after all, cleaning up your act, making yourself presentable to the proletariat.

For those who subscribe to the notion of the PMC, this would be a challenge indeed. For the notion is doubly elitist. In its capacity as capitalist functionary, the PMC is portrayed as being marvelously able to reproduce capitalist social relations, relatively unhampered by the opposition of those whom it is charged to control, the working class. Thus, the analysis minimizes the significance of very real and potent struggles against managerial authority and exaggerates the success of the middle class PMC. And in its role as PMC Left, the PMC is identified as "the Left itself" rather than, more correctly, as the Left with access to the media, with visibility, with the leisure to write social theory and with relatively little need to fear reprisals for being Left. Such a conception is hardly likely to encourage alliances with the not-so-lucky working class Left, whose existence the PMC Left denies. Thus, there is indeed much self-searching to be done. But for the Ehrenreichs the search for objective understanding has merely come full circle. Itself yet another affirmation of middle class elitism, the analysis closes with yet another call for humility. We have not travelled very far.

5

Between the Lines

Robert Schaeffer & James Weinstein

John and Barbara Ehrenreich's attempt to analyze the predicament of the working class movement commands attention because it strikes a familiar theoretical chord within the socialist left. The successive elaboration of "new" classes between the proletariat and bourgeoisie—new middle, new surplus middle, new bureaucratic, new petty bourgeois, new working, professional-managerial—has consumed the energies and absorbed the attention of activists and scholars throughout the last decade.[1]

The Ehrenreichs, like the others, have sought to determine the "objective" criteria that define classes—criteria that have essentially differentiated among groups of people. But this process of differentiation neglects the conditions shared among groups of people. Marx argued that class analysis proceeds from the abstract (the process of amassing similarities common to people) to the concrete (the process of differentiating between people). With the inversion of this methodology, by proceeding from the concrete to the abstract, class analysis in the United States has foundered on the reefs of bourgeois sociology. By elaborating a multiplicity of dicrete and antagonistic social classes based on their own arbitrary, concrete class determinants, the Ehrenreichs, like other left theorists, have contributed to the endless differentiation, stratification, and segmentation of people in capitalist society.

It is not accidental that the division and segmentation of classes in the United States should create a theoretical prison that reflects the left's political and practical isolation, and mirrors its division. The connection between the condition of the left and the position of left theorists is equally evident when we examine the Ehrenreichs' professional managerial class (PMC). In order to apprehend this connection we must first understand their political position. Their political convictions, after all, furnish the intelletual glue that holds the PMC together in the Ehrenreichs' minds.

The political convictions that weld together the theoretical construction of the PMC are both implicit and explicit. Their *implicit* outlook is the conviction that class struggles in China are relevant to the American situation. Drawing upon John Ehrenreich's analysis of class struggles in China, the Ehrenreichs graft a Chinese PMC onto the American class structure.[2] The Ehrenreichs' *explicit*, or ostensible political purpose is to criticise the New Left from a Chinese vantage point, to expose the radicals' connection with a class at odds with the proletariat and bourgeoisie.

In order to give substance to the claim that the class origins of student radicals undermined the social aims and compromised the political activity of the New Left, the Ehrenreichs trace this class back to the socialists and progressives of the turn of the century. By drawing a comparison between the Chinese PMC and its American counterpart, the Ehrenreichs implicitly admonish the New Left for failing to measure up to the standards set by the Great Proletarian Cultural Revolution and the Movement to Criticize Lin Piao and Confucious taking place at the same time in China.

1. A discussion of the various new class theories can be found in Robert Schaeffer's article, "A Critique of the 'New Class' Theorists: Towards a Theory of the Working Class in America," *Social Praxis,* Vol. 4, #1&2, pp. 71-95. The authors of the classes referred to here are: new middle (Carchedi), new surplus middle (Nicolaus, Anderson), new bureaucratic (Hodges), new petty-bourgeois (Poulantzas), new working (Harrington, Glaberman, Weir), and professional-managerial (Ehrenreich and Ehrenreich).

2. See John Ehrenreich, "The Dictatorship of the Proletariat in China," *Monthly Review,* (October 1975).

In the "Dictatorship of the Proletariat in China," John Ehrenreich presented an analysis of the political struggles in contemporary China. The focus of the struggle was a campaign by the popular masses aimed at preventing a class of revisionists from resurrecting capitalism in China. He argues that this class of revisionists was composed of educated, mental, unproductive managers and party bureaucrats who sought to establish for themselves a network of privileges, prerogatives, and power over others (what the Chinese called "bourgeois right") that could, in the end, resuscitate capitalist class relations.

Chinese society, John Ehrenreich maintains, "is characterized by three differences—the difference between city and countryside, between worker and peasant, and between manual and mental labor...." Only the last gap concerns us here, for in it we find the germ of the PMC. "Mental workers," John Ehrenreich insists, "managers, officials, professionals, technicians—earn more than manual workers, have higher educational levels, tend to have more interesting jobs, and are often in positions where they have power over manual workers...the advantages and power of mental workers clearly contain the roots of a 'new class' which could gradually take over real control of the means of production and restore capitalism."[3]

The similarities between this "new class" in China and what the Ehrenreichs later called the PMC in the U.S. are striking. Like the Chinese, the American PMC consists of educated, salaried, unproductive mental workers who control other workers as managers or confront them as experts. They also seek to extend their prerogatives and privileges as professionals—people who control "a specialized body of knowledge, accessible only by lengthy training." [p. 26]

They do, presumably, differ in one important respect. The "new class" in China, as a class seeking real control over the organization of the forces and relations of production, presents itself as a proto-bourgeois class. That is the reason for underlining the danger of a *capitalist* restoration. The PMC in America, on the other hand, is not seen by the Ehrenreichs as endowed with proto-bourgeois sentiments but rather is openly hostile to the bourgeoisie. Why the American PMC should differ from the Chinese in this regard is not explained but remains a curious anomaly in the Ehrenreichs' theorization.

The problem, however, is not what insights can be gained from the Chinese experience, but whether the Chinese class struggles are relevant to the articulation of classes in America. Three objections can be raised.

First, the Ehrenreichs depict the struggle between manual and mental labor and the rise of the PMC as a global phenomena: "Arab

3. Ibid., pp. 19-20.

Socialism, African Socialism, and military socialism (pre 1975 Peru) can be understood not as a petit-bourgeois socialism but PMC socialism, based on the rising class of civilian and military government mental workers." [p. 43] Thus the manual-mental distinction emerges as a primary contradiction on the geo-political terrain. The particular class struggles, social movements and national liberation struggles are subordinated to the conflict arising out of the emergence of a world wide PMC. Their emphasis on the primacy of mental labor obliterates the important economic, social and political distinctions between these movements. It distorts an analysis of their internal character to suit the exigencies of Chinese domestic and foreign policy. For anyone interested in setting these national movements against the backdrop of imperialism, the endemic economic crisis, and the capitalist world system as a whole, this subordination is untenable.

Second, by deriving the manual-mental distinction from the Chinese experience and then using it as a device for analyzing class struggle in America, the Ehrenreichs have created enormous historical and theoretical problems for themselves. To compare the struggles taking place in one part of the world, conditioned as they are by long and particular historical developments, with that of another without theorizing the unifying connection between these spatially and temporally diverse movements is unMarxist, ahistorical, and rudely simplistic.

The debate over manual and mental labor, red vs. expert, is taking place within the context of a socialist country during a period characterized by the "dictatorship of the proletariat." No such situation obtains in the United States. China has had a complex class structure: one that resisted colonial and imperialist penetration from the outside while at the same time resisting the transformation of forces and relations of production internally. By contrast probably no country in the world has been as thoroughly conditioned by capitalist production and bourgeois class relations as the United States. Nor can the United States be located in the same relation to the capitalist world economy as China. The U.S. is at the center of the industrial capitalist world; China is at its periphery. To insist upon the manual-mental distinction as a valid measure of class struggle in the two countries is to insist upon transcendental rather than materialist analysis.

Third, even if we take a more limited view, the Ehrenreichs' assessment that "the new left (in the U.S.), which is predominantly drawn from the PMC, must address itself to the subjective and cultural aspects of class oppression as well as to material inequalities; it must commit itself to uprooting its own ingrained and often subtle attitudes of condescension and elitism" [p. 45] belies their conviction that the new left failed to address the same problem or attain the same degree of success as the

Cultural Revolution in rooting out the ossification of leaders in the state and party apparatuses and in destroying the prerogatives and prerequisites of power. It must be noted that Communist Party bureaucrats and technical managers did not themselves initiate or uproot the "subtle attitudes of elitism and condescension." The attack on these attitudes was initiated by people outside (and above) their ranks and carried out under the watchful eye of the red guard and popular masses. The notion that one must undertake a thoroughgoing self-criticism is an idea proper to a revolutionary *party* that seeks to link its cadre to the conditions and aspirations of the popular masses. It is not the attribute of a social *class*.

Putting aside the problem of utilizing a Chinese model in examining the United States, let us examine the Ehrenreichs' definition of the PMC on its own terms.

Since the Ehrenreichs claim that their theory of the PMC is a departure from previous theories, in particular Mills and the new communist movements, we must first ask, "How is the theory of the PMC different from other middle class theories?" And since a body of literature exists addressing the rise of new middle classes, we must also ask, "What does the Ehrenreichs' theory of the PMC have in common with the other theories?"

If we put aside the obvious political differences and the Chinese origin of the PMC,[4] the Ehrenreichs' theory of the PMC differs from the other new class theories in several ways. The Ehrenreichs emphasize mental labor as a qualification more than Poulantzas and Gorz do, but the emphasis is a matter of degree, not substance. They also claim that the PMC has its origins in the progressive and socialist movements of the early 1900's. All the other theorists tend to think that the middle class is a relatively "new" phenomena, and for that reason undeveloped by Marx, emerging most clearly after World War II.[5] But these relatively minor

4. We don't mean to slight the political difference between people in the new communist movements, the remnants of the new left, and the Ehrenreichs. Their perceived differences are obviously important; however, we are not concerned with the political positions or strategic implications, but rather with the theoretical approach of these people. When one looks at that, the political differences tend to dissolve and, to our surprise and their astonishment, the analytic-methodological-theoretical similarity stands starkly revealed. See Schaeffer, *Social Praxis*.

5. Most theorists—Poulantzas, Hodges, Anderson, Gorz, Brudish, Carchedi, Nicolaus, Braverman, Sweezy—tend to see the new middle classes emerging along with the rapid expansion of the US on a world scale, and the expansion of the productive forces that accompanied the permanent war economy following the Second World War.

differences should not distract us from the fundamental similarity of these theories.

The Ehrenreichs' criteria for distinguishing the PMC from the working class are strikingly similar to the criteria used to determine class by other new middle class theorists. And they share a common failing. They begin by looking at the different forms that labor takes under monopoly capitalism, describing how they differ from one another and then deriving separate social classes according to the attributes of specific kinds of labor. We will argue that this is no different from the method employed by bourgeois social scientists whose differentiation between groups of people *preceeds* the abstraction of the amassing of similarities and common conditions shared among groups of people.[6] The choice of which attribute to assign importance in the "objective" determination of classes becomes purely arbitrary.[7]

Marx's Method

Marx's method of class analysis begins by abstracting people's common relation to capital (taken as a whole) and then demonstrates that the relation between capital and labor is based on abstract labor: "The production of surplus value is determined by the physical expenditure of living, abstract and homogenous labor in the sphere of production.[8] This relation is premised on the reduction of labor to a

6. Bourgeois social scientists, unlike the new class theorists, become so bogged down in differentiating that they have no time to abstract classes from their studies, nor do they care to. New class theorists readily elaborate classes out of their studies, but bourgeois social scientists are probably correct in pointing out that they have little justification for doing so.

7. The disagreement of these theorists over which criteria, which attribute or set of attributes to assign primacy provides an indication of the extent of the arbitrariness. The fractured theoretical disagreement more than anything else reflects the isolation from which the theory of the left in this country is conceived.

8. Quoted in Ernest Mandel, *Late Capitalism* (London: New Left Books, 1975), pp. 100-01. See also I.I. Rubin, *Essays on Marx's Theory of Value* (Detroit: Black and Red, 1972), pp. 140-41:

It is obvious that abstract labor is contrasted to concrete labor. Abstract labor is related to a definite social form, and expresses determined relations of man to man in the process of production. Concrete labor is the definition of labor in terms of its *material technical properties*. Abstract labor includes the definition of *social forms* of organization of human labor. This is not a generic and specific definition of labor, but the analysis of labor from two standpoints: the material-technical and the social. The concept of abstract labor expresses the characteristics of the social organization of labor in a commodity capitalist society.

Rubin illustrates the point that we are interested in: the organization of *social*

position of dependence on capital, which alone could provide it with a means of surviving.

This relation is not based on what Marx called concrete hetero-geneous labor (labor in all its complex and variegated forms)—labor with different skills performing different tasks within the capitalist division of labor. Marx insisted on the former, abstract labor, being the necessary tool of class analysis because capital continually puts living labor to different uses. And these uses change over time.

The particular kinds of labor, skills, and jobs employed by capital are always undergoing change. Capital is not tied to *any* particular kind of concrete labor, just as it is evident that no job is sacrosanct under capital. Capital can always subdivide or combine that labor, replace it with a machine, or give it to a new worker (peasant, immigrant, migrant, child, woman, black, etc.) and thereby change the character, attribute, type, intensity, location, duration and degree of skill of that labor.

When people base class analysis on the concrete labor or specific attributes of types of jobs employed within the capitalist division of labor, as the Ehrenreichs and the new class theorists do, the process whereby these forms of labor are produced, changed and reproduced anew, frequently under a new guise, completely eludes them.[9] By beginning with a process of differentiation and generating classes out of those distinctions, these theorists perceive only a partial view of the relation between capital and labor and their attempts to analyze classes in contemporary capitalist society are continually frustrated.

classes, not the material-technical or concrete properties of those classes. This, of course, is precisely the error the Ehrenreichs and the new class theorists make.

9. There have been two ways of approaching the transformation of concrete labor in capitalist society. The first way, generally adopted by the new working class theorists (Harrington, Weir, Mallet, Glaberman, Szymanski), has seen in the development of capitalist production a tendency towards proletarianization of all kinds of labor. The division of people into the two great classes—proletariat and bourgeoisie—has proceeded apace, usually at the expense of petty commodity producers and the petty bourgeoisie. Different social groupings are progressively fused into the condition of wage labor and expand the working class.

In contrast to this approach, a second group who we have described as new middle class theorists (Poulantzas, Hodges, Anderson, Carchedi, Nicolaus, Ehrenreich) view capitalist production evolving in quite a different way. Instead of a tendency towards proletarianization—the fusion of people into an expanded working class—they argue that the exigencies of capitalist production have created new classes between the proletariat and bourgeoisie. They characterize the dominant tendency in the development of capitalism as one that produces segmentation—the fission of wage labor into discrete, heirarchical, and, one might even say, stratified groupings—which creates classes orbiting somewhere between the two great poles.

Income Determinations: Salary and Wage

The Ehrenreichs "define the PMC as consisting of salaried, mental workers" who are "essentially non-productive...who do not own the means of production and whose major function in the social division of labor may be described broadly as the reproduction of capitalist culture and capitalist class relations." [pp. 12, 14] Salaried, mental, non-productive—all three are crucial for the identification of the PMC. They assume certain relations between people and imply others. Let us begin with the term salary. What kind of relationship does it presume and what is the implication of using it?

The category salary presumes a relation between salary and wage. It implies that they constitute a separate relation to the payer of income, the capitalist. The Ehrenreichs assume that PMC people receive a salary and working class people are paid a wage, and they imply that this separate means of payment constitutes a class distinction.

But what is the difference between a wage and a salary? The wage is paid hourly, daily, weekly, or bi-weekly; it varies according to the actual time worked, and sometimes varies according to the amount produced. The salary is usually paid monthly and does not vary according to the actual time worked, but presumes that the time will amount to 40 hours a week (or more) for the month as a whole. Why should the difference between getting a bi-weekly check and a monthly check substantially affect the character of labor? Conversely, why shouldn't we make a distinction between those who get paid at the end of the day (farm laborers for example) and those who have a more secure weekly income? For that matter, why not make a distinction between those who receive payments in kind, those who work piece rate, on commission or on a cost-

Both approaches are wrong; both are right. They are wrong in that they are partial; they are right in trying to apprehend the tendency of capitalist development. I would argue that the tendencies toward proletarianization and segmentation occur simultaneously, and are necessary and complementary tendencies within the context of the production, reproduction, and accumulation of capital. People are attracted from the periphery of capitalist relations (immigrants, contract laborers), from its center (young people, women, national minorities), from its intermediate strata (professionals, petty bourgeoisie, crafts people), and fused in to the common condition of wage labor so that they can be used and consumed in the expanded reproduction of capital. At the same time, workers are repelled from capitalist production through retirement (old people, workers with used-up labor power), by the introduction of machines that replace workers, and by shunting people into the reserve army (there to reenter the production process or to remain indefinately). The rythm of attraction and repulsion (proletarianization—segmentation) is the *normal* pulse of capital accumulation; wage labor is its life-blood.

plus contract basis? As Braverman has shown, salaried workers are frequently paid less than people who receive a wage and wage workers with unions frequently have greater job security. The only difference analytically is the frequency of payment, and that is hardly the basis of a class distinction.

When Marx talked about "wage labor" he was not talking about the laboring wage. The laboring wage and its mode of payment differs from worker to worker, firm to firm, and from country to country without ever affecting the character of wage *labor*—the need to sell one's labor power to the capitalist in order to survive. As Marx says, "Manufacture therefore develops a hierarchy of labor powers, to which there corresponds a scale of wages."[10] The amount of "wage," the price one can get from the capitalist, and the particular form the wage can take—paper script from the company; dollars, yen, marks, rubles; at the end of the day or the end of the year—varies widely under capitalism. It always will. It takes different forms and changes over time according to the demands made on capital by the workers and according to the prerogatives of the capitalist. That is why it is irrelevant to the determination of working class identity.

There is something else implied by salary when it is used in conjunction with the term unproductive. The Ehrenreichs, and most new middle class theorists, imply that the crucial difference between wage and salary is that a person receiving a wage is paid for *producing* surplus value, while a person receiving a salary is paid, at least in part, *from* the surplus value created by the wage laborer.[11] The Ehrenreichs argue that, "The PMC's existence presupposes that the social surplus has to be developed to a point to sustain the PMC in addition to the bourgeoisie, for the PMC is essentially non-productive." [p. 14]

10. Karl Marx, *Capital*, 3 Vols. (New York: International Publishers, 1967), 1:349.
   It has already been shown in general that wages of labor, or price of labor, is but an irrational expression for the value of labor, or price of labor power; and the specific conditions under which labor power is sold, have nothing to do with labor as a general agent in production. [Marx, *Capital*, 3:802-03]

11. See for example Hodges, Carchedi, Nicolaus and Anderson. For Donald Hodges classes are defined "in terms of relations of exploitation...which in turn are determined by the level of wages, by the share of income that is revenue—that part derived from the production of surplus value." The notion that income distribution determines class relations is shared by a number of writers in different forms. Carchedi talks about the two aspects of economic class determination being "the wage component and the revenue component." Nicolaus and Anderson describe the surplus class as being determined by the "consumption of

The Ehrenreichs assume that it is the working class who produces, both surplus value and the "social surplus," and imply that the PMC simply consumes part of it in order to survive as a class. But since they don't appropriate it directly (that's the job of the capitalist), how do they receive their share of the surplus value created by the working class? What is the mechanism, the mode of appropriation for this class? This is extremely important since it is through this mechanism that the PMC allegedly exploits the working class.

Though the Ehrenreichs don't spell this out as explicitly as other new middle class theorists, the answer is: through their salary. Their salary is the mechanism that enables them to share in the exploitation of the working class. It is also the mechanism that keeps them dependent on the capitalist class, since it is the capitalist who pays them a portion of surplus value through its revenue. In Marxist terms the Ehrenreichs are arguing that the PMC is paid a portion of *revenue* accruing to the capitalist class.

But the relation of the capitalist to the salaried worker is one where the owner of money (the capitalist) buys up, *prior* to the labor process itself, the title to the entire product of labor from the owner of labor power (the worker). The Ehrenreichs assume the opposite of this: they see the process as sequential and temporal—the capitalist extracts surplus value from the worker and *then* pays for the labor of the salaried worker from that same revenue or money fund. But this is not the case. Wage or salary is not a share of the return on the product of labor, rather it is the *price* of buying up every possible claim to a share of it; the capitalist does not share the revenue accruing to it (except with other capitalists, owners of land, sellers of its commodities.)[12]

If we agreed that salary represented a share of the surplus value, a

the surplus produced by the productive class." These writers share the view that salaried workers, workers who receive a portion of *revenue* are receiving a cut or share of the surplus value produced by others. but this is a misreading of Marx. Determining a class by the distribution of income assumes that distribution categories determine production categories—an inversion of production and distribution in the determination of wage labor. See Schaeffer, *Social Praxis*, pp. 80-81.

12. This (surplus value) like the portion of value which replaces the variable capital advances in wages, is a value newly created by the laborer during the process of production—congealed labor. But it does not cost the owner of the entire product, the capitalist, anything. This circumstance actually permits the capitalist to consume the surplus value entirely as revenue, unless he has to surrender parts of it to other participants—such as ground rent to the landlord, in which case such portions constitute a revenue of such third persons. [Marx, *Capital*, 2:387-88.]

portion of the revenue produced by the working class and accruing to capital, we would have to accept the logic of the bourgeois economic category of overhead. Overhead is a concept used by the capitalist to charge off some part of the labor force against some other part of the labor force, a ploy useful for disguising profitability and avoiding tax liability among other things. It seems ironic that left theorists should accept the logic of this and use it in their own analysis.[13]

The working class is made up of wage laborers, those who sell their labor power to capital at a price, and is determined by wage labor; it is not determined by the laboring wage, salary, commission, or piece-rate. The opposition of the categories wage and salary is a false dichotomy that vitiates class analysis.

Concrete Labor Determinations: Mental Labor

The Ehrenreichs use the term mental workers as a second distinguishing feature of the PMC. They argue that "technical workers, managerial workers, 'culture producers'—must be understood as comprising a distinct class in monopoly capitalist society." [p. 9] As *members* of this class they share a number of things in common, "a common relation to the economic foundations of society...a common lifestyle, educational background, kinship networks, consumption patterns, work habits, beliefs..." [p.11] But as *workers* they share one important attribute: they are all mental workers. Referring to "workers in the State and other ideological apparatuses—schools, government agencies, welfare agencies, (and) mass media," the Ehrenreichs conclude, "the problem then, is where to place these mental workers in the class structure of capitalist society." [p. 9]

If we take these workers in these jobs, in the schools and government agencies, we can certainly find other attributes *common* to them as *workers*. Most of them work in offices rather than in factories; most of them provide services rather than produce goods; few of them have to punch in or out at a time clock, few of them work in shifts around the clock or at night; and most of them wear white collars instead of blue collars. For years sociologists have used these attributes derived from different jobs to define separate strata and ascertain their status. The white collar-blue collar distinction was a favorite category, used by Marxists and non-Marxists alike for many years. But the distinction

---

13. Revenue for the worker is not the same as revenue for the capitalist; the first is determined by the price of labor power—the means of subsistence; the second is determined by the realization of surplus value embodied in the product of labor. [Schaeffer, *Social Praxis*, p. 81] See also Karl Marx, *Capital*, 3:817-18, 856.

between white and blue collar—now dissolving rapidly under the impact of leisure suits and double-knits—illustrates the difficulty of depending on job attributes to distinguish between classes in our society. Job attributes, the way a particular job is done, the particular relationship of the worker to the object of work—whether he or she uses hands or mind to shape the product of labor—is immaterial to the determination of class.

To what extent can we in fact distinguish between manual and mental labor? Gramsci for instance attacks the idea that *any* laboring activity can be arbitrarily rendered purely manual or purely mental under the aegis of capital. He says that people like Frederick Taylor tried to achieve just such a separation but failed because they could not (any more than capital) eliminate the human character of labor. The whole distinction is based on an impossibility. Capital cannot on the one hand employ pure mental labor since it would produce no commodity or surplus value and on the other hand it cannot reduce physical labor to that of a "Trained Gorilla" (Taylor's goal) without eliminating human labor completely. Gramsci, referring to manual-mental labor, pointed out:

> The most widespread error of method seems to me that of having looked for this criterion of distinction in the intrinsic nature of intellectual activities, rather than in the ensemble of the system of relations in which these activities have their place within the general complex of social relations. Indeed the worker or proletarian, for example, is not specifically characterized by his manual or instrumental work, but by performing this work in specific conditions and in specific social relations.... in any physical work, even the most degraded and mechanical, there exists a minimum of creative intellectual activity.... All men are intellectuals, one could therefore say: but not all men have in society the function of intellectuals. When one distinguishes between intellectuals and non-intellectuals, one is referring in reality only to the *immediate* social function of the professional category of the intellectuals.[14] (emphasis added)

14. Antonio Gramsci, *Selections from the Prison Notebooks*, ed. Quintin Hoare and Geoffrey Nowell Smith (New York: International Publishers, 1971), pp. 8-9. He also discusses the manual character of ostensibly mental labor in a passage that is one of our favorites:

Many people have to be persuaded that studying too is a job, and a very tiring one, with its own particular apprenticeship—involving muscles and nerves as well as intellect. It is a process of adaptation, a habit acquired with effort, tedium and even suffering....Many even think that the difficulties of learning are artificial, since they are accustomed to think only of manual work as sweat and toil. The question is a complex

Even if we cannot draw a hard and fast distinction between manual and mental labor, can we separate them by degree? Intuitively the distinction finds resonance in our experience even though it might not be theoretically useful. It is useful descriptively, as indeed all other categories of job attributes are intelligent as description. But description is different from analysis. The Ehrenreichs insist that manual and mental are distinguishable without showing why this should be so. They never spell out why mental labor differs from manual labor, but they infer that the cutting edge between them is education—whether or not one has been to college. They see college as the place where people are trained in the subtleties of mental labor and they imply that the working class consists of people who are "non-college educated." [p. 14] If that were the case then the working class would be shrinking since working class people now send their children to college. The Ehrenreichs also neglect to distinguish between the various tiers of collegiate education—some are the playgrounds for the rich, some are the sandlots of the poor—but they all get lumped together into training grounds for the PMC.

Does college education provide an analytic cutting edge between these two forms of labor? If it once did, its blade has in recent years become dull. Ernest Mandel offers a quite different perspective on the position of education and its relation to types of concrete labor in *Late Capitalism:*

> The hallmark of the growth of scientific intellectual labor—elicited by the cumulative growth of scientific knowledge, research and development, and ultimately determined by accelerated technological development—is the *massive reunification* (emphasis ours) of intellectual and productive activity, and the entry of intellectual labor into the sphere of production. Since this re-introduction of intellectual labor into the process of production corresponds to the immediate needs of late capitalist technology, the education of intellectual workers must be likewise strictly subordinated to these needs. The result is the crisis of the classical humanist university...the main task of the university is no longer to produce 'educated

one. Undoubtably the child of a traditional intellectual family acquires this psycho-physical adaptation more easily. Before he ever enters the classroom he has numerous advantages over his comrades, and is already in possession of attitudes learnt from his family environment, he concentrates more easily, since he is used to 'sitting still' etc. similarly the son of a city worker suffers less when he goes to work in a factory than does a peasant's child or a young peasant already formed by country life. [Ibid., pp. 42-43. See also p. 302 and pp. 309-10.]

men' of judgement and property—but to produce intellectually skilled wage earners for the production and circulation of commodities.[15]

Colleges are now producing "intellectually qualified wage labor" that can be fused into productive labor in industry.[16] Universities no longer exclusively produce educated entrepreneurs, independent professionals and ruling class ideologues, as was their main function in the last century. Now they are providing people with skills and outlooks necessary for production in modern capitalism. A situation has developed, as Marx maintained, in which "all the sciences have been pressed into the service of capital and in which invention becomes a branch of business and the application of science to direct production itself becomes a prospect which determines and solicits it."[17] As capital relies increasingly on the "wedding of the useful arts to industry" (to paraphrase David Noble), science and technology is transformed into capital, into instruments of production, and intellectual labor is reduced to the condition of wage labor.[18]

The Ehrenreichs insist that mental labor is the basis of a class distinction. But calling a particular kind of laboring activity "mental" is

15. Mandel, *Late Capitalism* (London: New Left Books, 1975), pp. 260-261: The more higher education becomes a qualification for specific labor processes, the more intellectual work becomes proletarianized, in other words transformed into a commodity....The further this process of proletarianization advances, the deeper the division of labor becomes entrenched within the sciences, accompanied inevitably by increasing overspecialization and "expert idiocy," and the more students become prisoners of a blinkered education strictly subordinated to the conditions of the valorization of capital....This is the underlying socio-economic basis of the spreading student revolt in late capitalism, and the mark of its objectively anti-capitalist drive." Ibid. See pp. 248-273 for a discussion of the role of technical, managerial, scientific and intellectual workers set in a wider context than the Ehrenreichs provide or would allow.

16. Mandel goes on to distinguish two groups of 'intellectually qualified labor' within society: 1) those integrated into the process of production, and 2) those integrated into the administrative and superstructural institutions. He argues that although the first group tends not to "identify subjectively with the interests of capital," and the second "typically induces a general identification of their function with the interests of the entrepreneurial bourgeoisie," neither identifies subjectively with itself as a class. Mandel, *Late Capitalism*, pp. 264-65.

17. Karl Marx, *Grundrisse*, trans. Martin Nicolaus (New York: Vintage Books, 1973), pp. 703-04.

18. See David Noble, *America by Design* (New York: Alfred Knopf, 1977).

arbitrary and descriptive. We can endlessly describe activities of labor employed by capital and insist that each task is different from all others. The choice as to which attribute to fix upon (mental, white collar, etc.) is, however, subjective. We cannot, by the Ehrenreichs' method, ever appreciate the similarities among workers or types of labor, and we cannot apprehend classes in capitalist society since concrete labor determinations slip through our analysis like so many grains of sand through a sieve.

Production Determinations: Unproductive Workers

The third feature of the Ehrenreichs' PMC is that it consists of "unproductive" workers. The concept of productive and unproductive is specific to Marx and to Marxism. Marx considered workers who produced surplus value for their employers to be productive. His initial use of this term was in regard to workers directly involved in production, but it included all those wage or salaried workers whose activity was necessary for the realization of surplus value by the capitalists. In Marx's view, this meant that engineers who rationalized the production process or refined products, supervisory personnel who increased the efficiency or output of the manual workers, maintenance workers who kept machines in working order, clerks who kept the flow of materials going were all productive.

Indeed, Marx went much further than this. He considered all workers who helped capitalists realize surplus value, whether the workers were involved in production or circulation, as productive. Thus in Marx's discussion of merchant capital, he wrote that while "the commercial laborer does not produce any surplus value directly," like the industrial worker, "the value of his labor is determined by the value of his labor power."[19] Further, the commercial workers (store clerks, etc.) added to the income of the capitalist "by helping him to reduce the costs of the realization of surplus value" and "in so doing, he performs partly unpaid labor."[20] Thus, while for "industrial capital, the expenses of circulation appear to be dead expenses," for the merchant they appear "as a source of profit." The investment made by merchant capital for the expense of circulation "is, therefore, a productive investment. And for this reason the commercial labor which it buys is likewise immediately productive for it."[21]

Marx argued that the labor of the "overlooker, engineer, manager, clerk, etc.—in a word, the labor of the whole personnel required in a

19. Karl Marx, *Capital*, 3 Vols. (Chicago: Charles Kerr, 1898), 3:353.
20. Ibid., p. 354.
21. Ibid., p. 356.

particular sphere of production...in fact add their aggregate labor to the constant capital, and increase the value of the product by this amount."[22]

The Ehrenreichs, following Poulantzas and Braverman, use the vulgar common sense meaning of productive, and do not use it the way Marx did. But the concept has no meaning outside of Marx. To define productive labor as that involved only in the production of commodities having apparent use value, as the Ehrenreichs do, clearly is at odds with Marx's conception.

Marx noted that commodities, embodying both use and exchange values, are not merely produced objects since the labor contained in them can be transformed into different physical and immaterial forms (as in the transformation of commodities into money or stock). What is important are the relations the commodity represents, not the function the commodity plays.[23] Marx insisted that "these definitions (of productive labor) are therefore not derived from the material characteristics of labor (neither from the nature of its product nor from the particular character of the labor as concrete labor) but from the definite social form, the social relations within which labor is realized."[24] He noted that, "This distinction between productive and unproductive has nothing to do with the particular specialty of the labor or with the particular use value in

22. Karl Marx, *Theories of Surplus Value,* 3 Vols. (Moscow: Foreign Languages Publication House, 1956), 1:160. See also Rubin, *Marx's Theory of Value,* p. 265:

> Intellectual laborers are supposed to be (for many theorists) indispensable for the process of production, and thus they 'earn' rewards for products created by physical workers. According to Marx, however, they create new value, from this value they receive a reward, leaving part of this value in the hands of the capitalist in the form of unpaid value, surplus value.

23. Intellectual labor necessary for the process of material production in no way differs from physical labor. It is productive if it is *organized* on capitalist principles. In this case it is completely the same thing whether the intellectual labor is organized together with the physical labor in an enterprise (engineering bureau, chemical laboratory, or an accounting bureau in a factory) or separated into an independent enterprise (an independent experimental chemical laboratory which has the task of improving production, and so on). [Ibid., p. 265.]

24. Marx, *Theories of Surplus Value,* 1:153. I.I. Rubin elaborates:
In other words, labor is considered productive or unproductive not from the standpoint of its *content,* namely in terms of the character of concrete working activity, but from the standpoint of the social form of *organization,* of its consistency with the production relations which characterize the given economic order of society. [Rubin, *Marx's Theory of Value,* pp. 261-62.]

which this special labor is incorporated."[25] And finally, he maintained that, "Included among productive workers, of course, are all those who contribute in one way or another to the production of a commodity, from the actual operatives to the manager or engineer (as distinct from the capitalist)."[26]

The production of commodities must be considered as a whole, not from the point of view of the individual laborer. Yet people who use the productive-unproductive distinction insist that people can be classified one way or the other according to their particular function in the production process. Production for the Ehrenreichs becomes confined to factory production, and commodity production becomes confined to the creation of use values.[27]

The proletariat itself is composed of both productive and unproductive workers. By productive we mean wage labor consumed by capital. However, the proletariat, people produced or reduced to wage labor in capitalist society, is always larger than the portion of wage labor employed by capital at a given time. Using the Ehrenreichs' criteria, however, we would say that the reserve army of unemployed is unproductive and should be excluded from the working class. But it is absurd to say that the unemployed automatically drop out of the working class simply because capital relegates them to the surplus population.

Marx never used productive-unproductive to distinguish between

25. Marx, *Theories of Surplus Value*, 1:156.

26. Quoted in Mandel, *Late Capitalism*, p.255. Mandel goes on to emphasize the importance of considering abstract labor above concrete labor and cites Marx:

> The functions of labor capacity are ranged beneath the concept of productive labor and its agents beneath the conception productive laborers, directly exploited by capital and subordinated to its valorization and to the production process as a whole. If we consider the total laborer who makes up this workshop, then his combined activity is directly realized materially in a total product, which is simultaneously a total mass of commodities, and it is a matter of complete indifference whether the function of the individual laborer, who represents only a limb of the total laborer, is more or less distant from the immediate labor done by hand. [Ibid., p. 95.]

27. The implication of this micro-economic performance principle in the determination of classes is that people like Kelly Girls would move in and out of the working class on a day to day basis. The wage labor of the same Kelly Girl, one day leased to a commercial bank for typing sales orders and the next day leased to a publishing house typing the manuscript of a book, would be considered unproductive of surplus value one day and productive the next. Their productiveness would depend entirely on the use of their labor by the customers of Kelly Girls.

classes.[28] In the first instance he used it to distinguish groups within the bourgeoisie—industrial, commodity, money capital—and their activity within the process of production as a whole. In the second instance he used it to describe the relation of wage labor, the proletariat, to these different forms of concrete activity. The use of the distinction by the Ehrenreichs violates the purpose of Marx's analysis and betrays the relevance of it. Instead of using this category in the spirit of Marx, they use it in the manner of bourgeois economists.

The Ehrenreichs' and new class theorists' usage of "unproductive" becomes virtually synonomous with the capitalist notion of "overhead."[29] Capitalists regularly charge the cost of service, technical, managerial and clerical personnel against the value added by another portion of the workforce. As we have mentioned before, capitalist methods of accounting—charging off part of the workforce against another part—disguise rather than identify class relations. "Value added" is not the same as surplus value, nor can overhead workers be considered unprofitable since their function is to insure and increase the production and realization of value. Under capitalist production relations any worker becomes "overhead" or "deadwood" as soon as the branch of a firm they work in, or the industry they work in, becomes unprofitable. In fact, even profitable plants are written off as losses when they absorb the losses of other branches within a conglomerate structure. Yet radicals accept this method of accounting and assume that the salaries of overhead-unproductive workers are a deduction from the production of surplus value. Capitalist accountants attempt to turn a portion of variable capital (overhead workers) into fixed or constant capital so that they can then depreciate (literally and figuratively) the value of that labor. But overhead workers are still part of variable capital, they still create surplus value for the capitalist even when they are placed in the debit column in the ledger.

Productive-unproductive, manual-mental, wage-salary are thus revealed to be partial, concrete determinations that are insufficient criteria for the determination of class in America.

---

28. If we insisted on this, as Poulantzas does, we would, as Eric Olin Wright has shown, be left with a working class comprising less than 20 percent of the American labor force. Wright, "Class Boundaries in Advanced Capitalist Societies," *New Left Review*, No. 98, (1976), pp. 21-22.

29. As Braverman says, the corporation has "given over the narrow and penny-pinching ways of its predecessors, whose first rule was to keep overhead (unproductive labor) down and devote all possible resources to production; 'spending millions to make millions has become the slogan'." Harry Braverman, *Labor and Monopoly Capital* (New York: Monthly Review Press, 1974), p. 416.

The Class Struggles

What is the purpose of providing this litany of objective class determinations—salaried, mental, unproductive—for the PMC? These "objective" determinations provide Marxists with the ingredients necessary for the construction of the class *in* itself (*an sich*). Without some kind of material-economic basis there would be no foundation to construct classes upon. The Ehrenreichs have dutifully approached the problem of structuring the class in itself, but as we have seen they have built the PMC on a foundation of sand. The second necessary element in the construction of classes, the political and social ingredients—the social cement as it were—holding together the internal structure of any class, is the articulation of the class *for* itself (*fur sich*). So far we have argued that the Ehrenrichs share with the new middle class theorists a conception of the class *in* itself. However, when the Ehrenreichs begin their historical discussion of the class *for* itself, they throw away the new middle class blueprints, part company with the new class theorists, and strike-out on their own.

The Ehrenreichs argue that the class struggle of the PMC, as a class for itself, consists of a simultaneous battle waged against the proletariat and the bourgeoisie. This is fair enough. If we review the historical record we can find instances where, for example, the rising bourgeoisie engaged several classes simultaneously. During the English revolution the bourgeoisie and Parliament struggled against a Royalist feudal aristocracy on the one hand and Levellers and Diggers on the other; likewise, during the French Revolution the bourgeoisie and the Convention waged a war against both Royalist conspiracy and foreign invasion with one hand while quelling peasant uprisings with the other hand. It should be noted that the rising bourgeoisie, itself a dense, compact social class, fought a total, all-out war for supremacy over the state and economy as a whole. It was able to sustain this intense onslaught, this all or nothing campaign, for only a brief period of time. Further, this class also enlisted the support of other classes, or fractions of classes, thoughout the society in order to gain enough social weight to tip the scales of fortune in its favor. To do this it had to put aside its internal disagreements and seize upon an identity of interests in order to weld itself into an effective political class. Marx describes the bourgeoisie in the *18th Brumaire* he says that, "as the party of Order they (the landed and industrial bourgeoisies) exercised more unrestricted and sterner domination over the other classes in society than ever previously." This class combativity, he argues, "was only possible under the form of the parliamentary republic, for only under this form could the two great divisions of the French bourgeoisie unite, and thus put the *rule* of their *class* instead of the *regime* of a privileged *faction* of it on the order of the day."[30] (emphasis added)

In other words, to act as a class meant to subordinate the differences within the class to the need for unity against, in this case, the proletariat. The differences within the ranks of the bourgeoisie were deep—between landed and industrial interests, between those who made their money from rent and those who made it from surplus value directly—at least as great as the differences the Ehrenreichs suppose to exist between the PMC and the working class. Similarly, their cultural values and traditions were deep, they lived in different places, yet they were able to set aside these material differences and recognized their interests as a class, set themselves to the task at hand, organize their domination of all other classes, and impress upon society the stamp of their rule.

Curiously, by comparison, the Ehrenreichs' PMC wages something less than an all-out struggle against capital and labor. It engages in a protracted, limited war with no clear aim or purpose in mind. Its aim is not to seize control of society as a whole and reshape it in its own image (as the aristocracy, bourgeoisie, and proletariat are wont to do), but rather it seeks to wrest a comfortable lifestyle from the bourgeoisie and acquire a measure of skill and a degree of deference from the proletariat. And it is content to do this over a long period of time, incrementally inching above the proletariat, but rising not so high as to threaten the bourgeoisie. How this kind of creeping insistence on half-measures can constitute the political and ideological basis for a social class is a question the Ehrenreichs never even think to answer.

Marx's theory of classes was composed with the idea in mind that a social class was a compact, ideologically unified, politically astute, and economically similar group of people who could represent itself as a force capable and willing to organize the whole of society, in its own image, for the benefit of all. Further, that in making this claim against the dominant social class (defined, at another time, by the same criteria) it must argue that this ruling class is decadent and incapable of exercising its function as the unifying force of political, social and economic society—later to be called the "nation."

We see no such claim on the part of the PMC. Since the Ehrenreichs insist that the PMC is dependent on the ruling class, it cannot lay claim to organizing society as a whole, nor can it describe the bourgeoisie as incapable of performing that function.

In order to circumvent this difficulty—the inability to accurately describe the PMC as engaged in a decisive or potentially decisive class struggle with either the proletariat or the bourgeoisie (since they can't

30. Karl Marx, *18th Brumaire* (Moscow: International Publishers, 1963), p. 48.

accurately characterize the PMC as a class *for itself*)—the Ehrenreichs attempt to define the PMC in its negativity. They argue that what defines the PMC as a class against other classes is that it is also a class *against* itself (*gegen sich*). This is either innovation or folly. In order to demonstrate that the PMC is a class for itself the Ehrenreichs sketch out a history of the progressive and socialist movements at the turn of this (students, children of the PMC) fighting *against* itself (its origins and parents). They say it was necessary for student radicals to "undertake a kind of negative class consciousness." [p. 39] Negative class consciousness? Class consciousness cannot be the negation of the class it is rooted in. The moment a class undertakes such a consciousness it dissolves as a class. And the moment the elements of the New Left arrived at such a position, they dissolved as a mass movement. Such an idea is a contradiction in terms, and is an abandonment of Marx's conception of class and class struggle. As Lukacs argued, to accept this kind of position "would be tantamount to observing society from a class standpoint other than its own. And no class can do that—unless it is willing to abdicate its power freely."[31]

Let us now look at the class struggles of the PMC. First we will examine the class for itself—the PMC as it has struggled with capital and the working class. We will argue that the Ehrenreichs' articulation of this struggle is inadequate, and fundamentally misrepresents the nature and consequences of the struggles they describe. And then we will turn to the PMC as a class against itself; we will look briefly at the Ehrenreichs' portrayal of the New Left, and the subsequent betrayal of its own class. We will argue that this characterization deprives what remains of the Left's real history, frustrates its present possibilities, and endangers its future aspirations.

The PMC As A Class For Itself: Against Capital

"From the beginning the nascent PMC possessed a class outlook that was distinct from, and often antagonistic to that of the capitalist class...the PMC was not merely a class of lackeys: the capitalists fought vigorously to block or modify those PMC reforms which they saw as threatening their interests. As for the PMC the very ideas...which justified their role to those capitalists inevitably led them to conflict with the capitalists." [p. 21] The Ehrenreichs seek to substantiate their claim that the PMC was hostile to capital by pointing to the political movements supposedly engendered by the PMC—progressivism and socialism.

31. Georg Lukacs, *History and Class Consciousness* (Cambridge, Mass.: MIT Press, 1971), pp. 53-54.

The Ehrenreichs try to establish the progressive and socialist movements at the turn of the century as class conscious expressions of the PMC as a class for itself, and as evidence of its anti-capitalist hostility. "The strongest expression of PMC anti-capitalist ideology was to be found in the explicitly socialist politics—which in the early 20th century meant the Socialist Party." [p. 24]

But progressivism was not a movement of the PMC. It was, to some extent, composed of truly middle class people. People whom the Ehrenreichs identify as PMC were actually petty bourgeois—small property owners, small manufacturers and lawyers. They were independently wealthy, not salaried workers dependent on employment for their survival. The other major component of the progressive movement was undeniably bourgeois.

What does it mean to say that many progressives were middle class—not PMC? It means, first of all, that it was predominantly a bourgeois movement. It also means that the reforms aimed at corralling the errant monopolies that were running roughshod over the state, small entrepreneurs and labor sprang from a real material base. This behavior threatened the social position and undermined the market strength of the middle class. They were anti-corporate but not anti-capitalist.

The sentiments of the middle class were regarded with favor by fractions of the haut bourgeoisie who sought to stabilize the political and social climate in order to proceed with a new rationalized program of economic expansion. This expansion could only succeed with a program of reforming the abuses, coopting the opposition and dampening the ardor for radical change. Ralph Easley, a leader in the National Civic Federation, one of the key organizational expressions of the corporate progressives, could legitimately say, "Our enemies are the *Socialists* among the labor people and the *anarchists* among the capitalists."[32]

The corporate progressives attacked these "socialists" and "anarchists" not from the point of view of a separate class, but with the intent of capturing the mantel of political and economic leadership. They coalesced around groups like the NCF in preference to the more resolutely anti-unionist, anti-reformist, National Association of Manufacturers. But if we look at the differences separating these two groups, their antagonism over political and economic issues, while acrimonious,

---

32. James Weinstein, *Corporate Ideal in the Liberal State: 1900-1918* (Boston: Beacon Press, 1968), pp. 19-20. Among the large corporations, such as US Steel, Weinstein argues, the anarchists tended to be those who came from the manufacturing end of the business—the old steel men—while the progressives were usually those who represented the banks, were second generation managers, or, most importantly, were identified with the Morgan interests and their assorted retinue of academic advisors and political hangers-on.

was confined within the parameters of capitalism and limited to those within the bourgeois and middle classes.

The bourgeoisie, like any ruling class, has its own internal conflicts, and it must rely on other sectors of the population to resolve those conflicts and to provide the social weight necessary to tip the balance of social forces in its favor. But why would the middle class ally with corporate capital in this endeavor? Why were they so reform minded? Because it was in the interests of the petit bourgeoisie, especially at the municipal level, to pursue a fairly wide vision of social responsibility. As participants in local chambers of commerce and boards of trade, local businessmen could identify the future of their cities with their own business interests. To rationalize and make more attractive a particular city meant more business for local entrepreneurs. The centralization of power, of the removal of decision-making from "politics," favored businessmen over workingmen *or* white collar employees. In no area of political or social reform did small business more clearly demonstrate the force of this logic than in movements for city commission and manager governments."[33] This was the basis of middle class support for corporate capital, and the basis of their mutual material interests. Contrary to the Ehrenreichs' position, the transformation of local and national government took place at the behest and under the aegis of capital (petit and haut bourgeoisie)—a union consumated and symbolized by the professor-President, Wilson—not the PMC.

As for the Socialist Party, though their claims that 90% of their membership was trade unionist were inaccurate since a large portion were impoverished tenant farmers in Oklahoma and Texas, the over whelming majority of urban members *were* workers and trade-unionists. As for the leadership of the party, probably two-thirds of the elected office holders were workers and union members, and the rest were middle class—Florence Kelley, J.G. Phelps Stokes, and Morris Hillquit to name a few. When the Ehrenreichs cite Morris Hillquit's boast, "In the U.S. probably more than anywhere else, socialism is recruiting heavily from the better classes of society," [p. 24] as proof of its PMC membership, they are misrepresenting Hillquit because the "better classes" he referred to were the propertied classes. And even this middle class contingent within the Socialist Party should not be overemphasized since its numbers were insignificant, and the role they played within the Party's NEC and national offices was not decisive.

The struggles that the Ehrenreichs are trying to pass off as PMC/ruling class struggles are really either inter-capitalist struggles,

33. Ibid., pp. 92-93.

between hard-line industrialists and corporate reformers, or struggles between the working class and the capitalist class. The struggles they seize upon to illustrate the class struggle of the PMC are trivial. How can we take seriously their attempt to portray the campaign for the conversion to the metric system as a matter of life and death importance to the PMC? Can we imagine the PMC swarming through the marbled halls of Congress, slide rules clenched in their upraised fists, voices cursing the rule (inch not metric) of capital, and see them as the vanguard of struggles for this aspiring class?[34]

The PMC As A Class For Itself: Against The Working Class

According to the Ehrenreichs, the PMC was responsible for three important developments in the early 20th century. Each development, a result of the conscious effort of the PMC, invariably pitted the PMC against the working class. The first development involved the "reorganization of the production process." [p. 24] "Science and its offshoot engineering were set to work producing technologies which undercut the power of skilled labor...in an effort to strip from workers their knowledge and control of the production process." [p. 14] Second, the development of the PMC required the expansion of the public or state sector into working class communities and resulted in the "emergence of mass institutions of social control." [p. 16] Third, the PMC spearheaded the "commodity penetration of working class life." [p. 16]

To the extent that these developments took place, they took place under the direction of capital, not the PMC. And to the degree that scientists and engineers participated in these processes they did so as representatives of capital, not in their own class interest. Let us take these three developments in turn.

David Noble describes the relationship between science and capital—engineers and capitalists—and the "reorganization of the production process" in a way that sharply contrasts with the Ehrenreichs:

---

34. David Noble, in *America by Design* (New York: Alfred Knopf, 1977) demonstrates that it was engineers sponsored by the new electrical and chemical industries who supported the conversion to the metric system. Opposing them were both owners and engineers of the metal working and machine tool industries that had invested heavily in English calibrated units. The opposition fought back conversion efforts in the 1890's and 1900's. When it was again raised as a possibility in the 1920's, it was again opposed, but this time by many of the same people who had supported it the first time around. Having since invested in English measured units themselves, the electrical and chemical industries now stood to lose by converting. The fight over the metric system was a fight amongst capitalists, and it can hardly be used as a measure (literally or figuratively) of the class struggle of the PMC. Ibid., p. 77.

Through control over the education process and licensing, the professional engineers gradually gained a monopoly over the practice of scientific technology. And through the massive employment of technically trained people, the industrial corporations secured a monopoly over the professional engineer.... In this way modern technology became a class bound phenomena, the racing heart of corporate capitalism.[35]

As engineers get pressed into the service of capital, their labor is turned into capital, and as Marx says, "Invention then becomes a business, and the application of science to direct production itself becomes a prospect which determines and solicits it."[36] engineers themselves realized that they stood within the ambit of capital and recognized that their interests lay either with capital or against it.

Tied as they were to the industrial organization which controlled the means of professional practice, most progressive engineers realized that anti-business political activity grounded upon engineering expertise led inevitably to political elitism and impotence, technical impotence, or both; radical engineers, they understood, had to choose between being radical and being engineers.... Thus the most radical and isolated segment of the engineering community remained on the periphery even when it surfaced briefly in the early days of the depression as a media fad and political dead end, technocracy.... The corporate engineers were most like the sophisticated, class conscious corporate liberals of the big business and banking community in their response to the various social currents of the day.[37]

The Ehrenreichs are correct in saying that the working class struggled against the degradation of work and against the people who introduced it—scientists and engineers—but they are not correct in saying that these managers and engineers struggled with the working class from an independent position. Noble points out that they did not constitute an independent technical force, rather they represented the interests of capital.

The second development the Ehrenreichs point to in order to substantiate their claim that the PMC struggles independently with the working class is the expansion of social services and "mass institutions of social control." But these social functions—from "technical education

35. Ibid., pp. xxiv-xxxv.
36. Marx, *Grundrisse*, p. 704.
37. Noble, *America By Design*, pp. 63-64.

for workers, kindergarten for their children, low-cost housing, recreational facilities and some aspects of public health programs, saving and substantiate their claim that the PMC struggles independently with the working class is the expansion of social services and "mass institutions of social control." But these social functions—from technical education for workers, kindergarten for their children, low-cost housing, recreational facilities and some aspects of public health programs, saving and lending money, insurance, pensions—were adopted *first* by the corporations and later adopted by the state at the behest of large corporations.[38] For example, the National Civic Federation, a representative of corporate liberalism, sought to develop "welfare work as an alternative to unionism. It groped towards sponsorship of social reforms acceptable to (but not initiated by) labor, the middle classes, and the corporations."[39] And the expansion of local governments was dictated not by professionals and managers looking for work in their hometown, as the Ehrenreichs claim when they say the PMC is a job creating class, but by the corporations who wanted to create the social and economic infrastructure necessary for their own development. Again, it was not a separate class of professionals who urged reforms that undermined the working class community, but the monopoly fraction of the ruling class who sought to stave off working class agitation and stabilize the economy.

As for "the commodity penetration of working class life," the Ehrenreichs are correct in saying that "an indigenous part of working class culture was edged out by commodities conceived and designed outside the class," but we must ask, "by what class?" Only the capitalist class had the wherewithall—the means (of production) and the ends (the accumulation of capital)—to undertake this massive commoditization of American life. But the Ehrenreichs regard this commoditization not as a process of the expansion of the productive forces and the accumulation of capital, but the accumulation of jobs and privileges for the PMC. But one must remember that this was also a period of the expansion of jobs for the working class and the beginning of massive internal migration seeking new job opportunities (Blacks moving North) instead of continued immigration from abroad. Yet nobody (on the left) would claim that Blacks wrested jobs for themselves at the expense of potential European immigrants. This, of course, is exactly what the Ehrenreichs maintain vis-a-vis the PMC. The expansion of jobs throughout the economy is but one aspect of the accumulation and expanded reproduction of capital during this period. The Ehrenreichs ignore that these wider developments misrepresent the impact of capital on the working class by

38. Weinstein, *Corporate Ideal*, pp. 19-20.
39. Ibid., pp. 37-38.

shifting the blame onto the PMC.

The Class Against Itself: The New Left

The Ehrenreichs' attempt to establish a historical connection between the class origins of the PMC—the progressives and socialists—and the expression of this class in the 60's—the New Left. In order to make clear the connection between these two movements, separated as they are by a gulf of 50 odd years, the Ehrenreichs have to define the New Left narrowly enough to keep other social forces from intruding onto the terrain of the PMC. In defining the New Left as essentially white, male, university students in SDS, they conveniently exclude from consideration the Civil Rights Movement and urban riots; Blacks, Indians, and Chicano minorities; the women's movement (for the most part); the counter-culture and its various incarnations (beatniks, hippies, freaks; rock and roll); and the anti-war movement (insofar as it represented soldiers and working class groups). These omissions do considerable violence to the unity of the constituent movements of the 60's, the outcome of which is to minimize their impact on the capitalist economy and society.

The Ehrenreichs' characterization of the New Left has many flaws. We will mention only a few. They misrepresent the crucial links between Black civil rights and the politicization of white radicals in the early 60's. The Ehrenreichs see them emerging as separate phenomena until the Black liberation movement "separated a chunk of the New Left from its own class." [p. 35] The links between these movements prior to and subsequent to this are conspicuously ignored. They also seek to separate the women's movement from its origins within the left so that its content will not be contaminated by the PMC (they consciously separate NOW and people like Betty Freidan from the women's movement proper, arguing that this group is merely an expression of the PMC). And they accept the bourgeois psychologists' commonplace notion, prevalent in the 60's, that "The gap between PMC elders and the children of the New Frontier in generational experience was too great to be bridged by abstract class interests." [p. 34]

More seriously, by arguing that SDS was the organization of class conscious PMC radicals, the Ehrenreichs wind up defending those who helped tear the movement apart, proclaiming that the betrayal of the left by itself, its self-destructive course, was a good thing. They implicitly agree with Weatherman's analysis, that radicals were burdened with white skin privilege: "There was an acute consciousness of privilege—a static and fragmentary prelude to the notion of class" and that "a critical self consciousness of the PMC itself" was a necessary thing for radicals to undertake, "a kind of negative class consciousness." [pp. 35, 39] They tacitly agree with the Weatherman position, because Weatherman, for the Ehrenreichs, correctly formulated the class position of white radicals as based on privilege, and then tried to uproot their "own ingrained and often subtle attitudes of condescension and elitism" through self-destruction. Of course as soon as Weatherman made this pronouncement they dissolved themselves as a national political movement and vanished into a subterranean political current, fashionable described as the Underground.

This historical revisionism represents a bankrupt political intent— to discredit the New Left as a serious political movement that contributed something to the working class movement in the U.S. and to the proletarian movement internationally (remember May '68; the victory in Vietnam?). The Ehrenreichs, it would seem, are content with the present state of the left—small, though not yet small enough since it still has some purging self-criticism to attend to—but in reality this complacency only reflects in *theory* the actual *practice* and *position* of the left in this country.[40] It is not surprising that this should be so, only sad.

To end here would be to acquiesce to the defeatism of the Ehrenreichs and the isolation of the left. The Ehrenreichs, to their credit, have sought to understand the transformation of labor into different forms and incarnations under capitalism. Though they have failed in nearly every respect, we think the project of understanding this transformation is an important one. In order to apprehend this essential process—the capital labor relation—it is important to remember that labor has a two-fold character; labor as a commodity, and labor as a means of producing value (use value, exchange value, and surplus value).

If we examine the first aspect of labor—labor as a commodity like any other commodity in capitalism—we are struck with the fact that labor has to be produced and reproduced as a commodity. Labor, like other commodities, has to be transformed from abstract labor—the raw material from which the worker as a commodity is shaped—into a particular, useful form, concrete labor—the form in which it can be bought, sold, used, consumed and exchanged for a price on the market. Like other commodities, labor too must go through successive transfor-

40. The Ehrenreichs seem to accept working class anti-communism as necessary since it flows out of an antagonism to the PMC, and they note with approval, "working class anti-communism...grows out of the objective antagonism between the working class and the PMC. Often enough it is mixed with a wholesale rejection of anything or thought associated with the PMC—liberalism, intellectualism, etc." [p. 43] This position is politically bankrupt. They seem to be trying to encourage the working class to smash all the communists and the leftists the Ehrenreichs don't like—the PMC radical especially.

mations at the hands of various social production processes. And each of the successive social production processes change the value, the physical attributes and dimensions, the interchangeability, the location, and the exchangeability of the concrete labor. The raw material, abstract labor, is transformed into a finished product—concrete labor that can be consumed by the capitalist in the process of production.

We must now ask, "What are the different social production processes that produce different kinds of labor for capital?" For starters there are the family and the schools. These social production units transform abstract labor power into quantifiable concrete labor with specific attributes (among them: discipline, the knowledge of rudimentary and sophisticated physical and intellectual manipulations). There are, in addition to the family and school, social processes that transform the character and condition of labor. The migration and movement of people, for example, transforms people with one kind of concrete labor—peasants, peddlers in Europe and Asia—into another form of concrete labor somewhere else—workers and laborers in America. Then, once employed in a relation with capital, the concrete labor of workers is transformed into labor that can perform the specific task at hand—welding, assembling, counting. How well fitted the concrete labor of the worker is to the task at hand, how much demand by capital there is for this labor, and how much time and energy will be demanded of this labor by capital are all considerations that assign value, price, marketability, and consumability to this particular commodity, labor.

We mention these various processes because Marxists tend to slight them. Marx himself was concerned primarily with the *initial* transformation of serf, peasant, and craft laborer into a commodity, abstract wage labor. This is the process of proletarianization. Marx focused on the initial separation of the laborer from the means of production because this produced a working class. Marxists, however, tend to ignore the subsequent transformations that continually produce and reproduce the proletariat anew. These transformations are important because the ways in which these social production processes produce concrete labor change over time as the result of struggles between labor and capital.

We can see, for example, how schools and education fit into the capitalist mode of production by thinking of education as a social production process producing various commodities that are conveniently packaged and labeled with different degrees in particular fields. Schools transform the labor power of young people—in varying degrees, in different ways, and in disparate locations—into various commodities that can, as concrete labor, be appropriated by capital. Naturally, since this is part and parcel of capitalist class relations, there is resistance and struggle over the manner in which the transformation process takes place, just as there is resistance to the way labor is transformed and appropriated within the production process proper. Students daydream, play hooky, flunk-out, drop-out and even rebel against the structures that commoditize them. They demand the elimination of grades, open admissions, free education, smaller classes, better teachers, more meaningful work—all the characteristics of any incipient movement of labor against capitalist relations. These struggles are all part of the resistance to the process of commoditization and the impending proletarianization of labor power.

By conceiving of the transformation of labor as a commodity, shaped and molded to fit the exigencies of capitalist production, yet resisting it at the same time, we can reconceptualize the relation between labor and capital in a way that will allow us to understand the family, education, migration, and the importance of struggles located within these social production processes. From this vantage point we can comprehend the distinguishing features of the New Left in a new light. The Black movement's migration from South to North; beatnik drop-outs and hippie migration "on the road;" student resistance to impending proletarianization and militarization; women's reconceptualization of their roles in the family and society and a host of other tangible and serious developments in the 60's take on a different meaning when we look at how these struggles shaped and reshaped the structures that produce and reproduce the working class in America.

As a larger project, we must rethink our ideologically compromised conceptions of class and reexamine our own history so that we may find a way *out* of the isolation and fragmentation we now face on the left.

6.

New Left Knots

John Welch

I

We are the New Left, grown up and grown older.[1] Our left carries on, led by and mostly made up from people who were radicalized in the 60s. We carry with us the faults, the problems, the questions, and the weaknesses of our beginnings. One of these is like a recurrent nightmare:

A construction worker flattens an anti-war medical student. It's the Southwest Side of Chicago at a central draft board, and boys from the Catholic high school across the street take draft resistance leaflets and burn them; then they burn the resistance leafletter with cigarettes. Rednecks put on white sheets. "Go back to Russia!" We hand the workers copies of *The Spark*, our faction's newpaper, but they drop them in the mud puddle by the factory gate. "Rednecks, white socks, and Blue Ribbon Beer." We stand at the Pentagon and stare down bayonets held by draftees. "I'm proud to be an okie from Muskogee." It's raining and we slip on the cobblestones as the police push us back from the doorway to the induction center, and when the inductees are driven through they look down at us with expressions of suspicious wonder. A racist, male chauvinist with a hard hat and a blue work shirt crosses his arms and says, "Well, what about me?"

John and Barbara Ehrenreich, in "The Professional-Managerial Class (PMC)" suggest some reasons for all this, arguing that the New Left developed within a new sort of middling class, one which came into existence to absorb the cultural and industrial autonomy of the working class. There are two connected questions behind PMC analysis: first, why has the U.S. working class had so little class consciousness, and why has socialism been so weak in America; second, where did the New Left come from if not from the working class?

II

Throughout the history of the New Left there has been this nagging question: what about the working class? From the beginning the Left understood that their movement was not a working class movement, and that their situation was different from that of all other radical movements of the previous hundred years. The immediate problem, wrote C. Wright Mills in 1960, is to find an agency for social change by working through parliament. Socialists had looked to the working class, organized into parties and unions. Mills comments, "I cannot avoid the view that in both cases, the historic agency (in the advanced capitalist countries) has either collapsed or become most ambiguous: so far as structural change is concerned *these* don't seem to be at once available and effective as our agency anymore."[2] According to Mills, we must not "write off" the working class—the situation may change—but for now we should look to the "cultural apparatus," to the intellectuals, for our "radical agency."[3] We must begin with the intelligentsia, "for that is what we now are."[4]

The New Left that followed was, of course, a student movement, and it remained centered on campuses. "We are people of this generation, bred in at least moderate comfort, housed now in universities, and

---

1. I will be talking about the *white* New Left in the U.S. The black New Left had different problems, different reasons for existing, and a different political trajectory.

2. C. Wright Mills, "Letter to the New Left," reprinted in *Power, Politics & People* (New York, 1963), pp. 254-55.

3. Mills, "Letter," p. 255.

4. Mills, "Letter," pp. 256-57.

looking uncomfortably at the world we inherit."[5] However, white New Leftists continued to worry about their missing "agency for radical reform," and about the relation of radical students to off-campus allies. Some white ex-students worked with the Student Non-Violent Coordinating Committee (SNCC) in the South, while others in the North sought, through ERAP projects to build an "interracial movement of the poor."[6] By 1965, SNCC had begun to suggest that whites should not be organizing black people. A SNCC working paper argued that—

> So far, we have found that most white radicals have sought to escape the horrible reality of America by going into the black community and attempting to organize black people while neglecting the organization of their own people's racist communities. How can one clean up someone else's yard when one's own yard is untidy?[7]

But poor whites had not radicalized quickly nor massively in the ERAP-targeted communities. So where did this leave SDS? Greg Calvert, the organization's National Secretary, summarized the difficulties and the possibilities in a speech in February, 1967:

> First, we have to admit that—like it or not—we live in urban industrial capitalist America, in white America, and not in the rural South. We owe SNCC a deep debt of gratitude for having slapped us brutally in the face with the slogan of black power, a slogan which said to white radicals, "Go home and organize in white America which is *your* reality and which only you are equipped to change." Secondly, we are thus forced to ask ourselves whether in white America there exists the possibility for organizing a truly radical, an authentically revolutionary movement for change. Finally, we must face the fact that unless such a potential exists, then the basic arguments of...Third World oriented groupings bear serious reading....The problem is a search for a constituency, for an agent of social trans-

5. *Port Huron Statement,* SDS, 1962.

6. The title of an important strategy paper by Carl Wittman and Tom Hayden, 1963. Reprinted in Mitchell Cohen and Dennis Hale, eds., *The New Student Left* (Boston: 1967), pp. 175-213. ERAP was the Economic Research and Action Project of SDS.

7. SNCC, "The Basis of Black Power," Winter, 1965-66. Reprinted in a Radical Education Project (REP), *SDS Goes to Work (Again),* compiled for the December, 1968, SDS National Council meeting.

formation, for 'the revolutionary class.' If no such constituency can be developed, then our only hope lies with external agencies, with revolutionary developments in the Third World.[8]

Revolutionary movements are not built out of the desire for more material goods, Calvert continues, revolutions are struggles for human freedom, "struggles born out of the perception of the contradictions between human potentiality and oppressive actuality."[9] Liberalism works from guilt, from the belief that others are unjustly denied the ability to be like oneself. Revolutionary consciousness begins from "the perception of oneself as unfree, as oppressed..."

> Revolutionary consciousness leads to the struggle for one's own freedom in unity with others who share the burden of oppression. It is, to speak in the classical vocabulary, class consciousness because it no longer sees the problem as someone else's, because it breaks through individualization and privatization, because the recognition of one's unfreedom unites one in the struggle of the oppressed, because it posits a more universally human potentiality for all men in a liberated society.[10]

The theory of the "new working class" offered SDS a revolutionary understanding of advanced capitalism. Most Americans, including student activists believe that they are part of the "middle class," and that, therefore, they are not oppressed. But, said Calvert, "the vast majority of those whom we called the middle class must properly be understood as members of the 'new working class': that is, as those workers who fill the jobs created by a new level of technological development within the same exploitative system."[11] Students are apprentice members of this new working class, so that their demands for "student control" over their university training would prefigure demands for worker's control, demands which their future employers, the great corporations, will be unable to meet. In fact, students are trainees to a "key group" in the new working class, because of the importance of technology within modern production.[12]

8. Greg Calvert, "In White America," *National Guardian,* 3/25/67. Reprinted by REP, but more available in Massimo Teodori, *The New Left* (New York: 1969), pp. 412-18.

9. Calvert, "America," p. 1.

10. Calvert, "America," p. 2.

11. Calvert, "America," p. 3.

12. Calvert, "America," p. 3.

Imagine, said Calvert and Nieman, an assembly-line worker at a Ford plant who stews in a traffic jam, having no more reasonable mass transportation, and whose job depends on the socially irrational need to sell more cars, which will make his highway even more crowded. This autoworker has a son, a college-trained engineer who has no more control over his job than does an autoworker. The son may even imagine that he is "middle-class," but this is false, one of the biggest of the lies that keep American workers quiet. What's more, it is the son, the engineer, who has the training "to design a rational and humane transportation system based on collective social need rather than profit motivation and organized individual compulsive consumption."[13]

This is theoretical dynamite: Calvert has found a revolutionary agency, and it turns out to include people just like those already in SDS. The new working class theory spoke to changes which were felt to have happened in advanced capitalism, and it spoke through a more modern and more human language than that of traditional marxism. No "downtrodden masses." What's more, the theory justified SDS's move back to campus, just where the anti-war movement had begun to grow, and where the Berkeley Free Speech Movement had suggested that some elemental force might be eating away at the multiversity. Technology, argued the theorists of the new working class, demands an all around education, an education "into the basic methods of scientific-technological research."[14] The multiversity fragments its academic training for the same reason that management fragments jobs: skilled workers possess a power that can be used against capital. This fragmentation produces alienation among student "trainees" just as it does among factory workers. Out of alienation, out of apathy, into movement; Calvert was arguing persuasively that SDS should quit being ashamed of organizing college students. Don't wait for Lefty: he's here already, down at the chem lab.

The student movement understood itself at last. Historians of the New Left usually pause over the 1966-1968 period, noting that finally SDS was developing some serious theory, becoming marxist in an innovative way, but complaining that the innovations quickly and unfortunately dissolved back into "the old crap."[15] The left was growing on campus and the "new working class" theory appeared to explain why,

13. Greg Calvert and Carol Nieman, "Socialist Consciousness and the New Left," in *Guardian,* 8/24, 8/31, and 9/7/68. Reprinted by New Left Education Project, Austin, Texas.

14. Andre Gorz, quoted by Carl Davidson in *New Radicals in the Multiversities,* SDS pamphlet, Chicago, 1968, p. 8.

15. See, for example, James Weinstein, "The Left, Old and New," *Socialist Revolution #10,* pp. 48-51.

but there were several problems with the theory.

If students were to be organized as technical-workers-in-training, what should one do with a movement of liberal arts and social science majors? My SDS chapter at the University of Chicago, for instance, had students majoring in history, political science, sociology, "philosophical psychology," urban studies, literature, maybe a few artsies, but almost no science majors. Those science majors who got radicalized tended to switch from math and physics to things like psycho-pharmacology and comparative religion. We went to the chem labs, but didn't find anybody called Lefty. Where were the students who were training in fields that might put them into the newly technologized production? At City College, for another instance, student politics usually polarized between liberal arts hippees and the North Campus ROTC fascists. Maybe the liberal arts hippees were not a revolutionary-class-in-formation but kids who had chosen to get as far as possible away from capitalist work and capitalist practicality. Maybe new working class theory explains why academics might hate their slot-minded training, but then these radical students would represent the last gasp of romanticism versus the money-grubbers; the theory had assumed that they would take their rebellion into technical training and demand control over that training and, later, their jobs.

Carl Davidson, then SDS Interorganizational Secretary, eventually suggested,

> We should reach out to engineers and technical students rather than to business administration majors, education majors rather than art students. From a national perspective, this strategy would suggest that we should place priorities on organizing in certain kinds of universities—the community colleges, junior colleges, state universities, and technical schools, rather than religious colleges or the Ivy League.[16]

But engineers would not organize: look at the size of the Committee for Social Responsibility in Engineering or Scientists and Engineers for Social and Political Action. And, though SDS chapters eventually grew up at some community colleges and at some less fashionable state universities, and even though the Kent State and San Francisco State chapters were hero-chapters during the last year of SDS, the national organization remained centered around the powerful chapters of its original base: elite private universities (such as Columbia, Chicago, or

16. Davidson, *New Radicals,* p. 18.

Stanford) and the great state universities (Ann Arbor, Madison, Berkeley). Leadership tended to come from these chapters; did the Chicago Regional Office pay any attention to the chapter at Chicago City College? But the students at Chicago City came from backgrounds most like those new working class members imagined by Calvert: children of blue collar workers hoping to prepare themselves for bottom-level white collar jobs.

The student movement that grew was an anti-war movement, a movement to throw the military off campus, to end university complicity with the war. "The Vietnam War continues filling our ranks with fresh recruits."[17] People opposed cozy relations between their universities and the big corporations, but not for the reasons new working class theory had predicted. Students threw rocks at recruiters for war corporations, but they tolerated other corporate recruiters. Davidson had hoped that SDS would be able to talk with recruits about their desires for craftlike control of their future work, but students responded to appeals about napalm and cluster-bomb-units. At best, it was possible, sometimes, to convince students that they were actually workers, but then what? It was very difficult to frame demands or suggest actions that might make a revolutionary movement out of new working class theory. Organizers could suggest that graduates join or form white collar unions, but that hardly seemed adequately revolutionary, especially to an organization that disliked unions in the first place.[18]

The movement ran out from under its "new working class" theorists.

These theorists had always argued that college-trained technical workers were a key sector within an expanded working class; a revolutionary movement would have to synthesize this new working class with the older blue collar working class and with the welfare poor (whose unemployment results from the automation which creates the technicians). What would the synthesis look like? The language in which this was discussed suggested that people envisioned the new, old, and unemployed sectors of the working class as if they were building blocks, with neat grooves at the edges, so that to synthesize them one merely slapped them alongside each other. But the blocks were people, and the war was a knife: blue-collar sons fought and bled. How do you synthesize induction with deferral?

17. Carl Davidson, "Towards Institutional Resistance," *New Left Notes,* 11/13/67.

18. Calvert and Nieman, "Consciousness," p. 6. For attempts to work out an organizing program, cf. Davidson, *New Radicals.*

There was non-cooperation, but this did not really solve the problem. Students held 2-S deferments, a class privilege, while working-class youth got drafted. Could students genuinely oppose the war if they were safe from having to fight it? Could draftees take that opposition seriously? And if radical students opposed elitism, how could they hide behind their deferment? But then draft resisters, once they'd given up the deferment, discovered that more and more draftable kids wanted to avoid the army in any way they could. These draftable kids could not understand why anybody would give up a clear deferment, and they found it just incomprehensible if a non-cooperator told them that he wanted to "share the fate of the less fortunate."

Black power had insisted that white radicals should reach and civilize white communities; with the war, the movement felt again the difference between who it was and where it had to be. Early on, some organizers argued that anti-war resistance had to reach into "poor white and lower paid working class communities...

> It is here that the war hits hardest. It is young men from these communities who do most of the dying in Vietnam...But it is here that the anti-war movement has had least experience and least success. Paradoxically, the people most brutalized by material and social exploitation, the people pushed unceasingly through the processing of school, military and job seem unmoved by the anti-war effort.

These organizers proposed community organizing, a sort of revived ERAP, focused against the war by way of draft resistance. Through the draft, the war hits everybody in these communities. The war will end someday and with it the movement that it created, unless that movement becomes "rooted deeply, not simply in communities, but in the lives and difficulties of people," and unless that movement develops the ability to resist real power.[19]

Good. But it was not enough just to admit that the movement had to reach working people: ex-student organizers would have to face and overcome the differences between their backgrounds and instincts and those of the people they wanted to organize. This is how a group of ERAP veterans, including several organizers, replied to the community-based resistance proposal described just above. "We welcome those whose radical work will not remain confined to the student community where too many 'radicals' often unconsciously believe what liberal America has told us—'poor and working people are the enemy'."

19. "We've Got to Reach Our Own People," *Movement,* November, 1967; reprinted in Teodori, *The New Left,* pp. 303-09.

However...

the authors talk of establishing roots in working class communities now, so that the people there will "be approached by
people who settle into their own communities, are familiar and
militant about their community problems, and who gain
respect and credentials in their community." This is an important and proper motivation, yet the would-be-organizer must
understand that sinking roots is extremely difficult and slow,
filled with the problems of people of DIFFERENT CUL-
TURES AND AT THIS TIME DIFFERENT INTERESTS
AND MOTIVATIONS checking each other out, growing
together and learning to understand and live with differences.
People who come out of the radical-student-hip culture will not
shed easily (even though they may desire to do so) some of what
must be shed or purged if they hope to become close or deeply
involved BOTH POLITICALLY AND PERSONALLY
with people in poor and working class neighborhoods...

Those who intend to leave the radical student community at this
time or in the near future must deal with the fact that their
concerns and style have developed in a social, political,
economic, and cultural scene very different from the one they
will face in the neighborhoods they select to live and work in.
The authors...define resistance as "an effort to impede and
disrupt the functioning of the military/political machinery
wherever it is local and vulnerable." Resistance, defined this
way, is a political concept, with an associated style that is carried
over from the student political scene WHICH IS A VERY
DIFFERENT PLACE FROM A UNIVERSITY. The would-
be organizer will be forced to learn that good! They have not
done their living-in research, are (by the sound of their article)
not sensitive to the dynamics of the places they intend to live
and work. It should be noted that NO WHERE IN THEIR
PIECE DO THEY SPEAK OF LEARNING FROM THE
PEOPLE THEY HOPE TO WORK WITH.[20]

***

The Progressive Labor Party began to gain followers within SDS,
partly because they attacked all varieties of new working class theory as

20. Junebug Bykin, Diane Fager, Mike James, et al., "Take a Step into
America," *Movement,* December, 1967. Reprinted in *SDS Goes.*

elitist, arguing that only the "old" working class could really be revolutionary. Students are petty-bourgeois, student power is student privilege. A turning point might have been the French "events" of May, 1968. As PL declared a few months later:

> France is the sharpest people's struggle in recent history in an advanced capitalist country. The theory that a "new" working class—professionals and technicians—is the key force did not materialize in practice. French students were very clear that while they could start the fight, the working class must finish it![21]

SDS dropped the "new working class" strategy very quickly, while the leadership tried to hustle up a pro-working class position to counter PL. In the summer of 1968 that leadership had presented an SDS convention with a grand strategy based on new working class theory, and Bernadine Dohrn had been elected a national officer partly because she had co-authored the paper (even though the strategy lost). By December, Dohrn was calling Greg Calvert a "social fascist."[22] Later that month SDS committed itself, through a national council meeting, to become a class-conscious youth movement:

> At this point in history, SDS is faced with its most crucial ideological decision, that of determining its direction with regard to the working class. At this time there must be a realization on the part of many in our movement that students alone cannot and will not be able to bring about the downfall of capitalism, the system which is at the root of man's oppression. Many of us are going to have to go through important changes, personally.[23]

The resolution, "Towards a Revolutionary Youth Movement" ("RYM"), called on SDS to "reach out to new constituencies both on and off campus," but the reasoning behind this call was distorted by the student perspective from which it was made. We have to reach blue-collar workers by way of blue-collar youth, it argued, because otherwise we won't be able to make our revolution. Whose revolution? Students, that is, appear to have discovered that they want and need to make a revolution: they can't do it by themselves, so they look around to see who will do it *for them.* Workers, being strategically located, carry the

---

21. Progressive Labor Party, "Student Labor Action Project," *New Left Notes,* 10/7/68; reprinted in *SDS Goes.*

22. *New Left Notes,* 12/18/68.

23. "Towards a Revolutionary Youth Movement," reprinted in *Debate Within SDS,* REP, 1969.

power to paralyze society, so students have to reach workers and persuade them to use that power to make a revolution. This was, actually, PL's argument (modified only by the RYMers' support for black nationalism); even the writing style now sounds like PL. And the RYM plan for reaching workers differed from that of PL mostly in that the RYMers had more sympathy for the youth culture which had spread downward to working-class kids: long hair and dope and rock & roll made what looked like a common culture for both radical students and "young workers." This would make it possible to communicate radical politics across the class gap. But communication, still, would be one-way. Us to Them. How, then, could students assume that their politics expressed anything vital in the lives of working people?

The later New Left was "pro-working class," and supposed the earlier New Left to have been "anti-working class;" yet each left was outside the working class and understood this. The proletarianizing New Left of 1969 acknowledged this even in the reasons it gave for wanting to proletarianize itself. However, neither new working class theory nor the new leninism which resulted from RYM recognized the hostility that had always festered along the gap between college left and blue-collar people. New working class strategy assumed that such hostility was a simple mistake, and could be overcome simply if college-trained technicians realized that they, like "real workers," also sold their labor for wages. The new leninists tried to avoid the problem completely: if anyone accepted proletarian ideology, if they let the proletariat into their hearts, then they were "communists," no matter what their background.

Sample a few weeks of the *Guardian*, the largest "new communist" paper. You will discover that the radicalizing ex-student faces no problem except the masterings of Marxist-Leninist thought. Passed masters, no matter who, are simply called "communists," and the *Guardian* soberly argues its positions as if such people were the old Flint autoworkers. Communists must say this, do that. The old CPUSA lost its revolutionary nerve in the '50s—no mention of its having lost its base in the labor movement—but now a real communist movement is growing again. Even if that new communist movement begins from New Left students and still consists largely of veterans of the '60s, there is no problem: they're all "communists,"and let's continue to "win" people to "communist ideas." The ideas are the same, even if now they are "put forth" by a radicalized doctor.

The new leninists read Lenin to mean that students could carry socialism to the working class, who, left to themselves, can attain only "trade union consciousness," whatever that is. Socialism, after all, was developed originally among cultured members of the bourgeoisie who went over to the proletariat. This was very handy. Whatever Lenin may have said or the Bolsheviks may have done, this might become for the new leninists a rationale for maintaining their distance from manual labor, for becoming the strategists for the working class. Meanwhile, the workers must learn to follow their orders. If the workers aren't obedient, then they have a diseased and "false consciousness."

In fact, Perry Anderson, an editor of *New Left Review*, argued along just these lines during a tour of the U.S. in the fall of 1969. We are all university educated, he suggested, and it is our privilege to have the free time and training to "do theory." Workers have no time, no space to think deeply for themselves, so revolutionary intellectuals must do it for them. This might seem elitist, and, in fact, it will give intellectuals great power within the party, but intellectuals should see this power as bringing an awesome responsibility: the college left must try humbly to serve the ignorant mass of workers. The Leninist party model fits perfectly around the real gap between students and proletarians.[24] It is only for the sake of those without brains that brains have been given to us.

III

So the New Left worried about its distance from working people. From the other direction, it was clear enough to working class kids like me that we were moving into a different class world when we became active in the left. It was not just that the politics was accompanied by a jargon and by customs different from those I'd been raised in; it wasn't just that becoming-lefties had to learn a special language. In fact, U.S. left language operates in ordinary academic syntax: the sentence structure is the same, and only a few key words are added. It seemed to me that New Left culture existed within a larger academic culture, one which I had been training to join since I'd been put into the college-prep track in junior high school. And it was clear that the New Leftists, like other students, had very different experiences and assumptions from mine, and especially that they had very peculiar notions of what working people were like.

It was clear, for instance, that ordinary students who were against the war thought that workers were all crypto-nazis. Many students and active leftists really did believe that "working people are the enemy." Of course leftist leaders knew better, and those who knew better were responsible for the GI coffeehouses and the anti-war marches that blamed the war on the politicians and the generals (and the "ruling elite") rather than on the draftees. Still, remember how many times you heard people call common soldiers "pigs." And even sophisticated leftists

24. Perry Anderson, *Leviathan,* October, 1969.

sometimes slipped, like the radical lawyer who once explained to me that "the workers are what's wrong with this country, they oppress everybody else."

It became obvious to me that most lefties had little sense of the lives of anybody but those whom are usually called "upper middle class," and whom the Ehrenreichs would call the PMC. Working people often were talked about as if they were fat and satisfied, pigs wallowing in warm mud. The working class has "sold out," it's been "bought off." It's off, out there, not visible nor worth investigating. Then, mostly later, workers became starving masses, shivering people begging for lumps of coal, people who sent their children to work in the mills at age six, people who were beaten by foremen with whips to make them roll out steel from sunup to sundown.

I never recognized myself nor my family in any of the New Left descriptions of workers.[25] During the "pro-worker" phase of the movement many student radicals "proletarianized" themselves by getting factory jobs. But then they often acted as if they'd been martyred. They let you know what giant sacrifices they'd made. They complained bitterly about people they felt had not sacrificed as much. They took the jobs due to strategic necessity, clearly hating what they were doing and tolerating it only because of the strategic payoff they expected. When the workers did not rise up, when the strategy did not pay off quickly, then they became even more obnoxiously self-righteous. But there was something weird even about the jolly proletarianizers, the ones whose joy at factory work seemed to come from outer space. I remember one guy explaining, with a look of robotoid bliss, that he loved getting up at five a.m because he drew strength and inspiration from being so close to the heart of basic production. This bozo apparently sang happy worker songs every morning to his machinery.

Student leftists, "middle class radicals," could never look at blue collar jobs and communities "objectively." They brought their apprehensions with them, and these apprehensions distorted their sensing. Working-class communities can be washed-out, boring places. Factory work is no fun: I grew up listening to stories about "the plant," and by the time I was about twelve I knew I wanted no part of it. I wanted any sort of job where I could get up at a human time, work someplace air-conditioned, come home clean, and have weekends off. Still, manual

25. As a partial test of the PMC thesis, I suggest that you ask New Leftists from blue-collar families if they ever recognized themselves in New Left theory. How many found a *class blindness* toward the lives of people from their background?

work never seemed like some humiliating fall from the civilized world. It seemed to be different for the "proletarianizers," and that told me I was dealing with people from a different world, a different *class* world from the one in which I'd grown up.

IV

Theorists from the Second International on down have repeatedly asked why socialism has been so weak in the U.S., and why its working class has not been class conscious. This question usually goes along with that of how to Americanize Marx. The U.S. lag behind the international movement led to the discussion in the late '20s of "American exceptionalism," and it led Corey, in the '30s, to investigate the importance of the "middle class."[26] While various Marxists worried about America's "exceptionalism," several generations of American sociologists have celebrated our almost-classlessness, have built careers and destroyed forests pinning down the ways in which our working class does not behave as Marx is supposed to have predicted. Everyone agrees: there is no (or not yet) class consciousness in the U.S.

At least, there is nothing like the European working class consciousness. There has been class violence in the U.S., more of it, maybe, than in most European counties. There is a terrific sense of class hatred here. People appraise each other carefully, they identify class origins, and they spit on each other across class bounderies. Ask a waitress. I learned, growing up, that there's Us and Them, ordinary people and "rich people." These rich people look down on our sort, and we hate them. Now, in the U.S. we never see the people who are really rich, so those people I called "rich" were actually the "upper middle class." The Scarsdale people, the PMC. They were the bosses that we saw; they were the schoolteachers who acted like missionaries bringing "culture" to the heathen. They tried to teach us to shut up and be obedient, and they tried to interest us in the elements of the "finer" culture outside. We made them miserable and they complained: "How did I get stuck teaching these dummies, why can't I get a job teaching in a *nice* suburb?"

Kids I knew aspired to open gas stations, or to become state troopers. Later, in high school, they aspired to the Marine Corps for manly adventure, or to the Navy to avoid the Army. If any of us aspired

---

26. For American Exceptionalism, cf. various articles by Jay Lovestone in CPUSA publications in the late '20s; also, the more interesting Leon Samson, *Toward a United Front,* New York, 1935; Lewis Corey, *The Crisis of the Middle Classes,* New York, 1935.

to go higher, we might hope to become a schoolteacher, just like the hated Mr. So and So. And that was a different world. It might be possible, in a country with a different sort of class-consciousness, to be a teacher who is working class. That would require a sense of once-a-worker-always-a-worker, an overarching sense of class identity. And this, in turn, would require a sense of class-mission, a sense that your social class was more than a rating or a category into which you were dropped. Millions of English workers have sung Blake's hymn:

> ...And did the Countenance Divine
> Shine forth upon our clouded hills?
> And was Jerusalem builded here
> Among these dark Satanic mills?
>
> ...I will not cease from mental fight
> Nor shall my sword sleep in my hand
> Till we have built Jerusalem
> In England's green and pleasant land.

Can anyone imagine American workers in the twentieth century singing a song like that? Here, again, we find the early New Left problem of "agency." The Ehrenreichs' "PMC" paper is part of an answer to the question of what happened to American working class consciousness. It explains, also, the hostility along the edges between working class and "middle class," and it explains where the New Left came from. All these are political questions, the traditional U.S. socialist questions.

Most discussion, so far, of the PMC thesis has missed the point. I've sat through several of these discussions: twice at meetings of chapters of New American Movement, once at a NAM convention, once at a "conference on dialectics," and once at a socialist school. And I read the letters that appeared in *Radical America* after that magazine published the essay. Leftists who came from blue-collar backgrounds tended to agree with the paper, saying that it made good sense of things they'd seen and felt in the movement. Of the other people, some took it as a personal insult, as if they were being called "pigs," and argued that they didn't like to be made to feel uncomfortable. A classic was the socialist editor who said that "if the Ehrenreichs are correct, then I should quit the paper and get a job in a factory and join the RCP [Revolutionary Communist Party]; I don't want to join the RCP and I don't want to work in a factory, so they must be wrong."[27]

The other, more serious, critics took the "PMC" paper as an exercise

27. NAM Convention, 1976.

in class definition, as a suggestion of various critieria by which one might define a social class. The Ehrenreichs had used the wrong criteria, they said, so they offered their own, alternative, ways to define a class. Most often they argued that a "Marxist definition" would derive a social class by extrapolating from Marx's equation, found in *Capital*, for the movement of surplus value. Only this extrapolation could get you down to Marxist basics, they argued, and any talk of the "social existence" or the "culture" of a class was bourgeois idealist and unmarxist and wrong.

Clearly, the article was not intended to add to the clutter of Marxist writings on how to define classes; the Ehrenreichs should, probably, have used the word "describe" instead of "define" to introduce their summary of the characteristics of the PMC there at the beginning of Section II (subtitled "A Definition"). In fact, it makes little sense to talk about definitions of social classes. Definitions are roughly timeless and imply that the things defined must *always* carry the characteristics of the definition or else, if their characteristics change, be different things. Definitions, then, are tricky to attempt to apply to that historical grouping of people called a "class." What's more, while a definition might help us to decide what sort of an animal we'd seen—this is a toad, that's a frog—there is no point to using definitions in a similar way on people. Classes define themselves. If a class does not exist until we define it, if people are not members of a class until we locate them in one, then there are really no classes.

Many of the critics seemed to believe that Marx had provided "the classic" definition of the working class, and seemed to believe that people had not known they were workers until Marx told them so. Marx, on this view, created "marxist analysis" and them applied it to society.[28] Marxism means "method" derived (with a twist) from Hegel. However, it seems more likely that English and French working class movements, having defined themselves, pressed "the labor question" into the middle of European politics and thereby created Marx. The labor problem even affected Germans, even cloudy Hegelian philosophers like the young Marx; why else did Marx begin to study economics?

One further problem: Marx never finished defining his social classes. There is no classical Marxist definition of the working class, at least no

28. The most sophisticated statement of this view is Georg Lukacs, *History and Class Consciousness* (Boston, 1971), especially the chapter, "What is Orthodox Marxism?"

definition done by Marx.[29] He began such a definition in the last pages of Volume III of *Capital*, and he had gotten as far as noting that having the same sources of revenue might constitute a group of people into a class. But, he adds, this will not work, and "here the manuscript ends." I do not believe that Marx could have finished his constitution of social classes. It's possible to see how he could move from the historical facts of the English capitalist economy to an abstract economic model behind it; but it is very difficult to see how he could have moved from the abstract model out through the complicated tangle of existing social classes to define anything as thick and rich as the life of a working class. And it may just be that this is the difficulty that kept him from finishing *Capital*: he didn't finish it because he couldn't.[30]

Having lost themselves in class models, the critics rarely thought to challenge the evidence on which the PMC had been based. The Ehrenreichs assume the work of Braverman, Lasch, Montgomery (and friends), who believe that there was, between 1890 and 1920, a thorough industrial and social reorganization of the working class, one that aimed to remove the working and cultural autonomy of the class. Montgomery, for instance, has found several strike waves fought, during this period, to retain as much control as possible over the work process. Somehow, none of the critics thought to attack "PMC" by attacking its sources in Braverman and the others.[31]

Many of the critics were upset that the PMC included professionals and managerials together. By ignoring the "social existence" of the class, as ephemeral superstructural fluff, they were able to argue that pro-

29. Nor can I find one in the available English translations of Kautsky. See, incidentally, Adam Przeworski, "Proletariat into a Class: The Process of Class Formation from Karl Kautsky's *Class Struggle* to Present Controversies," *Politics and Society,* VII (1977), p. 353. "The concept of the proletariat seems to have been self-evident to the founders of scientific socialism."

30. See, also, Edmund Wilson, *To the Finland Station* (New York: 1972), pp. 352-53.

31. Harry Braverman, *Labor and Monopoly Capital* (New York: 1974). David Montgomery, "New Unionism," *Journal of Social History,* 1974; and "Workers Control of Machine Production in the 19th Century," *Labor History,* Fall, 1976. Christopher Lasch, *New Radicalism in America* (New York: 1965); and *haven in Heartless World* (New York: 1977). Katherine Stone, "The Origins of Joab Structures in the Steel Industry," Review of Radical Political Economics, Summer, 1974. Bryan Palmer, "Class, Conception, and Conflict," RRPE, Summer, 1975. See, also, the discussion between Palmer and Jon Amsden at the Spring, 1977 MARHO Conference. For another critique of the Montgomery theory, see Jean Monds, "Workers Control and the Historians," *New Left Review #97.*

fessionals and managers did not belong in the same class, because they did different work. This, incidentally, sounds like just the sort of constituting of a class to which Marx was beginning to object in that last paragraph of *Capital*. The critics' objections would have been more convincing had they checked to see if professionals and managers often come from the same families; if they go to the same schools; if they marry each other; if they live in the same neighborhoods; if they read the same magazines; if they dress alike, in fashions promoted in those magazines; if they speak a similar language; if they belong to the same country clubs; if they take their vacations in the same places. If not, them the critics have a point. There is sociological data available on most of these, and, having gone through it, I'm convinced that managers and professionals are tightly connected; but, then, we know the answer to most of these questions without having to go to sociology for them.

V

The problem of the PMC is real. Ordinary people recognize the difference between the "upper middle class" and working people. So do advertisers (remember why the *Saturday Evening Post* folded?); so do bourgeois sociologists. Some people have claimed that "if the PMC is true, then it will be harder to make a powerful socialist movement here." But the problem is real, and leftists have worried about it for nearly twenty years, like some disease so awful that we don't want to understand how it works. The *class* conflict between the U.S. left and the U.S. working class will not disappear by itself; but we can't overcome it unless, first, we recognize it. The Ehrenreichs' article "The Professional-Managerial Class" begins that recognition.

7

Intellectuals and the Class Structure
of
Capitalist Society

Erik Olin Wright

Intellectuals have always had an ambiguous status both as actors in the history of Marxism and as categories within Marxist theory. On the one hand, the contribution of intellectuals to socialist movements is undeniable: as theorists, polemicists, revolutionary leaders. The most decisive advances in revolutionary theory have been made by men and women with considerable education, who spent a great deal of their time in intellectual activities. While it is unquestionably true that their ideas were nurtured through their contact with the masses, especially in the course of social struggles, nevertheless it is equally true that most important contributors to revolutionary theory were not themselves proletarians or peasants. They were intellectuals, and the systematic development of revolutionary theory is impossible to imagine without their contribution.

On the other hand, the very fact that most intellectuals are not unambiguously part of the working class has meant that they have always been viewed with some suspicion within revolutionary movements. Although as individuals, intellectuals might be totally committed to a revolutionary project, as a social category intellectuals occupy privileged positions within bourgeois ideological relations and often privileged positions within bourgeois economic relations as well. The common designation by Marxists of intellectuals as "petty bourgeois" reflects the reality of these privileges. The result is that while intellectuals as individuals have been essential for revolutionary movements, intellectuals as a social category have often impeded the growth of working class socialist struggles.

This essay will not attempt to sort out the complex ways in which intellectuals have furthered and hampered socialist movements. It will also not deal with the critical programmatic question of what precisely should be the role of intellectuals within contemporary revolutionary organization. Such issues are obviously important, but before they can be sensibly addressed it is necessary to have a more refined understanding of precisely what is the class character of intellectual labor itself. This will be the central focus of this essay: to unravel the location of intellectuals within the class structure of advanced capitalist societies.

Before proceeding it is necessary to define more carefully how I will use the expression "intellectual" throughout this discussion. The term "intellectual" has three interconnected meanings: First, "intellectual" designates a *general characteristic of all human activity,* namely that all activity involves in one way or another the use of the intellect, the mind. All activity, no matter how routinized, involves some mental processes. Second, "intellectual" designates a *specific type of laboring activity*: laboring activity which is involved in one way or another with the elaboration and dissemination of ideas (rather than simply the use of ideas). Third, "intellectual" designates a *category of people*: people whose activity is primarily that of elaborating and disseminating ideas.[1]

One of the central characteristics of the division of labor in capitalist society is the tendency for intellectuals as a category of people to replace intellectuality as a type of laboring activity. This is usually expressed as the tendency for the progressive separation of mental and manual labor within capitalist society, that is, for a progressive separation of the

1. Gramsci distinguished between the first two of these concepts of intellectuals and the third by saying that "All men are intellectuals, one could therefore say; but not all men have in society the function of intellectuals." (Antonio Gramsci, *Selections from the Prison Notebooks,* ed. by Quintin Hoare and Geoffrey Nowell Smith [New York: International Publishers, 1971], p.9). The "function of intellectuals" refers to the third of these definitions: people whose primary activity is the elaboration and dissemination of ideas.

activities of planning, designing, organizing, conceptualizing, from the activities of executing, producing, and directly transforming nature. Instead of the elaboration and dissemination of ideas being part of everyone's laboring activity, such activity becomes tendentially restricted to specific categories of people: intellectuals.

The analysis in the following pages will concentrate on the third usage of the concept of intellectuals, intellectuals as a social category. The basic task, then, will be to sort out the class location of individuals whose central activity or function is the elaboration and dissemination of ideas.

Within Marxist theory there are at least five broad interpretations of the class position of intellectuals: 1) all intellectuals who are wage-laborers are part of the working class; 2) intellectuals can be divided into three categories: those who are tied to the working class, those who are tied to the bourgeoisie and those who are tied to precapitalist classes; 3) intellectuals constitute one segment of the petty bourgeosie, sometimes referred to as the "new" petty bourgeoisie; 4) intellectuals largely fall into the "Professional and Managerial Class," which constitutes a distinct class, separate from both the working class and the petty boureoisie; and 5) intellectuals should generally be thought of as occupying contradictory locations within class relations at the economic and ideological levels. I will argue that each of these interpretations taps part of the reality of intellectuals in capitalist society, but that the fifth interpretation provides the most comprehensive basis for a rigourous understanding of intellectuals.

1) All intellectuals are workers. In this interpretation, the essential defining criterion for the working class is wage labor. Workers are defined as those people who do not own their own means of production, who are propertyless, and thus must seek employment from capital or the state in order to live. Regardless of what concrete activities they perform once they are employed, all people who have nothing to sell but their labor power are workers. In this perspective, while intellectuals may constitute a privileged stratum of the working class in terms of income, status, job security and other privileges, in terms of fundamental class relations they occupy the same position as industrial wage-laborers.[2]

There is a certain compelling quality to this simple polarization view of the class structure of capitalist societies and the treatment of intellectuals as workers. What it captures is the immanent tendency of capitalism towards polarization. The fundamental dynamics of the capitalist mode of production are embedded in the polarized relation of

---

2. A recent defense of this position can be found in an article by Francesca Friedman, "The Internal Structure of the American Working Class," *Socialist Revolution* #26 (1975).

labor to capital, and at the highest level of abstraction one can see all class positions in capitalist societies as being tendentially drawn into one polarized position or the other. But as an historical account of the actual class character of intellectual wage-labor, the view that intellectuals are firmly within the proletariat is inadequate for many reasons. Perhaps the most important issue in the present context is the assumption that the complex relationship between capital and labor can be captured by a single dimension, a single criterion: selling and buying the commodity labor power. The relationship between capital and labor is fundamentally determined by what Marxists call the social relations of production, and the selling and buying of labor power constitutes only one aspect—albeit a very important aspect—of these relations. Two other dimensions of the social relations of production are especially important: the social relations of control over the labor of others within the labor process, and the social relations of control over one's own labor within the labor process. If the social relations of production represent a complex combination of several dimensions of social relations, then workers cannot be defined simply as wage laborers, but as wage laborers who also do not control the labor of others within production and do not control the use of their own labor within the labor process. In these terms, many intellectuals would be excluded from the working class, even though they do sell their labor power as a commodity.

2) **Intellectuals belong to several different classes**. This position is closely associated with the work of Antonio Gramsci.[3] Gramsci identifies three categories of intellectuals: those intellectuals who are organic intellectuals of the working class, those who are organic intellectuals of the bourgeoisie and those whom he calls "traditional intellectuals," typically organic intellectuals of the feudal aristocracy. Rather than seeing the global category of "intellectuals" having any genuine class unity either as part of the working class or of some other class, Gramsci identifies the class character of intellectuals with the specific function they play in the class struggle. Those intellectuals who contribute to the hegemony of bourgeois ideology comprise the intellectual stratum of the bourgeois class; those intellectuals who combat bourgeois ideology and contribute to the counter-hegemony of the proletariat are part of the working class; and those intellectuals who embody backward looking precapitalist culture reflecting the world view of the feudal aristocracy, constitute the traditional stratum of intellectuals. In the course of capitalist development, this latter category tends to be absorbed into the capitalist system as organic intellectuals of the bourgeoisie, and thus

3. See in particular Gramsci's important essay, "On Intellectuals" in Gramsci, *Prison Notebooks*.

there is a general tendency for intellectuals to become polarized into two camps.

Gramsci's conception of intellectuals has the considerable merit of emphasizing the dynamic rather than static nature of class relations: class location must always be conceptualized in terms of class struggle, not simply in terms of a structure of positions. Nevertheless, it has a number of important limitations. In particular, by arguing that all intellectuals whose activity reproduces the hegemony of the bourgeoisie are part of the bourgeois class itself, Gramsci tends to minimize the objective antagonism between many of these intellectuals and the bourgeoisie. While it may be true, for example, that teachers contribute to the ideological hegemony of the bourgeoisie, it is also true that many categories of teachers are oppressed in various ways by the bourgeoisie. Some teachers, in fact, are even exploited by capital in the technical sense of producing surplus value.[4] Thus, while teachers may be *functionally* organic intellectuals of the bourgeoisie, *structurally* they are generally not members of the bourgeois class.

This conflation of functional and structural definitions of class location tends to obscure the concrete social relations within which intellectual labor is performed. It is one thing to argue, for example, that the director of a news network or a university is part of the bourgeois class, and another to argue that reporters and teachers are part of the bourgeoisie. It is of fundamental importance to distinguish between those intellectuals who control the apparatus of production of ideas (ideology), and those who merely work within those apparatuses. Once this distinction is made, it becomes possible to talk about the proletarianization of intellectual labor—the progressive loss of any control over the immediate conditions of work by intellectual wage laborers. And this in turn makes it possible to talk about the increasing *structural* basis for class unity between certain categories of intellectuals

---

4. Marx makes this point in a famous passage in *Capital* comparing teachers to workers in sausage factories:

> A schoolmaster is a productive worker when, in addition to belaboring the heads of his pupils, he works himself into the ground to enrich the owner of the school. That the latter has laid out his capital in a teaching factory, instead of a sausage factory, makes no difference to the relation.

(Karl Marx, *Capital* [London: Penguin/NLB, 1976], p. 644).

Such teachers could still function as organic intellectuals of the bourgeoisie even though they would be exploited directly by capital. This highlights the difference between an analysis of the structure of class relations and the functional roles in the class struggle. The complexity of the class analysis of intellectual labor, as we shall see in the discussion of contradictory class locations, comes precisely from the disjuncture between their structural and functional location within class relations.

and the working class, even though in functional terms they might remain "organic intellectuals of the bourgeoisie."[5] This is not to deny the value of Gramsci's insights about the roles of intellectuals within the class struggle, and in particular his insistence on the importance of organic intellectuals of the working class for any revolutionary movement. The point is that such an analysis of functional relations to the class struggle is not a substitute for a critical decoding of the objective class character of given structural positions held by intellectuals.

3) **Intellectuals are part of the petty bourgeoisie.** The dissatisfaction with the simple polarization view of the class structure has led many Marxists to treat intellectuals as one segment of the petty bourgeoisie. In order to distinguish this segment from the traditional petty bourgeoisie of small shopkeepers and artisans, the intellectual-petty bourgeoisie has often been called part of the "new petty bourgeoisie." One of the most systematic advocates of this position at the present time is Nicos Poulantzas, especially in his recent book *Classes in Contemporary Capitalism.*

The view that intellectuals constitute a new petty bourgeoisie rests on two complementary claims: first, that intellectuals cannot be considered part of the working class, and second, that they share a fundamental similarity in class location with the traditional petty bourgeoisie.

A number of arguments are used to support the first claim: in addition to the rejection of wage-labor as an adequate criterion for defining the proletariat, it has been argued by Poulantzas and others that intellectuals should be excluded from the working class because they are generally unproductive laborers and because they do not engage in manual labor.[6] While I agree with Poulantzas that intellectuals (or at least most intellectuals) are not an integral part of the working class, I disagree with the arguments he uses to defend this thesis.[7] Let us examine each of these arguments in turn.

5. This point will be further amplified in the discussion of contradictory class locations below.

6. Unproductive labor is being used here in the technical Marxist sense of labor which does not produce surplus value. This would include the labor of bank clerks, most sales workers, goverment bureaucrats, etc. To say that labor is unproductive in this sense is not to say that it is unuseful, but merely to say that it does not produce new value (surplus value) for capital. For a more elaborate discussion of unproductive labor, see James O'Connor, "Productive and Unproductive Labor," *Politics and Society* (1975).

7. For a much more detailed review and critique of Poulantzas' analysis of classes, see Erik Olin Wright, "Class Boundaries in Advanced Capitalist Societies," *New Left Review* #98 (1976). This essay has been substantially revised

In order to make the claim that unproductive labor as a whole is in a different class from productive labor, it is necessary to establish that this division corresponds to a division of *fundamental* class interests.[8] The essential method for assessing such divisions of fundamental class interests is to decode rigorously the social relations of production and analyze the locations of specific categories of labor within those relations. Categories of labor which occupy similar positions within the social relations of production share, at the economic level, the same fundamental class interests. In these terms it is very difficult to maintain that unproductive labor occupies a distinctively different location within production relations from productive labor: like productive workers, many unproductive workers have absolutely no control over their labor process, are completely subordinated to capital, have no capacity to control the labor of others, and so on. Now, it may be true that most intellectuals do not fall into the working class on these dimensions of social relations (indeed, this is what I will argue in the discussion of contradictory locations), but it is because of their location on these dimensions and not because of their status as unproductive labor per se that they should be considered outside of the working class.

Poulantzas' argument for excluding intellectuals from the working class because they are mental laborers is more complex. For Poulantzas, the division between mental and manual labor constitutes the basic relationship of ideological domination/subordination in capitalist society (i.e., manual labor is subordinated to mental labor at the ideological level). Since classes must be defined at the ideological as well as economic levels, it follows, Poulantzas insists, that since mental labor dominates manual labor at the ideological level it cannot be part of the working class. Since intellectuals are one category of mental labor, it also follows that intellectuals are outside of the working class.

While Poulantzas may push this analysis too far—arguing that even

and published as Chapter Two in Erik Olin Wright, *Class, Crisis and the State* (London: New Left Books, 1978).

8. Fundamental interests must be contrasted to immediate interests. Immediate interests are interests that are defined strictly within a given mode of production. They are interests which take a mode of production as a given. Within the working class, such immediate interests are defined primarily in terms of market relations. Fundamental interests, on the other hand, are interests defined at the level of the mode of production. They are interests which call into question the mode of production itself, posing choices between alternative social relations of production. To say that basic class divisions are defined by fundamental interest implies that classes are ultimately defined by interests in different modes of production, different kinds of social relations.

secretaries and routinized salesworkers are mental laborers and thus dominate the working class ideologically—nevertheless, the central thrust of his argument seems to me substantially correct. I would only modify his position in one important respect: It is not enough simply to do mental labor to dominate the working class (even at the ideological level). It is also necessary to occupy a position of domination within ideological apparatuses. A mental laborer (such as a secretary) who lacks any control over the process of ideological production does not dominate the working class ideologically. In these terms, most intellectuals—people engaged in the elaboration and dissemination of ideas—would have some degree of control over the production of ideology, and thus would occupy a position of ideological domination with respect to the working class. This point will be developed at greater length in the discussion of contradictory locations within class relations below.

It is insufficient, of course, simply to establish that intellectuals are not part of the working class; it is equally important to understand what class they are part of. Two different sorts of arguments have been used to support the claim that intellectuals share a common class positon with the petty bourgeoisie. First, as Judah Hill has argued, certain categories of intellectuals—especially professionals—can be viewed as "owning" their means of production even when they are employed by capital. That is, such intellectuals own their intangible intellectual skills (especially when such skills are certified in diplomas and licenses), and since these skills constitute the critical "means of production" of intellectuals, intellectuals should be seen as property-holders just like the traditional petty bourgeoisie.[9]

The central difficulty with this position is that it confuses an analysis of class defined in terms of market relations with class understood at the level of production relations. While it is certainly true, as Weber argued 50 years ago, that intellectuals possess certain special skills which give them certain advantages within the market, they do not necessarily have any real control *over the use* of those intellectual skills within production. Except in the case of self-employed professionals, most intellectuals give up considerable degrees of control over the use of their intellectual "means of production" when they accept employment by capital or the state. In order to maintain that certain categories of intellectual wage-laborers genuinely "own" their means of production, therefore, it is necessary to examine systematically the labor process within which they engage in intellectual labor and see the extent to which they actually retain self-direction of intellectual production. In general,

9. See Judah Hill, "Class Analysis: the United States in the 1970s," Pamphlet, Class Analysis, P.O. Box 8494, Emeryville, California, 1975.

intellectual wage-laborers wold have much less control over their labor process than the traditional petty bourgeoisie.

The second argument supporting the claim that intellectuals are part of the petty bourgeoisie centers on an hypothesized unity of the ideologies of new and old petty bourgeoisies. This theme has been stressed by Poulantzas in his various works. Poulantzas argues that the very character of intellectual labor and the organizational structures within which it is performed in captialist society guarantee that intellectuals will be characterized by the essential elements of petty bourgeois ideology: individualism, veneration of the state, careerism, etc. In spite of the fact that intellectual wage-labor is involved in entirely different social relations of production from the petty bourgeoisie at the economic level—the petty bourgeoisie consists of independent producers within simple commodity relations of production while intellectuals are subordinated directly to capital within capitalist relations of production—nevertheless, Poulantzas argues, the congruence of their ideologies is so strong as to weld them into a single class.

Again, as in the simple polarization view of intellectuals, there is a compelling quality to this analysis. Certainly in terms of class conciousness, there are clear tendencies in many capitalist societies for intellectuals to have similar world views to the petty bourgeoisie, and at least in certain circumstances, to adopt similar political orientations. And yet, in the end, the view that intellectuals fall firmly into the petty bourgeoisie is as unsatisfactory as the view that they are part of the working class. To begin with, the claim that the ideologies of intellectual wage-laborers are essentially identical to the traditional petty bourgeoisie requires a very limited reading of ideology. For example, while both categories may hold highly individualistic ideologies, the individualism of the traditional petty bourgeoisie (be your own boss, rugged individualism) is entirely antithetical to the individualism of the employed intellectuals (organizational competitiveness, careerism). To equate the two is to obscure the fundamentally different social relations within which these individualistic ideologies operate.

Even more importantly, even if it were the case that the ideologies of intellectuals and the traditional petty bourgeoisie were identical, it would be unsatisfactory from a Marxist perspective to give such weight to consciousness and ideology that they can utterly obliterate the fundamental differences in economic relations which characterize most intellectuals and the traditional petty bourgeoisie. While wage labor may not be a sufficient criterion for defining class, it is certainly an important criterion, for it determines the basic contours of the relationship to capital. This difference in the relationship to capital means that there are basic—not just marginal—differences in the relationships of the petty bourgeoisie and intellectual wage-laborers to working class struggles and struggles for socialism. Specifically, because they are small property-owners, the petty bourgeoisie have a much more contradictory relationship to socialism than do intellectual wage-laborers. This is not to say that the class interests of intellectuals and workers are identical—indeed, if they were we would say that intellectual labor was part of the working class—but merely that those interests are generally less opposed to each other than are the interests of the working class to those of the traditional petty bourgeoisie.

4) **Intellectuals are part of a Professional-Managerial Class.** If intellectuals should generally not be considered part of the working class, and if they are also not part of the petty bourgeoisie, then perhaps they should be considered part of a completely different class, a class which is distinct from the working class, the petty bourgeoisie and the bourgeoisie. This is essentially the claim of Barbara and John Ehrenreich in their analysis of the Professional-Managerial Class. They define the PMC as:

> consisting of those salaried mental workers who do not own the means of production and whose major function in the social division of labor may be described broadly as the reproduction of capitalist culture and capitalist class relations. [p. 12]

Most salaried intellectuals would certainly fall into the PMC by this definition. The question then becomes whether the PMC can be really viewed as a "class" in the same sense that the bourgeoisie and the proletariat are classes, or whether what the Ehrenreichs are calling class should be understood as some other kind of social reality. It is one thing to argue that the various categories grouped together under the label PMC have a certain internal unity, and another thing to identify the logic of that unity as a class unity.

The Ehrenreichs use two basic arguments to support the thesis that the PMC is in fact a class. First, they argue that the PMC is "characterized by a common relationship to the economic foundations of society—the means of production and the socially organized patterns of distribution and consumption." [p. 11] Second, they argue that the PMC is a class because it is "characterized by a coherent social and cultural existence," that is, that its members "share a common life style, educational background, kinship networks, consumption patterns, work habits, beliefs." [p. 11] This second argument is clearly dependent upon the first, for many other social categories which do not constitute classes are characterized by a coherent social and cultural existence (e.g., farmers, lumberjacks, sailors). It is only if it is established that the PMC in fact does occupy a common "relation to the economic foundations of society" that this second argument can be seen as reinforcing its existence as a class.

On what basis, then, do the Ehrenreichs argue that the PMC does constitute a distinctive location with respect to the means of production? Their essential argument is that the PMC is defined by a distinctive *function* in the social division of labor, namely the function of reproducing class relations. The concept of a common relation to the "economic foundations" of society is therefore identified with a common function in the division of labor, and positions which perform a common function are then viewed as constituting a class.[10]

As in Gramsci's analysis, the Ehrenreichs' discussion of functions is extremely important for any adequate understanding of intellectuals (or other members of the PMC), particularly in terms of their role in the class struggle. Nevertheless, such simple identification of the class location of intellectuals with their function in the social division of labor tends to collapse the structural and functional aspects of class into a single dimension, and this obscures rather than clarifies the essential class character of intellectual wage-labor. This is so for two basic reasons: 1) the problem of noncoincidence of structural positions with functions; and 2) the need to understand the social relations internal to the performance of functions. Let us look briefly at each of these issues.

Functions within a society, including the function of reproducing class relations, must be understood as *dimensions* of social relations, not *categories* or positions. While it is certainly true that some positions are more "specialized" than others in the function of reproduction, *every* position determined by capitalist relations of production to some extent or another contributes to the reproduction of those relations. Marx's analysis of commodity fetishism, for example, is in part an analysis of how the reproduction of capitalist relations of production is embedded in the very character of those relations rather than being simply the responsibility of some specialized occupations. Manual workers on the production line, therefore, also perform the "function" of reproducing capitalist relations of production simply by participating in capitalist production.

In spite of this, it is true that some positions do become specialized in this function of reproduction. But it is equally true that even these specialized reproductive positions are generally not exclusively reproductive. Engineers, for example, do not merely function to reproduce capitalist class relations. They also design bridges and in other ways perform clearly productive functions. Why should their class location be

10. For an extended theoretical defense of such functional definitions of class relations, see G. Carchedi, *On the Economic Identification of Social Classes* (London: Routledge and Kegan Paul, 1977).

defined exclusively by their reproductive function? On what basis is it possible to establish which function is "more" important? And even if this can be determined, why should the dominant function necessarily have exclusive sway in determining class location? These questions illustrate some of the difficulties in making any simple identification of class and function.

The problem with a simple function=class conception becomes even clearer when we examine the social relations within which the specialized function of reproducing class relations takes place. If we examine some ideological apparatus—a school, a newspaper, a church— it is immediately clear that not all positions within that apparatus have the same structural relation to the functions of that apparatus. Some positions are involved in the control of the entire apparatus. Others involve control over specific activities within the apparatus, perhaps simply the activity of the position itself, but no control whatsoever over the apparatus as a whole. And finally, some positions are excluded entirely from any control over either the apparatus or specific activities within it. In terms of their relationship to the class structure as a whole, *all* positions within an ideological apparatus serve the "function" of reproducing the capitalist class relations since the ideological apparatus itself serves this function. But clearly, different locations within the apparatus have entirely different structural relationships to this function than others.

The Ehrenreichs are quite aware of these gradations of positions within a single functional apparatus, and it leads them to argue that certain positions within the PMC are "closer" to the working class than others, while other positions are "closer" to the bourgeoisie. A registered nurse, for example, constitutes a position within the PMC close to the working class; an upper-middle manager in a corporation constitutes a position within the PMC closer to the bourgeoisie. The Ehrenreichs stress that the PMC is not a homogeneous class, but is characterized by an internal hierarchy of strata reflecting a range of structural locations within the common function of reproducing capitalist social relations.

Now, to say that both a registered nurse and an upper-middle manager are both members of the same class (albeit at different "ends" of the class) implies that they are "closer" to each other than they are to any other class. If this were not the case—if in fact registered nurses are "closer" to workers than to upper-middle managers—then it would not make sense to see them as being within the same class. A registered nurse and an upper-middle manager might still have a certain commonality within class relations, but that commonality could not be understood as defining them within a single, coherent class. This is not a problem in the ambiguities at the "bounderies" of classes, but of the very logic of designating a set of positions within the social division of labor as a class.[11]

The question of whether the PMC can be considered a class can thus be re-posed as follows: does it make sense to consider a set of positions that are in some sense situated "between" the working class and the bourgeoisie, in which some of these positions are closer to the working class and others closer to the bourgeoisie, a "class" in the same sense that the bourgeoisie and the proletariat are classes? There is a strong tradition within Marxism to assume that *every* position within the social division of labor *must* fall firmly into one class or another. If this assumption is accepted, then by default, all of the positions between the working class and the bourgeoisie must, of necessity, constitute a class.

But there is an alternative: instead of insisting that all positions within the social division of labor fall firmly into classes, some positions can be seen as *objectively torn between classes*. If classes are understood as social relations, not things, this implies that certain positions have a contradictory character within those social relations. On certain dimensions of class relations they share the characteristics of the bourgeoisie, on others they share the characteristics of the working class. If this stance is adopted, then it becomes very easy to talk about the sense in which some of these positions can be considered "closer" to the working class than others. They are closer precisely in the sense that their location within the social relations of production shares more characteristics with the working class than with the bourgeoisie. In this view, instead of seeing intellectuals as part of a distinctive class with its own coherence and unity, intellectuals would be understood as falling within a contradictory location within class relations.

5) **Intellectuals occupy contradictory locations within class relations.** Let me explain more rigorously exactly what I mean by the expression "contradictory locations within class relations." In a sense, of course, all class locations in capitalist society are "contradictory," since the very concept of class expresses fundamentally antagonistic relations. Some positions, however, are contradictory in a double sense: first, they reflect the basic antagonistic class relations of capitalist society, and second, they are objectively torn between the antagonistic classes of that society. Such positions do not have a class identity in their own right: their class character is determined strictly by their location between classes. It is because of this derivative nature of their class location that

11. For all the difficulties in rigorously defining the 'boundaries" of the capitalist class and the working class, no one suggests that the aristocracy of labor (for example) is "closer" to the capitalist class than is an unskilled worker. The spacial metaphor is simply inappropriate for discussing class relations. A highly privileged worker may be more integrated into capitalist society, may accept the ideological hegemony of the bourgeoisie in a deeper way, and so on, but they are not closer to capitalists as a class.

such positions are referred to as contradictory locations within class relations.

Since classes in capitalist society cannot be defined simply in terms of economic relations,neither can contradictory locations. It is essential to specify the contradictory character of certain positions at the level of political and ideological class relations as well as at the level of social relations of production. In the case of intellectuals, it will be especially important to examine their class location at the ideological level. In what follows, we will first examine contradictory class locations in terms of social relations of production, and then extend this discussion to class relations at the ideological level. The upshot, as we shall see, is that *intellectuals typically occupy a contradictory class location between the working class and the petty bourgeoisie at the economic level, but between the working class and the bourgeoisie at the ideological level.*

At the level of social relations of production, there are three basic contradictory locations within class relations in capitalist society:

1) *Managers* occupy a contradictory location between the working class and the bourgeoisie.

2) *Small employers* occupy a contradictory location between the bourgeoisie and the petty bourgeoisie.

3) *Semi-autonomous employees* occupy a contradictory location between the petty bourgeoisie and the working class.

These three class locations are schematically illustrated in chart 1. The third category is especially important in the present context since much intellectual wage-labor falls into this location. Let us look at it a bit more closely.[12]

In order to understand the semi-autonomous employee category—the contradictory class location between the proletariat and the petty bourgeoisie—we need to look at the characteristic labor process of the

---

12. Because of space limitations, we will not systematically discuss managers and small employers in this essay. For a detailed discussion of these contradictory class locations at the level of production relations, see Wright, *Class, Crisis and the State,* especially Chapter Two, "The Class Structure of Advanced Capitalist Societies." The essential character of these locations can be very briefly summarized as follows: small employers are like capitalists in that they exploit labor power, but they are like the petty bourgeoisie in that they and members of their family directly engage in production themselves so that much of the surplus labor generated in production comes directly from their labor rather than simply from their workers. Managers are like capitalists in that they directly control the laboring activity of workers within production and may control the use of physical capital, and in some circumstances money capital, as well. They are excluded from control of the overall accumulation process and they sell their labor power as a commodity to capital.

Chart 1) Contradictory Locations Within Class Relations at the Level of Social Relations of Production

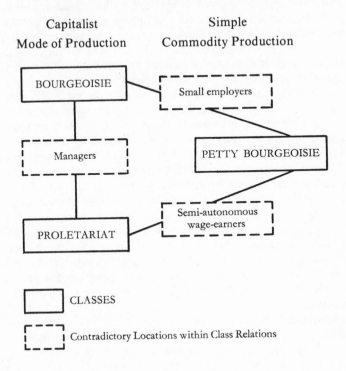

Capitalist
Mode of Production

Simple
Commodity Production

BOURGEOISIE

Small employers

Managers

PETTY BOURGEOISIE

Semi-autonomous
wage-earners

PROLETARIAT

☐ CLASSES

⌐ ⌐ Contradictory Locations within Class Relations

petty bourgeoisie and the proletariat. The distinctive thing about the petty bourgeois labor process is that the petty bourgeois producer directly controls that labor process. In common parlance, the petty bourgeois is his or her own boss. The pace of work, the tools and procedures used, the scheduling of work, the product produced, etc. are all under the control of the direct producer. In capitalist production, on the other hand, the worker has at most marginal control over the immediate labor process. In the extreme case of the production line regulated by principles of scientific management, the worker becomes a human machine with no autonomy whatsoever. In these terms, semi-autonomous employees represent those wage-laborers who, for a variety of reasons, maintain high levels of genuine control over their labor process. Like workers they are employed by capital (or the state), like workers they must sell their labor power in order to live, and like workers, they do not control the apparatus of production as a whole. But unlike workers, and like the petty bourgeoisie, they do have real control over much of their own labor process. This is often the situation of intellectual wage-labor. Perhaps the clearest example is an assistant professor, at least in an elite university. While assistant professors certainly do not have any control over the apparatus of education as a whole, they do have substantial degrees of control over what they teach, how they teach, what kind of research they do, how they spend their time, etc.

To describe a position as a contradictory location between the petty bourgeoisie and the working class means that such positions *simultaneously* share class interests with the working class and the petty bourgeoisie, but have interests identical to neither. They are objectively torn between the two classes. For such class positions, socialism simultaneously promises genuine liberation from the distortions and domination of capital and a reduction of the *individual* autonomy which they experience under capitalist conditions. That is, in a socialist society the labor process is controlled collectively by workers rather than either by capital or by individual laborers. This means that in many cases, especially for much intellectual labor, socialism implies a reduction in individual control over immediate laboring activity. It is in this sense that intellectual wage labor, to a greater or lesser extent, occupies a contradictory class location between the working class and the petty bourgeoisie.[13]

Intellectual labor, however, cannot be analysed solely in terms of social relations of production. As the Ehrenreichs correctly emphasize, intellectuals play key roles in the reproduction of capitalist social relations and capitalist culture, and this means that it is essential to analyse their class location at the ideological level.

To do this we must first identify the basic class relations at the ideological level. Without going into a great deal of detail on this question, three basic class locations can be identified at the ideological level:

---

13. The words "to a greater or lesser extent" are of considerable importance in this statement. Different categories of intellectuals will have different degrees of autonomy within the labor process, and thus accordingly will be closer to the proletariat or to the petty bourgeoisie. Ultimately, of course, it is rather arbitrary where one draws the line and says: this is a situation where autonomy has been so reduced that it is no longer a contradictory class location. There will inevitably occur class locations which are not only contradictory, but ambiguous, i.e., it is impossible to provide an abstract, a priori classification of such positions. What this indicates is the inevitable limitation of a purely structural analysis of class and class relations. In the end it is not the theoretical precision of the analyst which determines exactly how such ambiguous positions will be organized into classes, but rather the actual, historical course of class struggles.

1) The *bourgeois class* location at the ideological level consists of those positions involving control over the process of ideological production as a whole, i.e., control over the bourgeois ideological *apparatuses*.

2) The *contradictory class* location at the ideological level consists of those positions which are involved in the elaboration and dissemination of bourgeois ideology, but not in the overall control of the apparatuses of bourgeois ideology.[14]

3) The *working class* location at the ideological level consists of those positions which are excluded from either the control over the apparatuses as a whole or the elaboration and dissemination of ideology within those apparatuses.

In terms of the educational system, for example, the bourgeois position would be held by top education officials (boards of regents, chancellors superintendents of schools); the contradictory locations would be typically held by teachers; and the working class location would be held by secretaries, janitors, school cafeteria workers, etc.[15]

Let us now try to combine these two levels of analysis—contradictory locations at the level of production relations and at the level of ideological relations— in order to understand the class character of intellectual labor. So that this discussion will not be too abstract, I will focus specifically on the class location of teachers, although the analysis would apply to many other categories of intellectuals as well. By and large, teachers fall into the contradictory location between the petty bourgeoisie and the working class at the level of production relations. Historically, teachers have had fair amounts of control over their work process, but have generally had little to do with the control of the

14. In the present discussion I am restricting the notion of "elaboration and dissemination" of bourgeois ideology to *active* processes of elaboration/dissemination, that is, processes in which the actual *content* of activity is directly involved in the formation of ideology (e.g., writing advertising copy, teaching classes, engaging in sociological research, etc.). It is possible to extend the notion of elaboration/dissemination of ideology to include *passive* processes as well, that is processes in which the *form* of the relationship of the position to the working class reproduces bourgeois ideology regardless of the specific content of the activity of the position. For example, because of the ideology that only "experts" are capable of making technical decisions, that the relationship between experts and workers directly reproduces the ideological subordination of the working class even if the expert is designing a bridge rather than designing propaganda. This distinction between active and passive forms of the dissemination/elaboration of ideology is very similar to what the Ehrenreichs refer to as the "explicit" and "hidden" roles in the process of reproducing capitalist class relations and capitalist culture.

15. It is important to remember throughout this discussion that we are talking about the class character of positions. A teacher, for example, could be

educational system as a whole.[16] At the ideological level, on the other hand, teachers occupy a contradictory location between the bourgeoisie and the working class since teaching positions are one of the critical locations for the dissemination and elaboration of bourgeois ideology. Teachers are thus simultaneously located between the working class and the petty bourgeoisie and between the working class and the bourgeoisie.

This *disarticulation* between their class location at the economic and ideological levels has important consequences for the potential role of teachers (and other categories of intellectuals) in the class struggle. To the extent that teachers have a certain real level of autonomy at the level of social relations of (educational) production, they can potentially subvert bourgeois ideology at the level of ideological relations. There is thus a potential contradiction between the economic and ideological class location of educational workers, and this contradiction poses certain real threats to the bourgeoisie.

This potential contradiction is sharpest in institutions of higher education. In the United States at least, teachers in primary and secondary schools have much narrower autonomy in every respect than do teachers in higher education, and in particular they have less autonomy in terms of the ideological content of what they teach. In most places in the United States, if a primary school teacher were to attempt to seriously disseminate Communist ideas in the classroom, she/he would almost certainly be out of a job. In colleges and universities the situation is more complex, and the autonomy of teachers is more of a reality. In spite of its ideological functions in supporting liberalism and creating the

thoroughly engaged with working class struggles and even teach Marxist ideas in the classroom even though the teacher-position is a contradictory location at the level of ideology. Of course, in most circumstances there is a systematic relationship between the class affiliation of individuals and the class character of their positions—most teachers in fact teach bourgeois ideology. If it should happen that, as a result of class struggles, a large proportion of teachers within bourgeois educational apparatuses began to challenge bourgeois ideology, there would be a serious crisis of ideological hegemony. Under such circumstances one would expect extremely sharp struggles within the apparatus as attempts were made to re-impose bourgeois ideology on the teachers.

16. In an extremely interesing study of class struggles over education in Chicago, Julia Wriggley shows how in the first part of this century Chicago teachers attempted to establish parent-teacher councils which would have effective control over educational policy. These attempts were thoroughly repressed by the educational bureaucracy and the political apparatus. Many teachers were fired and it was made clear that teachers would have no organized role in educational policy making. (Julia Wriggley, "The Politics of Education in Chicago: Social Conflicts and the Public Schools," Ph. D. Dissertation, Dept. of Sociology, University of Wisconsin, 1977).

image of open and free discussion, "academic freedom" within the University does in fact create greater space for ideas which challenge bourgeois ideology. This is precisely why authoritarian regimes in capitalist societies are so insistent on imposing strict ideological controls within universities. If the relative autonomy of academics did not contradict their function at the ideological level, there would be no necessity for right-wing governments to purge so systematically the universities and schools. Conservatives may be somewhat paranoid in their estimation of the capacity of leftist academics to "poison" the minds of the young, but it is still true that the relative autonomy of teachers does create the possibility for real resistance to bourgeois ideology.[17]

If this analysis is correct, it might well be asked: Why doesn't the capitalist class simply eliminate this "petty bourgeois" autonomy of university teachers and other categories of intellectual wage-labor? There have been times, of course, when precisely this happens. The extreme case is authoritarian bourgeois states in which the detailed content of educational activity is dictated from above, but less extreme forms (such as McCarthyism in the United States) occur within bourgeois democracies as well. Still, in most circumstances academics have had a certain measure of real autonomy in advanced capitalist societies, and this needs to be explained. Several factors seem especially important. First of all, while the relative autonomy of academics and other intellectuals within the social relations of production poses a potential threat to the bourgeoisie, this autonomy is also useful for the bourgeoisie. The strength of bourgeois ideology rests in part upon the claim of liberal freedoms, and these claims are embodied in the relative autonomy of intellectuals, including teachers. Furthermore, the bourgeois class needs intellectual production, it needs scientific research and imaginative reformulations of bourgeois ideology, and such intellectual production needs a certain level of autonomy to be effective. Finally, the bourgeoisie would potentially face considerable resistance from certain sections of intellectuals as well as the working class if the autonomy of intellectual labor was seriously attacked. The capitalist class might want to erode the autonomy of intellectuals, but in some circumstances the political and ideological costs might simply be too high.

---

17. It is important to keep this argument in perspective. I am not saying that the autonomy of teachers is a primary determinant of the strength or weakness of socialist or communist ideology, either in the society as a whole or even in the university. It is still the strength of the working class, particularly as an organized political force, which is decisive in determining the strength of socialist/communist ideology in the university itself. The point is that the internal social relations within the university facilitate the penetration and consolidation of antibourgeois ideology.

As a result of these factors, the degree of autonomy of teachers within the social relations of production varies enormously across time and place. While teachers in general occupy a contradictory class location between the working class and the petty bourgeoisie at the economic level, certain teaching positions in certain times and places are much closer to the working class, other positions are much closer to the petty bourgeoisie. It is thus only a first step in the analysis to demonstrate that teachers occupy contradictory class locations. It is equally important to specify the variability within those relations and to examine the processes of change of the class location of given categories of teachers.

In the case of the United States, it appears that in the past decade and especially since the early 1970s, there has been a considerable proletarianization of many segments of teachers of higher education. Course loads have been increased, curriculums have been more administratively dictated, scheduling has been taken out of the hands of individual teachers, tenure-track positions have been replaced by short-term appointments with no job security, and so on. These transformations have produced a fairly deep bifurcation of the class situation of teachers in colleges and universities: in the elite institutions, proletarianization has occured at a much slower pace, or in some cases not at all; in junior colleges, community colleges and some undergraduate-oriented state universities, this erosion of the autonomy of teachers within the labor process has progressed very rapidly. Thus many teachers in such institutions have been drawn very close to the working class pole of the contradictory location between the working class and the petty bourgeoisie, while teachers at elite universities remain much closer to the petty bourgeois pole. As a result, one would expect very different patterns of class behavior on the part of academics in these two situations, in particular, very different possibilities for creating linkages between teachers and workers in various political and economic struggles. The much more successful unionization of university teachers in junior colleges and undergraduate-oriented state universities is one empirical indication of these trends.

At the ideological level, however, teachers remain in contradictory locations between the bourgeoisie and the proletariat in spite of the partial proletarianization of teachers at the economic level. While the autonomy within work may have decreased for many teachers, they still are actively engaged in the process of the elaboration and dissemination of bourgeois ideology. However, there are some developments within educational systems which indicate that teachers might be in a process of limited proletarianization at the ideological level as well as at the economic level. Perhaps the clearest example is the fairly extensive introduction of various forms of programmed learning through the use of computer technologies and other devices. Such machine-structured education undermines the role of teachers in the elaboration and dissemination of ideology. In the limiting situation, their responsibilities for actually disseminating ideology could be reduced to turning on machines rather than intervening as individuals within the process. Teachers would become machine-tenders rather than active participants in ideological production. In such a situation, the class location of teachers at the ideological level would move very close to that of workers (complete exclusion from the control over ideological production).

In more general terms, the variety of processes of routinization of the role of teaching in which the capacity of teachers to interject their own ideas into their teaching is reduced can be thought of as a process of ideological proletarianization within education. This does not mean that teachers simply dissolve into the working class at the ideological level, but it does mean that teaching positions play a less active role in the production of bourgeois ideology, and thus the situation of teachers at the ideological level would move closer to that of workers.

Such processes of ideological proletarianization of teachers should not be exaggerated. For the moment, most teachers still occupy a contradictory location within class relations at the ideological level. This generates a particularly complex set of pressures on teachers within the class struggle. On the one hand, although teachers occupy a contradictory class location between the petty bourgeoisie and the working class at the economic level, many teaching positions are unquestionably being proletarianized at the level of social relations of production. On the other hand, those same teaching positions still occupy contradictory locations between the bourgeoisie and the proletariat at the ideological level, and this location tends to tie them ideologically to the bourgeois class. The very ambivalent character of teacher unions and many teacher strikes reflects this disarticulation between the economic and ideological levels in the class locations of teachers.

Where does all of this leave us? In a sense, these efforts at developing a more differentiated way of analysing the class character of intellectual labor must be considered a prelude to the really important political questions facing progressive intellectuals: What is the role of intellectuals in the struggle for socialism? How can Marxist intellectuals serve the working class, both in the present period and in a longer-term revolutionary project? The central message of this paper is that in order to tackle these questions it is essential to recognize the complexity of the class character of intellectual labor and to avoid any simple reduction of intellectuals into the working class, the petty bourgeoisie or even a new class formation such as the Professional-Managerial Class. Only if the contradictory character of the objective class location of intellectuals is grasped can we begin to understand the contradictory character of their relationship to the class struggle. And only if this contradictory role in the class struggle is understood can we begin to develop appropriate political strategies for linking various kinds of intellectuals to socialist movements.

8.

The Professional-Managerial Class
or
Middle Strata

Stanley Aronowitz

There seems to be an unwritten rule that social and political theory is most orthodox when broad social movements are the least active. In the wake of the decline of the new left, the 1970s have been marked by a revival of the most sterile tenets of the old doctrines of Marx's survivors. On the one hand, there is the tendency to define the transition to socialism as an evolutionary process in which the contradictions between labor and capital are congealed more or less permanently in the struggle for reform. With the emphasis on a reform program to ameliorate the conditions of the working class and middle strata, the distinctions between workers and the middle strata are sometimes obliterated by claiming that the latter have become workers or that their interests are identical even if their class identities are different. On the other hand, next to this version of a moderate socialism, comes the sectarian attack against all reform, the denunciation of the petty bourgeois character of the left and of the trade unions, and the assertion of faith that the workers, and the workers alone, will make the revolution on the basis of the breakdown of capitalism, which is always just around the corner.

At last, in the midst of the dogged assertion of the two (or three) class model of the *Communist Manifesto*, John and Barbara Ehrenreich have given us a class analysis that offers historical as well as structural explanation for the rise of the professional and managerial groups to a new role of importance in modern society. Quite properly they have rejected the most recent efforts to preserve the old faith, notably the work of Nicos Poulantzas who declared that the creation of a new class within capitalism after the 19th century is "unthinkable."[1] Instead, they have described the principal features of what they call the Professional-Managerial Class (PMC) in terms of the development of monopoly capitalism as a qualitatively new stage in the history of the system. By monopoly capitalism they mean the stage of capitalism characterized by the concentration and centralization of capital into fewer hands, and a division of labor based, in part, on the necessity of creating new institutions of social power such as schools, hospitals and charitable organizations which reproduce capitalist relations and culture.

The formation of classes, according to the Ehrenreichs, cannot be discussed solely in terms of the abstract relation of social groups to the juridical relations of ownership of the means of production. For them, this structural relation only defines the necessary condition for class formation, but fails to specify the sufficient condition. Following Marx, they insist that a social group must share "a mode of life, interests and cultural formation" in order to constitute a class.[2] Thus, the major stumbling block to an adequate marxist theory of class relations in the modern era is avoided, namely, the penchant of the orthodox for formal spatial criteria for class membership. In these terms, the location of the PMC within the class structure, that is, their position as employees rather than owners, is not sufficient to define them as a class. For to conflate the PMC with the working class obscures their role in the division of labor. Their common interests are distinct from those of the workers, according to the authors, precisely because their functions are connected to the new

1. Nicos Poulantzas, *Classes in Contemporary Society* (London: NLB, 1976). Whence his designation of the employed managerial and professional strata as a "new petty bourgeoisie." There, of course, exists a petty bourgeoisie even in late monopoly capitalist society. It is the class of small and middle sized proprietors not connected with monopoly capital whose political expressions are largely within the two major political parties, but are often articulated as independent programs and anti-monopoly struggles, such as those of agricultural capital that is relatively speaking outside of the orbit of the large corporations.

2. Karl Marx, *18th Brumaire of Louis Bonaparte*, in *Surveys in Exile* ed. David Fernbach (New York: Vintage Books, 1974), p. 239.

requirements of capital for cadre to insure the reproduction of capitalist social relations as a concomitant to the reproduction of capital in the sphere of production.

The Ehrenreichs propose a further criterion of class formation: class members have a common formation, that is, they share education, life styles and professional ideologies. In their view, the PMC may be designated a class because its members are almost invariably college educated, share a common mode of life and engage in a series of functions which congeal in *interests* that are, at least partially, independent of both the bourgeoisie and the proletariat. On the lower side of its class boundary, its interests are not only independent but also antagonistic to those of the working class because its functions are chiefly to reproduce capitalist social relations and culture. Although the PMC frequently clashes with the capitalist class at the upper end, the authors have much greater difficulty showing that its clashes are truly antagonistic or that the PMC is independent of the capitalists.

The admirable attempt to discuss the specificity of the professionals and managers undertaken by the Ehrenreichs suffers some significant confusions and weaknesses. In the context of discussing these problems, I hope to make a contribution to the clarification of the marxist theory of class and unravel some of the difficulties in formulating a political strategy that is adequate to the changes that have characterized late monopoly capitalism.

Before proceeding, it may be useful to offer a theory of class as a basis for evaluating the position of professionals and managers and their role in contemporary capitalist social life. As is well known, Marx himself never offered a full-blown theory of class. The last pages of the third volume of *Capital* promise such a treatment, but the manuscript was left unfinished and the issue was never dealt with squarely.[3] The closest text we have to a definitive statement on the subject is the seventh section of the *18th Brumaire*. In the context of discussing the self deception of the French nation after the 1848 revolution and its sudden descent into what Marx called a "dead epoch" (after a revolution in which it imagined that it had propelled itself into a new era), Marx assesses the social forces leading to this counter-revolution. At one point in the narrative he was obliged to deal with the apparent passivity of the peasants. Upon this occasion, he was required to provide a definition of class, since his social theory is one in which class forces propel historical

3. See Karl Marx, *Capital,* 3 Vols., (New York: International Publishers), 1974, Vol. 3, ch. 52. In this chapter the landlords constitute the third great class of modern capitalist society. Marx got as far as arguing against the source of revenues among a social group as constituting grounds for class designation.

events and changes. It is worthwhile quoting this passage in full because it may illuminate a method for making class analyses in our own period.

> The small peasant proprietors form an immense mass, the members of which live in the same situation but do not enter into manifold relationships with each other. Their mode of operation isolates them instead of bringing them into mutual intercourse. This isolation is strengthened by the wretched state of France's means of communication and by the poverty of the peasants. Their field of production, the small holding, permits them no division of labor in its cultivation, no application of science and therefore no diversity of development, variety of talent, or wealth of social relationships. Each individual peasant family is almost self sufficient; it directly produces the greater part of its own consumption and therefore obtains its means of life more through exchange with nature than through intercourse with society.[4]

Marx goes on to illustrate this atomized existence. He then continues:

> In so far as millions of families live under economic conditions of existence that separate their mode of life, their interests and their cultural formation from those of other classes and bring them into conflict with those classes, they form a class. In so far as these small peasant proprietors are connected on a local basis, and the identity of their interests fail to produce a feeling of community, national links, or a political organization, they do not form a class. They are therefore incapable of asserting their class interest in their own name, whether through parliament or through a convention. They cannot represent themselves, they must be represented. Their representative must appear simultaneously as their master, as an authority over them, an unrestricted governmental power that protects them from other classes and sends rain and sunshine from above. The political influence of the small peasant proprietors is expressed as the executive subordinating society to itself.[5]

That this definition is offered in the context of a specific historical analysis allows Marx to discuss class as a living category rather than some arid sociological entity. But the theoretical content is quite clear. The

---

4. Karl Marx, *The 18th Brumaire of Louis Bonaparte* (New York: International Publishers, 1972), pp. 123-24.
5. Idem.

formation of a group of people within the social structure must be one that involves the following characteristics if they are to constitute a class: 1) They must enter into "manifold relations" as a consequence of the development of a) means of communication, b) division of labor, and c) a certain level of material culture that allows social intercourse; 2) they must have a *separate* mode of life interests and cultural formation that brings them into conflict with other classes; and 3) they must represent themselves politically, that is, speak in their own name.

The first condition implies a certain historical development, not only of the class in question, but of society's productive forces as well. The position of certain groups within the prevailing mode of production may cut them off from mutual and manifold relations, even if material conditions make possible the formation of classes in general.

The second condition states what the Ehrenreichs have noticed about the professionals/managers, except that they are *dependent*, not truly separate in their mode of life. Their cultural formation, their interests and their mode of life are still contingent on the requirements of capital, even if aspects of their functions within the capitalist division of labor mark them off from other classes.

It is for this reason that the third condition becomes so important. For if a class cannot represent itself politically, in its own name, as a consequence of its isolation or its dependence on other classes, it merely constitutes a stratum which must be part of the calculus of the rulers, especially if it possesses numerical strength and performs functions within society that are vital for society's reproduction. Its lack of self-representation makes it part of the state's claim to represent all classes. Strata which must be represented by their masters in order to be heard come to believe in the neutrality of the state, its station above social divisions in production and daily life and its legitimacy as an arbiter of social conflict, rather than as an instrument of class domination. In the development of U.S. capital, the petty bourgeoisie of small proprietors, including small farmers, merchants, artisans and small manufacturing employers, have constituted the mass base of the state. In the twentieth century, as the largest corporations have seized the raw materials, means of communications, machinery of production, and centralized distribution and marketing networks to a great degree, these strata have appealed to the state for justice. Of course, the irony of regulation in the era of monopoly capitalism has been that such measures benefit the regulated more than the middle strata who seek to use the state as an instrument of redress.

The PMC Is a Strata

Marx's categories are not arbitrary for determining the criteria for class formation. Methodologically he proceeds from an analysis of necessary as well as sufficient conditions for making his determinations. The Ehrenreichs have shown that the professionals/managers are products of a definite stage in the development of the capitalist division of labor and that they perform specific and separate functions within it. But the PMC lacks both the necessary and the sufficient conditions for class formation in so far as they have entered into purely local relations; that is, their national links are weak, still professionally determined. Moreover their autonomy from individual corporations and state bureaucracies is attenuated by the domination of capital not only over their functions but also their mode of life. Although the Ehrenreichs have ably demonstrated the efforts of professionals/managers to generate their own ideologies, there is no continous history of self-representation at the political level. Moreover their functions are themselves dependent. As the Ehrenreichs point out, the PMC owes its existence to the production of a large social surplus by the working class; and its emergence is an aspect of the rationalization of the division of labor. The PMC is, according to the Ehrenreichs, a product of the class struggle between the two principal anatagonists of capitalist society, the bourgeoisie and the proletariat. Within the framework of the extraction of larger quantities of relative surplus value from the workers, the PMC is called into being to perform three specialized functions: 1) to manage the class struggle at the point of production both by providing supervision of workers and by developing technologies of rationalization that strip workers of their skills, thereby divesting them of their autonomy in the production process; 2) to manage the reproduction of capitalist social relations and culture at the level of social institutions such as the family and schools that reproduce that labor force; and 3) to manage the production of class consciousness at the level of culture and ideology. But it is precisely these dependent functions, these aspects of the capitalist division of labor that, in my opinion, preclude the professionals/managers from constituting a class. They have failed to produce a "feeling of community, national links or a political organization," even though they have a common formation in the colleges, universities and professional training schools, and have common interests in so far as they perform separate and necessary functions.[6]

In the first place, there is a serious methodological confusion in the Ehrenreichs' designation of the professionals and managers as a class

6. Idem.

while at the same time asserting that their analysis "precludes treating it as a separate sociological entity." Since, according to the Ehrenreichs' perspective, the PMC "is in a sense a derivative class," the term "class" itself is a curious label for this group. Within capitalism, there are a number of derivative groups that are designated as strata, precisely because they are not independent of the principal class formations in the sociological sense. Although strata have distinct functions within the capitalist mode of production and occupy a unique position in the social structure, these characteristics are not sufficient to constitute a class.

Take, for example, the case of managers. The manager is a "company" man or woman. This means that after professional training this person exists at the sufferance of the corporation. Middle and top managers are typically "assigned" by the company to different locations at will. Their mode of life is not self-determined by anything resembling an autonomous culture, even though their formation has common cultural roots in the old petty bourgeoisie and prior generations of professionals and managers. The old school ties give way to company ties— their careers are determined within a hierarchy that is largely locally based, not on geography to be sure, but on the inner life of a single corporation or industry. Middle managers rarely leave the company that they have started with, although top managers are more peripatetic, not only between corporations and industries, but between the private and the public sector. Top management is certainly a class-in-formation because its links tend to be more global and self-focusing. But its dependency within United States capitalism is largely determined by the high level of integration among the owners of big capital. The sufficient condition for their ability to congeal as a class would be the development of a command state in which the interests of capital would be subordinated over the long run to the rule of a self-contained bureaucracy which was able to rule in its own name. Such a condition exists in times of emergency such as those that occur during wars and economic crises, but they are too short lived to permit the class latency of the managers to become manifest. The major attempts of modern times at the development of the command state, those associated with the rise of fascism, were too truncated to speak of the managers as a class.[7] Nevertheless it must be said that such possibility exists in a modern capitalist world that requires ever more global integration and finds its corporate structure ill-suited for such enterprises.

As for the middle managers it must be said that, as a mass, they do

7. Within the growing literature of fascism, the work of Franz Neumann (*Behemoth*) stands out in its attempt to assess new class forces brought into play by the rise of the command state.

not even approach the situation of the top executives. Their community is the company, not the city or town. Their professional interests seem feeble next to those of the corporations that they serve. While the Ehrenreichs have adduced impressive historical evidence for their efforts at self-determination, can it be claimed that the Society for the Advancement of Management and other professional groups are independent forces in the political structure? Those organizations that enter the political arena, such as the American Medical Association and the American Hospital Association, are so intertwined in their political functions with major industries and branches of the state apparatus that they can hardly be declared representatives of distinct class formations. Their influence is often considerable on government policy, especially in the medical field, but they are still particularistic in form and content.

The few organizations that attempt to represent their particular interests as the general interest, such as the American Association for the Advancement of Science, are signs that the professionals/managers at the middle level aspire for class identity, since they try to generate ideologies that can be taken as global, especially in the nuclear age where the problem of mass destruction has often appeared to be the overriding interest of society as a whole. Similarly, in the production process, in which the tendency for science and technology to replace human labor appears universal, those whose functions coincide with the changing technical composition of capital believe themselves to be a separate interest within society because their work has become increasingly central to capital's reproduction. The Ehrenreichs have documented the evolution and the decline of technocratic ideology and shown it to be a moment in the evolution of capital's hegemony—the moment of resistance among technical intellectuals to the domination of what seems to be an archaic form of social organization, a society dominated by the owners of capital.

But the impulse to ideological discourse is not a sufficient sign of class formation, only of desire. The managerial groups are still determined both in their objective relation to the social division of labor and their ideological and political role within late capitalist society by the hegemony of big capital. They are professional servants of a specific system of social relations which, the Ehrenreichs properly argue, requires new mediations such as organized attention to the social reproduction process as much as to the development of ideologies that neutralize technology and present it as a sign of progress for all classes within society. Managers and intellectuals charged with ideological production must have partial autonomy to generate new ideological paradigms that legitimate late   capitalism, specifically since the old ideologies of pluralism, individualism and natural right seem to have suffered eclipse as the monopoly stage renders them anachronistic. Such is the importance of concepts like "post-industrial society," and "service economy" or the preeminence of "expertise" as a means to legitmate the transformation from the competitive to the monopoly phase of capitalism.[8] That the older notions appropriate to early and middle stages of capitalist development survive is a testament to the ultimate impossibility of sustaining capitalist legitimacy except on the basis of the idea of the sanctity of the individual, the idea of freedom as autonomy from public contraints and the concepts of justice grounded in the notions of self-interest.[9] The new universals of capitalism are certainly bound up with the consciousness of these new strata since they have assumed growing importance in sustaining the social system. But technocratic ideology corresponds not to the formation of a new class, but to the degree to which capital is required to represent the technical and professional strata as much as itself.

The PMC Does Not Represent Itself

I suspect that a second problem in the Ehrenreichs' theoretical presuppositions about class is their failure to comprehend Gramsci's concept of hegemony. Their work mistakes signs of autonomy from its material conditions. While they have pointed to the incipient efforts of the professionals and managers to find a set of links, cultural identity and community ties, the professionals and managers have failed to produce a stratum of intellectuals who were successfully able to "exercise intellectual and moral leadership" that separated these strata from the bourgeoisie.[10] The intellectuals generated by monopoly capitalism tend to become a technical intelligentsia;[11] their functions are instrumental in character

8. See Daniel Bell, *The Coming of Post-Industrial Society* (New York: Basic Books, 1973); and Alain Torraine, *Post Industrial Society* (New York: Pantheon Books, 1972), for recent examples of attempts to generate these ideologies as new theories of social transformation. In both works, the professionals and managers play a key role in the new society, one in which problem solving rather than ideological combat plays a key role. The planner, the expert rather than the ideological intellectual, is thrust to the center of the historical stage. What is curious about these efforts is that they represent the persistence of ideology masked as social theory.

9. Thus the appearance of a kind of right wing anarchism in recent years. See the work of Robert Nosick, Murray Rothbard and other new apostles of a kind of anti-corporate egoism.

10. Antonio Gramsci, *Selections from the Prison Notebooks* (New York: International Publishers, 1972), pp. 56-57.

11. The term is used most felicitously by Andre Gorz, "The Technical Intelligensia and the Capitalist Division of Labor," in *The Division of Labor*, ed. Andre Gorz (London: Harvester Books, 1976).

and can only be understood within the parameters of the logic of capital. Because they are closely integrated by capital, their ideologies tend to express the needs of capital, even when they wish to produce their own intellectual culture.

For example, technocratic ideologies are generated out of the functions and the social position of that portion of the technical intelligensia that wishes to transform its own functions into a vision of society. But these are not oppositional ideologies to the dominant corporate bourgeoisie since capital at this stage of its development is in a constant search for new ways to eliminate living labor in the production process or to reduce it to a function of capital. The vision of the technical intelligensia within the professional and managerial strata is the vision of capital itself. At the level of social organization, it wishes to make capital even more rational than the vestiges of its competitive structure allows. And its concept of rationality varies not at all from the concept of capital. It seeks the integration of all aspects of production with aspects of of consumption so as to prevent disjunctures, crises and wars that result in the weakening and destruction of capital.

Even those ideologies that purport to oppose the rule of a technologically integrated capitalism find difficulty escaping from the vision of total administration. Thus, the irony of some tendencies of criticial marxism has been its inability to separate itself from the visions of late capitalism and its technical intelligensia. Critique appears as celebration; the hegemony of capital expresses itself as an idea of rationality whose inner logic appears seamless. Who can oppose a machine that frees us from back-breaking labor, or an economic plan that attentuates, even if it does not eliminate, economic crisis? After all, the crisis hits the workers and poor hardest, less than it reduces and declasses many among the intermediate strata. As much as critical theory rails against the production of waste, its awesome descriptions of the horrors of consumption do not free it from constituting a kind of technocratic ideology insofar as the images of domination appear ever more opaque.[12]

The passages from Marx that we looked at earlier make the concept of hegemony clear: a class becomes a class when its material conditions of

---

12. See Herbert Marcuse, *One Dimensional Man* (Boston: Beacon Press, 1964) for an acute example of this. Despite the power of the analysis, Marcuse finds difficulty separating his own perpective from that of technological domination since he is unable to locate oppositional forces within the parameters of his category of total administration. It is this positing of the end of the dialectic of history that results in the merging of critical theory with its antagonist, technologically dominating capitalism.

life and its social position make possible the creation of an intellectual and spiritual culture that contends for moral leadership within society. Gramsci's contribution to the marxist theory of class was to underscore the indispensibility of the formation of a stratum of intellectuals organically linked to a class who produce ideologies that become an essential ingredient of that class's self representation and claim for universality. The professionals and managers have formed such a stratum in contemporary society, but their intellectuals are servants of capital, not of the strata from which they arise. Among the reasons for this cruel course of events is that the intellectuals share the bureaucratic conditions of labor of the rest of the strata. Their work has been rationalized such that the question of moral leadership and a separate intellectual culture has become impossible. The professors and the research scientists in large universities share with those directly employed by private capital a purely instrumental role in the social division of labor. The rationalization of the academic disciplines, even the reduction of philosophy to a particular discipline constrained by a set of definite rules and limited to a technical sphere of discourse, has made it all but impossible for any group of bourgeois intellectuals to achieve a global vision, much less one that facilitates the representation of its own strata as a moral and intellectual force.

Of course, if the concept of class relies on the ability of a series of social strata to achieve its own cultural identity and political representation independent of, and antagonistic to, other classes of society, then the problem of the U.S. workers must be addressed in the same terms. For it must be evident that United States workers have failed to free themselves from the cultural and political domination of capital, even if their interests within society are independent and antagonistic to capital. Moreover, since the workers are represented by their masters "as an authority over them," except in those rare instances when the conditions of their existence force them into general strikes or industry wide strikes, workers have failed to achieve hegemony over any section of the intellectuals and to subordinate them to their interests. Under these conditions, marxism itself has assumed a putative character in U.S. society rather than being the living, vital ideology of a class which recognizes it as one of its own self-expressions. Consequently, the dogmatism and atrophy of marxism in the United States may be explained as a function of the domination of capital over the workers, as much as its own peculiar intellectual failing.

In the historical sense, the working class does not exist in the United States. It has failed to form a political party, and instead has remained within the calculus of the capitalist parties as an interest group that must be taken into account in the course of political affairs; but it need not be contended with for moral leadership of society. Further, class feeling and national links, the manifold interconnections that constitute the elements of class consciousness—that is, the recognition not only by the workers that they have distinct and antagonistic interests to those of capital, but that the realization of these interests must entail a fundamental change in social structure—has not developed in this country. It could be shown that the specific features of U.S. capitalist development, rather than external factors, were responsible for the failure of a working class formation in the classical European sense, but this is not the place to discuss them.

On the other hand, can it be claimed that there is not a U.S. working class? Does its high degree of integration within the hegemonic ideologies and culture of the bourgeoisie reduce the workers to a series of disparate strata whose internal connections are more or less arbitrary except in so far as they share a common relationship to the means of production? In terms of the so-called calculus of revolution such a statement is defensible. On the surface, it would appear that the U.S. working class and much of the European working class suffer from what Sartre called seriality. They have failed to fuse into a class capable of representing itself politically; its culture, national links and feelings of community are those of corporate capitalism, expressed most powerfully in the forms of the culture industry.

As dependent social formations, the professionals and the managers can never form a class. They will remain a more or less influential strata within capitalist society linked together by particular professions or by the forms of capital. That these types of linkages sometimes conflict with each other does not constitute a sufficient basis for calling either the professionals or the managers a class.

The case of the working class is different. In structural terms, the exploitation that inheres in the production process forces labor into an antagonistic relation with capital. Not only its relation to the ownership of property (a condition shared by the middle strata), but also its position within the social and technical division of labor constitute more than a local phenomenon in the sense described by Marx when referring to the small peasant proprietors. The interests of the workers are genuinely independent of those of capital because the gain of one constitutes the loss of the other. Only under specialized circumstances, such as occurred for the U.S. after the Second World War and extending to the late 1960s, does the community of interest between labor and capital appear permanent. Even in this instance, the underlying struggle for shares of relative surplus value between labor and capital resulted in more or less violent conflict. To the degree that both capital and labor have become collective, corresponding to the emergence of capitalism as a truly world system coordinated at both the political and economic level, the preconditions for wider links among the working class internationally have already appeared at the material base of society.

The character of labor as abstract, that is, as separate from its concrete technical character, has reached a high level of development in the late 20th century. The ideological and cultural mediations that prevent workers from achieving class consciousness, that is, from recognizing the domination of capital over their mode of life not only in the labor process but in the cultural and social spheres as well, cannot obviate the essential antagonism between labor and capital. The mediations assume enormous significance in the modern period where capital's internal contradictions have rendered the world system more unstable. Under conditions of capital's hegemony in the political and cultural spheres, the class struggle remains segregated in the economic sphere—it is intense, capable of changing the calculus of capital's reproduction, even determinant of the rate of technological change and the forms of political domination. But the weight of bourgeois hegemony remains so heavy that the class becomes opaque even to itself. Its political expressions, its public representations are fragmented even in comparison to the European workers whose communist and socialist parties are, after all, representations of its class interests, at least at the level of political rhetoric.

Nevertheless, the logic applicable to the middle strata, its dependent character, does not hold for the workers. Workers' ideological and cultural dependency is contradicted by the inexorability of their struggle that is rooted in the production process. And to the extent that the antagonism between labor and capital is inscribed in the conditions of capital's reproduction, capital remains dependent on labor. Its existence is contingent on labor, while the middle strata is contingent on it. This fundamental difference marks the class boundaries between the workers and the middle strata. The middle strata are created by the limit on the forms of surplus value extraction imposed by workers' organization and struggle, however reformist these may be. The proliferation of the middle strata is a form of resolution of the fundamental antagonism of the two principal classes of capitalist society. While the U.S. working class has not yet *constituted itself* as a class historically, as an historical subject, its manifold relations within the capitalist order mark it as an independent class formation.

Capital and labor are the universal forms of class antagonism under capitalism, because the commodity form and the capital relation penetrate into all corners of the social world, subsume nature under its signs, and tend to transform all distinctions based on age, sex, skill and race into dependent variables of the production and reproduction of capital. Since capital *is* an antagonistic relation, the existence of the workers as a class is implied by its sale of labor power and the conditions of the extraction of surplus value. Bourgeois hegemony at the cultural and ideological level can not prevent workers from engaging in the struggle against the effort of the boss to extract more relative surplus value. The limits upon class consciousness and class organization may prevent workers from becoming a class in terms of its historical tasks as defined by marxism, but the structure of capital implies the workers' antagonistic separation from capitalists. This is the contradiction that defines the historical ambiguity of the working class in modern capitalist society. The workers cannot fail to oppose their exploiters, no matter what the survey researchers find ("events belie forecasts" as Lefebrve has reminded us). At the moment when social scientists found "irrefutable" evidence that the working class is embourgeoisified by discovering that they are homeowners, are enmeshed in consumption patterns typical of the petty bourgeoisie and exhibit reactionary social attitudes, the workers confound these findings by going out on a wildcat strike, by engaging in acts of sabotage, or by forming a rank and file movement to oppose their class collaborationist union officials. The logic of capital forces them to fight, even if their awareness of the stakes of combat does not translate into political terms. Even if U.S. capitalism's genius has been to successfully segment the economic movement of the workers, to prevent it from becoming political by employing such devises as collective bargaining, company paid benefits, and systems of job hierarchies that divide workers by race, class, sex, and presumed skill, it cannot contain resistance and the struggle over surplus value.

The situation of the managers is also different. They are instruments of capital—their role is to facilitate the extraction of relative surplus value and to reproduce capitalist social relations. They were called into existence under two separate, but related conditions: first, management appears as a "science," as a new form of domination (disguised as "natural" domination) at the moment when workers by successfully fighting for the shorter working day, have limited the capacity of capital to resolve its expansion problems by further extracting absolute surplus value. The introduction of new machines is an aspect of the logic of capital that now requires the deskilling and elimination of living labor in order to increase the production of relative surplus value.[13] At the same time, capitalism cannot completely eliminate productive labor because the production of profit ultimately relies on living rather than dead labor.

13. See Karl Marx, *Capital, Volume One* (New York: Vintage Books, ch. "six," reproduced as an appendix to the new translation called the "Immediate Results of the Production of Relative Surplus Value."

The institutions that are generated to reproduce the labor force, capitalist culture and capitalist social relations at the secondary level, that is, at the level of ideological structures such as the state, social agencies, trade unions and above all schools, calls into existence a virtual army of medical doctors, social workers, teachers and bureaucrats. The management of political parties and the institutions of social reproduction must be added to the appearance of scientific management as constituting the new strata. In short, the existence of the managerial groups are aspects of the logic of capital and lack both the historical and the structural features of antagonistic autonomy. The Ehrenreichs are perfectly right to claim that managerial strata are antagonistic to the working class, but they are not antagonistic in the last instance to capital.

The PMC Conflates Professionals with Managers

A third serious problem raised by the PMC thesis then is its insistence that professionals and managers ought to be conflated into a single class. For apart from the question of what constitutes a class, to call professionals managers because they function to reproduce capitalist culture and social relations and therefore must be considered structurally antagonistic to the working class is telling only half the story. The authors are quite right in refusing an occupational basis for class standing. Their argument that persons within the same occupation may belong to different classes is well taken. Their example of nursing is very persuasive. Nurses, especially women with technical education who perform the most rationalized functions in patient care, occupy an ambiguous position in the class structure. So far, so good. But there the analysis goes in an entirely different direction. From this point on, the point about the ambivalent position of professionals is dropped.

For the rest of the theoretical argument, professionals are more or less identified with the category of mental labor which is, for the most, college trained. In contrast, the PMC is functionally specified by its function as management and as having "control or authority over labor." Presumably those who perform any of these functions may be considered a member of the PMC. Yet the Ehrenreichs have missed the point made by Eric Wright in his generally sympathetic review of Poulantzas' work. Wright's concept of "contradictory class locations" seems to me more appropriate than the conflation performed by the Ehrenreichs for classifying and assessing the significance of some strata which have emerged as professionals with the expansion of capital.[14]

The concept proposed by Wright recognizes the ambiguity inherent in the formation of social groups who, even though they are bereft of

14. Erik Olin Wright, "Class Boundaries in Advanced Capitalist Societies" *New Left Review, #98.*

property, exercise some of the functions of capital.[15] These strata are more or less aligned with capital depending on their role in the social division of labor. Managers are clear antagonists of workers, even if they are wage earners. But professionals, technicians, employees of various apparatuses of the state are in a far different position.

At the most basic level, if Marx's dictum is true that in late capitalism "knowledge has become a productive force," even the main productive force, engineers, technicians and some categories of scientists produce surplus value notwithstanding the control functions performed by their labor.[16] We may say that, as a social group, they embody within each individual both the functions of productive workers *and* the aspects of the managerial role. Insofar as their technical and scientific knowledge is imbedded in the machine and contributes to the productivity of labor as a whole, they are producers. Insofar as their work entails both the direct supervision of the less qualified laborers and the indirect deskilling of these workers and their consequent subordination to capital, they are managers. It is precisely these contradictory aspects of their position and of their function in the division of labor that prevent them from an unambiguously antagonistic relation with the working class.

The proliferation of administration and bureaucracy in late capitalism has tended to increase the number of those who may be called bureaucratic employees (about 1/6 of the labor force). Their recruitment is not from the old or the new middle classes alone. These functionaries are recruited from segments of the working class and constitute one of the options available to many workers in the face of diminishing number of manufacturing jobs in the economy.

For example, how are we to understand the entrance of large numbers of Italian and Irish men from working class backgrounds into the police force and other sectors of the state bureaucracy? Certainly as the state becomes more specialized and far reaching in its function, it requires more recruits, both from the working class and from those with college background, with presumed technical qualifications. That these qualifications are largely ideological in character (planners, social workers, parole officers, etc.) does not obviate the contradiction between their repressive function and the fact that these tasks are becoming increasingly rationalized, such that those who perform them are themselves subordinated to the state managers. Moreover, how can we be satisified with a designation of professionals as those who are college educated and perform mental labor, if almost all net increases in the number of jobs since the end of the Second World War can be explained

15. Idem.
16. Karl Marx, *Grundrisse* (New York: Vintage Books, 1974), p. 705.

in terms of increases in government employment, and other sectors that reproduce "capitalist social relations and capitalist culture?" The plain fact is that capitalism cannot survive without its socially reproductive functions because it is bound to eliminate ever larger numbers of so-called manual workers (a social and ideological category since all labor requires the coordination of hand and brain) as its labor saving machinery strives to overcome the resistance of living labor to the extraction of a higher mass of surplus value. The transformation of the majority of the working population into consumers and non-productive workers is a consequence of the historical tendency of capital to reproduce itself in labor and capital saving forms.

Of course, the Ehrenreichs would like to preserve certain occupations within state and private bureaucracies for the working class. Clerical workers, blue collar workers who are not productive but are certainly subordinate to the professional managers of public and private organizations, and even some "professionals" who they believe are granted such status only by courtesy (nurses, for example) may all be considered part of the working class. But those who have specialized and have long periods of training and are obliged to observe a "code of ethics" as a condition of their right to practice the profession may be considered managers and thus members of the PMC if they exercise, under the rule of capital, the functions of management, i.e., control and authority over labor.

The problem with this formulation is that the concept of authority and control within large bureaucracies has become ambiguous. As the integration and standardization of functions by such abstract processes as rules and qualifications increase, even those who perform menial supervisory functions, or whose work is tied to the control and rationalizing functions, find themselves controlled and managed. On the one hand, they have internalized the ideologies of professionalism, according to which they perform "service" functions or are engaged in scientific or technical research that is free of political and ideological constraints. On the other hand, they find their own professional tasks mechanized and subjected to external controls. Wage earning lawyers and engineers, are obliged to observe constraints that have robbed them of traditional autonomy. The rules of the job seem ever more restrictive and often violate traditional canons of professional ethics. In the process, ethics are overturned by inexorable requirements of profit and domination.

Under these conditions, the proletarianized professionals organize trade unions, or transform their professional organizations into collective bargaining agents. The professional ethics are increasingly employed as blatant instruments of self-interest and lose their universalistic claims.

This does not imply that the "new working class"[17] has been born from the subordination of the professions to capital. The control and authority functions remain, but they are considerably attenuated by the centralization of capital which deprives the mental laborers of their mythic autonomy.

It is for these reasons that I have concluded that class theory must separate the professionals and technical employees from the managers in the context of wage labor. The technicians, notwithstanding their training in colleges and universities, are certainly closer to the working class than the Ehrenreich's would allow. Their performance of "mental labor" does not in itself make them antagonists of the working class. Their work is clearly subordinated to the direction of management, even though these tasks are, in turn, controls on the efforts of manual laborers. Those who are called "professionals" by virtue of their credentials and qualifications increasingly find themselves reduced to technicians. The difference in their actual functions in an industrial setting from those of the technicians is progressively reduced except for those who take on direct managerial functions. As I have argued elsewhere, in the era of general degradation of skills, the distinctions between mental and physical labor and between professionals and technicians are maintained ideologically rather than in the actual performance of labor.[18] Moreover, the growth of administration has resulted in the hegemony of managers over the professionals. What is missing in the Ehrenreichs' analysis that prevents them from seeing these distinctions is a conception of bureaucracy adequate to the present era.

Bureaucratic domination has become a typical feature of all advanced capitalist countries. It is highlighted by the separation of administration/management, disguised as an "objective" system of rules and regulations, from the performance of the everyday tasks of the organization. Although the bureaucracy is certainly a part of the overall domination of capital, its internal differentiation on the basis of growing centralization of power places most of its operatives in a position of subordination even if they too participate in the general functions of control.

17. The term was coined, to the best of my knowledge by Serge Mallet. See his *Essays on the New Working Class,* ed. Dick Howard, (St. Louis: Telos Press, 1975).

18. Stanley Aronowitz, *False Promises* (New York: McGraw-Hill, 1973), ch. 3, contains a discussion on the ideological character of job and professional classifications in the age of degraded labor. I believe the Ehrenreichs have been taken in, to some extent, by the reified institutions of schools and professional associations and have failed to recognize the degraded character of much of what is called professional labor.

Thus, since professionals find themselves in the dual role of productive labor and of management in the production sphere, and are caught in similar contradictions in private and public bureaucracies, it seems better to retain the notion of the middle strata as those groups of professionals and technicians whose autonomy is systematically undermined by capital. Rather than regarding them as antagonists of the working class, I would propose that non-managerial middle strata may be considered likely candidates for new alliances with workers and underclasses in contemporary capitalist societies.

Let me summarize the argument against the notion of a Professional-Managerial Class. My chief objections concerns the rather loose way in which the concept "class" is used. The Ehrenreichs have expanded class not only to mean the common relationship of a group to the owners of the means of production, but also to a common culture and social formation. But they neglected the significance of political self-representation in the historical development of classes in modern society. The notion of a "political party" must not be understood in the electoral sense that the phrase connotes: classes may or may not contend for political power through parliamentary means, depending on conditions of time and place. Nor should the Leninist concept of a party as a band of dedicated, professional revolutionaries be generalized beyond the particular circumstances under which such formations have occurred in a colonial and neo-colonial countries. Under certain conditions, classes may represent themselves politically through trade unions, association of various types or even federations that have both trade union and political functions such as those formed by anarchists in Spain and Latin America at the turn of the 20th century.

Political self-representation means that a group defines itself as fundamentally antagonistic to the dominant class in society and is prepared to contend for power. Of course, its concept of power may or may not signify its intention to establish new social relations. But it will certainly develop ideologies (plural because various fragments of the class may see the question of political power differently) that both mobilize members of the class and constitute a way of seeing the world, that is, a world view that is hostile at many levels to the ruling ideas of the ruling class. If these requirements are necessary, the professionals/managers within late capitalism cannot be said to form a class. They have some of the features of a class and may even generate an intellectual stratum that wishes to represent its relation to the social and political reality ideologically. "Technocratic consciousness" may be understood as one example of the *possibility* of ideological development for the managerial stratum. To the extent that all problems are reduced to their technical dimension, managers do call into existence intellectual forms of their social practice. But these ideologies do not appear antagonistic to any major section of the capitalist class, except the small, old competitive sector.

In contrast to the working class which stands in *objective antagonism* to the big capitalists, the professionals/managers have a purely *local* basis for their antagonism. They do not challenge the economic hegemony of capital, only its political and ideological strategies for rule. Thus there may be a strategic difference between the managers and the owners of capital, but no fundamental historical difference.

Finally, I have argued that the technical and some sections of the professional strata cannot be confused with the managerial groups. Technicians and professionals occupy a position of *contradictory location* between the working class and managerial strata. They neither own nor control the means of production but are a part of the apparatus of control. At the same time, to the extent that knowledge has become the main productive force in late capitalism, their work is transformed into mental labor. For this reason, they are capable of organizing against capital as much as they are part of capital's domination over the working class and other subordinate strata of society.

II

The Ehrenreichs' willingness to jettison the entire corpus of new working class theory, in favor of an attempt to isolate the working class as the only possible progressive class in contemporary capitalism, bears no correspondence to the historical experience of the socialist and working class movement. There has never been a time when the working class could afford to dispense with alliances with other social classes in its struggle for liberation, for the road to revolutionary transformation is littered with stones and it curves rather than takes a straight path. Since the working class, in the Ehrenreich definition, comprises some 70% of the population, the implication may be drawn that the conditions for a go-it-alone policy have arrived. But such a position forgets that history demands different alliances depending on specific circumstances. At one moment, the workers may find themselves joining with agrarian classes against foreign imperialism, or, in the advanced countries, against the largest international corporations.[19]

At this historical moment when the centrality of the middle strata both to the process of production and to the configuration of the capitalist system as a whole seems indisputable, even for the Ehrenreichs, the attempt to lump the managerial strata with that of the professionals and to declare both antagonistic to the working class simply raises more problems than it solves. The task of a socialist movement is to draw in wider sections of those whose contradictory location in the class structure may make them important allies in the struggle for liberation, rather than to declare them antagonists before a concrete analysis is made.

To be sure, it does not follow that all professionals and technicians who perform contradictory functions in the social system may be

19. The reader will notice that this perspective differs in some respects from that advanced by William A. Williams, James Weinstein and other historians who only see the co-optation entailed in the populism of the early 20th century and of those following Rosa Luxemburg who oppose nationalism in third world countries unconditionally. To enter into an alliance does not imply the necessary surrender of the critical position of marxism towards both the doctrines of bourgeois nationalism and populism. Alliances are most successful when the autonomy of each partner is respected and becomes the basis of internal struggle within it. The popular fronts of the 1930's, where the communists tended to surrender their autonomy and the workers' interests were often compromised to bourgeois interests, have unfortunately become the models of alliances for our time. Naturally, this interpretation of the class alliance should be rejected. Moreover my concept of class alliance does not speak, as the CP did, of progressive sections of the capitalist class" as likely allies. Such notions are the theoretical basis of much of the reformism of the CP.

considered progressive. Under certain circumstances, such as a period during which the economy expands on the basis of higher rates of productivity that is the result of the work of the middle strata, particularly their role as knowledge workers, these groups may be hostile to worker's militancy. During times of économic expansion, the knowledge workers are particularly favored by the capitalists since their work is the basis of high profit rates. On the other hand, the world wide capitalist crisis currently in process has produced a major shift in the political loyalties and assessments of entire sections of professional and technical employees. As large corporations eliminate jobs by moving to low wage areas, not only for manual but also for mental labor, technical and professional employees tend to become more militant and seek alliances with the working class.

The experience of the Eurocommunist movements illustrates the possibilities, but also the problems of such class alliances. Beginning in the period just after the uprisings in France and Italy of 1968-69, large sections of the professional and technical strata left the Christian Democratic and Gaullist parties and joined the Communist and Socialist parties and, increasingly the Ecology party, which has been a surprisingly strong factor in recent municipal elections. In Italy, the Communists were the chief beneficiary of the shift of chunks of these strata leftward. The choice to go left instead of remaining on the right expressed the frustration of these groups with the manifest failure of pro-capitalist parties to solve their problems. One may say that the exodus of capital to less developed regions at home and abroad, combined with recessionary economic conditions, produced a recognition that the privileged position of the middle strata was threatened substantially for the first time since the end of World War II.

The turn towards socialism was by no means an unmixed blessing for the workers and socialist forces. The middle strata are not revolutionary. To some extent, they constitute a brake on the socialist character of the left programs in western European countries. Their consciousness remains profoundly technocratic and imbued with professional ideologies. Thus, they are frequently a force of moderation on the left rather than propelling it to bolder action. The mass influx of these strata in the Communist and Socialist parties is an internal pressure away from the old revolutionary rhetoric of these parties. The middle strata cannot adapt easily to the slogans of proletarian dictatorship or to the pro-Soviet orientation of the CP. Indeed it marches to a different tune than the old proletarian elements in the mass left parties.

But the question of the character of the struggle for socialism in the contemporary era is raised sharply by their growing social importance. If

Braverman,[20] Marglin[21] and others who have shown that the tendency of modern capital is to degrade labor by robbing it of its skill and autonomy are right, then what is called the traditional working class has been cut to ribbons by late capitalism. It is not only a case of the loss of the skilled workers' ability to direct the production process, even to the extent they enjoyed such autonomy in the mid-19th century, but also that the fundamental conditions for the formation of working class conscious-ness, the concentration of capital in ever larger units in centralized industrial cities, has been irreversibility undermined by the decentraliza-tion movement both to rural and other underdeveloped areas at home and abroad. The plain fact is that, despite marxist warnings that the ruling class cannot achieve its dream of world wide crisis-free rationality because of the irrationality of the system, world capitalism, under the hegemony of U.S. based multinationals, has embarked on the road to planning which entails a level of the integration of capital unknown in its history. Capital has been able to assess the strength of the workers' movement and adjust its investment programs accordingly. The failure of the revolution in the West after 1917 allowed capitalist technology to create a kind of spurious global village by means of transportation networks that were efficient enough to attenuate the old need to locate industries in a few large urban centers. The middle strata have functioned as the technicians of capital's ability to dominate the working class by depriving it of its centers of strength. Detroit is no longer the indisputable hub of the car industry; Pittsburgh has been relegated to a secondary steelmaking region and traditional steel cities like Buffalo and Youngs-town have been stripped of important plants; New York City was once the third largest machine tool manufacturing area in the country. Today, not a single major manufacturer remains. The deindustrialization of the northeast and even the industrial heartland of the nation—the Ohio River region of the midwest—signals the end of the industrial concentra-tions in a few major cities and regions. At the same time, it has meant that important centers of working class militancy have also been defused. While the task of organizing the industrial unions forty years ago could be compressed into the problem of reaching workers in Chicago, New York, Cleveland, Detroit and a dozen secondary centers, today the problem of working class solidarity is world wide. An automobile sold in a typical city or town may be assembled for the big three auto makers in any of a hundred countries around the world; Taiwan-made textiles and

20. Harry Braverman, *Labor and Monopoly Capital* (New York: Monthly Review Press, 1974).

21. Steven Marglin, "What Do Bosses Do?" *The Division of Labor*, ed. Gorz.

garments and Spanish-made shoes adorn shopping center stores, and German and Japanese steel are used to create U.S. products. The instrumentalities of these rapid and far reaching changes in the international division of labor and the mobility of capital are not only the managers of the multinationals, but the planners, scientists and technicians as well.

As the logic of capital requires a more minute division of labor, more sophisticated integrative mechanisms, enlarged state intervention into the economy, and a larger army of administrative workers, the size of the middle strata of professionals grows. At the same time, those lacking power and authority within the administrative and state sectors also grow. The army of clerical workers, operators of duplicating, accounting, bookkeeping, and other machines accompanies the employment of computer professionals, accountants, designers and other professionals.

Although clerical workers such as typists, secretaries and office machine operators are certainly part of the working class, their position is by no means unambiguous in the social structure. The institutions for which they labor are not aspects of the productive apparatus of capitalist society. Head offices of large corporations and state bureaucracies are apparatuses of bourgeois ideological hegemony as well as social domination. The institutions of schools, health care, and administration are giant in size in contemporary capitalist society and, as the Ehrenreichs correctly point out, function to reproduce capitalist social relations and culture, as well as facilitate the accumulation and realization of capital. Even those who perform degraded and repetitive clerical tasks in these institutions participate in the production and reproduction of capital and the social relations that sustain it.

What is more, often the clerical functions overlap with those of technicians and professionals. The number of "managers" of clerical workers is extremely high in proportion to those who are designated as "clerical" employees. For years, unions have fought attempts by middle and top managers to "promote" a significant proportion of clerical workers to low level supervisory positions as a means to insure against strikes or to otherwise weaken the union rolls. This tendency is particularly pronounced in telephone and other branches of the communications industry where the proportion of supervisors to workers is about one to three. In addition, many of those designated in the job categories as technicians and professionals find that, as mechanization replaces a large number of tasks that were previously skilled aspects of their professions, these college educated, professionally trained employees are reduced to clerical workers. Much of their time is spent performing tasks previously part of clerical workers' activities.

Concomitantly professional salaries in many large corporations are not growing as fast as they once did, or as fast as production workers'. The claims of management, that their skills have become degraded and that they should not be rewarded as they once were, has the ring of truth. Of course, such degradation has not prevented management from requiring incoming technicians and professionals to possess more credentials than ever before. Higher qualifications required for relatively lower paying jobs is a function of a glutted labor market rather than higher performance requirements. Where professionals have been able to command higher salaries such as doctors and engineers, these are results of strong professional association pressure to either limit entrance of new persons into the field, trade union-like activity such as strikes and collective bargaining, or the expansion of the industries in which they work.

The most striking aspect of the growth of planning, administrative and ideological institutions is that they have grown in proportion as the number of production workers in the economy has declined. The declining numerical strength of the old working class is, in a crucial sense, a function of the activities of engineers, designers, scientific and technical professionals and administrators. Thus, the composition of the working class has changed. Workers engaged in production and transportation number no more than 25% of the non-self employed labor force. If the Ehrenreichs are correct that 70% of the population belongs to the working class, many of those are located in functions and institutions whose role in the social division of labor corresponds to their designation "reproduction of capitalist social relations and culture."

After this long digression, an argument emerges for refusing the formulations of both Poulantzas' attempt to save orthodox marxism by the inventing the category of the "new" petty bourgeoisie and the Ehrenreichs' notion of the professional/managerial class. For imbedded in both theories is the romanticization of the old industrial working class. With Poulantzas however, unlike the Ehrenreichs, the new middle strata have political importance for the socialist movement. Indeed, in the context of the unfolding of the class struggle in western Europe, any political movement that refused all alliances with sections of the middle strata would be condemned to political irrelevance. In these countries, the question of the class alliance on the political level is a matter of immediate urgency. Whether one approves of the political programs of the organized left parties or not, the question of the class alliances must be addressed. Gorz, Mallet and, more recently, Poulantzas have tried to comprehend the theoretical significance of changes in the configuration of capitalism.[22] The Ehrenreichs, by their conflation of the professionals

22. Gorz' recent and unfortunate tendency to dismiss the middle strata,

with the managers, the positing of antagonistic relations between all parts of these strata with the working class, and, most importantly their profound misunderstanding of the marxian theory of class, refusing to relate it to the concrete conditions of political representation as well as to the problems of structural hierarchy and culture, have lapsed in their otherwise serious attempt to update marxist theory, into a position that lends itself to sectarian politics.

Perhaps one may account for this refusal to acknowledge a politics of class alliance on the basis of the reformism of the middle strata, not to mention this strata's furious efforts to hold on to professional privileges. In order to reject an alliance with sections of the middle strata, it would be necessary to show that the capitalist crisis has sufficiently matured so that the hierarchical organization of the working class has been sufficiently attenuated so as to make it more homogeneous. Under these conditions, revolutionary change would be on the agenda. Then the working class, as Marx predicted, would carry the burden of social transformation on its own shoulders, dragging the newly proletarianized elements of the middle strata kicking and screaming into the future.[23]

Unfortunately, history does not present ideal type situations for those engaged in political struggle. There has never been a time when the working class was able to carry on alone, even though the past century has shown that it is capable of representing itself, of creating its own political forms as well as trade unions to carry on the economic combat. Even the composition of socialist and communist parties has never been exclusively proletarian. A relatively substantial number of middle class professionals—in the first place, doctors, journalists and lawyers—have joined the parties and even become some of its most important leaders. This fusion of workers and middle class professionals has produced contradictions within the socialist movement throughout its history. Many periods of socialist history have been marked by the rise of a jacobin element within the parties, that is, the tendencies towards putschism, authoritarian internal party life, and concepts of leadership

especially the technical intelligentsia, as a potentially oppositional force ought not to obscure the substantial contribution his work has made to our understanding of the new features of class structure in contemporary society.

23. This position, most closely associated with the work of the early Karl Korsch, Herman Gorter and Anton Pannakoek was formulated most powerfully in the period just after the first world war when the crisis had, indeed, raised the question of proletarian revolution in its sharpest possible form. But as Theodore Adorno said, referring to this period, the attempt "miscarried," leaving capital the space not only to recover its hegemony over society, but to invent new forms of domination particularly in the technical cultural spheres.

that make the masses an instrument of the party's program rather than the other way around. These are just some of the deleterious consequences of the entrance of non-working class strata into the party.

Lenin's formula,[24] according to which those of non-working class origins lose their class identity when they become revolutionaries is more a case of wishful thinking than scientific analysis. Socialists of middle class origins not only bring their origins to the movement but their bourgeois ideologies are continually reproduced since in contemporary capitalist countries most of them do not become professional revolutionaries but retain their links to the middle strata.

The Ehrenreichs have shown how in the new left of the 1960's the course of the movement, indeed of U.S. history, was shaped by the problems associated with the class origins of the student and anti-war activists. Having said all that, however, it does not follow that a serious revolutionary movement can dispense with the concept of class alliance in the struggle for socialism.

For the prospects of worldwide capitalist breakdown, although not impossible, remain unlikely. The corporate bourgeoisie has achieved a degree of political and ideological coherence unknown before the 1960's. It is not a question of a new phase of crisis-free, organized capitalism. Rather, we may venture to say that contradictions are displaced in our era of capitalism: displaced to the third world as during the oil and food crises of recent years; displaced to the underclasses of capitalist societies, a permanent pool of marginal and unemployed persons who constitute both a permanent reserve army for capital's expansion on a world scale and a body of persons who labor at jobs where the rate of exploitation owing to low wages enables capital to recover its average rate of profit even in bad times; displaced to waste consumption, a way of disaccumulating that portion of surplus value that cannot be reinvested in productive industries; displaced to wars and to large outlays for military production that do not enter the process of circulation, except indirectly in the form of new means of production; displaced, finally, to the ideological and cultural sphere in the form of the production of strata supported by a portion of surplus value, whose role is to reproduce capitalist social relations.

Yet, the consequences of this displacement cannot be external to socialist strategy. For as capitalist rationality dominates even a segment of its own cadre, the contradictions between professionalism and the technical division of labor radicalize some cadre. At a certain point, these professionals are obliged to share the burdens of the crisis by accepting de

24. Most notably in V.I. Lenin, *What is to Be Done?* (New York: International Publishers, 1969).

facto wage cuts as inflation outruns salary increases, by accepting extended periods of unemployment as state and social welfare sectors cutback to permit capital accumulation during periods of intensified international competition, and by accepting the prospect that they may never work in the professions for which they were trained. During the 1930's these conditions forced many professionals to reconsider their hostility to radical and left movements within this country. In other countries, some of them went over to fascism as well. It was precisely because the radicalization of the middle strata might turn them to the right that the left has been aware of the importance of dealing with its problems; this is why purest proletarian ideologies that sustain themselves on half truths, that deny the contradictions in the position and the consciousness of the middle strata, must ultimately become a barrier to the building of a strong, socialist movement.

I am not speaking for a policy that would sacrifice the interests of the workers' movements on the altar of popular unity. As history shows, such policies do not effectively prevent the rise of authoritarian movements, nor are they effective in mobilizing large numbers of people to fight capital. In fact, they are the other side of the sectarian attacks on working with the middle strata in the name of proletarian revolution. This was the record of the left during the 1930's and seems to be the pattern emerging in the late 1970's as the high tide of popular resistance recedes. Marxist theory becomes a vehicle for the resurrection of the old time religion, or it is revised beyond a recognition in the name of building a broad movement against monopolistic capital.

The precondition of a class alliance capable of working within the contradictions of capitalism, as much as pointing towards social transformation, is a working class which recognizes the indivisibility of the economic and political struggle against capital. For us in the United States, the broad base of working class militancy at the point of production has never been our most important weakness, even if the movement has its ebbs and flows. Miners and teamsters are clear examples of workers willing to fight their union as well as the employer to combat the efforts of capital to take its own problems out of the workers hides. The workers' movement founders on the separation of the economic from the political struggle, its refusal to make the ideological jump to a class perspective on the whole society rather than confining its antagonism to the trade union level. Political class consciousness is the practical recognition that capital, rather than the boss, is the real enemy.

At present, the radicalized middle strata dominates the left precisely because it is engaged in a struggle against capital at the point of the displacement of systemic contradictions: where wars are employed to avert the crisis; where capital accumulation results in the destruction of the environment; where capital tries to overcome the problems arising from new world corporate arrangements by raising prices for oil, gas and electricity; where the state sector is hit with cutbacks and the professionals are mobilized to protect their job interests; where the political parties of capital begin to reject the split between the middle strata and the ruling class on these questions. The middle strata derive their power preeminently in the political sphere since their economic power is restricted by their location in secondary and tertiary sectors of the economy. With the notable exception of scientists, technicians and engineers who work in industry, most members of professional strata are in the state sector or quasi-state welfare and research organizations and universities. Politics is their very survival. While industrial workers have been able to win battles, at least in the short run, by such measures as strikes, sabotage and slowdowns, few state workers can avail themselves of such tactics without severe reprisals. Yet, a strike in the state sector is, perforce, a political strike and quickly becomes a public issue, while industrial strikes are merely news, unless they are prolonged. Moreover, professional associations and professional unions are obliged to wage continuous combat at the political level even when direct action is not indicated.

Is it any wonder that a left which in its very foundations argues for the politicization of cultural and economic struggles should find itself inundated with disaffected members of the middle strata? We must comprehend the specific historical conditions that produced a working class whose struggle was segregated at the economic level, rather than bemoaning the distorted composition of the left. Nor will the situation improve materially in the immediate future for recruitment of large numbers of workers into left movements or the transformation of unions into political instruments of workers' interests.

This is not the place to recite the reasons for the deep conservatism of U.S. workers or their unions. Suffice it to say that the left itself bears some responsibility for having failed to consistently fight for the politicization of economic struggle, just as it has all but ignored the problem of the cultural hegemony of capital and the attempts of women, artists and racial and ethnic minorities to struggle against cultural domination. The cultural and ideological hegemony of capital expresses itself as much in the economism of left militants as it does in the narrow social focus of U.S. unions, in which the left also has played important part. Too often the left played the role of organizing militant unions without raising the absolute need to transcend the shop and industrial level of struggle.

But there were objective conditions that failed to produce a politicized working class in this country that go well beyond the weaknesses of the left. The job is to understand these forces rather than attempting to account for all our contemporary problems as a movement by referring to the well-known weakness inherent in its low working-class composition. I would argue that instead of downplaying its middle class character, it would be better to focus instead on building the movements of middle strata—the ecology movement, the new anti-war movement, the alternative and appropriate technologies groups, and the womens movement— as allies of a working class movement.

The role of the left within these movements is to combat the tendency to define themselves as opposed to the trade unions and other organizations linked to the working class. Instead, the left must find connections to workers' interests, such as the counterposing of nuclear construction which benefits only a small section of workers to alternative decentralized energy technologies that may provide employment for a larger number of workers while meeting the demand for a clean environment, for adequate energy sources and for alternatives to war industries that meet popular needs.

None of these proposals obviate the need for a socialist strategy within the working class—the organization of clerical workers and other groups where women predominate; the patient, long effort to persuade workers that capital can no longer accommodate their interests through collective bargaining and that combat against such policies as the runaway shop, high taxes, inflation and worsening working conditions requires political action. The fight against job hierarchies, against technologies that further rationalize the labor process into more boring, repetitive tasks, and the battle to control the direction of investment in order to limit capital's freedom to move within and beyond national borders requires political intervention on the part of the working class. These areas cannot be left to the labor bureaucrats or its mechanisms of ideological domination. But as central as these concepts and interventions are to a socialist movement, we cannot abandon the work of defining theoretically and strategically the possibilities for class alliances in the struggle for social transformation.

A Ticket to Ride:
More Locations on the Class Map

Michael Albert & Robin Hahnel

Barbara and John Ehrenreich raise a "new complaint" against Marxist analysis: perhaps traditional class distinctions are insufficient. Perhaps people who receive a wage but perform the "mental labor" of "reproducing productive and cultural relationships" are themselves a "new class" with their own interests and ideology opposed to the interests and ideology of workers and capitalists.[1] What are the implications of this possibility for change in our society, for socialist tasks, and for socialist organization and program? Our paper addresses these questions while critically evaluating the Ehrenreichs' thesis.

1. We will use the phrase "professional and managerial sector" (PMS) instead of PMC so as not to prejudge whether this whole assemblage of people is in fact a class.

We organize the discussion into five major parts. First, "class analysis" means different things depending on one's theoretical premises. For instance, different views of the importance of the economic realm versus other realms, or of consciousness versus "material relations," lead to different kinds of class analysis. We begin by examining the premises behind the Ehrenreichs' view of class relations as well as the premises of those they critique, and by proposing our own alternative to both.

Next we review the Ehrenreichs' specific arguments concerning the existence of the PMC, and propose our own thesis regarding what we call the professional and managerial sector (PMS). In our opinion the PMS contains a new class of "coordinators" but also many people who are not members of the coordinator class but who occupy contradictory class locations between this new class and the working class.[2]

Third, we propose three areas for further investigation that might be useful in clarifying the worth of any "new class" hypothesis. The first has to do with the determination of the direction of development of modern technology, the second with the possibility of a mode of production other than socialist or capitalist which is dominated by and elaborates the interests of the "new class" into economic organization, and the third with the character of modern political organization and struggles.

We then elaborate our argument by applying our concepts to understanding the phenomenon of Eurocommunism—is it a sophisticated working class strategy to create socialism or is it the strategy of another class intent on coopting the working class and creating a form of economic organization opposed to workers' real interests? We argue for the latter interpretation and believe that the analysis is a very important point in favor of a new "class map" of modern capitalist societies.

And finally, we conclude our article with a short discussion of the New Left and the promise it offers of a powerful socialist movement of the future.

I   The Theory Behind Class Analysis

Class analysis searches out "collective agents" who might play central roles in historical change. According to orthodox Marxism, the economic realm is the base of all others. It has its own dynamic relations and its own tendencies toward development or stagnation. At the core of these tendencies is a contradition between the forces and relations of production. As this contradiction develops, the society matures and

2. The idea of "contradictory class locations" is fully developed in Erik Olin Wright, *Class, Crisis and State* (London: NLB, 1978). A group occupies a contradictory position in the class structure if it shares aspects of its character with more than one other class, and therefore tends to vacillate in allegiances.

finally enters a period of crisis and dissolution. In the "end" a new societal formation is established on the basis of new economic relations which resolve the particular contradiction of the previous mode of production.[3]

Class analysis seeks to discern collectivities who share economic situations causing them to react similarly to economic phenomena and to the ripening of the contradictions at the core of a society's mode of production. In finding these collective agents for the capitalist mode of production, one has ostensibly found the critical actors in capitalism's perpetuation or demise—in the classical view, the bourgeoisie and the proletariat.[4]

Although the Ehrenreichs criticize the particular way orthodox Marxists demarcate classes in modern capitalist society, it would appear, at least from their article, that they do not disagree with the orthodox focus on class as the only possible collective agent of history.[5] But we have another view.

As class analysis presupposes, the economic function of providing the material means of social livelihood is necessary to the reproduction of modern society. But can we apriori say that it is the only function necessary to societal reproduction? In fact, isn't the feature of production which makes economics so important the fact that beyond being necessary to social reproduction, economic activity occupies a great deal of our time *and* is necessarily social? To carry out production people must enter social relations and this makes possible the formation of important collective agents of history. Other activities are necessary to social reproduction—breathing being an obvious if rather trivial example. We spend a lot of time performing this necessary function but what distinguishes production from breathing is that production requires social interaction. Breathing doesn't lead to group interests and consciousness, and therefore it is of no importance to our attempt to determine collective agents of history. Seeing the social reason for the relevance of the economic realm to locating historical agents, can't we now see that other realms might be critical as well?[6]

3. Some readers may take offense at our "simple minded" rendition of orthodox Marxist notions, but these do form the basis for most arguments favoring a two-class polarity in modern society, and it is this position, whatever the range of its following, that the Ehrenreichs are attacking.

4. The Ehrenreichs present the two-class analysis as currently dominant, and while not wishing to deny the existence of many other approaches, we agree.

5. They do not, for example, make any significant mention of the autonomous importance of race, and even tend to imply that a "materialistic" approach to issues of sex would be sufficient, though in other writings they very explicitly call for an analysis of the independent and autonomous role of sexual and kinship dynamics.

6. For a fuller discussion of the relevance of these assertions see Michael

For example, for society to continue, the next generation must be conceived and socialized. Children must be brought into the world, nurtured and "ushered" into adulthood. Kinship relations between men, women and children are socially unavoidable. Kinship activity is necessary to societal reproduction and requires considerable social interaction. Perhaps in the dynamics of kinship we might also find cause for the formation of collective agents of history, i.e., groups of people who by virtue of their place in kinship patterns share certain interests and perspectives and react similarly to certain phenomena critical to social change.[7] Then, of course, with both kinship and economic relations important, fathers, mothers, uncles, sisters ... in a given class would face different situations as would people from different classes in the same kinship group. Each "core characteristic" (in this case, economic and kinship relations) would affect the contours of the other.

Similarly, people enter "community" and "decision-making" networks. Important "demarcations" can arise from people's attempts to attain self-respect through cultural involvements based on shared points of origin or ancestry, a particular belief, a physical attribute, a common enemy or some other "distinguishing" characteristic, especially when these factors lead to the formation of "communities" with specific ongoing social relations among members and between members and "outsiders". Racial, ethnic, religious and national formations are all thus included under our rubric of community relations. Decision-making relations, in contrast, derive from the collective implication of people's ability to consciously plan their own purposive activities. Such planning requires clarity about what others are doing, about what is allowable and what isn't, what is planned and what is not. Alternative decision-making structures, and the accompanying demarcation of various kinds of hierarchy, can lead to sectors which have different powers, interests, consciousness and historical roles. Considering the possibility that these community and authority networks may have dynamic attributes critical to the reproduction of any particular society, it seems reasonable to suggest that either might generate commonalities sufficient for the formation of important historical collective agents.[8] In the United States, for example, there is certainly reason to believe that racial community

Albert and Robin Hahnel, *Unorthodox Marxism,* (Boston: South End Press, 1978), pp. 58-64, 130-132.

7. See Gayle Rubin, "Traffic in Women" in Rayna Reiter, ed., *Toward an Anthropology of Women* (New York: Monthly Review Press, 1977); Batya Weinbaum, *The Curious Courtship of Women's Liberation and Socialism* (Boston: South End Press, 1978); and Albert and Hahnel, *Unorthodox Marxism.*

8. Note that just as there are people who develop class centered analyses, kinship centered analyses, and race centered analyses—Marxists, feminists, and

relations are critical and that black, third world people, and white people should be seen as important historical actors. The meaning of sex, class, race, and hierarchical affiliations is clearly dependent upon their mutual interrelations.[9] Further any person's full consciousness is a function of their position with respect to more than one network of social relations, and even their partial consciousness with reference to a single realm—for instance, the economic—is affected by their position in that realm, their class, and in other realms too—for example, by their race and sex. But what does this tell us about the process of finding potential agents of socialist revolution and about the character of class analysis?

If we assume economic relations are the key link in revolutionary change, the class or classes on the "side of history" would be the agents of revolution. Propelled by their economic interests they would eventually struggle for socialism. Their organizations would be the revolutionary organizations. The collective agents of history and the motive of revolutionary struggle would be found only within the economic realm, and search elsewhere would be secondary.[10] This is the attitude which gives a sense of unparalleled urgency to most activists' concerns with class analysis.

But what if the reproduction of current relationships was dependent upon dynamics manifested in a number of realms—for example, not only in economics, but also in kinship, community, and decision-making? And

nationalists, respectively—there are also people who develop decision-making centered analyses, the anarchists. Each may be more in touch with reality than any one gives the others credit for. Moreover, just as demarcating community and kinship realms calls into question the common practice of explaining racism and sexism derivatively from economic forces, so demarcating the decision-making realm questions the advisiblity of interrogating the state from a class perspective alone.

9. The immediate reaction of many orthodox Marxists might be to assert that it is economic forces which determine what we have called community, decision-making and kinship relations. But it is our contention that this is not necessarily so in all societies. In a particular society it may be necessary to take a totalist approach and not regard class as the sole critical social relationship. With kinship, community, and decision-making also achieving a central position, class analysis becomes a different process and the demarcation of classes carries a different meaning. This is the reason for the present discussion in this essay. We hope its brevity has not given the ideas an excessively mechanical tone. The views are developed more fully, with more attention to the obviously critical fact that workers are of different races and sexes, women of different classes and races, etc. in Albert and Hahnel, *Unorthodox Marxism.*

10. The assertion isn't that workers organize only on the shop floor or only around shop floor demands, but that all other dimensions of the struggle are seen as having their roots here.

what if it was impossible to reduce the dynamics of these different realms to any one of them alone? Then identification of a potentially revolutionary agent in any one realm would only represent the identification of a group who by its position, role, and interests *might* become an agent of revolution, and *might* develop an awareness extending from its realm to the totality of critical realms. The organizations of agents in one realm *might* be part of a broader federation of revolutionary organizations but there would most probably be many obstacles to overcome if this were to result. Most generally, particular groups in this view would be expected to attain revolutionary consciousness, if at all, by different paths.[11] And moreover, certain divisions within any one group would not be only "peripheral" to commonalities, and only of relevance as "divisive factors," but important in their own right as well.

For example, if kinship relations were critical to a social order, then women might very well occupy a central place in social change. This wouldn't mean that women were automatically revolutionary, nor that they would inevitably develop a full revolutionary awareness by pursuing only their kinship-defined interests, but more modestly that: 1) women identifying as mothers, daughters, sisters would likely share common reactions to many kinship phenomena; 2) they might develop their own organizational forms; and 3) they would develop a revolutionary consciousness and role, if at all, by routes generally other than those followed by men and other collective agents. Similarly, in a society with critically important racial community relations, oppressed racial groups would be key agents in creating a "totalist" socialist movement.

Of course we also fully expect groups sharing affinities arising in the economic realm, or classes, to be important agents of revolutionary change in modern capitalist societies, but even so our approach to class analysis is obviously very different from that of orthodox Marxism. For us class analysis is not a be-all, end-all affair. It is critical, but not alone critical. When we demarcate a potentially revolutionary class or classes, we have not found the sole agents of socialist revolution, nor have we found agents whose pursuit of their own defining interests will automatically generate a *full* revolutionary perspective. Nor have we identified agents whose organizational forms are the only vehicles of revolution. Rather, in naming a potentially revolutionary class, we

11. This is consistent with the efforts of women and third world people to argue the need for autonomous movements within a total revolutionary struggle. Further, any group's consciousness can be revolutionary but might also merely be rationalizations of their situation. There is no mechanical translation from the discovery of a group that may become a historical agent to the actual event of a revolutionary historical intervention.

demarcate a group whose position and role in economic affairs make 1) a progressive economic orientation likely; 2) the development of an overall revolutionary consciousness possible; and 3) the class's particular road to such a total consciousness different from that of other revolutionary agents.[12] The traditional working class, for example, may not necessarily develop an anti-sexist consciousness from its economic interests and position alone; political struggle with women who identify as women more than as workers and eventually following women's leadership may be necessary. Yet anti-sexist consciousness and practice may be essential to a total revolutionary perspective. Similarly, the road to an anti-racist, or anti-authoritarian consciousness (should these be required for revolution) would be different for workers than for other agents demarcated in other realms of society. Note, we mean here specifically people *identifying primarily* as workers. Obviously workers are not all white men, and workers of different race and sex develop their political orientation by different routes and often to different ends. Regrettably, in this article, we can only touch the surface of the complex entwined relations of race, sex, class and authority. We merely set out some of the abstract concepts; the problem of concrete analysis remains, especially investigation of the effect it has that each "collective agency" is stratified along criteria other than its defining one—thus classes along race, sex and authority lines, races along class, sex, and authority lines, and so on.

But all this said, we still don't know how to identify a class. How do we draw "boundaries" such that for purposes of political work it makes sense to treat the agents on either side differently? For this is simultaneously the purpose and critical result of the analysis of agents of history— finding one, we find a group which has its own interests, needs, views and potentials, at least with respect to one particular facet of social life, and which therefore will respond differently to political programs, have different organizational needs in political struggle, and deserve different "treatment" in political organizing than other collective agents (e.g. in different societies and epochs: mothers, fathers, blacks, Chicanos, Vietnamese, Chinese, Capitalists, workers, ...).[13]

12. We locate classes in terms of economic social relations which for us includes recognition that the development of a class is a cultural and ideological process, and that there are situations under which these so-called "subjective" factors will dominate what seem to be the implications of "material" factors.

13. Obviously people are often members of more than one historically important group. Membership in each group has implications for activity and consciousness in the realm with respect to which that group is defined— economic, kinship, etc. The "whole-person" is affected by and has aspects relevant to development along all these "realm-defined" dimensions. A full revolutionary stance must move beyond an interest group identification to take a

Marx has taught us much about criteria for discerning economic classes.[14] We want to distinguish groups who share interests, needs, and self-conceptions by virtue of their place in production and their economic roles.[15] We know from Marx that a person's position in the economy determines how one gets an income (from what source, in what amounts and by means of complying with what requirements) and one's power over one's own work and potentially the work of others as well. We also know from Marx that in their productive activity people produce their own characteristics as well as external material objects (or services). That is, within the constraints of our jobs—by what we do, how we do it, the mentalities we must employ, the skills we enrich or deny, and the energy we renew or squander—we in part determine our own personality, consciousness and needs. With a change in job relationships, even without any change in income and material needs, there may be a change in consciousness, personality, and subjective desires.

If we can find a group whose structural position in the economy gives it common material interests and powers and aligns it in pursuit of material advancement against others who would most often challenge or deny that advancement, and if by the social relations involved in the functions it fulfills the same group has the potential to develop a shared self-conception and way of viewing various economic relationships and other groups, then it would seem a very probable candidate for the designation "class". But classes are also expected to play a collective historical role, an accomplishment which requires self-consciousness and some form of organization, whether on-going, or simply established in the moment of the group's intervention in history. This suggests another dimension for examining prospective sectors to decide whether they constitute a class: Does the sector organize itself in any way? Have its members ever recognized and consciously acted upon their commonalities, or if they haven't, is there reason to expect that they will in the future, particularly in a revolutionary period?

A useful definition of class must incorporate recognition of the supposedly extreme aspects of three "polarities". First, a useful definition must include both an objective and a subjective aspect. A class must share material interests and powers due to its on-going position in the

stand along all the critical dimensions. This is more fully discussed in Albert and Hahnel, *Unorthodox Marxism*.

14. Marx never set out any precise definitions or methodologies of class analysis. We, like others, are only giving our own interpretation, no doubt determined by our own experiences and situations.

15. Later we will argue for the potentially autonomous importance of cultural relations, and for more on this see Marshall Shalins, *Culture and Practical Reason* (Chicago University Press, 1978).

functioning of the economy, but it must also at least potentially share a consciousness of that commonality and display some tendency to pursue activities based on such a common perception. The Ehrenreichs themselves are very clear on this point. Second, the demarcation of a class requires both an empirical and a theoretical justification. In addition to locating various commonalities, shared interests, and organizational potentials, one must also demonstrate the roots of these features in lasting underlying social relationships. Finally, our analysis must be both immediate and historical. Having a basis in current social relationships, any class we demarcate must also hold an economic position which will at least preserve its relevance throughout the period of our future concern. Only after ascertaining that a particular group fulfills objective and subjective, empirical and theoretical, immediate and historical criteria can we confidently assert that it is a class and investigate the implications for political strategy.[16]

II Capitalists, Workers and the "PMC"

Most Marxists neatly summarize the economic relations of capitalism with the symbolic formulas, C^1-M-C^2 and M-C-M$'$, representing respectively the social roles imposed by the mode of production on workers and on capitalists. The workers sell their labor power, a commodity (C^1), for a wage (M), and then buy the means of their subsistence and other commodities (C^2). The capitalists, on the other hand, use their money (M) to buy various commodities (C equal to labor power, intermediate goods, machinery, etc.) and then combine these in production selling the product for more money (M$'$). The laborer seeks the use value of the goods finally bought with the wage. The capitalist seeks to expand the exchange value he began with by appropriating the surplus value generated in production—the difference between M, the amount he starts out with, and M$'$, the amount he holds at the "end". Though highly abstract, for most Marxists this represents the basic dynamics of capitalism.[17] Is there any argument here that workers and

16. Our approach to discerning historical agents is not objective in the traditional, disinterested sense. It is rooted in the desire to change society. Perhaps the most alienating thing about many attempts at class analysis is the way they are divorced from activist concerns. A) Women, blacks, and working people discern differences between people which have immense impact upon organizing. B) "Movement writers" debate who does and who doesn't have the right definitions, which groups fit their definitions and which don't, all without discussion of perceived political relations. Where the theory should explicate experience and assist its enrichment, it is usually so unrelated to experience and so obscurely written that it can do neither. Overcoming such problems should be a priority task of all socialists, especially those of the PMS.

17. See Paul Sweezy, *The Theory of Capitalist Development* (New York:

capitalists should each be considered a class?

From their position in the economy workers derive an interest in the enlargement of wages per hour of labor power sold. Moreover, they also derive an interest in limiting the actual amount of labor the capitalist can successfully extract from their labor power. That is, the workers sell only their capacity to do work over a certain span of time, the work day. It is up to the capitalist to extract as much work as possible during that period and to modify the human characteristics of his work force so as to preserve this capacity in the future, while it is in the worker's interest to maximize his/her immediate fulfillment and future development or at least to minimize the drudgery, pain, and stultification resulting from time spent on the job. This gives the workers and capitalists opposing interests in controlling the pace and defining the character of work on the shop floor.[18]

Workers thus have shared wage and work organization interests with roots in the structure of the capitalist mode of production. The character of their daily interaction and activity can be expected to yield many common self-conceptions, and ways of viewing the economy and other members of society—employers in particular. Furthermore, history shows that workers easily discern at least some of their common interests and form organizations to pursue them, ranging from burial societies and drinking and sporting clubs to trade unions and political parties.[19] Finally, according to this Marxist analysis, contradictions in the economy are instrumental in socialist organizing and the socialist revolution, and it is the working class who is in the position of acting on these contradictions in the interest of attaining socialism. Workers thus have shared interests which they pursue within the contours of the system—the enhancement of their material position via the fight over wages and for control of the work day—and also occupy a position which makes attainment of a socialist practice possible, or in some views, inevitable.

So the workers are designated a class because they share needs and consciousness deriving from their position in the economy, because they

Monthly Review Press, 1942) for what remains one of the clearest and most instructive presentations of orthodox Marxist theory.

18. Herb Gintis has done a path-breaking job of elaborating the implications of this latter point in his unpublished essay "Theory of the Capitalist Firm", Harv. Disc. Paper No. 328, Oct. 1973, and this work is elaborated further in Albert and Hahnel, *Unorthodox Marxism,* pp. 149-157.

19. See E.P. Thompson, *The Making of the English Working Class* (New York: Random House, 1966) for a brilliant treatment of class as based in both objective and subjective aspects producing class as a historical outcome. The early burial societies and clubs are described by Thompson as historic progenitors of modern English trade unions and political parties.

share a common adversary and organize for wages and control, and because we can see their potentially crucial role in the struggle for socialism. Cut to its essentials, this is the logic of the Marxist demarcation of workers as a class.[20]

A discussion of capitalists is the obvious "other side" of the discussion of workers. From their position in the economy, capitalists recognize their common interests in enlarging profits and increasing control over the production process and organize in various business organizations, clubs and political parties to pursue them. They fight on a daily basis, seeking to retain control of the workplace and to expand profits; and they also fight in times of crisis, seeking to maintain the system by whatever means necessary.

The recognition of these two classes and of their long and short term struggles has helped Marxists understand many dynamics of capitalist economies and other facets of capitalist societies as well. Nevertheless, the importance of kinship relations, community relations and decision-making relations calls into question the orthodox claim that class analysis alone is enough to help us fully understand the totality of our society's laws of motion.[21] But where we have argued the insufficiency of class analysis in general, the Ehrenreichs' major point in the article in this book is to challenge the sufficiency of orthodox Marxist two-class analysis of the modern capitalist economy. They say, in essence, the C^1-M-C^2 and M-C-M' formalism is too narrow. Focusing only on the abstract quantitative exchange, it leaves out reference to the character of work activities and thereby causes us to overlook the possibility that not all people who sell their labor power for a wage should be included in a single class. It is here that the Ehrenreichs propose a new formulation, that there is a new class, the "PMC".[22]

In her autobiographical work, *Daughter of Earth,* Agnes Smedley describes her feelings as a working class socialist woman encountering

20. Of course the Marxist heritage includes many richer analyses, but nonetheless the orthodox two-class model remains the bedrock of most Marxist exposition and instructs most Marxist analysis.

21. Perhaps, for example, to understand the social relations in a U.S. factory, class analysis is insufficient. For in addition to reproducing class relations, maybe factory dynamics are historically structured to perpetuate, replicate, and even reproduce kinship, community, and decision-making relations which have their roots in other realms of social life. For a discussion of the factory and kinship see Weinbaum, *Curious Courtship,* and with reference to all three possibilities see Albert and Hahnel, *Unorthodox Marxism,* pp. 109-118.

22. The Ehrenreichs also challenge the notion that production relations alone determine class definitions as they accept Thompson's formulation that culture can have an independent impact.

certain New York socialist intellectuals for the first time:

> I do not know if they were superficial—or if they were wise. In any case they and their ways were strange to me. Their quick, humorous repartee left me silent....Many of them belonged to those interesting and charming intellectuals who idealize the workers, from afar, believing that within the working class lies buried some magic force and knowledge...I sat in beaten wonderment and confusion among them. When I was introduced to them they automatically extended a hand, but their eyes were on someone else and they were speaking to others. I might have been one of the chairs they were gripping in passing...I made no more impression upon them and their world than a stone makes when thrown into a lake. They left in me a feeling of confusion, of impotence, of humility and even of resentment. I did not know how to learn the things they knew, and they had not time or interest to tell me how.[23]

Is there just a temporary gap between Agnes Smedley and the intellectuals; are they aberrant—is she naive; or is this a meeting of people who simply come from "different places?" The last is the Ehrenreichs' answer.

Leftists generally agree that there exists a middle element, what we call the PMS (Professional/Managerial Sector), different from both workers and capitalists. However, most prefer not to demarcate this element as a class, arguing instead that it is a strata of one of the two main classes or that it occupies a "contradictory position" between these two.[24] The Ehrenreichs feel, on the contrary, that this group is autonomous and that it has a life and interests of its own. According to the Ehrenreichs, while the PMS shares some features with workers and some with capitalists, more importantly, it has characteristics unique unto itself. It has shared interests, plays an autonomous historical role, and can become an important agent in modern revolutionary struggles. For the Ehrenreichs, it is a class, the PMC.

> We define the Professional/Managerial Class as consisting of salaried mental workers who do not own the means of production and whose major function in the social division of labor may be broadly described as the reproduction of capitalist culture and capitalist class relations.[25]

23. Agnes Smedley, *Daughter of Earth* (New York: Feminist Press, 1973).

24. For example, Wright takes this view in *Class, Crisis and State.*

25. Barbara and John Ehrenreich, "The Professional-Managerial Class," p. 12 of this book. The Ehrenreichs extend the definition to include shared cultural features in many other parts of their essay.

The Ehrenreichs feel that in the socialist movement and in the definition of socialist relations, PMC politics are capable of dominating working class politics. It is this possibility, more than any other, which propels our interest in the Ehrenreichs' redefinition of class concepts.

Is the PMS really the PMC; is it only an assemblage of people in contradictory class locations; or could it be both at once? In the course of evaluating the Ehrenreichs' arguments we make a case for the third option, preserving the Ehrenreichs' contributions while hopefully overcoming some of the weaknesses in their presentation.

The Ehrenreichs assert that a class should be demarcated according to structural and cultural criteria. They seek to show: 1) that the PMS's position in the economy puts them in an antagonistic relation with both workers and capitalists; 2) that it also gives them certain interests of their own which are oftentimes elaborated in political struggle and visions of an alternative PMS dominated mode of production; and 3) finally, that the PMS has its own cultural relations internally and with respect to other groups as well. For these reasons, according to the Ehrenreichs, the PMS is really a class, the PMC.

The PMC is deemed to be those salaried mental workers whose "major function" is the reproduction of *capitalist* cultural and class relations, a full 20-25% of the population, including engineers, managers, professionals of all kinds, nurses, teachers, cultural workers, etc.[26] According to the Ehrenreichs, these people are antagonistic to capitalists in much the same way as traditional workers. Selling their labor power to capitalists they develop material interests contradictory to maximizing profits. Further, like the workers, they also develop an interest in controlling the character of their work situation; but because of their skills and intellectual training and because of their societal roles, they are in a much better position to pursue this struggle. As workers who are highly skilled they have exceptional bargaining power to attain autonomy; as workers who are highly schooled, intellectually active, and assertive, they have considerable self-confidence with which to pursue autonomy; and finally as workers whose role is mediating capitalist/ worker conflicts to the advantage of the capitalists, for their effectiveness it is important that their ties to capitalist authority be obscure, that their autonomy be real and evident.[27]

26. Actually the Ehrenreichs' estimate is too high even by their own figures as they fail to take proper account of the fact that many families will have more than one member occupying a PMC position.

27. The Ehrenreichs' definition and discussion suggests that they may feel that salaried vs. waged and productive vs. unproductive are distinctions which may separate the PMC from other workers. We see no reason to pursue these notions. Certainly, there is little to be found in the difference that comes with

But in the Ehrenreichs' view these "worker attributes and interests" don't constitute sufficient reason to call the PMS an unusual, privileged strata of the working class. Rather, the PMS is antagonistic to workers as well. The PMS exists only insofar as the working class was robbed of its own intellectual skills, and the role of the PMS is to manipulate the working class to the advantage of capitalists. The Ehrenreichs argue that with the development of monopoly capitalism the working class was denied all but the most mechanical role in production—it was the emergent PMS who took over the more administrative and cognitive tasks.[28] The relationship between the PMS and workers is therefore antagonistic, however much they may have in common in their opposition to capitalists.

To this point the PMS could be merely in a contradictory location, sometimes aligning against capitalists with workers, and sometimes against workers with capitalists. However, the Ehrenreichs go further: PMS members develop their own psychology, their own mode of life, their own conceptions of how to preserve their positions, enlarge their impact, and even initiate a new mode of production elaborating their own interests as those of all of society. The PMS describes "rational" organization as its primary virtue, and "efficiency" as a fundamental goal.[29] Profit, they realize, is but one of many ends their genius could serve, and not the most rewarding to their talents nor the most conducive to their advance or maximal contribution to society. To pursue alternatives, the PMS gradually develops its own professional organizations, both for defense and for the careful elaboration of new possibilities. Speaking of PMS "know-how", the Ehrenreichs quote Frederick Taylor:

> The same principles can be applied with equal force to all social activities: to the management of our tradesmen, large and small; of our churches, our philanthropic institutions, our universities and our government departments.... What other reforms could do as much toward promoting prosperity, toward the diminution of poverty and the alleviation of suffering?[30]

getting paid on different schedules; one is still selling one's labor power for a wage. Further, we see almost no way to even analytically distinguish between "productive" and "unproductive" workers, and even if such distinctions could be made, a) they would not be along the PMC worker boundary, b) it's not clear that they would have any implications for material interests or consciousness formation, and c) in a monopoly formation they would be dwarfed in importance by the effects of unequal exchange on income and relative interests anyway.

28. "The Professional and Managerial Class", pp. 22-23.

29. We should remember that this is an ideology, it means rational organization in the interests of the PMC, and efficiency toward PMC ends.

30. Ibid., pp. 22-23.

And they also quote Thorstein Veblin as he lays out a "technocratic" vision with even greater clarity:

> (Capitalists) have always turned the technologists and their knowlege to account...only so far as would serve their own commercial profit, not to the extent of their ability; or to a limit set by material circumstances; or by the needs of the community...To do their work as it should be done these men of the industrial general staff, i.e. engineers and managers, must have a free hand, unhampered by commercial considerations and reservations....It is an open secret that with a relatively free hand the production experts would today readily increase the ordinary output of industry by several fold—variously estimated at some 300 percent to 1200 percent of the current output. And what stands in the way of so increasing the ordinary output of goods and services is business as usual.[31]

Socialist movements, according to the Ehrenreichs, have often embodied this PMS technocratic vision.[32] It is at the heart of the aim to rationalize industry and manage the economy through central planning, and of the vanguard approach to "serving the people," and thus of Leninism itself.[33] Could it also have been at the heart of the Russian Revolution and many other liberation struggles in the Third World as well?[34] If this is the case, it would certainly be a powerful argument that the middle sectors indeed constitute an important class in history.

This represents the whole of the Ehrenreichs' argument. The middle sector is not a sector at all, but a new class, the PMC. Anti-capitalist but simultaneously elitist, it sometimes generates a populist politics, but in the end always gravitates to a technocratic solution to society's ills. By its knowledge, industriousness, and anti-capitalist interests, it can often find a home or even dominant place in workers' movements, but it often ends by subverting these movements to its own purposes. PMC interests are not the same as worker interests; PMC culture is not the same as worker culture. PMC dominated movements will often be unattractive to workers for just these reasons, but when conditions demand alliances, powerful "unified" movements may emerge. However, if these movements form under PMC leadership, even their complete victory will not bring workers' power nor a working class redefinition of economic relations.

31. Ibid., pp. 23-24.

32. The Ehrenreichs most often mean social democratic movements but also make references to communist movements.

33. For more on this see Albert and Hahnel, *Unorthodox Marxism,* Chapters Seven and Eight.

34. See Gerard Chaliand, *Revolution in the Third World* (New York: Viking Press, 1977).

The Ehrenreichs have made a case that has an undeniable ring of experiential truth. It corresponds nicely to the experience of Agnes Smedley (related earlier) and countless other workers in their relations with "experts" and on encountering the "socialist movement"—for this movement often seems to be the property of someone else, the workers feel like outsiders.[35] But for all the insights they have, the Ehrenreichs have still left a number of loose ends in their analysis. With a critical evaluation true to the original spirit of their inquiry, perhaps we can suggest some alterations and re-tie those dangling ends.

The problem with the PMC hypothesis is first that the Ehrenreichs' definition of the PMC is flawed, and second that the structural-functional aspects of the account are imprecisely worked out.

First the definition. For the Ehrenreichs the PMC are salaried mental workers primarily involved in the reproduction of capitalist relations. The aim of the definition is (or should be) to capture just those elements who can generate their own autonomous political vision and programs. These are the people we should want to give the "new class" label to. But by characterizing these people as engaged primarily in reproducing *capitalist* relations, the Ehrenreichs inadvertently undercut the whole thrust of their argument. For if that's the group's sole purpose, how can they possibly evolve an independent interest, organizational form, practice, and goal? The Ehrenreichs' definition of the PMC reduces it to dependence. Of course a group could *start* with a dependent purpose and evolve an autonomous interest later, but the original purpose can't be taken as the defining trait of the later evolving class. This problem, therefore, is not necessarily in the world but may merely be in the Ehrenreichs' poor choice of words for describing it—a view we shall argue shortly.

Second, and these are more serious problems with the Ehrenreichs' definition, *all* workers receive a wage or salary,[36] *all* employ mental abilities and energies, and *all* are engaged in the reproduction of societal (including class) relations. Capitalism certainly subsumes the craft workers of old to the logic of a vast system of deadening rules and regulations. It robs many workers' skills and it attempts to place conception, design and administration outside the worker's purview; but nonetheless, even today, all workers must still necessarily use their minds. Were assembly workers in a Ford plant to lose all their intellectual faculties while retaining all their specific work-task abilities, there would simply be no more Fords. Work to order, with no initiative of one's own,

35. It's impossible not to wonder how many workers would feel close to the analyses in this article, able to use them, able to "converse" with them, etc. The gap is one of language, culture, and style, as much as one of politics.

36. We mentioned above that we see little distinction between wage and salary.

is tantamount to no work at all. As Cornelius Castoriadis notes, it is ironic "that in real life, capitalism is obliged to base itself on people's capacity for self-organization, on the individual and collective creativity of the producers without which it could not survive for a day, while the whole 'official organization' of modern society both ignores and seeks to suppress these abilities to the utmost."[37]

There is nowhere to draw a sharp boundary between those who do intellectual labor and those who do manual labor. All work involves both moments, it is the balance and character of the two moments that varies from job to job, as well as the emphasis on "conception" as compared to "execution".[38] A computer programmer who solves preassigned problems, an ad writer, an assembly worker, and a teacher may all have very comparable situations in respect to the extent to which they execute tasks defined by others versus conceptualizing their tasks for themselves; and depending upon where they work, for whom, and on what, though their degree and character of intellectual involvement may vary, it can never drop to zero. Where would the Ehrenreichs draw a line to split off "intellectual workers" from "manual workers?" Still the fact that we can conceive of drawing a line between those who conceptualize their work in advance and those who merely exercise tasks conceptualized and defined by others suggests that a definition other than the one supplied by the Ehrenreichs may still salvage the prospect for a "new class". Similarly all work reproduces (or subverts) the contours of society's defining class (and other) relations. And here it is only a matter of form and not one of degree. For it is simply not useful to argue that advertisements, or psychological "cures", or even designs for new workplace technologies reproduce class relations more than successfully carried out work assignments in an auto plant. All work produces not only commodities for sale, but also human characteristics and social relations.[39] Work in a factory reproduces social relations not only by creating the products necessary to on-going social life, nor even only by "fueling" the accumulation process and continually reproducing the capitalist/worker relationship, but also, at least in the United States, by continually helping to reproduce patriarchal and racial community relations as well.[40] In this sense, as human activity, all work in the United States is enmeshed with and part of the same phenomena of societal reproduction and development. Defining class by its having a reproductive function is impossible.

37. Cornelius Castoriadis, *Workers' Councils and the Economics of Self-Managment,* Solidarity Pamphlet (London).

38. This distinction is fully developed in Harry Braverman, *Labor and Monopoly Capital* (New York: Monthly Review Press, 1975).

39. See Albert and Hahnel, *Unorthodox Marxism,* Chapters Three and Four.

40. Idem.

All economic actors have a reproductive function and so this characteristic can not help us distinguish one from any other.

As a result of the weakness of their definition, the Ehrenreichs speak clearly only to those who have strong experiential intuitions about what they are trying to say, to the Agnes Smedleys of the current left. To the Ehrenreichs' credit, such people immediately recognize something powerful in the new hypothesis. But for many others their definition doesn't delimit the PMC from all other workers and therefore leaves considerable confusion, and sometimes aggravation as well.[41]

In addition to defining the PMC poorly, the Ehrenreichs weaken their case further by arguing from economic structures and functions to class implications much too abruptly. So what if we can show that all PMS jobs exist as a result of the past expropriation of workers' skills (or, for that matter, if someone else can show that they have other roots)? This objective historical relationship may or may not have translated into a pressure continually separating PMSers from workers. It may or may not be continually reproduced in the present. The question is whether now and in the relevant future PMS relations to workers embody this anatagonism in a way that can propel the PMS to understand it and to elaborate their own class interests in light of it. This is a problem of concrete current relations—not of past relations, however much of a clue those origins may give to the current situation or the reasons for its existence. The Ehrenreichs' structural/functional argument is therefore unfinished; having laid a historical foundation, the Ehrenreichs should have also clarified the shared consciousness and interests of the new class by showing how they are generated by current production relations.

The Ehrenreichs are intent on finding a new class for compelling political reasons already mentioned. In surveying the PMS they recognize its great span of vocations and even the variations for people in any one vocation carried out in different institutional settings. For example, managers are different from lawyers, from psychologists, from social workers, from teachers, from engineers—and mechanical engineers in production are different from industrial engineers who design shop floor relations, are different from plant engineers who problem-solve with little autonomy at all—and professors with autonomy of choice and light course loads at elite universities are different from professors with heavy predetermined loads at state Junior Colleges, are different from public elementary school teachers. But feeling the pressures to demarcate a class, the Ehrenreichs argue that such "minor differences" should not blind us to the PMC's overriding commonalities. Here we feel the

41. See the interchanges in *Radical America* in the issues following publication of the Ehrenreichs' essay.

argument has been extended too far. If a nurse's situation is more akin to that of a worker than to that of a doctor or manager, why lump him or her with the latter? If the particular relations in one town make social workers there like other workers, while in another place they fill a more professional role and see their function as managing the lives of "incompetent indigents", why should we ignore this for the convenience of a simpler theoretical exposition? If trade union leaders in one sector play a bureaucratic role of keeping the lid on worker resentment while in another they identify as workers combating capitalist oppression because of the different social relations and history of the two sectors and their unions, why ignore this to preserve a fixed "vocational criterion?"

There are two points here. First, though a part of the PMS must be a class (exactly the subset which generates the technocratic vision and has no other comparable structural allegiances) there are also many people who simply occupy contradictory positions between this new class and workers. We call the new class the "coordinator class". We call the middle sector the "PMS" and we call the middle sector without the coordinators, the "contradictory middle strata" or "CMS". But now membership in these groups is not merely a function of vocation. It depends upon the actual social relations of work a person daily encounters as well as other cultural and historical factors.[42]

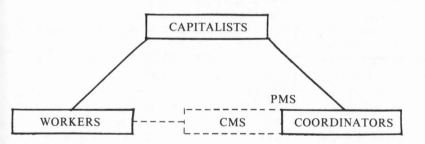

In our understanding, the coordinator class is characterized by their psychology of personal achievement and initiative, by their elitism and paternalism toward workers, and by their potential antagonism toward capitalists, all stemming from their economic position and reinforced by their cultural situation.

42. This last point is held in common with the Ehrenreichs though it takes us in a somewhat different direction.

Coordinators have significant *control* over their own labor and frequently over that of other people as well, generally *conceptualize* their work in advance and/or develop concepts which must be adopted by others, and finally have *authoritative* relations with traditional workers who are either their workplace subordinates or their clients. In short, the coordinators occupy economic positions which continually generate feelings of self-worth and capability, habits of command and also specifically anti-worker conceptions such as "workers are intellectually incapable or psychologically ill-equipped to administer their own lives without our compassionate aid." These are society's managers, its elite university professors, top industrial engineers and designers, many of its media people, union bureaucrats, psychologists, psychiatrists, and the like, and a much lesser percentage of its nurses, teachers, social workers, "problem solving" production engineers and technicians, who for the most part simply occupy contradictory positions in the class structure as members of the CMS. Nurses, for example, may come to identify as workers because of their subordinate position, or may feel professional and vacillate toward identification as coordinators, because of the authority they exert in their work—especially when the coordinators actively undertake to enact technocratic solutions to modern problems. The coordinators, however, are the members of the new class. They elaborate the new interests and organizations. The other elements of the PMS, who share much in the way of education and role definition with both coordinators and workers, may vacillate between, depending upon circumstances.[43] For example, in May '68 in France, the CMS aligned with the workers in pursuit of a real working class self-management solution to capitalist problems. Now, however, these elements are often aligned with a coordinator class project, the Eurocommunist movement, seeking technocratic solutions to these same problems.[44]

Our initial argument that coordinators constitute a class is just our translation of the case the Ehrenreichs have already largely made. Now, however, their historical evidence is a powerful guide, while current economic social relations are the root of the demarcation. The coordinators are found to occupy places in the economy giving them interests hostile to both workers and capitalists. They pursue wealth, autonomy and power against capitalists. They defend their skill, knowledge, and authority against workers. They have an ideology of achievement,

43. "Vacillation" is not the operative word, really. Rather what is critical is the fact that the CMS must vacillate between class positions elaborated by others—they develop no separate position of their own. Members of any group, may of course vacillate in their allegiances.

44. We will have more to say about Eurocommunism in a coming section.

initiative, and efficiency. They elaborate a self-interested technocratic solution to the problems of modern society, develop their own organizations to pursue these, and even elaborate their own kind of technocratic movements for "revolutionary" change. The CMS, on the other hand, occupies a contradictory class location, sometimes drawn to the workers, sometimes drawn to the coordinators. Their "class consciousness" is a mixed product. Their full consciousness is additionally affected by their positions in community, kinship, and authority networks.[45]

We should be clear that we do not mean to just "lump" these CMS people right back into the working class. No, there can be no denying that nurses, school teachers, advertizing people, technicians and the like are not simply of the working class. On average they earn considerably more and generally have more job security (though neither are always true), but more importantly the character of their work, their self-image, their culture, and their interactions with others are different than for members of the working class proper. They are between workers and coordinators. They are people we want to actively organize because their ultimate interests can be in socialism, but all the same to be part of the working class movement they and workers too must overcome certain past habits and views of each other. Further, these middle element people can become aligned to coordinators as many of their interests can also be propelled by a successful coordinator movement. They are simply in a multiple contradictory position—the boundaries to the "left" and "right" are porous, but crossing to develop one allegiance or the other is a complex journey. It is also very much affected, as we have mentioned elsewhere, but regrettably don't have space to investigate, by racial, sexual and authority factors.

The historical basis for the existence of the coordinator class and contradictory middle strata in any particular society is in some respects as the Ehrenreichs argued for the PMC. In any class stratified economy there will be one or more classes which produce what they themselves consume and a surplus appropriated by a ruling class. If these are the only classes, the conceptualization of work, its design and definition, and its administration will all be carried out by representatives of these (the expropriating and the expropriated) classes. However, historically it's often the case that experts of various types carry out these tasks, evolving in the process a position in the economy which engenders mixed pressures upon them. The reason for existence of this class is roughly as the Ehrenreichs' model asserts. The expropriated classes can't be given the intermediate positions as they might become too organized and turn on their expropriators. The expropriators, on the other hand, are

---

45. The distinction here between ourselves and E.O. Wright is our addition of the coordinator class and therefore also the different definitions of contradictory class locations.

too few in number and often too limited in skills to carry out these tasks alone, especially as the society in question becomes more and more complex. The "intermediate element" becomes the professional and managerial sector, out of which we believe there has emerged in the United States the coordinator class and the contradictory middle strata. What might alternatively be the case in other countries is a problem we cannot now address.

The case for our formulation is finished, but obviously incomplete. We present it only as a hypothesis aimed to preserve the advances embodied in the Ehrenreichs' work and to simultaneously correct some of its weaknesses—in particular, misdefinition, collapsing all middle elements into one class, substituting facts about historical origins and functions for an argument based on present social relations, and insufficiently recognizing that vocations alone incompletely identify class positions. Our arguments about the coordinator class and CMS obviously don't have the straightforward clarity that assertions about workers and capitalists have. Whether this indicates a tortured analysis, or that class texture is not so simple as we have always thought remains to be determined. But even if there is some agreement with our hypothesis, it will still be necessary to determine just who is a coordinator and which social and cultural relations are sufficient for defining coordinators, as well as who are the CMS and what exactly are their intermediate situations and likely political tendencies, as well as the racial and sexual composition of each group. Short of all this, however, we here merely suggest a few areas of investigation which can shed additional light on the problems of a "new" class analysis.

III Further Investigations In Class Analysis

Coordinator Class Technology?

Consider the process of technological development. Traditional class analysis explains its presence but not necessarily its direction. Capitalists must accumulate and invest in new technologies; but of all the technologies which are possible, how do we explain why some are pursued and the rest ignored? Are capitalist requirements the only ones which bear upon these outcomes?[46]

Capitalists hire scores of industrial engineers and scientists and indirectly mold research endeavors at many university and other non-

46. We have argued elsewhere that orthodox Marxism provides an insufficient theory of capitalist investment and that the recent debate among radical economists over the priority of "profit" and "control" criteria is badly misplaced. We also attempt to clarify the mechanisms of both qualitative and quantitative social reproduction—see *Unorthodox Marxism*, pp. 69-71, 153-57, and 129-79.

corporate labs.[47] The capitalist class puts its stamp on new technologies by its power over funds for their development and over the science responsible for their definition.[48] But the practitioners and direct administrators and planners of these projects, the managers, scientists, and industrial design engineers, are all coordinators. So how do we use class analysis to help us understand the direction of capitalist investment and the role of coordinators?

On the one hand we may argue that the coordinator's position is intermediate and completely dependent. In this case, subject to pressures from many directions, the coordinators would vacillate between a capitalist and a working class allegiance. Like other elements we've discussed, the coordinators would be only a contradictory middle sector. In this case, the capitalists alone would govern the coordinators' contribution to the development of new technologies. Carrying out the capitalists' orders and with no autonomous interests of their own, the coordinators would produce technological advances consistent with capitalist interests. Where there was more than one potential solution to a technical need, capitalists would make the choice between options and certainly no non-capitalist criteria would influence such decisions. To understand the direction of development of technology, it would be sufficient to do a traditional class analysis. Science and technology would be capitalist. The questions asked, the problems posed, the answers allowed—theoretically and practically—would be circumscribed by the capitalists' needs and desires. The coordinators would carry out a program designed by capitalists and subject to capitalist review at every step. The coordinators would have no "mind of their own" with which to inject the project with some contrary non-capitalist content.

On the other hand, what if the coordinators constitute a class between and autonomous from capitalists and workers?

The capitalists would still be the employers and administer the finances essential to research and development. But now the coordinators would have their own autonomous interests and politics. Could these be injected into the scientific project? Could the coordinators attain a position of such indispensibility and expertise in their own areas of work that they could sometimes influence these in their own self-interest? Might there be a coordinator science and technology as well as a capitalist science and technology?

Following the Ehrenreichs' analysis we found that coordinators have a relative monopoly on certain forms of theoretical understanding and skill, powers over their own and over other people's labor and

47. David Noble, *America By Design* (New York: Alfred Knopf, 1977).

48. Idem, and Stanley Aronowitz, *Science, Technology and Marxism* (forthcoming from South End Press).

corresponding interests in preserving these advantages and increasing their value as much as possible.[49] From this perspective, the coordinators would be wise to seek technologies which would increase societal dependence on the coordinator class itself. They might seek to extend divisions of labor and knowledge and to promote the importance of experts and managers, even beyond what the capitalists themselves would find most desirable.[50] Neither a necessary nor a sufficient condition that the coordinators should be deemed a class, nonetheless the existence of technological developments reflecting coordinator rather than capitalist or worker interests would provide evidence for this case. For if modern technology could only be understood using a coordinator class analysis, then the political importance of technological development would provide a good argument for the coordinators being considered a class.[51]

Coordinator Mode of Production?

Capitalist interests are embodied in the capitalist mode of production where it is they who appropriate the social surplus. And while the working class was also born of capitalism, their interests are ultimately in achieving a socialist mode of production where they can escape exploitation and attain power over their own lives. But what of the coordinators? Where are their interests located? If the coordinators are only an intermediate strata, they must choose between the capitalists and the workers' worlds. But if they are an autonomous class, they *might* seek a mode of production reflecting their own interests above all others. Do the coordinators have interests of their own which can become the basis for defining a future society's relations of production? If so, then in addition to worker and capitalist goals, the struggle over economic relations would have a third possible outcome, the "coordinator mode of production," and we would be on very firm ground calling the coordinators a new class.

49. Obviously we narrowed the Ehrenreichs' location of these traits.

50. One could also imagine similar phenomena in other spheres of economic life—perhaps in medicine, education, law, or even social work.... But perhaps computer technology provides the most likely field for further investigation.

51. The point here is that the fact that capitalists can or can't dominate the will of another sector cannot be taken as evidence concerning whether that sector should be considered a class. Were the dominance inevitable and permanent, were the sector totally dependent in its existence and ideology, that would be one thing. But that it is simply overpowered within a certain historical setting is another—and not at all an argument the sector shouldn't be taken as a class. There is also here the idea that among economic classes dominance and subordination is largely a function of whose interests are served and advanced by the criteria governing the allocation and use of labor power.

We feel that it's reasonable to argue that the technocratic economic forms we find in much of the "socialist world" are indeed versions of this coordinator mode of production.[52] The Russian model need no longer be classed as either capitalist or socialist, as a degenerate form of one (state, etatist, or bureaucratic socialism), or an advanced form of the other (state, bureaucratic, or planned capitalism). It is a well-developed example of the coordinator mode of production.

There is state ownership of the means of production. Planning is carried on by a bureaucracy of experts. Party cadre administer and simultaneously "serve the people." The state is supposedly an agency of workers but there is no real vehicle for workers to monitor state activity, nor any means at all for direct workers' self-management of the economy.[53] Instead, workers must labor in hierarchical firms with little say over what they do and how they do it, over what is produced and what isn't, and over the general policies of economic development. At best workers inform managers of production possibilities and make advisory suggestions about more or less preferred outcomes, but the local managers relay the information up to the planners, and the planners and party leaders do the deciding. And aren't the managers, planners, party leaders, and other experts just the coordinator class now at last in a position to administer society's welfare and appropriate its surplus in their own "rational" way? In this society there is an intricate entwinement of a new decision-making organization and a new mode of organization of economic activity.[54] This is the logical conclusion of our position and if it could be shown true it would serve as powerful evidence for the "new class" view.

Next consider the "two-line struggle" made famous by the experience of the Chinese Cultural Revolution. Assuming there is no such thing as a coordinator mode of production, the two-line struggle is well conceived. The only road to full socialism is by a progressive expansion of workers' power as against capitalists' power—and these are the only two contenders. The party, technical workers and administrative cadre can be vehicles for this process if they are vigilant in "serving the people" and avoiding "the capitalist road." Insofar as many of these people are no

52. See footnote "34".

53. Albert and Hahnel, *Unorthodox Marxism*, Chapter Seven includes a much more complete discussion.

54. This points to another problem in the Ehrenreichs' formulations. Using only a class analysis, their understanding of the "Russian Model" is marred. They overlook the importance of the political realm, and especially of the Leninist Party as a partner in the elaboration of this new social formation—indeed, historically, as the "senior partner."

longer workers but middle element people, they have no autonomous interests of their own. Eventually they must gravitate to the side of either the workers or the capitalists—for these are the only two roads in the transition stage known as socialism. Thus with proper accord to the importance of the two-line struggle against capitalist deformations, coordinator skills can be put to the tasks of development at the same time that the economy is brought over to the service of workers. The "proletarian line" can gain dominance over the "capitalist line." This analysis justifies and simultaneously qualifies the call for party cadre and other experts to take decision-making leadership in the development of socialist relationships.[55]

But what if the coordinators have their own interests and the potential to elaborate their own economic vision? Then there are three possible outcomes for the "transition stage." Will there be participatory planning by democratic councils, a rationalized technocratic coordinator organization operating in the presumed interests of "all the people," or a new form of profit-centered market economy? Imbued with a deep-seated disbelief in the masses' ability to administer their own affairs, the coodinators come to dismiss the first possibility as dangerous utopianism and see themselves as waging the only serious struggle against capitalist restoration. If in the end the coordinators win, the cadre, managers and planners become permanent administrators to "the people's" needs. The call for vigilance and for corrective movements from above and below lasts only until the new class stabilizes itself against both capitalist and worker opposition.[56]

But from the orientation of a class-conscious worker this outcome is a sham. Assuming the coordinators are a class, either of the non-working class outcomes is exclusive of real worker's interests.[57] In neither of the two proposed programs are there economic arrangements allowing direct collective self-management and overcoming divisions of conceptual and routine labor. In both cases the worker is relegated to a position of weakness and obedience: in one approach the capitalist has power, in the other the cadre does. In any case, however much may be gained by a victory of the "serve the people" cadre (especially in the third world), and

55. See Michael Albert, *What Is To Be Undone,* (Boston: Porter Sargent, 1974).

56. The Chinese do not speak about the cadre, managers, and planners disappearing; only about conquering their elitist tendencies and insuring that they truly learn to best "serve the people." This is certainly in tune with our analysis.

57. Note that we do not attempt to qualify the relative degrees to which a coordinator mode or a capitalist mode is oppressive to workers. The word "equally" is conspicuously absent from in front of "exclusive".

however much worker loyalty they can garner due to their commitment to societal advance and very real opposition to past injustices, their party's victory is not itself a victory of the working class.[58]

Which is the true picture? Council communists and certain workers' organizations in Russia at the time of the October Revolution argued against the Bolshevik model on grounds that it was simply a technocratic, centrist, elitist approach still foreign to real working class socialist aims.[59] However it is only recently that this argument has resurfaced and been linked to an understanding of capitalism and class analysis. Are the coordinators the ruling class of state "socialist" societies? Certainly this is a critical area of investigation for those who would pursue a third class position.

The possibility of three rather than two modes of production in modern societies, based on the rule of any of the three classes, suggests that just as a coordinator mode might have replaced the nascent socialist modes in the aftermath of the Russian Revolution of 1917, or even after the Great Proletarian Cultural Revolution in China, a coordinator mode might evolve out of a capitalist mode of production.[60] Although we leave consideration of this idea to our treatment of the current phenomenon of Eurocommunism at the end of this essay, it bears mentioning that an analysis of the more advanced forms of Social Democratic rule in countries such as Norway and Sweden as societies in which the coordinator class has gradually increased its dominance might shed more light on the dynamics of these economies than the rather sterile debates over whether such societies are capitalist or socialist. In the third world it might prove enlightening to view Nasserite Egypt and Perez's programs in Venezuela through the Ehrenreichs' looking glass.

The Problems of Socialist Organizing

Perhaps the major reason for controversy over the Ehrenreichs' hypothesis is a fear of its strategic implications and impact. People worry over what it would mean if the PMC were a class. Would PMCers still be eligible for membership in socialist organizations? Would socialists write off the PMC (and thus polarize it to the right), seek to develop

58. Fernando Claudin, in his new book *Eurocommunism and Socialism,* (London: NLB, 1978) p. 35, deals especially well with this point, though in reference to another context.

59. For relevant discussions see, Albert, *What Is To Be Undone,* and Maurice Brinton, *The Bolsheviks and Workers' Control* (Montreal: Black Rose, 1970).

60. We also see the possibility that three rather than two elements may be struggling for hegemony during the period of uncertainty about the direction of development of any modern revolution.

autonomous worker organizations and mixed worker/PMC organizations as well, or simply seek to incorporate the PMC in a working class left; and in each instance, how, and according to what guiding conceptions?

Many people's concern with the PMC as a possible class comes out of their own concrete organizing experiences. These people feel that the PMC has its own culture, needs, and outlook which both require specific organizing approaches, and endanger working class potentials (once PMC people become members of socialist organizations). We have accepted this general line of argument for a diminished PMC, the coordinator class, and have relegated other elements of the Ehrenreichs' class to the alternative category, contradictory middle strata. What are the implications for our view of strategy?

Revolutionary analysis must begin with the search for groups who are potential historical agents by virtue of their positions in the social relations of various life activities. Having found such an agent (whether it be a class, or race, or sex, or layer in a hierarchy) one has found a group which has its own interests and outlook and which must therefore be treated specially by socialist programs (around at least one realm of life). Moreover one may well have uncovered a group which is in a position to take the lead in socialist organizing around a particular aspect of the total struggle, or which is instead in a more intermediate or problematic position. For example, in analyzing kinship relations many have argued that women constitute a historical agent which has the potential to take a leading position in the struggle for new kinship relations in a new socialist society. Men, on the other hand, are seen to have mixed interests and to be capable of joining this struggle in either a reactionary or a revolutionary way, but never as the element bringing the issue to attention in the first place, nor as definers of the goal. Further, it is seen that there is need for autonomous women's organizations within the broader movement because this is the only way women can elaborate anti-sexist programs free of male dominance.

Anyone proposing a third class model would likely have something similar in mind for the economic aspect of the total struggle. Understood as a class, the coordinators are in a position of paternal dominance over the working class. They possess skills and experience the workers have been denied. Just as men will generally tend to pursue patriarchal ends so the coordinators will generally pursue technocratic elitist ends. As men's organizations may temporarily align with other progressive forces or even with women, so might the coordinator organizations vacillate in their alliances. As men in a mixed socialist movement where women had no special autonomy would tend to dominate and assert patriarchal rather than anti-sexist programs, so coordinators in a mixed socialist movement where workers had no autonomy would tend to dominate and propel a technocratic socialist model rather than one more in tune with real worker interests.[61]

Further, the various middle strata, subject to various contradictory pressures, would now have more allegiances to choose from. They might become allied with capitalists, workers, or coordinators. The socialist goal would obviously be to incorporate these strata into worker movements while at most only seeking careful alliances with class conscious coordinators.

But here lies the central reason for consternation about any third class approach. If all the middle elements are merely vacillating strata, all efforts should be made to avoid polarizing them to the wrong camp. The doors of all left organizations must be wide open to these strata lest they go to the side of the capitalists. All PMS skills must be extolled as critical to socialist needs or they may be lost to the socialist cause.[62] On the other hand, if a third class view is correct, then this approach would obscure an important reality and frustrate the potential to develop a real workers' movement for socialism. Either a movement of this type wouldn't embody workers' cultural forms nor address their most pressing needs and would therefore be unattractive to workers, or, if the economy got bad enough and workers were compelled to support such a movement, still it would be a movement for a technocratic mode of production and not for workers' self-managing socialism.

In our analysis, there is some truth in both views. On the one hand the Ehrenreichs have incorporated too many sectors in their PMC while, on the other, ignoring the third class (as most other analysts do) does obscure fundamental difficulties. The contradictory middle strata should however, *be organized directly into the socialist movement*—their skills and interests must be recognized and their roles discussed while their contradictory tendencies and habits are forthrightly opposed. This the Ehrenreichs (or at least people reading and liking their analysis) may

---

61. So a coordinator identifying as a coordinator won't be in the socialist movement, but a woman or black person of the coordinator class identifying not as a coordinator but as a woman or a black person might join the relevant autonomous movement and then the socialist struggle as well.

62. It is also interesting to consider why one attributes so much importance to many coordinator and CMS skills. Is it simply a matter of feeling that the old "expert practitioners" will be the only practitioners for an interim period while their skills are spread and re-defined as with medicine; or is it a concern that only the old practitioners can exercise these skills because the workers are simply incapable of it? And which skills are necessary—which oppressive? Are the answers different when we ask a class conscious worker than when we ask a CMS or coordinator, even one aligned with socialism?

overlook. But the coordinators are another matter. With them one may sometimes form principled alliances but *not a unified movement.*[63] The "other analysts" may overlook this.

The alternative strategy which arises from our approach would be to have economy-wide socialist organizations on the one hand, including all contradictory sectors; and factory working class organizations on the other, so that the CMS might simultaneously be a part of the socialist movement and yet not dominate its every contour. The workers would have the autonomy to develop their own position and to make it the cornerstone of socialist economic struggle.[64] Alliances with coordinator organizations would then also be possible, and of course individual coordinators would sometimes be welcome in the society wide movement, though not always in every factory and other local organization.[65]

But there would still remain the problem of how to address the middle elements. Does one argue that there will be an on-going need for "socialist experts," or does one argue that in breaking down skill monopolies socialism would simultaneously eliminate the coordinators as well as the CMS as independent privileged groups? The former approach would likely attract more PMS people of all kinds, but the latter is more in tune with our analysis, no matter how great the risk of alienating some of these people. There is nothing good to be said for building a bigger movement with compromised politics which can no longer hope to accomplish working class ends. Nor is there ever any point

63. Of course there is nothing here which disallows specific CMS or coordinators a place in worker movements. There is simply a vigilance necessary and perhaps some rules to maintain a proper balance and "exclusion" where necessary. Men can be feminists, for example, but most won't be till later in the development of the whole left, and even as more men become feminist there will still need to be organizational and practical guards against a diminution in women's roles in defining the anti-patriarchal struggle. The situation is similar with workers and other elements and the economic struggle.

64. A critical aspect of socialist struggle in the U.S. is going to be the process by which workers develop a clear program for struggle and socialist construction in the economy. This will require a full analysis of the structure of industry and of potential means of its reorganization. Many CMS elements will have to partake in this analysis and reconceptualization, essentially as aides providing knowledge that has heretofore been denied the workers, but it is the workers who will have to elaborate the new models. Thus we need to have CMS people in the movement while also having organizations where workers are free to develop their own confidence and goals.

65. This phenomenon has already been relatively common on the left. There have been any number of community organizing projects, for example, set up by well-meaning CMS people who were unable to develop "equal relations" with working people sufficient to the maintenance of the projects. Subsequently, "coordinators" have sometimes been consciously excluded.

in building a movement so fraught with unresolved tensions that as times of crisis and need arise, the movement "falls apart."

If strategic experiences can't definitively tell us which view is correct, they can give strong intimations in one direction or the other. For example, to the extent that women and third world people have successfully argued against the orthodoxy that kinship and community race relations are as core to society's definition as economic relations, it has been largely a result of concrete political experience. The same will likely be true for any future success or failure of a coordinator or other third class analysis. If the development of the left seems to reflect interests other than those of workers or if there develop schisms between workers and middle element CMS people or coordinators who seem to dominate the formulation of left strategies, then a new class analysis will gain many adherents, at least among those who seriously want to understand these occurences.[66] Hopefully, under such circumstances the spirit in which socialists accept a new class map will be one of aiming to enlarge and strengthen the base of the left, rather than unnecessarily fragmenting and weakening it.[67]

IV Eurocommunism: A Worker's Strategy to Win Over the CMS or a Coordinator Strategy to Win "Everything"

In *Eurocommunism and the State,* Santiago Carrillo of the Spanish Communist Party, has made a particular version of Eurocommunist strategy very clear.[68] Modern society is becoming progressively more

66. It is not unreasonable to wonder about who might actually fit this characterization. Certainly when women began to develop a critique of sexism and of the role of men in patriarchal society, movement men were too threatened to listen and carefully consider what was being said. Only later, realizing that the analysis didn't consign them to infamy, but only to a position requiring considerable self-conscious development, did some men come to understand and even act on the womens' analyses. Could there be a similar phenomenon now with the hypothesizing of a third class analysis? Moreover, since middle element socialists certainly dominate among movement writers and "theorists", ourselves certainly included, might there be a slowness to really appreciate the arguments. Where we have to argue abstractly, by example, and by analysis of experiences, workers themselves will argue from their own feelings and needs. This doesn't consign our arguments to irrelevance, it merely suggests that we be a bit humble and that we hold our opinions flexibly until activist socialist workers have had a chance to express theirs as well.

67. This desire was certainly behind the Ehrenreichs' project, even if we at least feel that the implications of their particular demarcation would hold little promise for a widening of the movement—this being a chief factor in our attempt to alter those demarcations.

68. Santiago Carrillo, *Eurocommunism and the State* (London: NLB, 1978)

polarized between the monopoly capitalists on one hand, and all other sectors on the other. The trend is felt particularly within the state as state employees are forced to act out anti-social policies.

> Despite ineffectual neo-capitalist theories, the state is becoming less and less a state for all, and more and more a state for the few....those who form the state apparatus—for the moment we are speaking only about a tendency—are becoming aware that authority uses them in many cases against the interests of society; they are beginning to recognize the contradiction between society which goes one way, and the state which goes another, and to regard state power as an arbitrary boss.[69]

The "sharpening of the differences between an oligarchic minority and the rest of society" is the focus of Eurocommunist strategy. The aim is to coopt the state (church and army) to the service of the people by appealing to the "national feelings" of the relevant employees.[70] According to Carillo, for example, state workers become restive—

> Not out of narrow professional interests, or of those of their own particular group, but from a clearer and more consistent conception of their relation to real society, a relationship which the monopoly capitalist state deforms and manipulates to its own ends.[71]

Interests of the whole society are posed against interests of the monopolies. The coalition thus engendered has popular rather than interest group politics and is able to win advances in each of society's institutions and in the electorate at large, but the ensuing peaceful march to electoral power is only the first step. The popular politics of the coalition become steadily more socialist, the economy is progressively socialized even while private and public sectors exist simultaneously. Shorn of all frills, this is the strategic scenario.

The lynch pin is the communists' ability to simultaneously maintain a working class base and also win support of all "middle elements." To accomplish this it is necessary to break all ties with past rhetoric and history that horrifies these elements, but even more, the middle sectors must be actively solicited. Carillo, for example, argues for military

---

69. Ibid., p. 24.

70. The definition of "relevant employees" is encompassing small capitalists in Italy and even elements of the right wing in Spain—Eurocommunism is perhaps better described as a movement which is dominated by coordinator consciousness, but still also susceptible to considerable capitalist influence as well.

71. Ibid., p. 54.

policies which can gather the allegiance of professional soldiers and also offer an important place to managers and engineers:

> This road opens up the possibility of incorporating in the new society, not only the mass of scientists and technicians, but also that new figure in modern industry to whom the term 'executive' has been applied, always providing that he values his function in a professional capacity more than his share, if any, in the ownership of the enterprise. Under social and political democracy, and in the socialist society as well, the functions performed by the executive—naturally with certain differences—will also be needed.[72]

The logic of Carillo's approach is clear enough. In context of the division between monopoly capitalists and everyone else it should be possible to create a broad coalition which can contest the capitalist parties for political power. Managers who identify with profit would hurt such a movement and are unwelcome; managers who identify as professionals, the new executives in service of society, are welcome. Indeed, by supporting certain middle element values and properly respecting the future contributions these people can make, it appears true that such alliances can be achieved.[73] And after this, in Carillo's view, the problem is to have the full socialist perspective achieve hegemony in the new coalition. Without this the movement will simply reform the system to the capitalists' advantage, while with it the revolution can finally come to an advanced capitalist country. If the workers' allegiance can be preserved while the professionals, managers, and other middle elements are courted, then in the end the workers' interests will come to the fore. For theirs is the only coherent vision counter to that of the capitalists and will therefore inevitably become this anti-capitalist movements' ideology. The similarity to the logic of the "two-line struggle" as discussed earlier is clear.[74]

But the third class analysis suggests another problem. Yes, one pitfall is that the workers' support may be lost in the shuffle. Yes, another problem is that the whole movement may be coopted by the capitalists and middle elements who identify as capitalist rather than as professionals in service to the people. But additionally and even more importantly for calling the whole Eurocommunist strategy into question,

72. Ibid., p. 81.

73. Witness the growing electoral power of the Italian and French Communist Parties—when they don't take power it is considered a failure.

74. Another problem, abstracting monopoly relations from capitalism, we don't have the space to discuss here.

it is also possible that the movement may become (or even start out as) a coordinator project. Having been courted, the coordinators (along with the party bureaucrats) may well become dominant partners in an unbalanced marriage with workers. The result may be a technocratic "solution" to society's ills. The coordinators retain their initiative as experts and extend their power beyond all prior capitalist restraints. The coordinators win the allegiance of all other contradictory middle strata precisely as their programs begin to dominate. The resulting coordinator-party-CMS societal organization proves not to be a socialism of the workers at all. Serving the whole society is once again a mask for serving a segment, and this is so however peaceful, democratic, and even worker supported such a Eurocommunist success might be.[75]

In fact, the left does have to develop programs which can attract CMS elements, but such a task must not be undertaken while ignoring the existence of a third class, much less catering to its interests. The need to incorporate contradictory middle strata is real. Alliances with coordinator organizations may sometimes be possible, but the rush to incorporate coordinators (or even, in the extreme, non-monopoly sector capitalists) into the movement can be disastrous. It is a natural outgrowth of the construction of a movement which reflects coordinator culture, organization, and values.

What exactly is the change then from the Bolshevik road to the Eurocommunist one? In Carrillo's analysis, the Bolsheviks had no choice but to assault the state head-on, and because of World War I, they were in a position to do so effectively. Today, Carrillo reasonably argues, such a frontal strategy is hopeless. Only by organizing a majority coalition and by burrowing through the state from within can the left possibly succeed.[76] And this means fostering unity with all possible middle elements around "society-wide" interests. It is this last step which is too much.

For according to the logic of our analysis the story is more complex. In the Russian revolution, coordinator ideology and interests were embodied, however unconsciously and "innocently," in the Bolshevik Party. The state and army were relatively impotent defenders of the status-quo. Beyond imperial intervention and Civil War, an additional problem for the Bolsheviks was that the workers themselves were well organized and beginning to express their own interests in self-managing the whole economy.[77] Whatever the workers' loyalty to the party due to

75. Worker support obviously doesn't mean a worker outcome—witness the English Labor Party, among many other examples.

76. While this perspective is largely correct, the accompanying Eurocommunist disavowal of need to prepare for a confrontation is misguided.

77. See Footnote 59

its role in the struggle against the Czar and the war and its commitment to serving the people, such self-management desires were not compatible with the party's own program to itself administer the new society, albeit in the name of the workers. In this view the history of the early years might be understood as a struggle for dominance between capitalists supported from without; the coordinators aligned with many contradictory middle strata and having allegiance from many workers, all led by the party with its own emerging "political elite;" the peasants on the land, in soviets, and in agrarian movements; and many other workers in their own soviets and other local organizations.[78] The party won and the result was a technocratic solution calling itself "socialist" for legitimacy. The myth indeed went a long ways to the retention of worker and international support.

In the modern European era, still according to this "extended PMC" analysis, the situation is altered. The state is a powerful opponent. The coordinators compose a much broader class and have organizations of their own as well as the potential to capture leadership in workers' movements and to win allegiance from contradictory middle strata. And finally, at least in Europe, workers appear to be unsure of their own potential and quite willing to consciously coalesce with coordinators. Even with a working class base the party remains the incarnation of coordinator values and leadership, though in the party the social relations responsible for creating "coordinator cadre" are political, those of the movement itself, and within the decision-making realm rather than the economic realm. The resulting coalition is not designed to create participatory socialism by progressively winning contradictory middle strata to the workers' cause, but instead is a movement led by party cadre, bureaucrats and coordinators and aimed to coopt the working class to the creation of a technocratic mode of production.[79]

What is the truth? What does the future hold for Eurocommunism? The one indicator we would like to point to, here, in lieu of the capacity to make more detailed concrete analyses, is the internal structure and practice of the communist parties themselves. So long as they are hierarchical and without full workers' democracy at the base, all the words of praise for democratic rights in the society at large can only be rhetorical.[80] It is the social relations of the party which give rise to its

78. This view offers much more than most other approaches—as an alternative, see, for example, Charles Bettleheim, *Class Struggle in the USSR* (New York: Monthly Review, 1976).

79. As mentioned earlier the self-consciousness of coordinators won't be so crass. Feeling theirs is the only realistic struggle against capital, they will present it as a struggle in the interests of all of society.

80. Even the necessary disavowal of East European modes of production,

leadership becoming similar in their thinking and attitudes to the (economically defined) coordinators. With the hierarchy intact, coordinator authoritarian mentalities will continue to dominate left thinking and practice. Only a democratically organized party, no longer seeing itself as the "sole" repository of socialist strategy could hope to continue to elaborate a socialist bloc capable of winning a democratic struggle for socialist self-management. For only such a party could hope to coalesce all the various women's, community, minority, youth, and other movements now prevalent into a "totalist struggle" not subsumed to the exigencies of any single particularist "vanguard" analysis. And this highlights another dimension of the weakness of Eurocommunism and even of our analysis of it. Even after developing a broad framework in the first section of this paper, we have here come at Eurocommunism "economistically", using the lens of class analysis alone, however much we have adapted that lens to current requirements. Clearly it is analysis of the political decision-making network (here as in the discussion of modes of production earlier) which is critical to an understanding of the weakness of the Eurocommunist "democratic centralist" party structure; and it is decision-making, community, kinship, and class analysis together which could prove necessary for uncovering the real narrowness of form of the Eurocommunist movement, its organizations, and its programs. Constrained by space and ignorance of the European situation, it would be ridiculous to even attempt such a broad analysis here. But it should be clear, even short of such an analysis, that until the Eurocommunists present a model for their vision of socialism and unless that model makes explicit the means by which workers themselves will directly manage factories and the whole economy, as well as the means by which new decision-making, community, and kinship networks will be elaborated, we can't help but believe that the aim is for something very different—and therefore also feel that whatever fine tuning, correction, and cautious development it may require, a new type of "collective agent analysis" is a potential microscope we should bring to bear on the European drama, and on our own U.S. drama as well.

In our view the Ehrenreichs' analysis of the PMC has opened many new conceptual doors, introduced many new practical problems and opportunities. We find it necessary to divide the group, when they take it as a whole, but in either case it seems to us that the implications for socialist program and strategy are considerable.

the much-needed admission that they simply do not constitute *socialist* models at all, will be rhetoric till internal reorganization occurs.

10.

Women as a New Revolutionary Class in the United States

Ann Ferguson*

Socialist feminism in the autonomous women's movement takes as its starting point the view that both class and sex oppression determine the position of women in U.S. society today.[1] The standard marxist position is that sexism is a by-product of class societies which will lose its material base under communism.[2] The radical feminist position, on the contrary, seeks to show that classism is a byproduct of the first and underlying social contradiction between men and women.[3] Socialist feminists have argued that there are two interlocking and mutually dependent systems, capitalism and patriarchy, which together reinforce the continued existence of classes and male dominance.[4] But there are many different views within the socialist feminist camp of what patriarchy is, why it continues, and just how it connects with capitalism. What I shall do in this paper is present one type of marxist-feminist analysis which clarifies the base of patriarchy, explains its persistence, and draws the conclusion that the changing position of men and women in the family and in the economy creates the possibility of women as a new revolutionary class in contemporary U.S. capitalism.

There are two elements in my position which distinguish it from other socialist feminisms: 1) I adopt a dialectical materialist approach to understanding women's oppression but my application of the method led me to different conclusions than Marx and Engels as to the origin and persistence of patriarchy; and 2) I accept the importance of a "new class" analysis to understand developments in our present system, which I characterize as "advanced patriarchal capitalism." Like the Ehren-reichs in their lead article in this volume, I think it is important to stress the emergence of a new social grouping: what they term the "professional managerial class." I agree with them and Erik Olin Wright[5] that advanced capitalist production has created "class contradictory" positions, i.e.,

*This paper is the product of several years of thought which has not been done in isolation but in connection with political work in the autonomous socialist feminist women's movement and with theoretical work with various study groups. Unpublished papers by individual members of the Marxist Activist Philosophers (MAP), Paula Struhl and Linda Nicolson, were important in the seminal thinking, as was the workshop on Socialist Feminism given by the Women's Caucus of MAP. I want to give special thanks to Nancy Folbre and Sam Bowles who have given extensive comments and helped with numerous revisions. Thanks to Pat Walker and Rick Edwards for valuable editorial comments. Particularly helpful were seminars in which the paper was discussed: Bowles' graduate seminar, Marx II, the summer 1977 Women's Caucus of MAP meeting, and the Fall '77 MAP Conference. An earlier version of this paper was read at the Spring '77 Hampshire College Socialist Feminism Conference.

1. Many socialist feminists include racial oppression as a concept of equal importance in understanding the social conflicts basic to U.S. capitalism. However, I know of no one who presents a historical analysis which makes clear how *race* fits in as a basic social division between people rather than as an effect of capitalism and/or patriarchy. A worked out theory would have to develop an analysis of the special position of minorities in class and sex struggles, something I cannot do in this paper, in part because I don't know the best way to do it.

2. Cf. M. Cornforth, *Historical Materialism* (New York: International Publishers, 1954). C. Guettel, *Marxism and Feminism* (Toronto, Women's Press, 1974); J. Stalin, *Dialectical and Historical Materialism* (New York: International Publishers, 1972).

3. The classic statement of the position is in S. Firestone, *The Dialectic of Sex* (New York: Bantam, 1970).

4. Cf. for example, Linda Phelps, "Patriarchy and Capitalism," *Quest,* v. II, no. 2 (Fall 1975); or Zillah Eisenstein, ed., *Capitalist Patriarchy and the Case for Socialist Feminism* (New York: Monthly Review, 1978).

5. E. O. Wright, "Class Boundaries in Advanced Capitalist Societies," *New Left Review* no. 98 (July/August).

positions which fall outside the capitalist or working class in that their role in production gives them some interests in common with each of these focal classes but interests which are identical to neither. I am less concerned with the issue of a correct classification of this group (i.e., are they a separate class? or a strata of the working class? or a group "between" classes?) than I am with the issues that are raised about the marxist criteria for class identity, and the implications for understanding the changing position of women. I agree with the Ehrenreichs' characterization of professionals and low level managers as a class, their historical sketch of the development of special functions of this group in social reproduction, and their emphasis on the cultural and historical cohesiveness of this group. But I maintain that their application of a broad concept of class does not go far enough, for an approach analogous to theirs would conclude that women are a class. Although the Ehrenreichs, as self-identified socialist feminists, have written other articles about the oppression of women and their function in social reproduction in the family and the economy, they do not draw on these insights here to tie in these points to a general theory of social reproduction in capitalism and the classes it produces. Perhaps they do not do this because they consider that there is an important political distinction between oppressive work defined by a sexual division of labor in the family and oppressive work in wage labor. In any case, I reject that invisible line: so my analysis differs from theirs.

What I shall argue is that the standard marxist idea of an exclusive class position for each individual no longer captures the reality of productive relations in advanced patriarchal capitalism. Rather, there are at least *three* different class relationships that can characterize a person at the same time: *sex class, family class,* and *individual economic class.* I argue that there is a family mode of childrearing, sexuality, and affection which I call "patriarchal sex/affective production" and that men and women are in *sex classes* relative to their positon of power and appropriation in that mode of production. Patriarchal sex/affective production is also an essential area for social reproduction in our society.

A person's *individual economic class* is defined by their individual relation to production, if they have one: e.g., a person is an individual member of the working class if s/he works for wages in a factory. However, not all members of society have an individual economic class: for example, full time housewives are defined by their husband's relation to production, and minors are defined by their parents' relation to production.

Whether or not a person has an individual economic class, they do at least (and in addition) have a *family class,* that is, a position in a family whose individual "breadwinner(s)" bear a certain relation to production.

One of the confusions about class identity comes from the situation where an individual whose family class as defined by the father's work is different than their individual economic class as an adult, or their new family class, if they marry a man with a different economic class position than their father's.

In the early stages of industrial capitalism the situation used to be less complicated than it is now, for then wives characteristically did not work outside the home after they were married. Family class for everyone in the family was defined by the husband's individual economic relation to production. Now that 47% of women work outside the home the situation is more complicated. However, since *class* as a concept involves historical and cultural self-identity: i.e., education, lifestyle, social identification and social bonds, we cannot simply see family class as an additive function of the individual economic relations of husband and wife. So, a man may own a small grocery store and his wife may work part time in a factory, or she may be a full time housewife. In either case because of the cultural implications of the man's position and money, the family class of the couple would likely be *petit bourgeois*.

I shall use this tripartite division of class relationships to show that it is developing contradictions between these class positions due to changes in the family and the economy that create the potential for women to become a new revolutionary class in the U.S. I hope that my analysis provides a methodological framework for socialist feminist intuitions that male control in the family is just as important as capitalist control of economic production. My view implies that the social relations between men and women in the family are just as much a part of the material base of society as are the social relations of economic production. We must understand developing contradictions between sex, family, and economic class as instabilities around which it is important to focus our political organizing as marxists and as feminists. I also intend my analysis to retain the distinction between the base and superstructure, unlike the marxist feminist model for the oppression of women proposed by Juliet Mitchell in *Women's Estate*. I shall discuss this distinction further later in the paper.

At this point I would like to begin the argument for the position that women and men are in sex classes by reviewing different criteria for class identity that have been proposed or assumed by marxists. My general strategy is to show: 1) my agreement with the Ehrenreichs that new economic class positions are forming in advanced patriarchal capitalism; and 2) that women constitute a revolutionary sex class according to *all* of the plausible criteria for class that have been maintained by marxists.

I. The Concept of Class

Are women a class? In order to answer this question we must define and justify a concept of class. One of the strengths of the historical materialist approach to understanding society and revolutionary change is its ability to explain revolutionary change. Marx and Engels justify their theory that class struggle is the moving force of history by using a class analysis to explain the transition from feudalism to capitalism, the French Revolution, the Paris Commune, etc. The concept of economic class that they develop is not simply an intellectual starting point which must be assumed in order to accept the rest of their theory. Rather, they show us the use of their concept by applying it in a way that helps us make sense out of a period of revolutionary change. And not only does their concept seem to work to explain past historical change, but the concept is in addition a political one, that is, it gives us a method for identifying those groups who may be key political agents for revolutionary change in present society. A problem with attempting to apply the marxist concept of *class* to analyze new developments in advanced capitalism is that the cluster of criteria which are associated with the applications Marx and Engels made of the concept to understand feudalism and early capitalism now may no longer identify one unambiguous group in the social relations of production. We need, therefore, to unpack the marxist concept of *economic class* in order to see which of the traditional criteria still apply.

The common core of the marxist concept of economic class is a group defined in both political and economic terms, that is, a *class* is a group of people who because of the kind of work they do and the power relations involved in that work in relation to other groups have a common interest, either in maintaining the system or in overthrowing it. *Class*, thus, has to be specified in terms of certain relations to production which individuals bear to each other in a given mode of production.

We need to specify more clearly what the relevant relation to production is, and what sort of power relations are involved in order to make the concept of *class* concrete. We can isolate at least six different criteria of *class* which have been given or assumed by marxists in their discussions of class differences. The first three criteria are clearly part of the basic conceptual apparatus of the classical marxist theorists: Marx and Engels, Lenin and Stalin.

Criterion 1: **Exploitation Relations**. According to this criterion, the exploiting class in a society is one which owns and/or controls the means of production in that society in a way which allows it to expropriate the social surplus of the society (whether that is defined in terms of surplus labor time or surplus value will depend on what specific mode of production, e.g., feudalism, capitalism, etc. is involved). The other classes of society are then defined in contrast to the exploiting class: that is, producers who are not owners but who have rights to appropriate part of their product (e.g., peasants), producers who sell their labor as a commodity (proletariat), etc. I shall call this criterion the economic criterion of class.

Criterion 2: **Political Relations**. Central to the classical marxist conception of history is the idea that class conflict is the moving force for social revolution. Classes thought of as political entities are defined in terms of their potential as a cohesive reactionary or revolutionary force, that is, groups which because of their economic relation to production as defined in criterion 1 are expected to develop cohesive interests and a common self-consciousness. The four thinkers mentioned above all seem to have held an inevitability thesis with respect to the relation between criterions 1 and 2 for *certain key classes*. Certain groups with objectively similar relations of exploitation in production, a "class in itself," would come to be a "class for itself," a group which is conscious of its common situation, and which comes to identify itself as a political group fighting for the same interests. Not all economic classes would come to be political classes; as we shall see, for example, Marx did not think that peasants could become a political class, hence a revolutionary agent. The key to whether an economic group will come to be a political group seems to depend on the existence of historical and social conditions which give the group *historical cohesiveness*. This we can call the third criterion of class:

Criterion 3: **Historical Cohesiveness**. This criterion stresses the point that classes are not simply abstract collections of individuals who fit under certain labels because social scientists find it helpful to so describe them. Rather, they are groups of people who share a common historical background, a common culture, common values, and therefore in one way or another some collective self-consciousness of themselves as members of a group sharing a common identity and common interests. The way I see it, there may be both structural and accidental historical reasons why an economic class does not develop the historical cohesiveness which is a necessary condition for further development into a political class "for itself." Marx appears to be giving some structural arguments why peasants do not form a class, according to criteria 2 and 3, in this quote from *The Eighteenth Brumaire*:

> The small-holding peasants form a vast mass, the members of which live in similar conditions but without entering into manifold relations with one another. Their mode of production isolates them from one another instead of bringing them into

mutual intercourse. The isolation is increased by France's bad means of communication and by the poverty of the peasants. In so far as there is merely local interconnection among these small-holding peasants, and the identity of their interests begets no community, no national bond and no political organization among them, they do not form a class. They are consequently incapable of enforcing their class interests in their own name, whether through parliament or through a convention. They cannot represent themselves, they must be represented.[6]

There are plausible historical reasons why the U.S. working class has not developed the class unity necessary to meet criteria 2 and 3, e.g., ethnic differences due to successive waves of immigration from different cultures; and work patterns of noise and isolation which make it difficult for workers to communicate on the job.

An implicit appeal to the criterion of historical cohesiveness as a way to group individuals who otherwise have disparate relations to production (hence don't meet criterion 1) seems to underlie Poulantzas' categorization of salaried teachers, entertainers, middle managers, etc. as the "new petty bourgeoisie." Though they are not self-employed, as are the "old" petty bourgeoisie, they share the values and ideological outlook of this group, i.e., they are individualistic, educated, defenders of the values of "free enterprise."

The second set of criteria for class has been developed by neo-marxists out of the criteria that may have been implicit in some of the classical writers, but were never spelled out. It seems fair to summarize the historical function of these criteria for marxist theory by saying that they all attempt to account for the failure of the working class in advanced capitalist countries to become a unified revolutionary class. Either they stress the relations of political *domination* and *submission* between capitalist and working classes due to the growth of the state and ideological institutions. Or they isolate some new class which has a privileged position in the new social relations of production by virtue of its control and *autonomy,* and whose ideological and *social function* perpetuate the status quo. We can spell out these criteria as follows:

Criterion 4: **Domination Relations.** This criterion for making distinctions between classes is based on relations of domination and submission, primarily tied to authority and control of the process of work. Those who control the labor power of others are in one class,

6. Quoted in A. Cutler, B. Hindess, P. Hirst, A. Hussain, *Marx's Capital and Capitalism Today*, Vol. I (London: Routledge and Kegan Paul, 1977), p. 171.

while those who do not are in another. People who are supervisors, managers, or foremen are obvious examples of those who control other workers. Less obvious examples are doctors' control of nurses, teachers' control over their students who can be seen as "workers in training," welfare officials' control of recipients' "work" in childraising, men's control of women's work in the home, and parents' control of children (future workers). Some of these examples would be disputed by those marxists who still hold that exploitation relations are the only way to distinguish classes. They would deny that work in the home or work in learning at school fits into the category of "productive work," i.e., work which produces surplus value. They would thus hold that such domination relations cannot be seen to be "exploitative" in the important sense which constitutes a class distinction.

Another aspect of work relations closely related to domination/submission is autonomy, i.e., how much autonomy does a worker have in producing his/her product and shaping the work process relative to other workers? This suggests a fifth criterion:

Criterion 5: **Autonomy**. We might want to maintain that those who control their own labor and the product of their labor are in one class, while those who are controlled are in another class. This group overlaps but is not quite co-extensive with the distinction between dominating and dominated classes. A person might control their own labor, as in a free lance photographer, and not control the labor power of others. Conversely, a person might be a dominator, as in a foreman or policeman, but yet not be autonomous in their work, if they in turn are controlled by their own bosses.[7]

A final criterion for class identity is that used by both Poulantzas and the Ehrenreichs, that of the major social function of the work performed:[8]

Criterion 6: **Political and Ideological Social Function**. A group whose work performs a key social function in reproducing capitalist relations of production should be distinguished as a separate class from those whose work does not perform this function, according to these

7. Andre Gorz in *Strategy for Labor* (Boston: Beacon, 1967) argues that technicians and professionals are a key strata of the "new working class" precisely because their autonomous work conditions create an attitude of their competence to control the work process which is increasingly in conflict with the interests of the capitalist class to control production arbitrarily for profit considerations. Although Gorz does not draw the conclusion that this group is a separate *class,* it is their special relation to production which gives them their focal position, and that is based on their relative *autonomy*.

8. Nicos Poulantzas, *Classes in Contemporary Capitalism (New York:* Humanities Press, 1975).

authors. Poulantzas distinguishes two important aspects of work that connect to this social function: 1) the distinction between supervisory and nonsupervisory work, which he takes to serve the *political* function of reproducing capitalist relations; and 2) the distinction between mental and manual labor, which he takes to serve the ideological function of excluding the working class from "secret knowledge" of the production process and justifying the mythology that experts are needed to make important decisions. This also serves the function of reproducing capitalist relations. By the use of this criterion, both Poulantzas and the Ehrenreichs conclude that mental and manual salaried workers fall into different classes, even though they share the same economic relation to production by criterion 1 (i.e., they all sell their labor as a commodity). They disagree about whether *all* mental workers can be said to fall into the PMC, and whether this group constitutes a class distinct from the "old" petty bourgeoisie. But, essentially, the argument boils down to the problem of how to determine precisely which workers have as their major function reproducing the capitalist relations of production (e.g., do clerical workers?).

II. Is the PMC a Class?

If we use these categories, the PMC as defined by the Ehrenreichs as the groups of "salaried mental workers who do not own the means of production and whose major function in the social division of labor may be described broadly as the reproduction of capitalist culture and capitalist class relations," [p. 12] are clearly a separate class which has the power either to challenge or support the system.

Teachers, entertainers, physicians, administrators, and the professionals have privileges unique to the capitalist system that connect to their relative autonomy in work, their relative job security, and for many, their control over the labor power of others (students, nurses, other workers). These privileges would be undermined by transition to a socialist system, not only because of explicit attacks on the division between mental and manual labor (e.g., in Cuba physicians are expected to do cleanup work that here would be done by hospital orderlies), but also because of democratic decision making by workers, students, etc., which would not leave the decisions in the hands of the "mental experts." These interests clearly are reactionary, i.e., tie this class to the defense of the status quo. On the other hand, the class is becoming increasingly proletarianized. Autonomy, job security, and domination are being increasingly diminished for those members of the class which work in state sector jobs. These tendencies support interests contrary to the defense of the status quo, and provide the base for elements of this class to develop a progressive consciousness. The Ehrenreichs present a historical analysis which suggests how the class developed in accord with the needs of capital to discipline and hierarchically structure the work force. Their analysis also provides the groundwork for the argument that the PMC is historically cohesive, that is, members of the group have a common culture and common social bonds, including intermarriage, common educational level, etc. The PMC group meets all our criteria for class identity cited above, so it is plausible to call them a class.

The PMC are a class then, but, I would argue, not for all the reasons cited by the Ehrenreichs. In particular, I would support Wright's rejection of criterion 6 as a distinguishing characteristic of *class*. It is not because the PMC performs a key social function of reproducing capitalist relations that they are a social class distinguishable from the working class. Rather it is because of the fact that the present organization of the work of education and administration of the work force allows educational and administrative workers special powers and privileges, i.e., relative autonomy and domination of others in the process of work. It is this fact which sets them against the working class. It is precisely when these powers are eroded, e.g., for elementary and secondary teachers being proletarianized, that elements of the group, *even though their jobs continue objectively to perform the function of reproducing capitalist relations of production*, may become allied with the working class. I would argue that criterion 6 is, in any case, too vague a concept to pick out one group from others, (e.g., do organized workers, in reactionary unions, constitute a class because their unions' primary function may be said to reproduce capitalist relations of production?), and should be rejected.

Although I reject the social function criterion as a criterion for class identity, I do think it is an important concept to consider in understanding the political position of a class. Since the PMC as a whole performs essential reproductive work for the capitalist system, work without which it could not continue to function, they can be said to be a *pivotal class* in political terms. Thus, those members of the PMC whose autonomy, and domination and job security are being eroded, and who thus have an increasing interest in opposing the capitalist system, are an important political force for progressive forces to organize. Later in the paper I shall argue that women as a sex class are a pivotal class in ways analogous to the PMC because of women's key role in reproductive work.

III   Patriarchal Capitalism

The assumption of all the writers we have considered in formulating criteria for class identity seems to be that one's class position in capitalism is determined by one's individual economic class, that is, whether one is a wage laborer or a capitalist, whether one controls one's own work and / or others in wage labor, etc. But this leaves out a whole sphere of work relations: those involved in the sexual division of labor in the family. By implication, any woman who is not a paid wage laborer but who works in the home and is supported by her husband has an ambiguous class location.

The reason for this omission is probably because most marxists tend to think of the family as involving a set of social relations that are not basic causative factors in the mode of production of society. The family is thought of as a way of organizing production only when the household is the center of productive efforts, e.g., in independent rural production. Industrial production is thought to have removed the center of production from private families and socialized it so that it occurs in factories and shops. The family is thus seen as part of the superstructure; i.e., relations in the family determine property relations and inheritance rights among members, the family "reproduces labor power" for the capitalist and performs the ideological functions of teaching the children individual values.[9]

This way of viewing the family is a mistake, for it ignores the fact that the family is a historically developed vehicle to satisfy key human needs— needs whose satisfaction is just as basic to the functioning of human society as is the satisfaction of the material needs of hunger and physical security. The satisfaction of these other key human needs: sexuality, nurturance, and children, is still basically produced in the family Furthermore, any conflicts between the social relations involved in producing these key human goods and the social relations of the production of material goods and services may provide a base for social change in society. Thus, I shall argue that a complete understanding of power and class relations in human production in capitalism must include an analysis of class relations of *family production*. A more general way to put this is that I view the "economic base" of society as that set of social relations of production which has primacy in providing a context in which other social relations of society and other human needs are developed and met. It must be seen to include both the social relations of production of goods and services for exchange on the market, *and* the

9. Cf. for example Eli Zaretsky, "Capitalism, the Family and Personal Life," *Socialist Revolution*, (January / June, 1973).

social relations of what I term "sex/affective" production, a system of meeting human needs which is centered in the family.[10]

The idea that social relations in the family are part of the core economic relations in our society is one that many marxists would reject. For them historical materialism as a method is usually interpreted in such a way as to imply that relations in the family are primarily derivative from, rather than co-constitutive with, core economic relations, as are other social relations involved in "superstructural" institutions, e.g., schools, churches, the legal system, the political system, and the state structure. There is a reading of the "laws" of historical materialism as sketched in Marx and Engels' *The German Ideology* which supports my "expanded base" theory, however. They claim in this work that the first premise of human history, the "first historical act," is the production of the means to satisfy the needs of "life," that is, eating and drinking, a habitation, clothing, etc., and that these key material needs lead humans to enter into "modes of cooperation" (i.e., modes of production) in order to satisfy them.[11]

But there are other basic needs that humans must also satisfy by developing modes of cooperation which are implicitly referred to in *The German Ideology*. The third law of human history is that humans biologically reproduce themselves (presumably as a result of the satisfaction of sexual needs), and must thus have mechanisms to deal with childcare and the training of new generations to survive and satisfy their needs. We can for the purposes of analysis distinguish two aspects of the production involved in satisfying these basic needs: 1) material production (the production of clothes, food, houses, etc.); and 2) sex/affective production, which I define as the system of production which organizes social modes of satisfying the needs of sexuality, nurturance,

10. My view differs here from Juliet Mitchell's view in *Women's Estate* (New York: Random House, 1972) in that she takes women's position in a society as determined by their relative power or subordination vis a vis men in the relations of *sexuality, socialization of children, biological reproduction* and *production*. I agree with her that these relations are key to understanding the position of women. However, Mitchell is not clear about whether these relations are primarily determined by economic relations or not. At times she seems to suggest they are, as when she relegates the family to an ideological function serving to promote the interests of the dominant economic class. At other times she seems to eliminate the base/superstructure distinction and emphasize a structuralist approach like Althusser. Here I part company with her, for I find the material base of these key relations to be centered in family relations between men and women, which I see as a basic (base) institution involved in sex/affective production.

11. Karl Marx and Friedrich Engels, *The German Ideology* in *Karl Marx: Selected Writings*, ed. D. McLellan, (Oxford Univ. Press, 1977), p. 165.

and children. The form in which these relations develop is through kinship and later family relationships. Marx and Engels acknowledge this and the early primacy of family relationships in social organization. Where they err is to assume (as they seem to) that the family loses its primacy when it loses its position as key economic unit in material production.[12] This ignores the importance of sex/affective production. Such a perspective falls into the trap of accepting the distinction between public and private life, as it is mystified in our society today. Needs for sexuality, nurturance, affection, and children are not seen as important levers for social action because they are satisfied in the private sphere of the family.

One way to characterize the interdependence between social relations of production in the family and the economic system as a whole is to start with the concept of *social formation*. A social formation is a system of production in use in a society at a specific time that may contain within it several different historically developed dependent modes of production. The social formation is characterized by a dominant set of social relations which control and often redefine social relations in the other subordinate modes of production. A historical example of a social formation is the combined U.S. capitalist/slave modes of production before the Civil War. I maintain that our present U.S. economic system can be thought of as a social formation consisting of capitalist and patriarchal modes of production. It has a co-dominant set of relations: 1) those between Capital and Wage Labor; and 2) those between men and women in patriarchal sex/affective production based in the family. It also has a subordinate set of class relations characteristic of welfare state capitalism, e.g., the existence of a class of institutionalized "poor," that is, those subsidized by the state on welfare or unemployment, and a dominant mode of production controlled by larger corporations, with a small sector of "family businesses," which has become a subordinate mode of production.

I need to defend my claim that the social relations of sex/affective production are *as formative* in shaping the other social relations of

12. Their words are as follows:

The third circumstance which, from the very outset, enters into historical development, is that men (sic) who daily remake their own life, begin to make other men (sic), to propagate their kind: the relation between man and woman, parents and children, the family. The family, which to begin with is the only social relationship, becomes later, when increased needs create new social relations and the increased population new needs, a subordinate one (except in Germany), and must then be treated and analysed according to the existing empirical data, not according to the "concept of the family," as is the custom in Germany. [Ibid., p. 166]

society as are the social relations of material production. I also must make clear why I hold that the modern family is still patriarchal, in light of the fact that fathers can no longer control their children's marriages, and that women can now own property and work independently of the family in wage labor. "Patriarchy" I shall define as a system of social relations in a society such that those who perform what is regarded as the "male" role (e.g., do "male" work) have more social power than, *exploit* and *control* those who perform, what is regarded as the "female" role (i.e., do "women's" work).[13] This use of the concept is somewhat broader than the original use of the concept, in which it meant "role of the father." I use the concept of *patriarchy* rather than the vague concept of *male dominance* because in my view the origin and persistence of male power and domination of women in all the institutions of society stems from male dominance and exploitation of women in the family and/or associated kinship networks.[14]

An argument for the claim that male/female social relations are co-dominant with other social relations of production is the universal presence in all human societies of what Gayle Rubin calls "sex gender" systems, that is, culturally defined male and female roles children come to

13. This definition has an important caveat: technically it should include the restriction that those who perform the male role have more power than those who perform the female role *only if* all other social factors are equal, viz., provided the individuals involved are not from different economic classes, races or castes.

14. Gayle Rubin points out in "The Traffic in Women" in *Toward an Anthropology of Women*, ed. R. Reiter, (New York: Monthly Review, 1976) that not all societies in which men dominate women are organized into separate nuclear or extended families. Nonetheless, the men seem to dominate through their control of the communal activities of the society, e.g., religious rites, trading, etc. On this basis she questions the use of the term "patriarchy" to explain male dominance. However, if we agree with Levi-Straus in *The Elementary Structures of Kinship* (Boston: Beacon Press, 1962) that one of the key mechanisms of male dominance in early societies is the male exchange of women in marriage, then the point can still be made: here men dominate women in the kin network as uncles and brothers because they *play the same social role* as the father plays in patriarchal families when he disposes of his daughter's hand in marriage. Because of the structural similarity of the mechanisms of male dominance I call them all patriarchal.

One of the important aspects of patriarchal relations is the fact that they are *socially*, not biologically, defined. Although it is almost always men who occupy the male role and women the female role, this is not always so: there are societies in which a woman can become a husband if she has the bride price, and societies like Mohave Indians in which homosexuals are accepted as male or female regardless of biological sex, depending only on the sex role they desire to play. Cf. Ann Oakley, *Sex, Gender and Society* (Harper and Row, 1972).

learn as part of their social identity.[15] The sex gender system organizes material work and services, by defining what is culturally acceptable as man's and woman's work. It also organizes nurturance, sexuality, and procreation by directing sexual urges (in most societies toward hetero-sexual relations and non-incestuous ties), by indicating possible friendships, and by defining parenthood and/or kinship ties and responsibilities.

Such a universal sexual division of labor, and societies with communal modes of production in which the sexual division of labor nonetheless gives men more power than women, suggests that Engels' historical hypothesis that the oppression of women begins with the development of class society is mistaken. A counter hypothesis is offered by Levi-Strauss, who argues that women are the first property, traded to cement bonds between tribes before the development of classes. Another hypothesis compatible with Levi-Strauss' is that societies developed matriarchal, egalitarian, or patriarchal kinship arrangements fairly haphazardly throughout the period of human prehistory when tribes were isolated from each other. When societies began to overlap, however, and to compete for hunting areas and land, those which were organized patriarchally were able to overcome matriarchal and egalitarian societies, and to impose their form of male-female patterns on those conquered.[16]

One important advantage of the theory that sex/affective and material power relationships are co-determinant of the other social institutions of society is that it helps us to understand how it is that patri-archal relations between men and women can shape the economic structures as well as the form and content of religions. These relations have persisted through many different modes of production, including socialist modes of production such as those in Russia and China. The

15. Rubin, "The Traffic in Women."

16. Cf. Friedrich Engels, *The Origin of the Family, Private Property and the State* (New York: International Publishers, 1972) and Levi-Strauss, *The Elementary Structures of Kinship.*

Patriarchal forms of organizing society have two advantages in survival terms when they compete with non-patriarchal societies: 1) they can create very efficient armies; and 2) they can generate a high population rate to replace fallen soldiers and/or to provide laborers for production. We can find a direct correlation between high birth rate and high degree of male control over women in historical societies, which suggests that when women have the power to decide their own pregnancies they tend to keep the birth rate low. If we extrapolate this information to prehistoric societies, we can surmise that many egalitarian or matriarchal societies were not able to compete with militaristic, high population-producing patriarchal societies. (I owe this line of thought to Nancy Folbre.)

content of the sexual division of labor will vary (e.g., in some systems men work for wage labor and women do not, while in others, e.g., feudal production, neither men nor women work for wages). Other relations of exploitation will vary as well (e.g., whether it is a feudal lord, the family itself, or a capitalist who is benefiting from the reproduction of labor power in the family).

Patriarchal family production involves unequal and exploitative relations between men and women in domestic maintenance and sex/affective work. However the *amount* of power the man has in relation to the woman in the family will vary with their relation to the dominant mode of production. So, if the woman has an individual economic class (e.g., if she is working for wage labor, or has an independent income) and if she is making equal wages it will be harder for the man to appropriate the surplus in wages after basic family needs are met. In general the typical nuclear family in the U.S. is less patriarchal than in earlier periods, and there are a substantial minority of households which are not patriarchal (i.e., are woman-headed). Nonetheless, the prevalence of the patriarchal family and the sexual division of labor has historically determined a male-dominated sexual division of labor in wage work in which women's work is paid less, is usually part time, and has less job security than men's. Those woman-headed households, then, cannot be said to be matriarchal, for the women in them do not have more power than the men they relate to.

The fact, then, that men have more power than women in all of the social formations in which family patriarchal sex/affective production is included gives us an insight not only into the persistence of sexism across changes in the dominant modes of material production, but also a way of understanding how the family as an economic unit has been the key mechanism in which patriarchal social relations have been reproduced.

IV   Women as Sex Class in the Patriarchal Nuclear Family

I want to argue that men and women are in *sex classes* in capitalist society today, classes which are defined by the sexual division of labor in the patriarchal family but which also appear in the sexual division of wage labor. In this section I shall present my arguments to show that women are exploited relative to men in the patriarchal nuclear family, that they are dominated and have little autonomy.[17] They must meet

17. I reject other marxist-feminist analyses because they do not draw this conclusion. For example, Margaret Benston in "The Political Economy of Women's Liberation," *Monthly Review* (September 1969) holds a view similar to mine about household work, but she fails to draw the conclusion that men exploit women in the present social formation. She argues that historically the

criteria 1,4, and 5 for class identity. In the last section, "Women as a Revolutionary Class," I will discuss the historical cohesiveness of the class (criterion 3) and the implications of whether women can become a "class for itself" (criterion 2).

By the "Capitalist Patriarchal Nuclear Family" (or CPNF), I understand an economic unit of man, woman, and possibly children, in which the man works full time in wage labor (is thus the main breadwinner), while the woman works as the primary domestic and childcare worker in the home.[18] If she is employed in wage labor, she is not employed more than part time. Although many families are not of this sort (e.g., female-headed households, or families where both husband and wife work full time), it is this arrangement to which schools,

development of capitalist industrial production rearranged the sexual division of labor in the household so that the woman continues to produce use values in the home, while the man now works for exchange values, working for a wage outside the home. Since only wage work provides social power in the capitalist social formation, the woman domestic use producer loses power in relation to men. This argument fails to explain a) why *women* continue to do use production in the home while men do not; and b) it assumes that men and women are not social actors who struggle for power in relation to each other when there are shifts in the mode of production. Rather, men come to benefit through an automatic process in which they have no say, but even a cursory look at the way male-dominated unions have sought to exclude women from wage labor casts doubt on this approach.

Maria Dalla Costa in *The Power of Women and the Subversion of the Community* (Bristol, England: Falling Wall Press, 1974) presents a view of women's work in the family in the capitalist mode of production which stresses women's role in producing the commodity labor power (by bearing children, doing maintenance work and nurturing children and husband in her role as family domestic worker). She thus indirectly produces surplus value for the capitalist. By her work in the home she becomes a non-wage earning member of the working class. It is not her husband but the capitalist who exploits her work there to make a profit. Dalla Costa's analysis ignores the special patriarchal features of household production. The husband is seen as a product and not as an agent who himself gets benefits and power from the sexual division of labor in the family. Furthermore not all work which is necessary for the production of surplus value is work which places one in the working class. It can be argued that members of the PMC, teachers, social workers and managers do training and organizational work necessary for the production of surplus value, yet have interests which contradict those of the working class.

18. This characterization raises some questions for I have excluded patriarchal nuclear families of the capitalist class by assuming the man must work full time in wage labor. We could include them by defining the family so that the male is the main "breadwinner," where that can include supporting the family from capital investments. But my tendency is to exclude them, on the grounds that male-female relations are sufficiently different because of their economic

jobs, and many social services (e.g., welfare, social security, etc.) are coordinated. Those who do not live in a patriarchal nuclear family are not only inconvenienced but suffer a loss of status. For many female-headed households, they suffer a loss of family class: their new individual economic class is lower than their family class was, defined in terms of their father's or former husband's relations to production.[19] If we can show that men exploit women in the CPNF, we will have provided a material basis for the general exploitation of women by men in society at large.

How then do men exploit women in the CPNF? There are four goods produced in sex/affective production in the family: domestic maintenance, children, nurturance, and sexuality. Since a sex/affective productive system is a system of exchange of goods and labor, we can classify such systems in terms of power relations involved, that is, is there an equal exchange between producers? If not, who controls the exchange? Patriarchal sex/affective production is characterized by unequal exchange between men and women: women receive less of the goods produced than men, and typically work harder, that is, spend more time producing them. The relationships between men and women can be considered *exploitative* because the man is able to appropriate more of the woman's labor time for his own use than she is of his, and also he gets more of the goods produced. It is *oppressive* because the sex/gender roles taught to boys and girls to perpetuate the sexual division of labor

means as to not be patriarchal. After all, if the men don't have to work, neither do the women: they can hire nannies for the children, and maintain separate vacation houses for their lovers, so it is unclear that the women in the capitalist class should be thought of as part of an exploited sex class. Divorced women from this class never lose their family class, due to alimony and child support settlements, trust funds, etc. The men, on the other hand, are still members of the exploiter sex class, for their relation to the means of material production allows them the power to exploit women from subordinate family and economic class positions.

19. It is important to note that a female-headed household in a predominantly patriarchal society cannot be defined as matriarchal, for the concept of *matriarchy* implies that women have more power than men; something certainly not true in a society where women must depend either on men for secure economic position (family class) or else be relegated to the lowest paid sex-segregated wage labor. The racist implications of the U.S. capitalist patriarchal social formation is evident in race-segregated wage labor and welfare systems that have created urban third world families where both men and women are powerless. In terms of *family class*, they are in the lowest sectors of the working class and poor, and the men, in addition, have no material base for patriarchal power in the family, although they have an emotional need for this power to maintain sex status in a patriarchal society. This situation leads to increasingly violent sex class conflicts between working class minority men and women.

develop a female personality structure which internalizes the goal to produce more for men and accept less for herself.[20]

What evidence is there for the view that men exploit women in family sex/affective production? There is clear evidence that women spend more time on housework than men do on wage labor. The figure given by the Chase Manhattan Bank survey is that a full time housewife puts in an average 99.6 hours of housework a week.[21] We also know that the inequality in relations to hours of work a week put in by husband and wife persists even when the wife is working in wage labor as well, for in that situation, studies have shown that the wife still puts in roughly 44 hours of housework a week in addition to her wage work, while the husband only puts in 11 hours of work in addition to his wage work.[22]

There is a problem with simple time comparison of work in family sex/affective production as a way to measure exploitation. What is exchanged is use values not market values. It could be argued that housework is less alienating than wage work: that the relatively greater control and autonomy the woman has over her workday at home makes longer hours of this work a reasonable exchange for alienating wage work. After all, the husband is not like the capitalist or foreman who attempts to increase the rate of exploitation of his wife's labor power by speedup, reduced pay, etc., and the man in the CPNF is subject to a greater percentage of his work being done under conditions of capitalist exploitation (this point of course excludes nuclear families of the capitalist class, which we excluded for considerations raised earlier).[23]

To answer this objection I shall argue that although housewives may seem to have more autonomy than wage earning husbands, they in

20. Since this is not commodity production, we can't talk of a rate of exploitation, for there is no quantitative way to measure and compare the values of these goods. Nor does it make sense to speak of the man "building up capital" with his human goods. Nonetheless there is a way we can approximate quantitative measurements of the inequalities involved in the exchange, and that is by adding the market commodity costs of the equivalent amounts of sexuality, childcare, maintenance and nurturance that are done by men and women.

The exploitative relation between men and women in the family Engels calls "slavery," and describes the sense in which the woman is the *property* of the man:

This latent slavery in the family, though still very crude, is the first property, but even at this early stage it corresponds perfectly to the definition of modern economists who call it the power of disposing of the labor power of others. [Marx and Engels, *The German Ideology*].

21. Chase Manhattan Bank Survey, quoted in Alain Girard "The Time Budget of Married Women in Urban Centers" in *Population*, (1968).

22. Cf. Mary Ryan, *Womanhood in America* (Franklin Watts, 1975).

23. Cf. footnote 18.

fact have less autonomy overall: less control, less "job security," and a lesser amount of the human goods that the sexual division of labor for domestic maintenance is designed to provide. The evidence for this inequality I base on three arguments.

The economic argument is that men, as the dominant wage earners, control the family income and have more power to dispose of any surplus as they wish. Connected to this is the relative economic dependence of women. Given that women overall can make only 60% of what men can make in wage labor, it follows that women are not equal to men in their options: they are less able to protest male choices for the use of surplus income because the possible breakup of the marriage "contract" or living agreement would disadvantage them much more than the man. They often stand to lose their family class.

The *sexual argument* and the *nurturance argument* overlap, the arguments being that women receive less sexual satisfaction and less nurturance from men than they give in patriarchal sex/affective productive systems. The reason that the arguments overlap is that women's inequality in sexual exchange and in receiving nurturance have one common cause: the "woman as nurturer" sex gender ideal. This in turn is based on one of the key material bases of patriarchy: that women are the primary childrearers.[24] The sexual division of labor in which women are responsible for the major care of children under six teaches children that women are nurturers (mothers) and men are achievers. Girls learn as part

24. As chief nurturers, women have been the sex to which both boys and girls have had to look for the satisfaction of their nurturance needs, and the ones towards which anger and frustration have been directed when all their needs cannot be met. Both anthropological and psychological studies suggest that female and male personalities develop differently as a result of this situation. Cf. K. Horney, *Feminine Psychology*, (Norton, 1967); N. Chodorow, "Family Structure and Feminine Personality," in *Women, Culture and Society*, ed. M. Rosaldo and L. Lamphere, (Stanford Univ. Press, 1974) and D. Dinnerstein, *The Mermaid and the Minotaur* (New York: Harper and Row, 1976). The anger toward the mother is turned against themselves in girls, who identify with the mother, and thus develop masochistic, self-sacrificing personalities; whereas the anger toward the mother is directed toward women by boys, who tend to develop misanthropic, narcissistic personalities.

The material base of patriarchy here becomes the fact that the sexual division of labor in the family is based on the creation of male and female personalities in which the male receives more nurturance because he has learned to expect and demand more, and the female gives more nurturance and receives less because she also has learned to expect less. The culturally developed difference between male and female personalities and skills has become, in Wilhelm Reich's words, a "material social power" which perpetuates the patriarchal sex/affective production in the family. Cf. W. Reich, *The Sexual Revolution* (New York: Simon and Shuster, 1974).

of their sense of self-identity that they are successful as people primarily if they are good wives and mothers; and good wives and mothers are those who are able to manage harmonious relationships for their husbands and children in the family. They are taught to find satisfaction in the satisfaction of others, and to place their needs second in the case of a conflict. Boys, on the contrary, learn that it is only if they are successful achievers that they can be successful men. They learn that the needs of others (wife, children) depend on their achievement, and to be a successful achiever they must be aggressive, competitive, put themselves first at school and later in business. In sexuality men are taught to be the initiators, women the receivers. Sexual success and work success are so much part of the sex/gender ideal taught to men that women as the nurturers have a large incentive to fake orgasm, to ignore sexual incompatibilities, in order to nurture the man's sense of self. No wonder, then, that the Hite Report, although clearly unsuccessful as a statistical sample because of its middle class bias, shows evidence that 80% of women do not regularly experience orgasms in sexual activity with men.[25]

The consequences of the "women as nurturer" sex gender ideal is the production of women who develop nurturing skills and a passive inability to demand nurturance from men; and the production of men who learn such skills are women's work, learn to demand nurturance from women yet don't know how to nurture themselves. There is a paradox involved here: women have had a near monopoly on nurturance skills, which produce a basic human need; yet the social relations of its production render them powerless to demand their fair share. I shall discuss how the situation is changing when I speak of women as a revolutionary class.

There are two other causes for the sexual inequality between women and men. These are "double standard monogamy," also incorporated with sex gender training, and women's role in procreation.

From the colonial period forward in U.S. history, men have always been freer to indulge in nonmonogamous sexual activity than women. During the Puritan period there was more equality, but the change from rural independent production to capitalist production brought a growing inequality. Because of the sexual division of labor in family production women of all classes became more dependent on men as wage earners and/or breadwinners than men were on women, for men no longer required the help of a wife and children to survive as they had in rural independent production. Thus, it is no surprise that the expansion of prostitution in the U.S. parallels the development of the separation between the home and the world of capitalist material production, with

25. Cf. Shere Hite, *The Hite Report* (New York: Dell, 1977).

the wife stuck in the home as the spiritual and moral guardian of the husband and children, and the husband free to indulge his sexual appetite outside the home.

The fact that women are the biological childbearers and not men puts women on an unequal footing in any system of sexual exchange in which they do not have access to control of their bodies to deal with the unwanted consequences of this connection of sexuality with procreation. The only recourse for women in such a situation is often abstinence, in order to avoid unwanted pregnancies, but this tactic requires that women suppress their sexuality. The fertility decline in the Victorian period in the U.S. suggests that many women did use this method.[26] We can see this as evidence of sex struggle in the mode of patriarchal sex/affective production. The problem is, that a sex strike as tool of sex struggle is unlike a work strike for wage workers as a tool of class struggle. It requires that women deny their sexual needs in a situation where men need not deny theirs, and there are always scabs (i.e., prostitutes) available to men to get those needs met.[27]

The relations of patriarchal sex/affective production for sexuality put women in a position of unequal exchange. They have less economic and legal power than men to demand an equal share of sexual satisfaction. Hence it is plausible to say that women have been the sexual property of men: that men own the means of producing and controlling sexuality in a way that women do not. No wonder that popular wisdom has it that women want to possess men, while men want freedom: the point is that because of the power relations between men and women, men already do or can possess women, so naturally they struggle to avoid the claims of women to equalize the possessive aspects of the relationship.

Let me sum up the points presented about the inequalities between men and women in patriarchal capitalism in relation to the criteria for class identity in order to show why I maintain women and men form sex classes.

Use of the first criterion, exploitation relations, usually assumes exploitation involves ownership and/or control of production. I have argued here that men in the CPNF own the wage and thus control sex/affective production in such a way as to be able to expropriate the

---

26. Cf. L. Gordon, "Voluntary Motherhood: The Beginnings of Feminist Birth Control Ideas in the U.S" and D. Scott Smith,"Family Limitation, Sexual Control and Domestic Feminism in Victorian America," in *Clio's Consciousness Raised*, eds. M. Hartmann and L. Banner, (New York: Harper and Row, 1974).

27. This assumes men are still able to get their nurturance needs met because women still depend on them economically. The situation today is changing. See the discussion in the section "Women as a Revolutionary Class."

surplus: surplus wages, surplus nurturance, and sexuality. The fact that the CPNF is the dominant unit of domestic maintenance and sex/affective production in patriarchal capitalism has also shaped the wage labor market so that women can be said to be an exploited sex class relative to men there.[28] This is a concrete case of reciprocal exploitation relations: how patriarchy in the family reproduces and reinforces itself by male domination in the social relations of public production.

The fourth and fifth criteria, Domination and Autonomy relations, can be shown to apply to men and women as sex classes in the family. If we remember that we are comparing power relations not only in the spheres of housework vs. wage work, but also sex/affective work, it becomes clearer how the analogy holds. I have argued that men dominate and control women in sexual activity and in nurturance.[29] It can be argued further that men are more autonomous in their sexual activities because they do them as consumers and not as part of their sex gender-defined work in the family.[30] Also men who happen to pick up some

28. According to S. Bowles and H. Gintis in "Heterogeneous Labor and the Labor Theory of Value," *Cambridge Journal of Economics*, v. 1, #2, (1977) different rates of exploitation can be assigned to different types of labor within the wage labor force. Once we can say some workers *exploit* others, we can go on to argue either that these sectors of the working class occupy class-contradictory positions (using Wright's approach), that they occupy different classes (the Ehrenreichs and Poulantzas' approach), or that people can occupy more than one class at a time, and *sex class* is one of these (my alternative).

29. Other feminists of course have made these points. Those who come closest to formulating the arguments presented here are Barbara Deming in "Love Has Been Exploited Labor" *Liberation* (May, 1973); and Meredith Tax "Women and Her Mind: The Story of Everyday Life," New England Free Press pamphlet, (1970).

30. Here is a quote from a worker at Fisher Body Plant about the connections between his sexuality and his wife's:

Because my need to be sexually revitalized each day is so great, it becomes the first and most basic part of a contract I need to make in order to ensure it.

The goal of this contract is stability, and it includes whatever I need to comsume: sex, food, clothes, a house, perhaps children. My partner in this contract is in most cases a woman; by now she is as much a slave to my need to consume as I am a slave to Fisher Body's need to consume me. What does she produce? Again, sex, food, clothes, a house, babies. What does she consume for all this effort?—all the material wealth I can offer plus a life outside of a brutal and uncompromising labor market. Within this picture, it's easy to see why many women get bored with sex. They get bored for the same reason I get bored with stacking bucket seats in cars. [J. Lippert, "Sexuality as Consumption," in *For Men Against Sexism*, ed. J. Snodgrass, (Times Change Press, 1977).

nurturance skills in spite of sex gender restrictions are more autonomous in their use: freer not to use them in ways which may be self-destructive of other needs.

We have shown that three of the five criteria we accepted for class identity apply to women and men as sex classes. Now we need to consider whether women as a group have the sort of political potential Marx and Engels originally foresaw for the working class in capitalism. Are women a revolutionary class? Do they have historical cohesiveness (Criterion 3)? And can they become a "class for itself" (Criterion 2)?

V   Women as a Revolutionary Class

The theoretical framework I have advanced here allows individuals to be members of overlapping classes: *family class*, *sex class*, and *individual economic class*. We need to know what class an individual will be likely to identify with if s/he is a member of several classes whose interests are in contradiction to each other. Are there laws of motion of advanced capitalist patriarchal social formations that can indicate where key contradictions will develop that allow for membership in one class to supersede in political importance membership in another class? One of the advantages of restricting the marxist concept of class to exploitation relations in wage labor (Criterion 1) is that those who are exploited here are also those who play a key role in the capital accumulation process. Therefore the implications of the laws of value and capitalist development seem to indicate why this class is of key political importance. Can we do something analogous with the analysis of *sex class* and *family class* in our society?

I maintain that we can. The task is to show that women are unlike Marx's characterization of peasants and like his characterization of the working class. Women have to be able to identify with sex class over family class, to be aware of themselves as a historically cohesive group, with a common culture and common interests by virtue of their position in the sexual division of labor in the family and in society. We need evidence of the existence of different men's and women's cultures, as well as some understanding of how growing contradictions between *sex class* and *family class* identification for women will push women to identify with the first.

There is certainly evidence of separate men's and women's cultures which is more distinctive the more patriarchal the society. By "culture," I have in mind a very broad concept that includes accepted patterns of acting, ways of treating each other, values, aesthetic and expressive forms, preferences for friendships, etc. The evidence presented by conservative writers such as Tiger about male-bonding supports the idea that men act as a sex class, and there is also evidence that women bond, although in strongly patriarchal societies this tends to be restricted to female kin and bound up with the family.[31]

Historically, however, there are few occasions in which sex class bonding has taken precedence to family class bonding; and those have often occurred, as in the "first wave" women's movement in 19th century America, when family class positions as well as male/female roles were in a state of transition because of changes in the mode of material production.[32] That movement failed to sustain the connection between middle class and working class women because the family class identification of the middle class women (primarily petty bourgeois and wealthy farmers) prevented them from challenging the economic class structure.

This is not surprising, for the family is the economic, sexual, procreative, and nurturant unit in a system of patriarchal sex/affective production. Men and women within families have seen as basic their common interests in raising children together, satisfying their material, nurturant, and sexual needs together, and amassing property that is used as collective security though it may be controlled by the man. Thus each individual tends to define his or her individual interests as that which promotes the family's interests.[33] For women this tendency is even stronger, given her sex/gender ego identity which is bound up with family tasks. The sexual division of labor in patriarchal sex/affective production reinforces this identification of individual with family interests. In previous social formations it was not economically and socially feasible for individuals to live outside of families and expect to get their material, nurturant, and sexual needs securely met. It is not then surprising that both men and women have identified themselves primarily with a common family class, defined typically by the male's relation to material production, with a common culture, values, and interests connected to other families in the same position.

The situation is changing, however, in advanced capitalism. There are increasing contradictions developing between the social relations of capitalist production and the social relations of patriarchal sex/affective production in the family. The economic material conditions for these

31. Lionel Tiger, *Men in Groups* (New York: Random House, 169). For other evidence that women bond, consider the U.S. Women's Movement. For an anthropological example see N. Teis, "Women in Groups: Ijaw Women's Associations," in *Women, Culture and Society,* eds. Rosaldo and Lamphere.

32. Cf. Alice Rossi, "Social Roots of the Women's Movement in America," in *Feminist Papers,* ed., Rossi (New York: Bantam, 1974).

33. Cf. Jane Humphries, "Class Struggle and the Persistence of the Working Class Family," *Cambridge Journal of Economics,* v. 1, # 3 (September 1977).

developments are: 1) the existence of wage labor jobs for women which will pay a subsistence wage; 2) the existence of welfare which will support women and children without a husband; and 3) inflationary pressures on family income which cause women to seek part time or full time wage work to supplement their husband's income.

What results from these conditions is an increasingly high rate of instability in patriarchal nuclear families: increasing high rate of divorce, less communal moral sanctions about "keeping the family together for the children," and more of an emphasis on the individual happiness of each partner. U.S. individualism, which always encouraged men to "do their own thing" is now increasingly an acceptable value system for women unhappy in marriage. This shift in morality parallels the change in material conditions that allow for the possibility that women can support themselves outside of the family. Inequalities in patriarchal sex/affective production have historically been maintained because most women have not had many viable options outside the nuclear family except prostitution. But the increasing number of state sector, clerical, and service jobs defined as "women's work" has now provided women with such an option. Even those women who are not seeking to stay single or to break out of unhappy marriages can become caught up in the contradiction that occurs between the wage labor job they take to increase their family's income, and the strain that now occurs in family relations because of the *increase* in the unequal division of labor this causes. (Is the husband now going to shoulder more housework? Are the kids? How will they deal with less attention from wife and mom?)

It is not only the new available options for work outside the family that is relevant to women's changing position. The fact is that with the increased instability of nuclear families, women can no longer count on being maintained in families as non-wage earning housewives, and thus achieve the old "wife-mother" sex gender ideal.[34] This makes it more likely that women will relate to sex class rather than family class as their prime source of identity. As wage workers women are thrown into proximity with other women not in their family. Due to sexual segregration of the work force into men's and women's jobs, women can come to identify with other women and put sex class identification as primary.

Another reason that women are forced to rely more on their sex class identity than their family class identity is that many women have to face the likelihood that they will lose their family class. Most wage labor possibilities for women are working class jobs. If a woman remains

34. For some American subcultures, e.g., black urban Americans, this has long been true.

single, she must either take a working class job or be "poor" (i.e., go on welfare, an option open only to single mothers). If a woman marries, it is likely that she will be divorced at least once in her lifetime, in which case she faces the same possibilities. Many family class PMC single and divorced women now are members of the working class as defined by their individual economic class; and increasing numbers of family class working class women are poor, i.e., on welfare.

Alimony and child support do not cushion women from these hazards of being a woman in U.S. society today. Only 14% of divorced women in the U.S. in 1976 were even awarded alimony by the courts and only one half of that number collect it regularly. As for child support, a full one half of the men ordered to pay child support are paying "practically nothing," and 90% of women receiving child support do not receive it regularly.[35] Furthermore, a homemaker is not entitled to social security benefits if divorced, so she has no prospects of a pension to support her in old age. A middle-aged divorcee is often a person thrown on the streets after years of homemaking with no marketable skills and not the energy or sense of self to start from the beginning to make a new life for herself.

Not only can women not count on wife and motherhood as a life concentration that will allow for a secure economic future but they cannot count on an easy way to care for their children. There is a contradiction between capitalist production demands and the existing patriarchal sex/affective system for handling child care. Inflation requires many women to supplement the husband's income by wage labor, yet there is little available child care for children under six. Working class mothers can't afford expensive child care so capitalist child care endeavors don't meet the demand: not profitable enough. There are 27.6 million children of working mothers who are under six years of age (public school age), yet there are only one million licensed day care slots available for these children.[36] Both single and married working mothers thus can increasingly identify around the sex class issue of child care.

There are other contradictions present in some superstructural institutions in society, e.g., the schools and media. These institutions are undermining the reproduction of patriarchal social relations by encouraging contradictory patterns and values. Two of the most important are the educational training of women and the emphasis on sexual consumerism by the media. The educational system is sexist in many ways, but

35. Cf. "Women and Poverty," in *Women's Agenda* (June 1976).
36. Cf. "Women and Childcare" in *Women's Agenda* (March/April 1976).

it does encourage the idea that women too may develop skills through education that would prepare them for a career independent of the family related goals of wife and motherhood. It thus develops an alternate sex gender ego ideal for some women, typically PMC family class women who go to better high schools and whose families can afford to send them to good colleges. Access to an alternate sex gender ideal is extremely important as a tool to allow women to challenge the system. It should come as no surprise that the vast majority of those involved in the current Women's Movement are college educated women.

There has been an increased emphasis on sexual pleasure by the media as a way to sell products. Although one result may be what Marcuse calls "repressive desublimation," another is that people come to an increased acceptance of the idea that women have a right to equal sexual freedom and satisfaction.[37] This also suggests modification of the sex gender ideal for women in ways which weaken the social relations of patriarchal family production. Both of these superstructural contradictions (in education and in the media) tend to weaken women's allegiance to family rather than sex class, if there is a conflict of interests.

I have given reasons to believe that women are a sex class which is developing historical cohesiveness because of contradictions appearing in the social relations of material and sex/affective production and between superstructural trends and existing male/female relations. But is this enough to make women a revolutionary class?

The PMC is a pivotal class in terms of the work it performs in reproducing capitalist relations of production. But so are women as a sex class in patriarchal family production! Women are the "culture-bearers" of family class *and* sex class values. They teach children expectations and goals, train them in rules of obedience to authority (acting as their first and most important role model in this area), and in general as the major child rearers do essential work in child socialization necessary to continuing capitalist and patriarchal culture. Secondly, men depend on women for the reproduction of their labor power by continued women's work in domestic maintenance, nurturance, and sexuality.

Women as a sex class, then, do have potential disruptive power because of their work in sex/affective production and capitalist patriarchal reproduction. If women refused to do their work as presently organized, neither capitalism nor patriarchy could continue to function.

Unlike the PMC, which is a mixed political class because it has contradictory interests, some in maintaining the system and some in challenging it, women are a revolutionary class because they have no objective interests as a sex class in maintaining the present system. Thus

37. H. Marcuse, *One Dimensional Man* (Boston: Beacon Press, 1964).

when women organize with other women in sex class identification, they can use the pivotal power gained by the importance of their social function in reproducing patriarchal capitalism to challenge continuance of the patriarchal family, and to raise the progressive aspects involved in family class identification for members of the PMC, working class or poor. The fact that women as a sex class cut across the divisions of PMC, working class, and poor can be a key to organizing progressive class alliances between these groups. Progressive feminists have been effective in communicating to many members of the autonomous Women's Movement that the objective conditions for women's liberation require the overthrow of *both* capitalism and male domination. There has also been some effective consciousness-raising about the issue of economic class: how family and individual economic class distinctions continue to divide women from each other and from true sisterhood.[38] There is some indication in political developments that the increasing consciousness of class issues is allowing the Women's Movement to correct some of its earlier PMC-focused approach; for example, broadening such demands as right to abortion and birth control to include opposition to forced sterilization, and the development of working women's unions (9 to 5 in Boston, CLUW, WAGE in California).

Two further points about the strategic position of women. First, the breakdown of the family has an increasing tendency to cause new women from the PMC and working class to enter the working class and poor. These women are usually angry because of defeated expectations, and can be an important group for raising both sex class and family class issues: issues like the right to free quality child care and health care, welfare payments to all women for housework, affirmative action for women in wage labor, etc. But many of the members of this group as single women and mothers need economic and cultural support *outside* of the institution of the patriarchal nuclear family in order to be able to do ongoing political work. In this context the cultural developments and support systems of the autonomous Women's Movement are important and show the falsity of the idea that cultural revolution must wait until after the economic and social revolutions occur.

Some examples of these developments are as follows: 1) the increasing frequency of women-headed households of unrelated adult women and sometimes children gives women the alternative of living with women (rather than in a nuclear family) and pooling economic

---

38. Cf. for example *Class and Feminism,* eds. C. Bunch and N. Myron (Oakland: Diana Press, 1974).

income and sex/affective work for each other and for children;[39] 2) Lesbian feminism as a viable cultural alternative to heterosexual love allows some women the possibility of gratifying affection and sexual needs without the need to deal with the exploitative relations existing at present in heterosexual family relations; 3) the rise of an independent cultural apparatus defining a new women's culture (music, poetry, theatre, visual art, restaurants) which is explicitly anti-patriarchal and (somewhat less explicitly) anti-capitalist gives a feeling of solidarity with a women's community which is struggling to redefine a formerly debilitating sex gender identity; and 4) transition homes for battered women and support groups for rape victims give victims of male violence the idea that other women will support them in fighting a passive acquiescence to such brutal treatment.

My final point about the strategic position of women concerns PMC women whose wage labor work directly involves them in the reproduction of capitalist relations. If such women are feminists, and even better, socialist feminists, they can use their relative autonomy and position of authority to undermine capitalist relations; can make conscious efforts to overcome the hierarchical relations between themselves and their poor working class or PMC students or clients or patients and begin to deal directly with elitism and other attitudes that continue to debilitate working class and poor people and to set them against PMC members. The contradictory position of such women (discrimination on the job, problems with the sexual division of labor at home, etc.) make them likely candidates for effective political work.

Conclusion

I have argued that women are a potentially revolutionary class. But they are not the only one. The working class is potentially revolutionary also, as are elements of the PMC. Indeed, because of the complicated objective contradictions between PMC and working class, and between sex class, family class, and economic class, a socialist and feminist revolution in this country is not possible at this time without *class alliances* of progressive people who identify the joint social formation of capitalism and patriarchy as the enemy. It stands to reason that different people will take different issues as their primary focus for organizing: some identifying working class, some women's issues, some racism and some joint PMC-working class issues. It is unclear at this point what kind

---

39. Ryan, *Womanhood in America* reports that one quarter of the families in a low income housing project involved two or more unrelated women (and many children). This shows that alternatives to the CPNF are increasingly sought for survival reasons, and not just by counterculture people and feminists.

of structure—coalitions, a party, grass root organizations, caucuses—is needed to produce the ideal alliance. The practical implication of this paper is that only an analysis which takes into account objective contradictions between classes in the U.S. today and the two, and sometimes three, overlapping class positions occupied by women and men can provide us with the understanding necessary to engage in the kind of practice that will teach us how and who to organize in the fight against capitalism and patriarchy.

III

Rejoinder

Barbara & John Ehrenreich

This book gives us an opportunity to clear up some points in our original article and to do what is seldom very easy to do when an idea is first formulated—to situate it in a particular set of activities and debates. We will not attempt to respond to each of the preceding articles, trusting that the reader will use his or her judgement in weighing them against our original article. Instead we will try to reflect on the entire subject and the debate it has provoked.

We are struck, in reading the more critical responses to our article printed in this volume, by the disparity between the issues which we were concerned with when we wrote the original article and the issues which most of our respondents dwell on.[1] So great is this disparity that it seems necessary to start this concluding essay by going back to *before* the original article was written, and giving the reader an explanation of what prompted us, sometime in late 1975, to undertake the research and discussion which led to the writing of "The Professional-Managerial Class."

In default of any explanation from us, some of the writers in this book have not hesitated to offer their own: that in times of minimal activity leftists occupy themselves with aimless theorizing; or that we hoped to "save" the socialist movement from the domination of the PMC, etc. In fact, the years between the decline of the university-based anti-war movement in the early 1970s (all too often mistaken for the decline of all oppositional movements) and 1976 were years of intense, if not always media-worthy activity: the continuing growth of the feminist and environmental movements, the emergence of scores of local community and workplace organizing projects, the development, in the wake of SDS's collapse, of the first fragile national New Left-descended organizations. There was no problem in this period of what to *do* but of how to make all the things that were being done add up to some sort of socialist, feminist, anti-racist and generally liberatory *movement.* So it was not a period of post-sixties idleness which inspired us, but a new phase of activity, which raised a new set of challenges and issues, quite different from those raised by the sixties New Left, Civil Rights, and anti-war movements.

One of the issues which loomed largest as the mid-seventies approached was the issue of *class*—class as a theoretical concept, class as a sort of demographic category to be compared to race and sex, class as a personal attribute by which individuals and whole organizations could be judged. The immediate signal for the left's preoccupation with class was the economic downturns of 1971 and 1974, which forced millions of U.S. workers into unemployment or underemployment. Within the women's movement, the response to these conditions was an upsurge of *socialist* feminism, as many previously non-left women's groups began to study Marxism and address themselves to issues related to work and income. Within the left, there was a turning-away from both internationalist and "cultural" issues and a rush towards the kind of Marxist-Leninism which had once been associated (unpleasantly in our experience) with the "old left." The "New Communist" ("Maoist," "Marxist-Leninist") groups which grew rapidly in this period advanced a politics in which production was seen as the touchstone of social life; party building was the key to

1. We were also struck by the disparity between what we wrote and what some of our critics seem to think we wrote. One of the reasons we decided not to reply to the critics article by article was the amount of space that would have to be devoted to simply listing the misunderstandings and distortions of our position. Schaeffer and Weinstein are especially guilty of this, replying in large measure to an article which we never wrote. Let the reader beware.

socialist strategy; and class was the "primary contradiction"—outweighing race, sex, etc., as a propellant towards revolutionary action.

The New Communist groups retrospectively turned on the New Left for its failure to consistently acknowledge the working class as the agent of revolutionary change. The New Left, they argued, had had no clear class analysis—only a series of political fads, in which, at various times, poor people, students, "youth," Third World people and the "new working class" of intellectual workers had each temporarily occupied center stage. Furthermore, according to the New Communist critique, the New Left had in practice been either contemptuous or indifferent toward the working class. This critical omission explained what was now described as the New Left's "failure," and succeeding revolutionaries were advised to return to the straight and narrow path of Marxist orthodoxy.

Under the influence of the New Communist line, scores of left groups now sought to purge themselves of non-working class ideology and leadership. People who were not authentically "working class" in background and occupation were lumped together as "petty bourgeois" and urged to remold their thinking and their lives. Qualities attributed to the "working class" were seen as wholesome and revolutionary; those attributed to the "petty bourgeoisie" were decadent and counter-revolutionary. At various times during 1975 and 1976, feminism, homosexuality, marijuana, the New Left, trade union leadership, liberalism, ultra-leftism (the list could be extended considerably) were branded as "petty bourgeois."

Unfortunately, the sheer silliness of these polemics over class had the effect of immunizing many sober people against the recognition that there might indeed be some kinds of "class problems" on the left. For despite the puerility of the New Communist Movement's polemics on class, they contained more than a grain of truth. There *is* a problem of class on the left, and one which has been difficult and painful to come to grips with.

Perhaps the problems had always been there but couldn't surface until the shock of the left's encounters with racism, and then sexism as internal problems on the left had died down a little—there actually were, proportionately speaking, more working class people in left and feminist organizations by the mid-70s. The expansion of higher education in the 60s and 70s and the G.I. anti-war movement had brought many young men and women from blue collar backgrounds into contact with the New Left and the feminist movements. Then the economic contractions of 1971 and especially of 1974 sent many of the same people back into blue collar or clerical jobs—creating a large number of left-leaning, "over-educated" young workers. At the same time, left and feminist organizations were expanding their outreach activities towards working class people—unemployment counselling projects, rank and file organizing, tenant organizing in working class neighborhoods, etc. The result was that while left groups in the late 60s had often been more or less homogenously composed of college-educated people from middle class backgrounds and usually with middle class career expectations, left groups in the 70s were likely to include people from a wide spectrum of family backgrounds, educational levels and occupations. For example, a local group which we had helped to organize contained at one point in 1976 a tenured professor, a warehouse worker, a practical nurse, a social worker, a writer, a locksmith, a librarian, a psychotherapist, and a skilled factory worker.

This kind of mix was seldom a comfortable one. Probably the most common pattern within the organized left was for the working class membership to drift away, repelled by the college seminar style which the left clung to as its *modus operandi*. "I felt I had nothing to contribute. I just don't have the background;" or, "It's just too exhausting to go to a meeting after working all day;" or, "I didn't feel people were interested in what I had to say". But in other cases there were (and continue to be) overt clashes, sometimes abetted by the current Marxist-Leninist notions of class, sometimes not. Usually the "working class" faction took the initiative in these clashes, expelling the "petty bourgeois" elements or splitting to form a new organization.[2] For example, the Minneapolis chapter of the New Amerian Movement (NAM), which had been the most influential left group in the city, destroyed itself in a spectacular split in 1976 which pitted relatively newer, working class recruits against older members, many with New Left and/or middle class backgrounds. In our own local group, it was a group of the professionals who took the initiative, walking out with the charge that the group's politics had been hopelessly diluted by the addition of certain new (working class) members. Outside of the left, numerous feminist projects were torn by conflicts between working class women and (as one put it to us) "the professionals and businesswomen/men who think we're dumb klutzes."

The tensions and clashes that went on in the mid-70s did not just re-

---

2. We by no means intend to suggest an identification of "working class" with "Marxist-Leninist" politics. The charge of "possessing petty bourgeois traits" was often traded amongst equally middle class, professionally accredited people. For example, one of the leaders of a "Marxist-Leninist" split in one Boston area group—an admirer of the "disciplining" influence of industrial labor—was a 22-year-old Harvard graduate. Conversely, many indisputably working class radicals were repelled by the "Marxist-Leninists" no less than by New Leftists. As we suggested in our original article, "Marxism-Leninism," as practiced by the New Communist Movement, was far from a repudiation of PMC ideology.

present, as it sometimes seemed, some kind of self-destructive disorder which had overtaken the left and feminist movements. Clashes between working class and professional-managerial kinds of people go on every day—in schools, in factories, in clinics, in hospitals, in neighborhoods. What was peculiar about the left as a setting for interactions between the two kinds of people, was that a certain artificial equality had always been *assumed.* As the sixties went by, race and sex inequalities within the left were acknowledged, at least verbally, but there has been almost no recognition of this other, less physically visible difference: a man who had spent the day unloading freight with constant harrassment from a supervisor and a man (just to keep the genders the same) who had spent the day lecturing to admiring students and anticipating a promotion were supposed, at the end of the day, to engage in political work together on a basis of comradeship and trust. The class conflicts which emerged within the left in the mid-70s were in some ways analogous to the sex conflicts within the anti-war and civil rights movements in the 60s: In the same way that the left served as an incubation chamber for feminism—by preaching egalitarianism while perpetuating the real inequalities between women and men—the left in the 70s bred a new kind of "class consciousness." And, as had been the case with feminist insights, the new awareness was not satisfactorily explained by conventional left theory.

The turmoil over class within the left opened up some disturbing questions—at least for those of us who were not satisfied with the contemporary "Marxist-Leninist" accounts of the situation. Why was the left, especially the white left which emerged from the 60s, so overwhelmingly middle class in composition—to the point where the theoretical standard bearers of socialism, the working class, had become a problem for outreach"? Was the anti-communism of much of the U.S. working class really just a product of cold war propaganda (as we had been led to believe in the 60s), or did it have something to do with the antagonisms which we had seen develop, in miniature, within left groups? Was this antagonism simply a matter of "style" (which in itself would have to be explained), or did it reflect some deeper features of American society?

In our particular case, these questions intersected with some apparently unrelated sets of concerns. We had both been activists and journalists in the area of health care, and since the early 70s we had been especially interested in medicine as a profession—its emergence as a modern profession near the turn of the century (at the expense of the working class tradition of lay healing), the ideological content of medical science, and the role of medical care as an instrument of social control. These interests were stimulated by the rapidly emerging women's health movement, which challenged the monopolization of skills by physicians and other "experts" and asserted lay people's right to reclaim vital areas of technology. From medicine, our interests branched out to other areas of professional domination. From 1974-1978, one of us (BE) was working (with Deirdre English) on a lengthy historical study of a number of kinds of professional experts (physicians, psychologists, home economists, etc.) who had come to have a defining influence on women's lives and work. Among other things, these studies led us to reject the common left view that these professions were simply tools of the ruling class. Instead it seemed that they had their own class interests, distinct both from those of the bourgeoisie and from those of the proletariat.[3]

In addition to this research and our experience as activists, we had both had the opportunity to visit China during a time (1974-1975) when the themes of the Cultural Revolution were still inspiring mass discussion and conflict. The political campaigns which we were lucky enough to glimpse during our visits—the "Campaign to Criticize Lin Piao and Confucius" in 1974 and the "Campaign to Study the Theory of the Dictatorship of the Proletariat" in 1975—addressed themselves to the inequalities which had persisted under socialism: between women and men, city and country dwellers, and manual laborers and professional-managerial workers. We were especially interested in this latter form of inequality, and curious about how the Chinese intended to avoid the development of a Soviet-style technocratic and bureaucratic elite. We

---

3. See Barbara Ehrenreich and Deirdre English, *Witches, Nurses and Midwives* (Feminist Press, 1972), *Complaints and Disorders* (Feminist Press, 1973), *For Her Own Good* (Doubleday Anchor, 1978); Barbara and John Ehrenreich, "Medicine and Social Control," *Social Policy* (May-June 1974), Helen Marieskind and Barbara Ehrenreich, "Towards Socialist Medicine," *Social Policy* (September-October 1975). Inspired by the same research, we also started to question the analysis of the Progressive movement, as developed in the late 1950s and early 1960s by Gabriel Kolko and James Weinstein, among others—an analysis which credited Progressive Era reforms largely to the efforts of the new class of corporate capitalists. This "corporate liberalism" thesis had been an important corrective to liberal interpretations of Progressivism, but it was one-sided. In particular it seriously underestimated the significance of the emergence to self-consciousness of the new professionals and managers. It also removed the "Progressive" actions of corporate leadership from their real context—bitter, often violent working class struggle, the rise of American imperialism, the hardening of nativism and racism. David Noble's *America By Design,* cited both by Noble and by Weinstein and Schaeffer in this volume, continues the same one-sidedness. In his concern to show that the engineers are lackeys of big capital, Noble seriously underemphasizes the internal struggles within the engineering profession and between engineers and manufacturers (the latter themselves often "shop-trained" engineers), over precisely the question of the degree of independence engineers might have.

were excited about the on-going efforts to break down professional hierarchies within health and education institutions, to democratize factory management and to reform the educational system so as to prevent the development of a semi-hereditary elite of professionals and managers—all efforts, we should note, which appear to have been abandoned or reversed since Mao's death.[4]

Our exposure to the tail end of the Cultural Revolution in China and our involvement in the developing feminist critique of professionalism here fed into our thinking about the class dynamics of the American left. On the one hand, China highlighted the conflict between manual and mental workers, and showed that this conflict could reach the proportions of what might be called class struggle. (No homology between the class structure of the U.S. and that of China—a largely peasant country—is suggested here or was suggested in the original article, contrary to Weinstein and Schaeffer's interpretation.) On the other hand, our readings on the history of the professions showed that the modern professions, including "professional" management, arose through the suppression of skills and functions which had been indigenous to working class women and men.[5] These disparate observations made us all

4. See not only "The Dictatorship of the Proletariat in China," by John Ehrenreich (*Monthly Review,* October 1975), which Schaeffer and Weinstein make much of in this volume, but also "Democracy in China," by Barbara Ehrenreich (*Monthly Review,* November 1974), which they overlooked in their zeal to discover the origins of our ideas on class.

5. David Noble, in criticizing this assertion, argues against us that engineers do not simply do "what workers used to do without them." The engineers, says Noble, are themselves "productive" and most of their specific functions are new ones, not ones "formerly performed by workers." We agree. However, Noble confused the change in the overall social division of labor with the change in the specific, immediate techniques, content, etc., of the various parts of the process of production. It was the *professions,* not their present-day *skills and techniques,* which arose through the suppression of skills and functions formerly indigenous to working class people.

To give an obvious example: doctors have certainly developed new obstetrical techniques over the last 75 years (with not unmixed results for women and infants!). They have also eliminated midwives and removed childbirth from its historical setting in the home, the family and the community. If we emphasized the importance of changes such as the suppression of the midwives at the hands of the doctors rather than changes in technology, it was because we were writing an article about changes in the class control of technology and expertise, not because we were unaware of the technical change characteristic of modern capitalism. As for the engineers, our point is precisely that they *are* productive in Noble's sense: they actually *design the production process*—i.e., they are the immediate determiners of the labor process which workers carry out. Moreover, for the most

the more dissatisfied with the usual explanations of the class tensions within the American left—both those which waved the whole thing away as a matter of "style" and those which relied on class categories such as the "petty bourgeoisie."

We thought that it was possible to understand these internal tensions—and, more important, the gap between the left and much of the working class in general—in a much more thoroughgoing and enlightening way. Furthermore, we thought it was *necessary* to do so, in however tentative a way. Not necessary, as David Noble suggests, because we were driven by an abstract search for order and certainty. Not necessary, as Howard and Cohen propose, because we wanted to impose a working class "metaphysic" on the left. And not necessary, as Albert and Hahnel intimate, because we hoped to purge the left of middle class dominance. But necessary because we *started* with the assumption that any successful socialist movement in this country will include—must include—both "working class" and "middle class" people, manual and mental workers, laborers and professionals, etc. Anyone who shares this assumption—and this includes almost all the contributors to this book—is *obliged* to try to understand the tensions and differences which tend to separate working and middle class people into different universes so that we might, at least within the context of a socialist movement, try to overcome them.

So this is what we must set out to do. We wanted an analysis which would bring into sharp focus the class tensions in and around the left. And, we wanted one which would, at the same time, acknowledge and help account for the fact that, in this country at least, the middle class has been a perennial source of progressive movement. To put it in terms common on the left in the mid-70s, we had no use for the wishy-washy "expanded working class" theories which denied that there were any tensions, other than those arising from false consciousness. Nor did we have much use for the "Marxist-Leninist" theories which simply castigated the "petty bourgeoisie" and all its radical manifestations, from the student left to the feminist movement. Neither approach drew seriously on the left history of the 60s and 70s, and neither pointed the way to any solution to the isolation and turmoil the left has experienced in the 70s. There needed to be a new way of understanding things that

part they are (or are on the way to becoming) managers. To ignore the concentration of these functions in a distinct group of people, separated from other "productive" workers by education, income, life style, autonomy and power, would indeed be, in Noble's words, to "muddle the analysis from the start."

would lead to a better way of *doing* things.

All the above could have served as an introduction to our original article. The reader is already familiar with the content of that article—our attempt to understand, as unflinchingly as possible, the "working class" *vs.* "middle class" antagonism, to use this analysis to take a fresh look at some U.S. left history, and our tentative conclusions about building a broad-based socialist movement. We turn now to the rest of the book, and the major problems which it addresses.

The Perils of Class Analysis

It is necessary, in turning to the bulk of this book, to throw in a subheading and mentally draw a line, because this book as a whole is not about what our original article was about. That article took off from a problem facing the U.S. left; its project, or purpose, was to develop a framework for understanding that problem (or, at the very least, to raise consciousness about the existence of the problem). Most of the essays in this book, however, do not address this project and barely acknowledge the problem. They are (with some interesting exceptions) concerned with a problem of a wholly different nature—a problem which belongs less to the struggles of a living movement than to the annals of academic Marxology. And that is the problem, above all, of what a "class" is, and secondly, of whether the social group variously described as the "middle class" or the "middle strata" truly comprises a "class."

This preoccupation with definitional questions at the expense of political issues is in itself worth some sort of historical comment. We described some of the challenges confronting left activists in the 70s. While all this was going on, another development was in progress, which has since been described as the "academicization of Marxism." A number of people who were influenced by, if not participants in, the movements of the 60s and early 70s, have become in the natural course of their careers college professors. Others, many of them younger, have been introduced to left thinking on the relatively inactive campuses of the mid-70s and are also pursuing academic careers. The influx of radicals to academia, combined with a slight post-60s decline in overt anti-communism among liberal academics, has resulted in a certain acceptability of Marxism as an intellectual orientation. The positive side of this development will be obvi-

---

6. Avowed Marxists continue to face harassment and discrimination from their colleagues and from college administrations, and the revival of Cold War-style anti-communism in previously left-ish journals such as the *New York Review of Books* has occurred simultaneously with the proliferation of Marxist academic journals and conferences. The change is one of degree, not of kind.

ous to most readers. The danger, however, is that the "academicization of Marxism" will require that Marxism remold itself to resemble an academic discipline, cut off from radical activity and venerating its own specialized terms and "methods" and patriarchate of contributors. It seems to us that our critics' preoccupation with the *definition* of class reflects precisely this kind of academicized thinking, a kind of thinking in which *political* questions are subordinated to questions of orthodoxy and of abstract theory.

But since the question of definition has become almost the major theme of this book, it is only fair that we expand on some of our own thinking on the meaning of class.

If the PMC paper skips over this subject all too quickly, it is because we did not start with the idea of coming up with a new class analysis or with some kind of abstract grid to superimpose on events. We started with the recognition of a certain *group of actual people*. We could see commonalities in their occupational roles and in their historical and present relations to both the working class and the capitalist class. We were convinced that the best way to understand these relations was with some sort of class analysis.

But here we at once ran into trouble. Despite the association of Marx with "class analysis," Marx himself nowhere clearly and unambiguously defines class. His one direct and extended effort, in the last chapter of the final volume of *Capital,* breaks off in the middle (after discarding a simplistic definition in terms of type and source of income) with Engels' heartbreaking editorial insertion: "Here the manuscript ends." Elsewhere Marx is thoroughly inconsistent: in one place, "class" is little more than a synonym for "group;" in another it is determined by the relationship to the means of production; in yet another it stands for a group with a common role in society as a whole; in still another it depends on consciousness of common interests *vis a vis* another class.

None of these definitions is easy to apply. How, for example, do you gauge a group's consciousness of its common interests? What can we mean by a *common* "relationship to the means of production" in a workforce which is as heterogeneous as that of a modern industrial nation? The simple and unambiguous criterion of "ownership" of the means of production mixes together, on the one side of the "relation" wealthy financiers and the holders of ten shares of stock, on the other side the salaried top executives and the machine operators. But as soon as we admit of other criteria than juridical ownership, the way is opened to endless debate about the proper boundaries of the word "common." Then there is the problem of the relationship between these various kinds of definitions: How does a group's relation to the means of production come to express itself in a common consciousness? What if a group having a "common" relation to the means of production just doesn't have a "common consciousness?" Perhaps our greatest mistake, in the original article, lay in not *acknowledging* our own queasiness about Marxist class theory, and simply hurrying along, after adding a few makeshift definitions to the main story. (We thank Albert and Hahnel for their attempts to make our definitions more acceptable to the academic reader.)[7]

These gross definitional problems would possibly be enough to discredit Marx himself, if he were to be resurrected and were to appear incognito at a contemporary gathering of the Union for Radical Political Economics or a similar group. But the truth is that if Marx did not bother to define class in a simple formulistic way, it was because he didn't think it important to do so. He lived at a time when certain classes *were defining themselves*. It was not abstract deduction but the actual emergence of the working class, self-defined by militant socialist currents within it, which led Marx to Marxism. So it is futile to look to Marx for a "scientific" definition of class. Marx's legacy is more demanding: it enjoins us to comprehend the social reality of which we are a part and to seek out the basic antagonisms, the contours and fissures which prefigure change.[8]

7. Dick Howard and Jean Cohen, who are perhaps the most abstract of our critics, seem to argue that it is "manipulative," "metaphysical," "economistic," "dogmatic," and several other bad things to seek to develop "a theory *for* realizing a pre-given end" (e.g., a mass movement for socialism). If we interpret them correctly (and we confess to some difficulty in understanding them), they are providing a perfect rationale for fully academicized abstract speculation.

8. For an extended discussion of Marx's varying usages of "class," see Bertell Ollman, "Marx's Use of 'Class'," *American Journal of Sociology 73*, no. 5 (March 1968), 537-80; reprinted in *Social and Sexual Revolution* (South End Press, 1979), pp. 42-43. Ollman concludes:

The interwoven criteria Marx used for understanding what constitutes a class represents the results of his empirical social studies. It is only, in other words, because Marx found groups in his society with different relations to the prevailing means of production, sets of opposing economic interests based on these relations, a corresponding cultural and moral differentiation, a growing consciousness among these groups of their uniqueness and accompanying interests, and—resulting from this consciousness—the development of social and political organizations which promote these interests, that he constructed his peculiar concept of "class." Of overriding importance is that "class" in Marxism is not just a label for groups carved out of society on the basis of a discernable set of standards, but expresses as well the involved

There is another problem with Marx's (or perhaps we should say "Marxist") notions of class. It stems from the fact that neither Marx himself nor other early Marxists anticipated that capitalism would survive for another hundred or more years. The bourgeoisie and the proletariat were locked in struggle which he believed would lead, sooner rather than later, to the abolition of all classes. Thus Marx's description of the classes' various relations to the means of production, their consciousness of their own interests, etc. was in a sense a *snap-shot* description. It contains no premonition that the classes would go on to reproduce themselves for four or five generations; that they would in fact assume a *caste-like* character, with workers procreating workers just as surely as capitalists procreate capitalists.

To put it another way, Marx expected the revolution to come, if not in his own lifetime, then very soon thereafter. The "contradictions" between workers and capitalists, between the "forces of production" and the "relations of production," have been with us for well over a century. But socialist revolution has not succeeded in any developed capitalist country. Why not? Confronting this question leads us again to the problem of how capitalism reproduces itself. The first step towards an answer has to be to throw out some of the fetishized abstractions of "Marxist" social theory and replace them with a realistic analysis of society. "Classes" do not make history; "contradictions" do not make history; "forces" do not make history: in the end, *people* make history. How people actually live, what they believe, etc., must be among the starting points of analysis. "Class" and similar terms are tools for making sense out of the common experience of many people; they are not *a priori* categories into which people's experience, behavior, beliefs, etc., must fit.

We would have assumed that this is obvious. But David Noble thinks differently: "The contradiction between the two poles of social production—forces of production and social relations—is less apparent now than in Marx's time....[*But*] *appearances do not exist; they are perceived.* The contradictions between forces of production and social relations has not disappeared: our perception of it has faded." (Emphasis added). What can Noble possibly mean? In people's making of history,

interaction which Marx believed he uncovered between these standards. When critics...ask complainingly for Marx's definition of "class," they are asking, in effect, for the latter's analysis of capitalist class society; and it is understandable that Marx had difficulty in reconstituting this analysis in the form of a definition of "class."...Does Marx provide an adequate account of social relations in capitalism? It is on the answer to this question that the utility of Marx's concept of "class" hinges.

"appearances" (i.e., what people perceive, think, believe) certainly "exist." If people don't "perceive" the contradiction after a hundred-plus years, we had better ask in what sense the contradiction really exists. And if we conclude that it *does* exist (and we think it does), we have to ask *why* it does not "appear" to people. Noble's argument simply eradicates these questions. If we do face them, we are led to an inquiry into the *mediations* which prevent people from comprehending the "contradictions," "forces," etc., which are theoretically immanent in the capitalist mode of production.

Now these mediations are not to be found solely within the realm of production. They are to be found in the family, in the community, in health and educational institutions, in mass culture, in consumption, in sexuality, and they are not reducible to production relations in any simple and immediate sense. The failure to recognize the significance of the "cultural" sphere (that is, the realm of experience outside of production) in advanced capitalism leads to a kind of "class analysis" which is at once economistic and whimsically idealist. Instead of class analysis as an analysis of the totality of social relationships among groups of people, it becomes an analysis of people's relationship to the inanimate means of production. Class is then perceived as primarily a matter of occupation, and the questions which are asked are: "which class are registered nurses in?" or "what will librarians do as a group?" or "what is the political orientation of computer programmers?" Eric Olin Wright's analysis of "contradictory class locations" is a typical example of this approach. To Wright, for example, the determinants of "class location" lie entirely within the sphere of production. The social purpose of one's work and relation inherent in this work to other classes are of no concern to Wright. The use of "relation-to-the-means-of-production" as the sole determinant of class is a classic (if not widely appreciated) example of what Marx called the "fetishism of commodities": the social character of people's relationships with each other is disguised as an objective relationship between them and things.

This wholly vocational approach to class leaves out everything else which shapes a person's political consciousness and loyalties—their experience of other classes, their family and friendship ties, their experiences as a consumer of services, their notion of their "community." Thus a person may be at one time a factory worker, at another time a gas station manager, and at another time a bar owner without ever leaving the cultural milieu which most people would recognize as "working class." A class which has been in existence for generations shares more than a "relation to the means of production;" it has a social and cultural existence which is shaped both *by* and *in opposition to* the other classes of society.

The "snap-shot" conception of class, which sees class as a cluster of occupational groupings, leaves the entire areas of culture and of private life—family, community, etc.—in darkness. Albert and Hahnel recognize this problem, but can see no way out of it than to posit some separate realm of human relationships which can include kinship, ties, community, etc. In their formulation, kinship becomes a "structure" on a par with "the economy," and even competing with it for centrality in the social order. This leads them to the curious notion that in societies where economic relations are especially important, classes are the important agents of change, but if "kinship relations [are] critical to a social order, then women might very well occupy a central place in social change." But what can this mean? Since when are women not part of classes, or men not part of kinship relations? And where is there a society in which kinship relations are *not* critical to the social order? Or to economic relations?

Another mystery which arises from a purely vocational approach to class is that of the class position of housewives—a subject which has filled numerous articles over the last 10 years. Is their class conferred on them by their husbands (or, more precisely, by their husbands' occupations), or can they be said to have an independent relation to the means of production, based on their domestic work? The mysteries disappear if we simply acknowledge that classes ("economic" classes) which have been around for a few generations have a *social existence*. Kinship, for example, is not some autonomous "structure." People marry largely within their classes, and classes are held together by these kinship ties as well as by bonds of similar labor or income. Unpaid housewives are not classless creatures; they are central to the network of kinship and community which define a class's social existence and its members' identity and expectations.

If the acknowledgement that classes have a social existence is what Howard and Cohen describe as the "dash of academic sociology" which we have added to the Marxist stew over class, we have no apologies for it. How else are we to account for the cultural and psychological aspects of class which Carter describes so forcefully? Any notion of class which leaves out so much of people's direct experience (not to mention potentially leaving out millions of women, children, retired people!) can have, to put it as gently as possible, little explanatory power.

We have, we hope, convinced you that there is no "correct" and "scientific" definition of "what a class is." This book itself stands as proof: it abounds with so many mutually contradictory notions of class that its main value may be less in what it says, from a Marxist point of view, about the world, than in what it says, unwittingly, about the state of contemporary Marxist class theory. Aronowitz attempts to apply the "classic" Marxist definition of class to the working class, only to discover that under this definition the working class itself does not exist as a class—a conclusion he recoils from with evident embarrassment. Howard and Cohen seem to alternate between arguing that class is an outdated historical concept, and suggesting that we use the term to describe the most politically promising group at any particular time—students, technicians, etc., in the 60s, perhaps European migrant workers in the 70s. Ferguson suggests that "class" is used in several different ways, one of which would allow women to be considered a class, or "sex-class." Schaeffer and Weinstein insist that Marx's idea of class is a "compact, ideologically unified, politically astute, and economically similar group of people who could represent itself [sic] as a force capable and willing to organize the whole of society in its own image for the benefit of all," a description which would admirably fit the editorial collective of a small left journal. Noble believes that class is "the relation between dialectical opposites" or, somewhat incomprehensibly, "a way of grounding Hegel's Spirit in history, in 'sensual' reality while retaining a sense of motion..." And so on.

Is the PMC a Class and What Does It Matter Anyway?

Our critics' preoccupation with the question of what exactly is a class is largely a *distraction* from the political questions we raised about the PMC. When they do approach the problem of the PMC, they turn to pure *denial*: "The PMC is not really a class," or "not really a single class," they argue. And in any case, they insist there are no serious or necesary conflicts between the groups we have called the PMC and the working class.

Turning to Marx again, we find no firm guidelines on how to deal with these middle strata. If Marx did not leave us with an adequate definition of class, neither did he leave us with an adequate theory, analysis, or even description of the "middle strata" or class. In his view, the principle "middle" class on the scene, the petty bourgeoisie, had an even shorter life expectancy than the bourgeoisie. The petty bourgeoisie would be proletarianized or swept up into the wage system along with the existing proletarians. So unimportant did the middle classes or class appear to Marx that in the third volume of *Capital*, where he lists the "three great classes of capitalism," they turn out to be the bourgeoisie, the working class and—not the middle class at all, but—the landlords.

Marx did not give the middle class short shrift because there could only *be* two classes, as Noble seems to argue when he tells us that classes must be "opposites" and negations of each other. There is no serious basis in Marx for such an assertion: where it seems to be implied by Marx (e.g., in the *Communist Manifesto*) it is clearly either rhetorical or a remnant of Hegelian metaphysics. In his historical analyses (including *Capital*), Marx allows for a number of major and minor classes within capitalist society: peasants, landlords, capitalists, workers, petty bourgeois, lumpen proletariat, even God help us! the "ideological classes." More directly, in his most explicit statement on all class in all his writings, in *The Eighteenth Brumaire of Louis Napoleon,* Marx says a class exists when "millions of families live under economic conditions of existence that divide their mode of life, their interests and their culture from those of the other classes, and puts them in hostile contrast to the latter." (Emphasis added. In passing we also note Marx's emphasis on "mode of life...interests...culture"—i.e., not on an abstract relation to the means of production.)

The explanation for Marx's neglect of the middle class (or classes) does not lie in Hegelian dialectics but in the simple fact that the salaried middle class was *not* yet an important factor on the scene. The only group which might be considered homologous to today's "middle class," the classical petty bourgeoisie, seemed to be dwindling numerically, and the appearance of the modern salaried professional-managerial class still awaited the emergence of modern corporations, institutionalized non-violent efforts to control the working class, the expanded state apparatus, etc. So how then are we to answer the question of whether the PMC is "truly" a class? The truth is, as the reader may be beginning to suspect, the question of whether or not the PMC is a class is neither very interesting nor very meaningful. Nor would it become much more interesting or meaningful if we could all agree on a "scientific" definition of class (which would have to include the dimensions of economic relations, social existence, and consciousness plus the connections between these). We agree with those of our respondents who rail against the notion that, by defining a set of static categories, and then stamping them onto reality, one can claim to have arrived at an explanatory theory. Now this kind of sterile definition is not, in fact, what our paper on the PMC offers. Our own definitions of class and of the PMC (which were admittedly hasty and provisional) were intended largely to counter the prevailing Marxist usage in which class was defined simply by "relation to the means of production." We were laying claim to the right to use the word "class" in a way that has more to do with actual experience, and we did this only as a preliminary to talking about an actual group of people, in relation to other social classes.

When all the quibbling about definitions has been put aside, this remains the reality that we have to concern ourselves with: that, in all modern industrial societies, there exists a group of people whom everyone, speaking colloquially, would distinguish from the working class, and no one, speaking technically, would confuse with the capitalist class or with the traditional petty bourgeoisie. That the members of this group are employed in occupations which share certain common features as to their nature, status, history, purpose. That they have elements of a common social existence such as a tendency to intermarry, to live in the same neighborhoods, to display a distinctive pattern of consumption, etc. That, if their own commonalities sometimes escape them, they are clearly visible *from the outside* (as Carter's essay brings home).[9] That from the outside, i.e., from the working class perspective they are viewed with hostility and fear as well as with envy and respect. And finally, that the hostility creates a problem for the left. Our critics in this volume have raised some interesting questions about class. *But none of them have raised any evidence or analysis which would lead us to deny this reality.*

What Are The Real Issues

Leaving aside the largely sterile debate about whether the PMC is in fact a class, let us return to the political questions that we raised in our original essay about the PMC and its relation to the working class. Underneath the verbal tonnage devoted to definitional problems, our respondents do, of course, have something to say about these questions. In this last section we will try to uncover their positions and compare them to our own.

First it should be observed that when most of our respondents do think strategically, they do so within a theoretical framework which has little to do with U.S. reality. The strategic question which lurks in the essays by Albert and Hahnel, Aronowitz, Wright and several others is the

---

9. Of course this group is far from homogeneous. Its members range from primary school teachers to tenured professors, from civil servants to civil engineers, from accountants to Marxist sociologists. Nor is it static: at various times its ranks have been swelled by recruits from the working class or thinned as occupational slots diminish. But this heterogeneity hardly makes it beyond the bounds of a class analysis. After all, it is neither less homogeneous nor more variable than what we commonly recognize as the "working class." The latter ranges from unskilled workers, paid at minimum wages, to highly skilled craftsmen, often paid an amount which any assistant professor would envy; from slum dwellers to residents of tree-lined working class suburbs; from elementary school drop-outs to community college graduates. And whatever politics we may find immanent in the working class by virtue of their relation to the means of production (as Aronowitz is concerned to establish), in practice the various parts of the U.S. working class are and have been politically and culturally divided and even mutually hostile.

question of *whether the PMC will be a reliable ally of the working class movement.* Is it, in a revolutionary sense, "good" or "bad?" Or can we, using the geometric formulations offered by Wright, determine which parts of it are potentially "good" and hence worth our time as organizers.

Now these are very important questions—at least in those situations where there is a coherent working class movement to be an ally of. These are questions which have rightly preoccupied the leadership of the Italian and Spanish Communist Parties, which represent massive working class movements. But this is not the situation in the United States. There are scores of working class struggles which one could point to at any one time, but there is no powerful working class left movement (despite Noble's wistful suggestion that its absence is only an illusion fostered by PMC control of the media). And there is certainly no revolutionary working class party for which we may imagine ourselves to be the strategists—sitting in party headquarters, deciding which elements of the "middle strata" we should bother making alliances with.

Our problem, if we are willing to accept the political realities of the United States today, is that we are members of a left which (in addition to being numerically all too small) is still largely PMC in composition. If we assume, as we and most of our respondents appear to, that any mass revolutionary movement in this country will be composed of both "middle class" and "working class" people, then the question which faces us is: what are the obstacles to building such a broad-based movement? Or, put another way, why has this situation arisen—how do we account for the narrowness of the left's class base?[10]

As we have said above, most of our critics do not address these questions in any direct or explicit way. But by looking carefully at the various class analyses they offer, it is possible to deduce what their answers might be. On the whole, they seem to be saying either a) there *is* no problem (i.e., our description of the situation of the U.S. left is inaccurate); or, b) if there is a problem, there are no obstacles to solving it which are worthy of analytic attention (i.e., the narrowness of the left's class base is a more or less accidental condition).

Schaeffer and Weinstein represent the first of these responses. In their class analysis, the working class has been expanded to include all those "who sell their labor power to capital at a price." Thus the groups we have called the PMC are actually in the working class; the present left

10. These are of course the questions which our original article addresses, and we are baffled by some of our respondents' misreadings. For example, Schaeffer and Weinstein find us "content with the present state of the left," while Aronowitz accuses us of being guilty of a "refusal of a politics of class alliance."

is homogeneously "working class;" and there is no real problem. Where there are obvious tensions, the Schaeffer and Weinstein analysis tends to dissolve them. For example, they describe students' resistence to the school's processing as an "incipient movement of labor against capitalist relations." But they completely leave out of this account the immediate agents of the student's oppression—the teachers, counsellors, etc. Since Schaeffer and Weinstein have harmoniously blended all the antagonists into the same expanded working class; they can cheerfully ignore the obstacles to any real unity among the two groups.

Wright's class analysis, on the surface much more sophisticated than that of Schaeffer and Weinstein, annihilates the political problems even more swiftly.[11] In his analysis, groups of people occupy class "locations," which may be "determinate" (in which case the group's class interest and its basic political orientation are fixed by the group's relation to the means of production), or "contradictory" (in which case the group's political orientation is "indeterminate," or open to ideological influence. The working class occupies a "determinate class location"—hostility to the bourgeoisie and a fundamental interest in achieving socialism is built into its economic situation. Now, unless we gravely misread Wright, this theoretical assignment of the working class to a "determinate class location" in one stroke "solves" the most serious problem of the U.S. left—simply by *positing* that the working class is inherently socialist.[12] This leap of the imagination (which most Marxist Leninist groups make with Wright) reduces the tasks of the left to providing the correct leadership for the working class in its march toward socialism.

Having posited a left-oriented working class, Wright has already departed from the U.S. scene, but it is still worth considering what he has to say on the problem of inter-class relationships. First we find that the people we have called the PMC are split—along purely vocational lines—into several subgroups, each occupying its own "location."[13]

---

11. In addition to his article in this volume, see Wright's essay in *New Left Review*, No. 98. Wright's argument is explicitly accepted, in varying degrees by Aronowitz, Albert and Hahnel, and Ferguson.

12. See Wright's article in *New Left Review*, No. 98, especially p. 41. It is worth noting that neither Wright nor Schaeffer and Weinstein ever consider the role of imperialism in shaping working class politics in the United States. The possibility that imperialism could create a common interest between the bourgeoisie and elements of the working class is never even raised in these essays.

13. Among other things, the purely vocational approach used by Wright omits all working class-PMC contacts other than those between bosses and workers. Professional-client contacts, which are important in shaping the

Managers are "located" between the working class and the bourgeoisie, professionals between the working class and the petty bourgeoisie, etc. Set off in their separate "locations," the managers, professionals, "intellectuals" and other PMC fragments have no possible *common* interest which might divide them from the working class, or *common* attributes which might be visible *from* the working class. In fact we find that the most interesting distinction between the (now divided) PMC and the working class in Wright's scheme is that the PMC groups all occupy *contradictory* class locations. Unlike the working class, which is stolidly rooted in its "determinate class location," PMC members can more or less decide which of the major classes (bourgeoisie, working class and traditional petty bourgeoisie, according to Wright) to line up with.[14] Hence the problem of building inter-class alliances hinges solely on the choice of the PMC groups: the possibility that the working class might have something to say about it, or that the PMC groups might have some "determinate" interests of their own, has been excluded.

Syzmanski offers a very different kind of class analysis, but in the end he too dissolves away the problem that our original article addressed. In his analysis, as in our own, the professional-managerial groups comprise a class distinct from the working class, which he calls the "new petty bourgeoisie." But because he denies the historical function of the PMC in relation to the working class (or at least denies it's being of any relevance to a class analysis), his new petty bourgeoisie exists in no particular *relation* to the working class: it is just a sociological entity, peripheral to the major class polarization of capitalist society. Furthermore this new petty bourgeoisie is in the process of being "proletarianized" itself, ie., it is subjected to increasing workloads, declining autonomy and material privileges, etc. There are, then, no real obstacles to the inter-class unity. As for the narrow class base of the existing left (which Syzmanski appears to acknowledge), this is no cause for worry, since the working class will need a vanguard composed (initially at least) of "socialist intelligentsia."

relationship between working class and the PMC, are invisible in his scheme. Wright's unwillingness to contemplate such PMC-working class antagonisms appears boldly in his treatment of schools. Recall that Schaeffer and Weinstein's schools lacked teachers; Wright's schools lack students! To Wright, schools are simply the workplaces for teachers. We must assume that their relations with students are benign, of interest only because the teacher has the opportunity to subvert the formation of bourgeois values in the students.

14. Wright's category of intellectuals, enjoys the most freedom in this regard, being doubly undetermined: they "typically occupy a contradictory class location between the working class and petty bourgeoisie at the economic level, but between the working class and the bourgeoisie at the ideological level."

So at last the real political difference between ourselves and the majority of our respondents should be clear. We say that a certain problem exists, that it is not accidental and temporary, but rooted in the organization of monopoly capitalist society; that the problem is an urgent one; that its solution will require a searching re-evaluation of the assumptions and institutions of the U.S. left. Our critics, in various ways, say that there is no problem, or that it is not a very serious one, or that it is going away anyway. They ask, with unexpected irritation: why do you bring this up now? Why make such a fuss about it? Why maximize this one problem? And we have to ask them in return: why do you minimize the problem, retreat from it into abstractions, or simply deny its existence? That—unfortunately little more than that—is the political dialogue which occurs in this book.

Why *do* they minimize the problem which seems so starkly clear to us (and to Carter and Welch)? In some ways, it would be surprising if they did not. We recall when the problem of sexism on the left was first raised by women in SDS and SNCC. The response of the men was not only an attempt to defend male privilege (though there was plenty of that), but an effort to *deny there was any problem at all.* The class problem seems to provoke a similar kind of defensiveness on the part of the still largely PMC left: if theory tells you that the working class is the agent of revolution, yet everyday experience tells you that you are not yourself "working class," then what are you to conclude about your own political role? The absurd anxiety arises that you may be doomed to historical irrelevance. Better perhaps to deny what everyday experience tells you and claim membership in an hospitably "expanded" working class (Schaeffer and Weinstein's approach). Or to find that you are not in a determinate class at all, but in a "contradictory class location"—from which you can freely choose your class position (Wright's approach). Or to find that people precisely like yourself are potentially the "vanguard" the working class movement needs (Szymanski's and the usual "Marxist-Leninist solution).

It also seems to us, that, underlying our critics' refusal to acknowledge any "class problem" on the left, there may be almost a fear of finding themselves someday in a left which is truly dominated by working class people, rather than radicals from the PMC. Thus Schaeffer and Weinstein imagine that we are "trying to encourage the working class to smash the...PMC radicals...in order to clear the field for genuine revolutionary, working class Maoists." Syzmanski worries that we may be encouraging the idea that "expertise and vanguard organizations are...obstacles to the development of revolutionary consciousness." Albert and Hahnel insist that the "skills and interests" of the PMC (or parts of it) "must be recognized." And Aronowitz admonishes us that the working class can't "carry on alone." It hardly needs to be said that the possibility of PMC radicals (with all their "skills and interests") being lost within a mass working class socialist upsurge is the least of the dangers facing the U.S. left at this time.

To pick up the other side of the dialogue: why did *we* choose to highlight the class issue—to call attention to it and attempt to place it in a historical framework? Not, as some of our critics would seem to suggest, to exacerbate the problem and contribute to the immobilization of the left. Rather, our work was motivated by one clear conviction—a conviction which grows out of the left's confrontations with racism and sexism over the last decade: that the problems we do not face up to and attempt to overcome will inevitably overcome us. The only way to transcend the narrowness of the left today lies through a profound understanding of the class forces which have up till now limited our outlook and strategy. As we argued in our original article, the New Left, at its best came close to understanding this. It is an insight which we owe to succeeding waves of radical movement.

Contributors

Pat Walker is a collective member of South End Press. He has been actively involved in community and tenant organizing. Pat teaches economics at the University of Massachusetts at Boston, and is working on his dissertation, "The Economic Decline of Massachusetts," at the Economics Department of the University of Massachusetts at Amherst.

Barbara Ehrenreich is editor of *Seven Days Magazine;* and a co-author with Deidre English of *For Her Own Good: 150 Years of the Experts Advice to Women.*

John Ehrenreich is an associate professor of American Studies at the State University of New York at Old Westbury. He was active in the anti-war and radical health movements. He edited *The Cultural Critique of Modern Medicine,* co-authored *American Health Empire: Power, Profits and Politics,* and co-authored *Long March Short Spring: The Student Movement at Home and Abroad.*

Al Syzmanski teaches at the University of Oregon in Eugene, Oregon. Al is the author of *The Capitalist State and the Politics of Class,* and is just finishing a study of the class nature of the Soviet Union (forthcoming from ZED Press).

Jean Cohen is completing a dissertation entitled, "The Crisis of Class Analysis in Late Capitalism," at the New School for Social Research. She is an associate editor of TELOS, as well as a member of the New York *Kapitalistate* group. Her active participation in the anti-authoritarian New Left movements of the 1960s (both the women's movement and the anti-war movement) informs her theoretical approach to the analysis and critique of contemporary forms of domination be they in the name of Marxism, or democracy, or both.

Dick Howard teaches at the State University of New York at Stony Brook. He is editor of *Selected Political Writings of Rosa Luxembourg,* co-editor (with Karl Klare) of *The Unknown Dimension: European Marxism Since Lenin,* co-editor (with Dean Savage) of *The New Working Class: Selected Writings of Serge Mallet,* and author of *The Development of the Marxian Dialectic,* and of *The Marxian Legacy.* Dick wishes to thank the "Research Institute of International Change," at Columbia University for the assistance received as a Senior Fellow for the Spring of 1978.

Sandy Carter currently teaches social psychology part-time at Cambridge-Goddard graduate school in Cambridge, Massachussetts. During the last ten years he has worked at various factory, construction, warehouse, and hospital jobs. More recently, he has worked as a counselor at hospitals in the Boston area. During these years he has been active in organizing around workplace, community and mental health issues. He is currently writing a book concerning mental health in capitalist society (forthcoming from South End Press).

Robert Schaeffer is a graduate student in Sociology at the State University of New York at Binghamton.

James Weinstein is editor of *In These Times*, and author of *Corporate Ideal in the Liberal State: 1900-1918*, *The Decline of Socialism in America: 1912-1925*, and *Ambiguous Legacy: The Left in American Politics*.

David Noble is an historian who is presently working on the social history of technology—the design and development of automated means of production technology—trying to understand how the means of production reflect the social relations of production. He is an assistant professor at MIT, and is author of *America by Design*.

John Welch is a taxi-driver in New York. He was a draft resistor, a member of SDS, a hospital worker, a member of the New York Taxi Rank and File Coalition, and a member of the New American Movement.

Erik Olin Wright, after spending a year as student chaplin at San Quentin Prison, helped write a book on prisons, *The Politics of Punishment*. He presently teaches sociology at the University of Wisconsin at Madison, where he has helped launch a new graduate level program within the sociology department in Marxist social science called the "Program in Class Analysis and Historical Change." He is the author of *Class, Crisis and the State*, and *Class Structure and Income Inequality* (forthcoming from Academic Press). He is coordinating editor of the journal *Politics and Society*.

Stanley Aronowitz is professor of Comparative Culture and Social Science at the University of California at Irvine. He is the author of *False Promises*, and *Science, Technology and Marxism* (forthcoming from South End Press).

Michael Albert is a collective member of South End Press, and is a part-time economics teacher at the University of Massachusetts at Boston, and at Norfolk State Prison. He has been active in socialist movements for the past eleven years and is the author of *What Is To Be Undone?*

Robin Hahnel is a member of the Economics Department at American University in Washington, D.C. He has been active in both national and community organizing.

Michael and Robin co-authored *Unorthodox Marxism*, and are now working on a joint project concerned with the character of socialism as it can be in the United States.

Ann Ferguson teaches philosophy at the University of Massachusetts at Amherst. She was a member of the founding collective of the Valley Women's Union, an autonomous socialist-feminist community women's organization, and has been active in progressive struggles in the Pioneer Valley area. She teaches music and is a parent in a third world progressive alternative school, the Che-Lumumba School. She is a member of the MAP (Marxist Activist Philosophers), and is currently working on a book on women as a revolutionary class in the U.S.

9